COMPARATIVE AND INTERNATIONAL EDUCATION

COMPARATIVE AND INTERNATIONAL EDUCATION
Issues for Teachers

SECOND EDITION

EDITED BY
KATHY BICKMORE
RUTH HAYHOE
CAROLINE MANION
KAREN MUNDY
ROBYN READ

CANADIAN SCHOLARS
Toronto | Vancouver

Comparative and International Education: Issues for Teachers, Second Edition
Edited by Kathy Bickmore, Ruth Hayhoe, Caroline Manion, Karen Mundy, and Robyn Read

First published in 2017 by
Canadian Scholars
425 Adelaide Street West, Suite 200
Toronto, Ontario   M5V 3C1

www.canadianscholars.ca

Copyright © 2017 Kathy Bickmore, Ruth Hayhoe, Caroline Manion, Karen Mundy, and Robyn Read, the contributing authors, and Canadian Scholars. All rights reserved. No part of this publication may be photocopied, reproduced, stored in a retrieval system, or transmitted, in any form or by any means, electronic, mechanical, or otherwise, without the written permission of Canadian Scholars, except for brief passages quoted for review purposes. In the case of photocopying, a licence may be obtained from Access Copyright: One Yonge Street, Suite 1900, Toronto, Ontario, M5E 1E5, (416) 868-1620, fax (416) 868-1621, toll-free 1-800-893-5777, www.accesscopyright.ca.

Every reasonable effort has been made to identify copyright holders. Canadian Scholars would be pleased to have any errors or omissions brought to its attention.

Library and Archives Canada Cataloguing in Publication

Comparative and international education : issues for teachers / edited by Kathy Bickmore, Ruth Hayhoe, Caroline Manion, Karen Mundy, Robyn Read.
—Second edition.

Includes bibliographical references and index.
Issued in print and electronic formats. ISBN 978-1-55130-951-4 (softcover).—ISBN 978-1-55130-953-8 (PDF).—ISBN 978-1-55130-952-1 (EPUB)

1. Comparative education. 2. International education. 3. Education—Cross-cultural studies. I. Bickmore, Kathy, 1957-, author, editor II. Hayhoe, Ruth, author, editor III. Manion, Caroline, 1974-, author, editor IV. Mundy, Karen E. (Karen Elizabeth), 1962-, author, editor V. Read, Robyn, author, editor

LB43.C666 2017   370.9   C2016-907008-5   C2016-907009-3

Cover design by Gord Robertson
Text design by John van der Woude, JVDW Designs

Printed and bound in Ontario, Canada

This book is dedicated to the memory of Professor Joe Farrell, co-founder of OISE's Comparative International Development Education Centre, former president of the Comparative International Education Society, and a beloved mentor and friend to many of the authors of this volume.

TABLE OF CONTENTS

Preface ix
List of Abbreviations xi

Chapter One: Why Study Comparative Education? 1
Ruth Hayhoe, Caroline Manion, and Karen Mundy

SECTION I: (RE)FORMING SCHOOLING: PHILOSOPHY, POLICY, AND SCHOOL ORGANIZATION
Chapter Two: Philosophy and Comparative Education: What Can We Learn from East Asia? 29
Ruth Hayhoe and Jun Li
Chapter Three: Reinventing Schooling: Successful Radical Alternatives from the Global South 59
Joseph P. Farrell, Caroline Manion, and Santiago Rincón-Gallardo
Chapter Four: Understanding Pedagogy: Cross-Cultural and Comparative Insights from Central Asia 88
Sarfaroz Niyozov
Chapter Five: Comparative Perspectives on School Improvement 119
Stephen Anderson and Malini Sivasubramaniam

SECTION II: JUSTICE, KNOWLEDGES FOR CHANGE, AND SOCIAL INCLUSION
Chapter Six: Comparative Indigenous Ways of Knowing and Learning 155
Katia Sol Madjidi and Jean-Paul Restoule
Chapter Seven: Gender and Education 183
Kara Janigan and Vandra Lea Masemann
Chapter Eight: Human Rights Education for Social Change: Experiences from South Asia 211
Monisha Bajaj

Chapter Nine: Global Citizenship Education in Schools: Evolving Understandings, Constructing Practices   234
Mark Evans and Dina Kiwan

Chapter Ten: Conflict, Peacebuilding, and Education: Rethinking Pedagogies in Divided Societies, Latin America, and around the World   268
Kathy Bickmore

SECTION III: EDUCATION IN THE WORLD SYSTEM: GLOBALIZATION AND DEVELOPMENT

Chapter Eleven: Education for All: Comparative Sociology of Schooling in Africa and Beyond   303
Karen Mundy and Robyn Read

Chapter Twelve: The Internationalization of Schooling: Implications for Teachers   335
Julia Resnik

Chapter Thirteen: International Education Indicators and Assessments: Issues for Teachers   363
Anna K. Chmielewski, Karen Mundy, and Joseph P. Farrell

About the Contributors   393
Index   399

PREFACE

The first edition of this anthology grew out of a collaborative effort among faculty in the Comparative, International, and Development Education Centre at the Ontario Institute for Studies in Education, University of Toronto (OISE, UT). Convinced of the value of introducing pre-service and practising educators to comparative and international educational research linked to their professional concerns, we produced a text that offers broad exposure to international issues and explores education in diverse cultural settings.

In this second edition we have expanded our scope, adding nine new authors, including some pre-eminent comparative education scholars from around the world. All chapters have been updated and revised. We have added two entirely new chapters: one on human rights education (Chapter Eight by Monisha Bajaj); and one examining the internationalization of education (Chapter Twelve by Julia Resnik). Additionally, this second edition includes a more specific definition of the field, addressed to teachers and their interests (see Chapter One); more on teachers and their involvement in international education; and a stronger focus on issues of diversity and social justice education. In this new edition, we have organized the chapters into three thematic sections, to facilitate critical comparative thinking: (I) (Re)Forming Schooling: Philosophy, Policy, and School Organization; (II) Justice, Knowledges for Change, and Social Inclusion; and (III) Education in the World System: Globalization and Development. Through these in-depth portrayals of educational issues, perspectives, and practices in a wide range of world contexts, we hope to stimulate readers to think comparatively and critically about their own educational practices and experiences.

The book is designed as a resource for initial and continuing teacher education and graduate education. Each chapter introduces major issues within the field of comparative and international education, highlighting significant research contributions, educational practices, and implications for teachers within each topic. The authors draw on comparative research from the Americas, Australia, Africa, Asia, Europe, and the Middle East. We have used the Canadian context as a case study in a few chapters; however, the concepts presented are easily extended to various North American and even global contexts.

Instructors who wish to use this book as a class text may choose to follow the given order of chapters and sections, or to change the order according to their course objectives. There are cross-references throughout the text to link learning across the various chapters and to highlight common themes. At the end of each chapter, key questions for reflection and discussion, along with a list of suggested readings, are intended to stimulate discussion about the chapter contents in relation to learners' own experience and teaching goals. Each chapter is also paired with at least one suggested audio-visual resource, carefully selected to provide students with an opportunity to "experience" education in other cultures and contexts without having to leave the classroom. In our own courses using this text at OISE, UT, the films provoked animated debate and discussion, offering participants a visceral feeling for the challenges and rewards of exploring educational issues through a comparative lens. The authors have provided a description of each film, as well as details on how to obtain these and other recommended resources. We have also produced a website of resources to support and enrich the use of this text: www.oise.utoronto.ca/cidec/Research/Issues_for_Teachers.html. On the website you will find links to relevant websites and online curriculum and teacher resources, as well as short video clips of some of the authors, and full-length video of some authors' lectures and PowerPoint presentations. We hope that you will find this book makes a valuable contribution to your teaching and learning and look forward to hearing your responses to it.

LIST OF ABBREVIATIONS

AEFE	Agence pour l'enseignement français à l'étranger
ASEAN	Association of Southeast Asian Nations
BIA	Bureau of Indian Affairs
BRAC	Bangladesh Rural Advancement Committee
CEDAW	Convention on the Elimination of All Forms of Discrimination Against Women
CIES	Comparative and International Education Society
CIESC	Comparative and International Education Society of Canada
CSR	Comprehensive School Reform
DP	Diploma Programme
EFA	Education for All
FPE	Free Primary Education
GCE	Global Citizenship Education
GCSE	(International) General Certificate of Secondary Education
GER	Gross Enrolment Ratio
GERM	Global Education Reform Movement
GMR	Global Monitoring Report
GNI	Gross National Income
HRE	Human Rights Education
HRLE	Human Rights and Legal Education
HRLS	Human Rights and Legal Services
HRW	Human Rights Watch
IB	International Baccalaureate
IBE	International Bureau of Education
IBO	International Baccalaureate Organization
IEA	International Association for the Evaluation of Educational Achievement
ILSAs	International Large-Scale Assessments
IMF	International Monetary Fund
INEE	Inter-Agency Network for Education in Emergencies

IPC	International Primary Curriculum
ISCED	International Standard Classification of Education
LCP	The Learning Community Project
MDGs	Millennium Development Goals
MoE	Ministry of Education
MYP	Middle Years Programme
NAFTA	North American Free Trade Agreement
NGOs	Non-governmental Organizations
OECD	Organisation for Economic Co-operation and Development
PALF	Pearson Affordable Learning Fund
PEF	Punjab Education Foundation
PEMLE	Program for the Improvement of Educational Achievement (Programa para la Mejora del Logro Educativo)
PISA	Programme for International Student Assessment
PLC	Professional Learning Community
PLN	Professional Learning Networks
PYP	Primary Years Programme
SACMEQ	Southern and Eastern African Consortium for Monitoring Educational Quality
SBM	School-Based Management
SDGs	Sustainable Development Goals
UDHR	Universal Declaration of Human Rights
UIS	UNESCO Institute for Statistics
UN	United Nations
UNESCO	United Nations Educational, Scientific, and Cultural Organization
UNICEF	United Nations International Children's Emergency Fund
UWC	United World Colleges
WISE	World Innovation Summit for Education
WOMP	World Order Models Project
WSIP	Whole School Improvement Program

CHAPTER ONE

WHY STUDY COMPARATIVE EDUCATION?

Ruth Hayhoe, Caroline Manion, and Karen Mundy

What is comparative education, and why study it? The answers to these questions are rich and varied, as we hope you will discover through this introduction to the field. For centuries, educators have acted on what we might call the "comparative" impulse: attempting to understand and improve their systems of learning by looking at others. This impulse is captured in the title of one of the most popular and enduring books in comparative education, *Other Schools and Ours* (King, 1979). Throughout the 20th century the comparative impulse fed wide-ranging efforts to solve problems of economic development, social conflict, and social inequality through educational reform. It also spawned important critical comparisons of such efforts, leading to pioneering work on the role played by education in the construction of global and national social systems.

There is no one answer to the question of what comparative education is, though many scholars have attempted to define the field over the years (see, for example, Bray, 2003; Crossley & Watson, 2003; Manzon, 2011). Some definitions are quite simple: "comparative education has developed as a field devoted broadly to the study of education in other countries" (Kelly, Altbach, & Arnove, 1982, p. 505, cited in Kubbow & Fossum, 2003, p. 5). Others focus on the element of change and the use of comparison to understand and modify our own educational policies and practices based upon lessons learned from others and other systems:

> By the expression "comparative study of education" we mean a systematic examination of other cultures and other systems of education derived from those cultures in order to discover semblance

and differences, and why variant solutions have been attempted (and with what result) to problems that are often common to all. (Mallinson, 1975, p. 10, cited in Crossley & Watson, 2003, p. 17)

At its most basic, comparative education offers a starting point for improving our educational systems and our classroom practices. It also challenges us to think broadly about the link between local practices and global issues, and to explore the overlapping values and social systems that underpin the educational enterprise itself. For teachers, an understanding of the comparative education literature helps for reflection on issues of concern in their own classrooms such as diversity, conflict/peace, teaching approaches, curriculum, and classroom organization in a wider global context, and for learning from the innovations, experiences, and practices of other teachers, schools, countries, and regions.

Comparative education has been developed over a period of nearly two centuries, and its rich literature constitutes a resource for teachers that is now more accessible than ever before, through the availability of web-based materials. The purpose of this text is to introduce you to the main ideas and literature of the field, and to give you a taste of comparative educational analysis in the twelve theme-based chapters that follow this introductory chapter. We have selected themes relating to teaching and learning, the child's right to education, alternative schooling, gender, curriculum and pedagogy, school improvement, Indigenous knowledge, multiculturalism, conflict resolution, and global citizenship, all topics important for new as well as more seasoned teachers. We have invited experienced scholar-educators to present comparative analyses that will enable you to see how much can be learned from attention to education in one or several other societies, nations, regions, or civilizations.

In this introductory chapter, we will begin with an overview of the early history of comparative education, then look at how the field developed in the 19th and 20th centuries, and how it expanded to include international education after the Second World War. We also suggest that socio-cultural, economic, technological, and political changes and processes associated with globalization have impacted comparative education research and practice. And finally, we look at the ways in which educators have contributed to the development of the field, and its close links with such international organizations as UNESCO and the World Bank.

THE EARLY HISTORY OF COMPARATIVE EDUCATION

Comparative education developed along with such other social sciences as sociology and psychology in Europe in the early 19th century. However, the field had many early antecedents in the experiences of learning across regions and civilizations that can be found throughout ancient and medieval history. Plato's famous masterwork, *The Republic*, drew upon some ideas of education and society he found admirable in the city state of Sparta, which he saw as having greater discipline and order than his native Athens. The Greek scholar and general Xenophon introduced Persian education to Greece through the biography he wrote of the magnanimous King Cyrus. Subsequently during the Roman Empire, the famous scholar Cicero made a comparison of Greek and Roman education systems, and concluded that a state-controlled education system was superior to a family-centred private system, since it nurtures bonds with the state that are important to a democracy (Jones, 1971; Trethewey, 1976).

Over the same period, Chinese thinkers developed educational ideas and texts in the Five Classics, compiled by Confucius and later philosophers, which formed the core of a uniquely Chinese approach to education. While teaching and learning took place largely in family- or clan-based schools at the local level, the imperial government administered examinations at prefectural, provincial, and national levels to select the most knowledgeable and talented young people for government service. This very early meritocracy attracted attention from such nearby states as Japan, Korea, and Vietnam, resulting in profound educational and philosophical influences from China on these societies, including the adoption of the Chinese ideographic script. China also remained open to learning from its neighbours to the west, sending numerous emissaries to India to bring back ideas and texts from Buddhism. Hundreds of texts were translated into Chinese and had a long-lasting influence on education and society in the whole East Asian region for many centuries (de Bary, 1988).

The medieval period saw the beginning of travel and interchange between Asia and Europe, over the fabled Silk Route and by sea. Marco Polo's account of China in the 13th century tells little about its education system, since the civil service examinations had been halted under the Mongol dynasty. Later European visitors, such as the Jesuits of the 16th and 17th centuries, however, wrote admiring accounts of Chinese education that had considerable influence in Europe. One result was the development of highly selective examinations in France for entry to the Grandes Écoles, which in turn assured employment in the nation's civil service. While the Enlightenment and the emergence of modern science and industrialism are often regarded as European achievements, comparative education explorations make it clear that diverse educational contributions, such as mathematics from India, and optics and medicine developed by Arabic scholars, were essential foundations for European science (Hayhoe & Pan, 2001).

COMPARATIVE EDUCATION IN THE 19TH CENTURY

Marc Antoine Jullien, who is often regarded as a founder of the field of comparative education, was born in 1775 and experienced the French Revolution as a teenager. Always a democrat in spirit and orientation, his liberal ideas were unacceptable to Napoleon, and he was given low-level positions in the inspectorate that required travel to Holland, Germany, and other countries of Europe. He became more and more interested in education, visiting progressive educators such as Johann Pestalozzi and Philipp von Fellenberg in Switzerland, and corresponding with leaders as distant as Czar Alexander of Russia and Thomas Jefferson of the United States.

After years of travel, observation, and writing, Jullien developed a plan for comparative education, which he published in 1816. In it he called for the establishment of a Normal Institute of Education for Europe, which would educate teachers in the best-known methods of teaching as a model for Europe. The institute was to publish a regular bulletin to encourage periodical communication among "all informed men engaged in the science of education" (Fraser, 1964, p. 39). It was also to stimulate the writing of "elementary books...in the different branches of science, which can direct childhood and youth from the first elements to the most advanced steps of human knowledge...by a continuous series of well-linked exercises" (ibid., p. 40). Finally, education itself was to be developed into a "positive science" through the collection of facts and observations from different countries and their arrangement in analytical charts, which "permit them to be related and compared, to deduct from them certain principles....This would ensure that teachers were not abandoned to narrow and limited rules, to the caprices and to arbitration of those who control [education]" (Fraser, 1964, pp. 40–41).

Jullien died in 1848, at the age of 73, never having been able to realize this dream of an international institute for comparative education. Those who did carry forward the work of comparative education were mainly educators involved in developing new state systems of education, who looked to societies other than their own for ideas that would help in this process. Victor Cousin, who became minister of public instruction in France in 1840, found inspiration in the Prussian system of primary education, and in approaches to technical education in Holland (Brewer, 1971). Horace Mann, who was the first secretary of the Board of Education of Massachusetts, made a six-month tour to Europe in 1843 and wrote a report comparing educational systems in Scotland, Ireland, France, Germany, Holland, and England. This report greatly influenced the development of common schools for all children in the United States.

K. D. Ushinsky, a Russian reformer who lived from 1824 to 1870, wrote extensively on educational practices in European countries and the United States, seeking to identify principles that would facilitate educational reform. Sir Michael Sadler, a British scholar and educator, who lived from 1861 to 1943, was responsible for an Office of Special Reports for the British government between 1897 and 1903, which published studies of education in Germany, India, and many other countries. Sadler is best known for his warning against the borrowing of educational patterns from one society to another, and his insistence that educational institutions need to be understood first in relation to the culture and society in which they are found (Bereday, 1964a; Jones, 1971).

> "We cannot wander at pleasure among the educational systems of the world, like a child strolling through a garden, and pick off a flower from one bush and some leaves from another, and then expect that if we stick what we have gathered into the soil at home, we shall have a living plant."
>
> —Sir Michael Sadler (cited in Crossley & Watson, 2003, p. 6)

While European, American, and Russian educators had a degree of freedom in their search for educational ideas outside of their own societies, Japanese and Chinese educators worked to create modern systems of education under a tremendous sense of threat and pressure. They saw modern education as essential for strengthening their nations from within so that they could resist the forms of colonial domination and control that they saw imposed on many other regions of the world. In 1870, the Japanese government drafted a policy for sending students abroad, which identified those areas of strength that Japan wished to emulate—engineering and commerce from Britain; medicine, economics, and some basic sciences from Germany; mathematics and basic sciences from France; architecture and shipbuilding from Holland; and agriculture from the United States (Nakayama, 1989, p. 100). This pragmatic form of comparative education laid a sound basis for Japan's economic development while maintaining fundamental aspects of the Japanese spirit and cultural identity.

A few decades later, Chinese thinkers and educators also tried to study the educational systems of countries they might emulate and to select those patterns that would help them establish a strong modern nation. Unfortunately, their political and economic progress was hindered by Japanese as well as Western imperialism. Nevertheless, they had the opportunity to experiment with educational patterns from Europe, Japan, and the United States. By contrast, places such as India, Vietnam, the Philippines, and much of Africa had modern education systems imposed by Western colonizers. A darker side to comparative education emerged through the increasing use of comparative research in the design and reform of colonial education in the early 20th century (Advisory Committee on Native Education in British Tropical African Dependencies, 1925; White, 1996).

COMPARATIVE EDUCATION IN THE FIRST HALF OF THE 20TH CENTURY

Only in the 20th century did comparative education begin to be taught in universities as an academic field of study, in spite of the fact that Jullien had laid a foundation for the field even earlier than Auguste Comte's work in founding sociology as a discipline. Many of the pioneering scholars of comparative education were either refugees or émigrés who had personal experience of education in several different societies. In England, Nicholas Hans wrote one of the early textbooks, in which he emphasized the importance of understanding factors such as religion, language, geography, and economy, which shaped the educational patterns of each nation differently. Hans had left Russia and moved to London at the time of the Russian Revolution of 1917. He maintained a great interest in Soviet education and society, nevertheless, and his comparative analysis of national education systems included England, France, the Soviet Union, and the United States (Hans, 1967).

The counterpart to Hans in the United States was Isaac Kandel, who was the leading comparativist at Teachers College, Columbia University, from 1921 to the early 1950s. Kandel was born in Romania and did a master's degree at Manchester University in England. He then immigrated to the United States and did a doctorate under John Dewey at Columbia University. Like Hans, Kandel hoped to see comparative education develop as a positive science, with appropriate use of statistical data on education in various countries of the world. He emphasized the importance of understanding the contexts of education in different societies, especially the impact of different political systems on educational development. He felt the distinction between highly centralized systems of education, such as that of the Soviet Union, and decentralized ones, such as that of the United States, was of great significance. His comparative education textbook, first published in 1933, covered education in England, France, Italy, Germany, the Soviet Union, and the United States (Kandel, 1933).

Kandel also identified what was to become a central issue within the study of comparative education: the importance of education in the construction of world peace. This is a topic dealt with in Chapter Ten of this volume. At the end of the First World War, women's suffrage organizations, international teachers' associations, and progressive educators each advocated the formation of an educational body within the League of Nations, to promote peace through international understanding and the expansion of educational opportunity. Among them were two women, Beatrice Ensor of England and Elisabeth Rotton of Germany, who went on to found the International League for New Education in 1921, and to promote the Geneva Declaration for the Rights of the Child in 1922. Comparative and progressive educators on both sides of the Atlantic were convinced that educational systems played a part in the development of what Kandel described as "sinister" forms of nationalism (Kandel, 1933, p. xxiv). British and American governments, however, rejected an educational role for the league, arguing that education was a purely national concern.

Despite the absence of a footing inside the League of Nations, progressive educators went on to build the first international educational organization. Founded in 1929 and based in Geneva, the International Bureau of Education (IBE) came into being as an independent professional organization whose goals included the promotion of public education for all and the enhancement of education for international understanding.

Operating under the leadership of noted Swiss psychologist Jean Piaget from 1929 to 1967, with Spanish comparative educator Pedro Rossello as vice-director, the IBE gained the status of an intergovernmental organization and developed many of the functions later taken on by UNESCO after the Second World War. It hosted an Annual Conference on Public Education that brought together leaders from national educational systems, and collected and published educational statistics from as many nations as were willing to contribute information. In 1933, it launched an International Yearbook of Education as well as four bulletins per year. The IBE was merged with UNESCO in 1967 (Suchodolski et al., 1979).

Published histories of comparative education between the two World Wars have tended to focus on prominent scholars in Europe and North America, yet comparative education was also being developed and taught in other parts of the world. The first comparative education textbook in the Chinese language, for example, was published in 1928, five years before Kandel's famous textbook. It was written by Zhuang Zexuan, a professor of education at Zhejiang University. Three other books on comparative education were published in China between 1930 and 1934, showing the great importance this field was given in Chinese universities of the time (Jing & Zhou, 1985, p. 241). Like Hans and Kandel, Chinese scholars were trying to understand the broad principles of education that could be learned from comparative study. They also had urgent concerns about China's survival as a modern nation. Many Chinese educators had studied with John Dewey at Columbia or at other American universities, and there was huge interest in progressive child-centred education, with many experimental schools established in the Chinese coastal regions. However, it was extremely difficult for these ideas to be widely disseminated in circumstances of national economic collapse and a looming military invasion by Japan.

Chinese educators were also interested in the centralized French system of education, since it had succeeded in a geographic distribution of educational facilities throughout the country. This was a matter of great concern for China, where most of the modern schools were located in coastal areas and hinterland areas lagged far behind. At the same time, educators feared their nationalist government would use educational centralization as a means to suppress freedom of thought and to exert direct political control over schools. Comparative education studies provided important contextual analysis to help them wrestle with these difficult questions.

COMPARATIVE AND INTERNATIONAL EDUCATION IN THE SECOND HALF OF THE 20TH CENTURY

After the Second World War, comparative education developed very rapidly as a field of research and practice. The development of the United Nations Educational, Scientific, and Cultural Organization (UNESCO, f. 1945) and the gradual inclusion of education in the work of other international development organizations, such as the World Bank, UNICEF, the United States Agency for International Development, and the Canadian International Development Agency, created a new demand for comparative educational research. The Comparative and International Education Society (CIES) of the United States was founded in 1956, and the Comparative and International Education Society of Canada (CIESC) in 1967, and many other national societies came into being over these years. In 1970, the World Council of Comparative Education Societies was established, with its first congress held in Ottawa in 1972. In addition to the many national societies that belong to the World Council, regional comparative education societies such as the Comparative Education Society in Europe and the Comparative Education Society of Asia are also members. Many national societies have their own academic journals, and participate actively in various kinds of international work, including liaising with such international organizations as UNESCO. Because they give equal importance to the academic work of comparative education analysis and to active involvement in international development concerns, many have broadened their description of the field by using the term *comparative and international education*.

The intellectual development of comparative education reflects the developments that one can see in such major social science disciplines as sociology, political science, and anthropology. In the first two decades after the Second World War, its focus was almost entirely on the relationship between education and national development. Great attention was given to ensuring that comparative education be made fully "scientific," given the availability of more reliable and comprehensive educational statistics and the possibility of large-scale quantitative analysis using computers. This "positivistic" phase gave rise to lively debates over the purpose and method of the field.

By the mid-1970s, however, it became clear that many of the findings of comparative education had limited relevance for developing nations of the Global South. Most had gained political independence but their educational systems were still dominated by the ideas and influences of former colonial powers. Dependency theory and world systems theory, both rooted in neo-Marxist scholarship, helped to identify barriers to independent and culturally authentic educational development in the structures of the world capitalist system.

Processes of globalization, an economic and technological phenomenon with political and socio-cultural dimensions, alongside the collapse of the Soviet Union in 1991, have spawned a new era of contention in the field of comparative education (Crossley & Watson, 2003). For two centuries comparative education tended to draw its analytic frameworks from Western civilization. In the most recent period, however, comparative education has emerged as a stage for an enhanced dialogue among peoples and civilizations. Examples of this are evident in many chapters of this textbook, which bring forth perspectives from Indigenous peoples, women, and multicultural communities, as well as from different geographical regions, such as Africa, Asia, and Latin America. Current debates are coloured by theories of postmodernity and postcolonialism, and by heightened awareness of global topics such as equality, peace, and cultural and ecological sustainability. The brief overview of three widely debated approaches to comparative education that follows offers a critical perspective on its literature.

COMPARATIVE EDUCATION AS A SCIENCE?

One of the most influential comparative educators of the early postwar period was George Bereday, an immigrant from Poland, who succeeded Isaac Kandel at Teachers College, Columbia University. His 1964 textbook, *Comparative Method in Education*, laid out a systematic approach to collecting facts about different educational systems, juxtaposing them in tables or diagrammatic representation and then identifying principles or laws of education and societal development through inductive logic. Bereday recognized the difficulties of collecting comparable data and emphasized the need for comparative education researchers to learn the languages of the societies they studied and to limit their analyses to four or five countries. His book included comparative analyses of educational issues in Poland, the United States, the USSR, England, France, Germany, and Colombia (Bereday, 1964b).

Bereday stimulated others in turn to reflect on how comparative education could become a science. In 1969 Harold Noah and Max Eckstein, two scholars who had immigrated to the United States from Britain,

CHAPTER ONE: Why Study Comparative Education? 11

published an influential book entitled *Towards a Science of Comparative Education*. In this book they proposed an approach to comparative education that would make it possible to use educational data from a large number of countries in order to discover causal relationships between desired educational outcomes, and the educational and societal inputs that were responsible for them. The more countries whose data could be used for these large-scale studies, the more "scientifically" reliable would be the findings, they suggested. With the dawning of the computer age, it was seen as less important to study the languages and historical contexts of different education systems—rather, the essential data about education and its relation to societal development could be quantified and expressed numerically (Noah & Eckstein, 1969).

Two major questions have occupied the attention of comparative educators working in this positivistic mode from the 1960s to the present time. The first explores the relation between education and economic development. What kinds of investment in "human capital" will produce the highest "social rates of return" (benefit to the economy) or "individual rates of return" (income for the individual)? Economists are also interested in cost-benefit analysis and what are called "production function" studies, in which the unit costs of inputs are weighted against the outputs of schools. For example, is teacher training or the purchase of textbooks a better investment? These types of study are of particular importance for development agencies, such as the World Bank, whose educational loans are premised on successful economic outcomes, and the ability of the borrowing country to pay back the loans over time. In spite of increasingly sophisticated scientific techniques of analysis, however, these studies are far from precise.

The second question, which is of even greater interest to educators, is what factors in both school and society have a significant causal relationship with high educational achievement. What teaching styles produce the best results in mathematics? What size of class is optimal for high achievement in physics? What types of curricular organization result in most effective language learning? Beginning in the 1960s, the International Association for the Evaluation of Educational Achievement (IEA) began a series of studies to address these questions. Over the years, more and more countries have participated, and alternative international studies of achievement, such as the Programme for International Student Assessment (PISA), have been developed. Chapter Thirteen of this text, by Anna K. Chmielewski, Joseph P. Farrell, and

Karen Mundy, introduces the methods and findings of these large-scale cross-national studies.

Not all comparativists of the 1960s and 1970s agreed that comparative education should try to become "scientific" in its methodology. British scholar Edmund King believed that human society could not be compared with the workings of a machine. It was more like the exchange of ideas in a conversation than the interaction of forces in a physical system. He thus put great emphasis on a comparative understanding of core concepts of education in different societies and nations.

King's textbook, *Other Schools and Ours*, was first published in 1962, and reappeared in five subsequent editions. King dealt with Denmark, France, Great Britain, the United States, the USSR, India, and Japan in this text (King, 1979). In his approach to research, King rejected the kinds of neutrality and objectivity that characterized scientific method, and emphasized subjective understanding of the hopes and expectations of teachers, students, and administrators as vitally important inputs for educational policy. In the early 1970s, he carried out a large-scale comparative study of schools, teachers, and students in England, France, Germany, Italy, and Sweden, with a focus on gathering ideas for a new approach to post-compulsory education. This was a time when universities were still highly elitist institutions, admitting only about 2 percent of young people aged 18 and above (King, 1974; 1975).

Although King was not an anthropologist, his attention to the ways in which students and teachers understood and constructed their social worlds anticipated the kinds of approaches to social theory associated with phenomenology and ethnography. One of the most influential comparative educators of a later period, Canadian scholar Vandra Masemann, developed an ethnographic approach to comparative education that attends to the ways in which human beings create meaning through education in different cultural contexts. Masemann describes her approach to comparative education as critical ethnography: she views neo-Marxism as an essential frame for a critical analysis of oppressive structures in the global economic

> "It is not only the top-level planner who is so engaged nowadays, but the teacher in the classroom too, and also the parent or politician or employer who may be no expert in comparative studies *per se*, but who has an *experiential* contribution to make to the world's comparative analysis."
> —Edmund King (1979, p. 20)

CHAPTER ONE: Why Study Comparative Education?

system whose influence reaches right down to local schools (Masemann, 1982). In recent years, there has been increasing attention given to what actually happens within schools, including the organization of learning, teaching practices, and efforts at school improvement, as demonstrated in Chapter Three by Joseph P. Farrell, Caroline Manion, and Santiago Rincón-Gallardo; Chapter Four by Sarfaroz Niyozov; and Chapter Five by Stephen Anderson and Malini Sivasubramaniam.

Another challenge to comparative education as a "science" came from Brian Holmes. He did not reject scientific method, but claimed that Bereday, Noah, and Eckstein were following an outmoded approach to science in their focus on causality. Holmes' problem approach to comparative education followed Karl Popper's idea of science as a series of imaginative conjectures that are subjected to rigorous testing in the specific conditions of the laboratory experiment. Those hypotheses that survive rigorous testing can be considered tentatively true until such time as they are proven false (Popper, 1963). Holmes felt comparative educators should identify important problems in education, look for solutions in the experiences of different societies, then predict which solutions would produce desirable educational results in the specific conditions of one society. These predictions would be tested not in the laboratory, but in the future unfolding of educational developments. For Holmes, the most significant elements in these specific conditions were cultural. He suggested ideal types as a sociological tool for taking into account deep-rooted religious and cultural beliefs about human persons, the nature of society, and the nature of knowledge. He thus developed a methodology that he regarded as scientific in a post-positivist way, and which gave great importance to non-quantifiable religious and cultural values (Holmes, 1981).

> "[A]ttempts to equalize educational opportunity on a global scale have led to the ignoring of local cultural values and traditional forms of knowledge and ways of thinking, which are in danger of becoming extinct."
> —Vandra Masemann (2013, p. 128)

Lê Thàn Khôi and Gu Mingyuan challenged the limited notion of comparative education as a science from a different direction by demonstrating the deep historical and cultural roots of non-Western educational systems—systems that could not be simply engineered through positive science. Both come from East Asia: Lê from Vietnam and Gu from China. Whereas Lê had spent much of his career in France and written mainly in French, Gu studied in the Soviet Union in the 1950s, then returned to China to revive the field of comparative education there, beginning in the early 1960s.

Lê Thàn Khôi's work suggests that comparative education could make possible a general theory of education derived from an in-depth study of the reciprocal relations between education and society in different types of civilizations over human history. Such a theory would achieve a universalism that acknowledges how the achievements of modernity were derived from multiple civilizations, not only that of Europe. Lê's approach to comparative education thus looks back into history, and recovers aspects of human heritage that have been forgotten in the rush to constitute comparative education as a science (Lê, 1986).

Gu Mingyuan's approach to comparative education developed in a very different context. He entered university in the year of China's successful Communist revolution. After two years of study in Beijing, he was sent to study in the Lenin Normal College in Moscow for five years. On return to China in 1955, he was full of enthusiasm for all that Soviet ideas could offer to China's socialist educational development, only to face disappointments and setbacks as China's new leaders rejected Soviet assistance as social imperialism in 1958, and threw the country into turmoil by unleashing a cultural revolution in 1966. The centre and journal that Gu had established for the study of foreign education in the early 1960s were closed down, and he was sent for hard labour in the countryside. Only after Deng Xiaoping came to power in 1978 was he able to draw upon his extensive comparative knowledge of education systems in different parts of the world to advise China's leadership on educational reforms that would make possible the modernization of China's economy and society (Hayhoe, 2001).

Gu's first approach was to introduce human capital theory, and to show how this was not the preserve only of capitalist countries but was used by Karl Marx in *Das Kapital*. Gu presented a comparative analysis of the modernization experiences of Western countries and the Soviet Union, which drew on extensive empirical data. On this basis, he persuaded the Chinese government to invest heavily in education (Gu, 2001a). Mingyuan's scientific approach to comparative education proved liberating to educators who had long felt themselves the victims of political movements outside of their control. They were delighted to be freed from "the caprices and…arbitration of those who control

CHAPTER ONE: Why Study Comparative Education?

education," to use a phase from Jullien's *Plan for Comparative Education* (Fraser, 1964, pp. 40–41).

Gu was not satisfied, however, to stay with this Western approach to comparative education. He developed a long-term research project to explore China's own cultural and educational traditions, and to identify educational patterns and ideas that would provide an indigenous basis for China's educational modernization (Gu, 2001b). He has also stimulated Chinese educators to reach out to the world and explain the unique educational ethos of East Asian countries, where Confucian traditions have been strong, and what this ethos can offer to educators elsewhere. Chapter Two of this volume, by Ruth Hayhoe and Jun Li, deals with this topic from a comparative philosophical perspective.

> "Neo-classical development theory views schooling as being a 'liberating process,' in which the child is transformed from a 'traditional' individual to a 'modern' one....But in dependency theory, the transformation that takes place in school cannot be liberating, since a person is simply changed from one role in a dependent system to a different role....The kind of economic structure able to absorb all the educated is not possible under conditions of the dependent situation. Thus a system of schooling which complements all people's social utility is also not possible."
> —Martin Carnoy (1974, pp. 56–57)

COMPARATIVE EDUCATION, IMPERIALISM, AND THE WORLD SYSTEM

In 1974, a book entitled *Education as Cultural Imperialism* by Martin Carnoy exploded like a bombshell in comparative education circles. Up to this time, the main units of comparative education analyses had been nation-states and national systems of education, with educational systems in Europe and North America tending to dominate the literature. Carnoy's book showed how difficult it was for nations in the Global South to develop modern schools to serve their own social, political, and economic development. Much that went on in schools in Africa, India, and Southeast Asia was not decided by their own educators but was determined by the languages, curricular patterns, and approaches to school organization that had been left behind by their colonizers. Educational policy was also shaped by ongoing dependence on development aid, which was described as "neocolonial."

Dependency theory was a form of neo-Marxism that had been developed by economists in Latin America to explain the widespread experience of underdevelopment or distorted development in countries of that region. They saw the cause for this in their role as peripheral parts of a world economic system controlled by centre countries in Europe and North America. Their education systems, which were dominated by European concepts they had inherited, served to make this subservience appear a normal and unavoidable stage of development. The Brazilian educator Paulo Freire was one of the first to challenge this educational imperialism with his idea of "conscientization." He sought to stimulate Latin American young people and adults to see with their own eyes and to struggle for independence, dignity, and self-determination (Freire, 1972). Freire's work has had wide-ranging influence, most notably among educators interested in transformative and liberatory approaches to learning (Schugurensky, 1998). The spread of Freirean pedagogy illustrates an important development in the field of comparative education: the expansion of South-North flows of educational ideas.

Some of the best-known scholars who pioneered this approach to comparative education are Robert Arnove, Philip Altbach, Gail Paradise Kelly, and Nelly Stromquist. Robert Arnove worked to relate comparative education to world system theory, another form of neo-Marxism which is based in a historical analysis of the development of the capitalist world system, and looks at the way core, semi-peripheral, and peripheral regions are shaped by economic and capital flows (Arnove, 1980). Gail Kelly is recognized as one of the early women pioneers of the field of comparative education. As co-editor with Philip Altbach of the important book *Education and the Colonial Experience*, she built on her early research on education in Vietnam and French West Africa, where one could see the persistence of French colonial influences, to develop a critical approach to education in Southern countries (Altbach & Kelly, 1984). She also became a leading figure in feminist approaches to comparative education, editing several important studies on women in education in different parts of the world (D. Kelly, 1996; Kelly & Elliot, 1982). Similarly, Nelly Stromquist sought to blend dependency and feminist theories, documenting the nature

> "For feminist scholars of education in the Third World, our goal is to find ways in which schools can be made a force to better women's lives."
> —Gail Kelly (cited in D. Kelly, 1996, p. 37)

of gender inequality in education first in Latin America and later at the global level (Stromquist, 1995). Grace Mak has carried forward this work in Asia, with titles such as *Women, Education and Development in Asia: Cross-National Perspectives* (Mak, 1996). Chapter Seven of this volume, "Gender and Education," by Kara Janigan and Vandra Masemann, deals with this literature.

Another critical approach to problems of education and imperialism came from a group of scholars who initiated the World Order Models Project (WOMP) in the late 1960s and described themselves as non-Marxist socialists. Johann Galtung, a Norwegian who held one of the world's first chairs in Peace Studies, developed a structural theory of imperialism. He identified structures of domination in political, economic, communications, and cultural arenas, and proposed ways of countering them through solidarity among nations in the Global South (Galtung, 1971). Chapter Ten by Kathy Bickmore gives many insights into the field of peace studies pioneered by Galtung and its importance for education.

The loosely organized group of sociologists, educators, and political scientists associated with the World Order Models Project created space for visioning a more just and sustainable world order. They brought ideas from the civilizations of India and Africa into the mainstream of Western social sciences. While there were not many comparative education scholars among them, one article that became a classic in the field was Ali Mazrui's "The African University as a Multi-national Corporation" (Mazrui, 1975). The more recent scholarship of George Dei, with its focus on understanding the roots of African culture and spirituality as a source for educational innovation, is another important contribution to the goal of inter-civilizational dialogue and sustainability envisaged by the WOMP scholars (Dei, 2002; 1994).

COMPARATIVE EDUCATION AND GLOBALIZATION

Perhaps more than any other theme, globalization has provoked expanding interest and lush debate within the field of comparative education. Most definitions of globalization begin with the idea that the integration of human societies across pre-existing territorial units has sped up, assisted in part by the development of new information, communication, and transportation technologies that compress time and space (Mundy, 2005). For some authors, the main motor of integration is economic—the expansion of truly global chains of commercialized production and consumption and the development of a knowledge economy. Others focus on the cultural and political drivers. Whatever the focus, central to all theories of globalization is the notion that interregional and "deterritorialized" flows of all kinds of social interaction have reached new magnitudes in recent history. Conceptually, globalization challenges comparative education's traditional focus on national systems of education. It also creates new opportunities for understanding those aspects of the educational enterprise that transcend national borders.

Several dimensions of engagement with the issue of globalization in the field of comparative education are worth highlighting. First, comparativists have been at the forefront of scholarship that shows how economic globalization has contributed to increasing fiscal constraint among states—with profound implications for the funding and organization of national systems of education (Carnoy, 1999). Escalating pressures for the expansion of free trade and global competition have forced national governments in all parts of the world to reposition their economies. They find themselves under pressure to view education more as an investment in human capital for competitiveness than as part of a range of measures of social provision and protection to ensure the welfare of all citizens. Economic globalization raises demand for skills and qualifications, but reduces the state's capacity to meet it. This creates new openings for the expansion of private educational services, particularly at higher levels, and new incentives for efficiency reforms at lower levels. Reduced budgets and increased migration and cultural exchange have also challenged the state's ability to use education to achieve social cohesion (Green, 2002).

Many scholars in comparative education have begun to document how a common set of educational reforms, organized around goals of market-like accountability and efficiency, have spread around the world (Ball, 1998; Steiner-Khamsi, 2004). In this volume, Chapter Five by Stephen Anderson and Malini Sivasubramaniam, and Chapter Thirteen by Anna K. Chmielewski, Joseph P. Farrell, and Karen Mundy explore two aspects of these global reform agendas: the heightened effort to engineer school effectiveness and improvement, and the expansion of international testing regimes. Comparativists have also studied the expanding influence of key intergovernmental organizations—the Organisation for Economic Co-operation and Development, the World Bank, the World Trade Organization, as well as regional organizations such as the European Community, the Association of Southeast Asian Nations (ASEAN), and

CHAPTER ONE: Why Study Comparative Education? 19

the North American Free Trade Agreement (NAFTA) (see, for example, Dale & Robertson, 2002; Henry et al., 2001; Mundy, 1998; Robertson, Bonal, & Dale, 2002). They have begun to make sense of the expansion of other transnational flows—for example, the growth of transnational social movements, teachers unions, and non-governmental organizations (NGOs) advocating for a universal right to education (Mundy & Murphy, 2001); and the implications of expanding transnational flows of students and transborder delivery of services in higher education.

The infusion of postmodernism and postcolonial theories into the field of comparative education has profoundly shaped the field's engagement with the concept of globalization. Postmodern and postcolonial theories challenge the assumption that globalization is mainly an economic process. Instead, globalization is understood as a cultural process, in which Western modernity, science, and rationality play a powerful role in the subjugation of other peoples and cultures (Crossley & Tikly, 2004; see also Paulston, 1996). In turn, postmodern and postcolonial scholars focus attention on the subversive and hybrid nature of local responses to cultural globalization, using ethnographic and subjective approaches to research (Hickling-Hudson, 2006). In the recent work of Kathryn Anderson-Levitt, Michel Welmond, Anne Hickling-Hudson, and Amy Stambach, among others, we see how local communities engage and reshape globalization in the everyday practices surrounding the school (Anderson-Levitt, 2003). In comparative education, postmodern and postcolonial scholarship has promoted the inclusion of diverse perspectives and ways of knowing, drawing upon Freirean pedagogy, transformative learning, and the experiences of Indigenous and subaltern cultures. Chapter Seven by Kara Janigan and Vandra Masemann, and Chapter Six by Katia Sol Madjidi and Jean-Paul Restoule, bring forth some of these perspectives by highlighting the comparative study of gender in education and of Indigenous ways of knowing and learning.

Today, most research in comparative education still acknowledges the importance of national governments in shaping the educational destinies of the world's people. However, globalization has stoked interest in what Arnove, Torres, and Franz have described as the "dialectic between the local and the global" (Arnove, Torres, & Franz, 2013). The field is now animated by questions of whether and why systems of education are homogenizing or retaining their local characteristics (Baker & LeTendre, 2005; Ramirez & Boli, 1987), and whether national educational systems can enhance social equality and social cohesion in the context of globalization (Green, 2002). Joseph P. Farrell, Caroline Manion, and Santiago Rincón-Gallardo (Chapter Three), Sarfaroz Niyozov (Chapter Four), and Karen Mundy and Robyn Read (Chapter Eleven) each tackle these questions in quite different ways in their contributions to this volume. These include the rise and spread of a global "Education for All" movement, alternatives to traditional schooling, and the influences of developing country cultural contexts on teaching practices. In Chapter Two by Ruth Hayhoe and Jun Li, we will learn how educational traditions in East Asian countries have shaped their response to globalization.

Comparativists also remain deeply concerned with the role that education can play in the normative construction of society both globally and locally, and are exploring educational practices that can enhance opportunities for dialogue among peoples, cultures, societies, and civilizations and prepare active, self-reflexive global citizens. The growing comparative study of civics and moral education, multicultural and anti-racist education, conflict and peace education, and education for global citizenship has reached an all-time high, as will be demonstrated in Chapter Eight by Monisha Bajaj, Chapter Nine by Mark Evans and Dina Kiwan, and Chapter Ten by Kathy Bickmore (see Steiner-Khamsi, Torney-Purta, & Schwille, 2002).

Why study comparative education? We hope this chapter has given you a sense of how understanding education in other cultures, regions, and contexts may enable you to think freshly and differently about the curriculum, classroom organization, and approaches to teaching commonly used in North American schools. We hope that the approaches to comparative education we have introduced will enable you to reflect critically on widely held assumptions about education and society that may need to be questioned. Most of all, we hope you will be stimulated to develop your own principles of education in dialogue with educators and scholars who have developed the field of comparative and international education over the past century and a half.

QUESTIONS FOR REFLECTION AND DISCUSSION
1. What experiences of cross-cultural learning are you aware of from ancient or medieval history? In what ways is comparing a natural aspect of human learning?

2. What role has human immigration played in comparative education? Do you think it is still important in the present period? Why or why not?
3. Which names of educators and educational issues in this chapter were already familiar to you? Which of those new to you attracts your interest, and why?

SUGGESTED AUDIO-VISUAL RESOURCES
The Finland Phenomenon: Inside the World's Most Surprising School System, by Bob Compton (2011). Part 1 of 4 available at: www.youtube.com/watch?v=VhH78NnRpp0
This 60-minute film comparatively explores the Finnish and US education systems, the former being among the highest performing systems in the world. Using observation and interviews with students, teachers, parents, administrators, and government officials, the film seeks to highlight the factors of success characterizing the education system in Finland and then use these to suggest gaps or areas where the United States may learn and improve. Topics include, but are not limited to, teacher recruitment and training, curriculum, organization of schooling, pedagogy, system reform and vision, and the wider policy, socio-cultural, economic, and political context. The film can serve as an excellent resource for studying and thinking about what makes an education system "successful" and the challenges of applying lessons learned from one system to another.

SUGGESTIONS FOR FURTHER READING
Adamson, Bob. (2012). International comparative studies in teaching and teacher education. *Teaching and Teacher Education, 28*, 641–648.
Alexander, Robin J. (2001). Border crossings: Towards a comparative pedagogy. *Comparative Education, 37*(4), 507–523.
Ball, Stephen. (1998). Big policies, small world: An introduction to international perspectives in education policy. *Comparative Education, 34*(2), 119–130.
Carney, Stephen. (2008). Negotiating policy in an age of globalization: Exploring educational "policyscapes" in Denmark, Nepal and China. *Comparative Education Review, 54*(4), 577–601.
Dei, George. (2002). Learning culture, spirituality and local knowledge: Implications for African schooling. *Internationl Review of Education, 48*(5), 335–360.

Hickling-Hudson, Anne. (2006). Cultural complexity, post-colonialism and educational change: Challenges for comparative educators. *International Review of Education, 52*(1), 201–218.

Lê, Thàn Khôi. (1986). Toward a general theory of education. *Comparative Education Review, 30*(1), 12–29.

Masemann, Vandra Lea. (2013). Culture and education. In Robert Arnove, Carlos Torres, and Stephen Franz (Eds.), *Comparative education: Dialectic of the global and the local* (4th ed.) (pp. 113–132). Lanham, MD: Rowman and Littlefield Publishers.

Mundy, Karen. (2005). Globalization and educational change: New policy worlds. In Nina Bascia, Alister Cumming, Amanda Datnow, Kenneth Leithwood, and David Livingstone (Eds.), *International handbook of educational policy, Part I* (pp. 3–17). Netherlands: Springer.

O'Sullivan, Margo C., Wolhuter, Charl C., and Maarman, Ruaan F. (2010). Comparative education in primary teacher education in Ireland and South Africa. *Teaching and Teacher Education, 10*, 775–785.

Schugurensky, Daniel. (1998). The legacy of Paulo Freire. *Convergence, 31*(1–2), 17–29.

Vavrus, Francis, and Bartlett, Lesley. (2012). Comparative pedagogies and epistemological diversity: Social and materials contexts of teaching in Tanzania. *Comparative Education Review, 56*(4), 634–658.

REFERENCES

Advisory Committee on Native Education in British Tropical African Dependencies. (1925). *Education policy in British tropical Africa*. London: Her Majesty's Stationery Office.

Altbach, Philip, and Kelly, Gail P. (1984). *Education and the colonial experience*. New Brunswick, NJ: Transaction Books.

Anderson-Levitt, Kathryn. (2003). *Local meanings, global schooling*. New York: Palgrave Macmillan.

Arnove, Robert. (1980). Comparative education and world systems analysis. *Comparative Education Review, 24*(1), 48–62.

Arnove, Robert, Torres, Carlos, and Franz, Stephen. (2013). *Comparative education: Dialectic of the global and the local* (4th ed.). Lanham, MD: Rowman and Littlefield Publishers.

Baker, David P., and LeTendre, Gerald. (2005). *National differences, global similarities*. Palo Alto, CA: Stanford University Press.

Ball, Stephen. (1998). Big policies, small world: An introduction to international perspectives in education policy. *Comparative Education, 34*(2), 119–130.

Bereday, George. (1964a). Sir Michael Sadler's "Study of foreign systems of education." *Comparative Education Review, 7*(3), 307–314.
Bereday, George. (1964b). *Comparative method in education.* New York: Holt Rinehart and Winston.
Bray, Mark (Ed.). (2003). *Comparative education: Continuing traditions, new challenges and new paradigms.* London: Kluwer Publishers.
Brewer, Walter, V. (1971). *Victor Cousin as a comparative educator.* New York: Teachers College Press.
Carnoy, Martin. (1999). *Globalization and educational reform: What planners need to know.* Paris: International Institute for Education Planning (IIEP).
Carnoy, Martin. (1974). *Education as cultural imperialism.* New York: D. McKay Co.
Crossley, Michael, and Tikly, Leon. (2004). Postcolonial perspectives and comparative and international research in education: A critical introduction. *Comparative Education, 40*(2), 147–156.
Crossley, Michael, and Watson, Keith. (2003). *Comparative and international research in education: Globalisation, context and difference.* New York: Routledge and Falmer.
Dale, Roger, and Robertson, Susan. (2002). The varying effects of regional organizations as subjects of globalization of education. *Comparative Education Review, 46*(1), 10–36.
de Bary, William Theodore. (1988). *East Asian civilizations: A dialogue in five stages.* Cambridge, MA: Harvard University Press.
Dei, George. (2002). Learning culture, spirituality and local knowledge: Implications for African schooling. *International Review of Education, 48*(5), 335–360.
Dei, George. (1994). Afrocentricity: A cornerstone of pedagogy. *Anthropology and Education Quarterly, 25*(1), 3–28.
Fraser, Stewart. (1964). *Jullien's plan for comparative education 1816–1817.* New York: Teachers College, Columbia University.
Freire, Paulo. (1972). *The pedagogy of the oppressed.* London: Sheed.
Galtung, Johan. (1971). A structural theory of imperialism. *Journal of Peace Research, 8*(2), 81–117.
Green, Andy. (2002). *Education, globalization and the role of comparative research.* Centenary Lectures. London: Institute of Education, University of London.
Gu, Mingyuan. (2001a). Modern production and modern education. In Gu Mingyuan (Ed.), *Education in China and abroad: Perspectives from a lifetime in comparative education* (pp. 27–51). Hong Kong: Comparative Education Research Centre, University of Hong Kong.
Gu, Mingyuan. (2001b). Modernisation and education in China's cultural traditions. In Gu Mingyuan (Ed.), *Education in China and abroad: Perspectives*

from a lifetime in comparative education (pp. 101–110). Hong Kong: Comparative Education Research Centre, University of Hong Kong.

Hans, Nicholas. (1967). *Comparative education*. London: Routledge and Kegan Paul.

Hayhoe, Ruth. (2001). Introduction. In Gu Mingyuan (Ed.), *Education in China and abroad: Perspectives from a lifetime in Comparative Education* (pp. 5–24). Hong Kong: Comparative Education Research Centre, University of Hong Kong.

Hayhoe, Ruth, and Pan, Julia (Eds.). (2001). *Knowledge across cultures: A contribution to dialogue among civilizations*. Hong Kong: Comparative Education Research Institute, University of Hong Kong.

Henry, Miriam, Lingard, Bob, Rizvi, Fazal, and Taylor, Sandra (Eds.). (2001). *The OECD, globalisation and education policy*. Oxford: Pergamon Press.

Hickling-Hudson, Anne. (2006). Cultural complexity, post-colonialism and educational change: Challenges for comparative educators. *International Review of Education, 52*(1), 201–218.

Holmes, Brian. (1981). *Comparative education: Some considerations of method*. London: George Allen and Unwin.

Jing, Shi-bo, and Zhou, Nan-zhao. (1985). Comparative education in China. *Comparative Education Review, 29*(2), 240–250.

Jones, Philip E. (1971). *Comparative education: Purpose and method*. St. Lucia: University of Queensland Press.

Kandel, Issac. (1933). *Comparative education*. Boston: Houghton & Mifflin Co.

Kelly, David (Ed.). (1996). *International feminist perspectives on educational reform: The work of Gail Paradise Kelly*. New York: Garland Publishing.

Kelly, Gail P., and Elliot, Carolyn M. (1982). *Women's education in the third world: Comparative perspectives*. Albany: State University of New York Press.

King, Edmund. (1975). *Post-compulsory education II: The way ahead*. London: Sage.

King, Edmund. (1974). *Post-compulsory education: A new analysis in Western Europe*. London: Sage.

Kubbow, Patricia K., and Fossum, Paul R. (2003). *Comparative education: Exploring issues in international context*. Upper Saddle River, NJ: Merrill/ Prentice Hall.

Lê, Thàn Khôi. (1986). Toward a general theory of education. *Comparative Education Review, 30*(1), 12–29.King, Edmund. (1979). *Other schools and ours* (5th ed.). London: Holt, Rinehart and Winston.

Mak, Grace (Ed.). (1996). *Women, education and development in Asia: Cross-national perspectives*. New York: Garland Publishing.

Manzon, M. (2011). *Comparative education: The construction of a field*. Hong Kong: Comparative Education Research Centre and Springer.

Masemann, Vandra Lea. (2013). Culture and education. In Robert Arnove, Carlos Torres, and Stephen Franz (Eds.), *Comparative education: The dialectic of the global and the local* (4th ed.) (pp. 113–131). Lanham, MD: Rowman and Little Field Publishers.

Masemann, Vandra Lea. (1982). Critical ethnography in the study of comparative education. *Comparative Education Review, 6*(1), 1–15.

Mazrui, Ali. (1975). The African university as a multi-national corporation. *Harvard Educational Review, 45*(2), 191–210.

Mundy, Karen. (2005). Globalization and educational change: New policy worlds. In Nina Bascia, Alister Cumming, Amanda Datnow, Kenneth Leithwood, and David Livingstone (Eds.), *International handbook of educational policy, Part I* (pp. 3–17). Netherlands: Springer.

Mundy, Karen. (1998). Educational multilateralism and world (dis)order. *Comparative Education Review, 42*(4), 448–478.

Mundy, Karen, and Murphy, Lynn. (2001). Transnational advocacy, global civil society: Emerging evidence from the field of education. *Comparative Education Review, 45*(1), 85–126.

Nakayama, Shigeru. (1989). Independence and choice: Western impacts on Japanese higher education. In Philip G. Altbach and Viswanathan Selveratnam (Eds.), *From dependence to autonomy: The development of Asian universities* (pp. 97–114). Dordecht, the Netherlands: Kluwer Academic Publishers.

Noah, Harold, and Eckstein, Max. (1969). *Towards a science of comparative education*. London: MacMillan.

Paulston, Rolland (Ed.). (1996). *Social cartography: Mapping ways of seeing social and educational change*. New York: Garland Publishing.

Popper, Karl. (1963). *Conjectures and refutations*. London: Routledge and Kegan Paul.

Ramirez, Francisco, and Boli, John. (1987). Global patterns of educational institutionalization. In George M. Thomas, John W. Meyer, Francisco O. Ramirez, and John Boli, *Institutional structure: Constituting the state, society and the individual* (pp. 150–172). Newbury Park, CA: Sage.

Robertson, Susan, Bonal, Xavier, and Roger Dale. (2002). GATS and the education service industry: Politics of scale and global territorialisation. *Comparative Education Review, 46*(3), 472–496.

Schugurensky, Daniel. (1998). The legacy of Paulo Freire. *Convergence, 31*(1–2), 17–29.

Steiner Khamsi, Gita (Ed.). (2004). *The global politics of educational borrowing*. New York: Teachers College Press.

Steiner Khamsi, Gita, Torney-Purta, Judith, and Schwille, John (Eds.). (2002). *New paradigms and recurring paradoxes in education for citizenship*. Oxford: Elsevier Science Ltd.

Stromquist, Nelly. (1995). Romancing the state: Gender and power in education. *Comparative Education Review, 39*(4), 423–454.

Suchodolski, Bogdan, et al. (1979). *The International Bureau of Education in the service of educational development*. Paris: UNESCO.
Trethewey, A. R. (1976). *Introducing comparative education*. Oxford: Pergamon Press.
White, Bob. (1996). Talk about school: Education and the colonial project in French and British Africa, 1860–1960. *Comparative Education, 32*(1), 9–25.

SECTION I

(RE)FORMING SCHOOLING: PHILOSOPHY, POLICY, AND SCHOOL ORGANIZATION

CHAPTER TWO
PHILOSOPHY AND COMPARATIVE EDUCATION: WHAT CAN WE LEARN FROM EAST ASIA?

Ruth Hayhoe and Jun Li

INTRODUCTION

This chapter begins with some reflections on philosophy and comparative education. The philosophical ideas of East Asia are taken as an "other," from which to look comparatively at some of the fundamental values that underlie educational thought in the West. Given the history of European colonization, and the attraction European models had for modernizing countries that were never colonized, these values became the foundations for modern systems of education. State schooling systems were first put in place in newly emerging European nations of the 18th and 19th centuries, as we have seen in Chapter One.

Ideal types will facilitate this comparative reflection on Europe and East Asia. German sociologist Max Weber developed ideal types as a way of identifying the distinctive contributions of differing religious and philosophical value systems to the process of social change. Weber (1994) defined ideal types as "an attempt to analyse historically unique configurations...by means of genetic concepts" (p. 266). He suggested that ideal types require a high degree of logical integration to be meaningful. Brian Holmes pioneered their use in comparative education as a way of probing the deep-rooted value orientations of different education systems.

Part one of this chapter gives a comparative overview of ideas of society, knowledge, and the human person in classical China and Europe. It highlights the profoundly different implications of these philosophical traditions for education. The patterns and underlying values of two important models of modern education, the American and the Soviet, are also presented.

Part two traces the historical development of modern educational systems in East Asia, showing how they absorbed the Western patterns that had been borrowed or imposed. Japan was the first to surprise the world, with its remarkable recovery after the Second World War, and the development of a strong economy and democratic polity. It was followed by the "the four little dragons" of South Korea, Taiwan, Singapore, and Hong Kong, whose development stimulated lively debates over an emerging East Asian model of capitalism (Vogel, 1991). Subsequently Mainland China and Vietnam adopted the idea of a "socialist market economy" and achieved remarkable reforms.

Part three offers reflections on East Asia's modern educational experience within the three paradigms of comparative education introduced in Chapter One: comparative education as a science; comparative education and imperialism; and comparative education and globalization, or the dialogue among civilizations. In taking each framework as a lens to analyze the East Asian experience, we will discover similarities and differences with education in other parts of the world. We will also explore some fascinating paradoxes that reflect deep-rooted philosophical differences between East Asia and the West.

Part four addresses the important question of what the West can learn from the educational ideas of East Asian societies, which share a common Confucian heritage, though they have developed under diverse experiences of imperialism, colonialism, capitalism, and socialism. Since the end of the Cold War and the beginning of a dialogue among civilizations in the 1990s, space has finally been created for the inheritors and admirers of East Asian civilization to introduce its educational values to the global community. The same is true for other civilizations, such as those of South Asia, the Middle East, and Africa. Later chapters of this text will explore some of their unique contributions to educational thought.

COMPARING CHINESE AND WESTERN EDUCATIONAL VALUES

Brian Holmes suggested the use of ideal types as a way of identifying contrasting values about society, knowledge, and the human person. In his 1981 textbook, he sketched out ideal types for comparing European,

CHAPTER TWO: Philosophy and Comparative Education   31

Soviet, and American education by summarizing the views of Plato, Karl Marx, and John Dewey (Holmes, 1981, pp. 111–175). Holmes was fully aware of the extreme generality of these types. His purpose was not to simplify complex educational phenomena, rather to identify deep-rooted differences, and interpret educational debates at a profound level.

Here we will give a brief consideration to the ideas of the Greek philosopher Plato (427–347 BCE), which had a long-lasting influence on the development of European education. We will view them in comparison to Chinese classical thought, which was shaped primarily by Confucius (551–479 BCE), Mencius (372–289 BCE), and Xun Zi (313–238 BCE), and also by the moderating influences of Lao Zi, the founder of Daoism, and by the ideas of Buddhism, a religion which was introduced to China from India in the first century CE.

In his wonderfully reflective volume, *The World of Thought in Ancient China*, Benjamin Schwartz explains the ideas of society, knowledge, and the human person in the dominant Chinese tradition, showing how different they were from parallel ideas in Europe. In Confucian thought, the ideal family is "the ultimate source of those values which humanize the relations of authority and hierarchy that must exist in any civilized society" (Schwartz, 1985, p. 70). In the family, human beings learn those virtues which redeem society. Authority comes to be accepted and exercised through the binding power of religious and moral sentiments based on kinship ties. The rites or ceremonies established by the classical texts thus hold together an entire normative order, which is derived from the relations of the ideal family. This concept of social order was accepted and embraced across the entire Chinese Mainland, as well as by nearby societies such as Korea, Japan, and Vietnam.

By contrast, in the city states of Greece, Plato outlined the good society as one which was ruled by guardians or philosopher kings. They belonged to the highest of three classes of people, with warriors maintaining order and workers seeing to the mundane needs of society. The philosopher kings accepted a pattern of life that had no place for the family, which was viewed as particularistic and limited in its moral value. They were devoted to a vision of good that was attained through abstract mathematical thought rather than practical life experience. By the same token the good society was to be regulated by impartial laws, which ensured the fair and just treatment of individuals according to their place in a fixed social order (Boyd & King, 1975, pp. 32–36). Schwartz (1985) suggests one of the reasons for this fundamental difference in emphasis lay in the character and size of the Greek city state, compared to the Chinese empire (p. 69).

Confucius viewed knowledge as beginning with the cumulative understanding of masses of empirical particulars, then linking these particulars to one's own experience, and subsequently to an underlying unity that tied everything together. By contrast, Plato saw knowledge as created through abstract mathematical reasoning and the perception of eternal forms, something that only philosopher kings could do, through a rigorous process of deductive logic. For Plato, knowledge had to rise above the limits of ordinary human experience. For Confucius, knowledge "does not rise from the chaos of the world of particulars to a world of eternal forms, since...the way remains indissolubly linked to the empirical world" (ibid., p. 95).

As for the human person, Confucius called for a lifelong pursuit of human heartedness, a learning for the sake of the self. The self, however, was viewed as a flowing stream, and human development as a way of harmonizing the self with the family, society, and the world of nature (Tu, 1998, pp. 13–14). Traditional Chinese society had four classes— scholar-officials, merchants, craftspeople, and farmers—yet Confucius made the important statement that in education there are no class distinctions, and stressed the unlimited potential of each person for development through education. Later philosophers debated whether human nature was fundamentally good, as proposed by Mencius, or basically evil and needing to be controlled by law and punishment, as taught by Xun Zi. Nevertheless, all agreed on the importance of education. The concept that "everyone is educable, everyone can become a sage, and everyone is perfectible forms the basic optimism and dynamism towards education in the Confucian tradition" (Lee, 1996, p. 30).

By contrast, Plato's view of the human person put more emphasis on innate characteristics, suggesting that human beings were born to be philosopher kings, warriors, or workers, and should be educated to fulfill their ordained roles, in order that a society of justice and order could be maintained. Intelligence was not only inborn, but also passed on by heredity, in Plato's view. The philosopher kings were therefore given favourable conditions to ensure the continuance of a line of "superior" leaders. The ideal society maintained the distinction among the three classes, and there was no encouragement to educate either workers or warriors in ways that would enable them to become leaders (Boyd & King, 1975, p. 36).

CHAPTER TWO: Philosophy and Comparative Education   33

Plato's ideas were challenged almost immediately, in the work of his disciple Aristotle (383–322 BCE), and that of many later educators. Yet they expressed an idea that has persisted in Western educational thought—that there are certain innate qualities and abilities that no amount of education can change. By contrast, the Confucian view of the human person emphasizes the perfectibility of each person, if maximum effort is put into learning, with full support from family and community.

This Chinese conviction about human potential was further strengthened by Daoist ideas put forward in Lao Zi's *Classic of the Way*, which emphasized the relationship between human persons and the world of nature (Ames & Hall, 2004). Buddhism was later introduced to China from India, and this strengthened the Daoist understanding of the interconnection between human psychology and the natural world. It envisions a society where there are neither social nor cultural identities among its members (Weerasinghe, 1992, pp. 49–50).

The main motivation for learning in Chinese culture was intrinsic, a learning for the sake of the self, to develop one's full humanity. There was also an extrinsic motivation for learning in the famous civil service examination system, which took shape in the sixth century CE. It offered the opportunity for all male children to demonstrate their knowledge and ability through a series of examinations held at local, provincial, and capital levels throughout the empire. Those who succeeded in these examinations were given the opportunity to serve as scholar-officials. The competition for such opportunities was fierce, yet there was a significant record of social mobility in traditional Chinese society. Nearly every village had at least one example of a boy whose study efforts had enabled him to reach the top (Lee, 1996, p. 38).

By contrast, oral rather than written examinations were used in early European education. The medieval universities gained papal charters for a degree of autonomy and academic freedom from the 12th century CE, but their students were largely male clerics. Only in the 16th century with the Protestant Reformation were opportunities for literacy and self-advancement opened up to wider populations, beyond the land-owning aristocracy. When European Jesuits went to China in that same century, they were greatly impressed by the Chinese system of government. They wrote admiring accounts of educational practices that enabled the emperor to draw upon talented people from all classes who had been educated to a very high level (Llasera, 1987).

To complete the circle of comparison between East Asia and the West, we will consider two other ideal types. John Dewey's idea of society, knowledge, and the human person gives insight into the fundamental values underlying American education, which would influence Japan, South Korea, and Taiwan. Karl Marx's ideal society found expression in the patterns of modern Soviet education, and from there influenced such socialist countries as China and Vietnam.

In contrast to Plato's static view, John Dewey saw society as being in continuous change, and democracy as "a mode of associated living, of conjoint, communicated experience" (Holmes, 1981, p. 146). Human beings, as members of society, should jointly find solutions for the problems that emerged in social development, through the application of a scientific understanding of the natural and social worlds. Dewey believed that intelligence could grow as the individual grew, and "the basic freedom is the freedom of mind and of whatever degree of freedom of action and experience is necessary to produce freedom of intelligence" (Holmes, 1981, p. 148). Dewey saw the future as open, for people to create according to individual or shared visions.

Dewey viewed the human person less as an individual with intrinsic rights and abilities than as "an organism continuously interacting with a natural environment." He believed "[t]he individual and the social should not be set against each other as separate entities, for without one the other has no existence. Therefore, under changing circumstances, individuality takes on new forms, and in doing so, further modifies the circumstances" (ibid., p. 145). Holmes defined Dewey's ideal person as a reflective individual in a changing environment.

Dewey's idea of knowledge was strikingly different from Plato's. Knowledge is advanced through problem solving in the social or natural world, and predictions about the most effective solutions to problems are tested by experience. There is no authoritative body of knowledge, but established disciplines should be taught "in connection with [their] bearing upon the creation and growth of the kind of power of observation, inquiry, reflection and testing that are the heart of scientific intelligence" (ibid., p. 156).

Karl Marx's view of human society also emphasized change, a process of social transformation from capitalist to socialist to Communist forms of society determined by a science of history. With the revolutionary overthrow of capitalism, it was thought possible to construct a socialist polity under working-class rule, with the Communist Party as its vanguard. The abolition of private property and the shared ownership of the means of production would make possible an egalitarian society, in which all worked according to their ability and had their needs provided for collectively.

Within Communist society, human persons were to be educated and re-educated, until their consciousness was freed from the exploitative social relations of the prior capitalist society. Each person could then serve the best interests of the collective in the distinctive roles and functions assigned by the state, and enjoy the benefits of an equitable set of social relations. The human person was thus seen as part of a collective that was defined by class identity, rather than by a relationship within family, community, or the world of nature.

Within Soviet Communism, knowledge was seen as encyclopaedic, embracing all of the subject matter developed over human history. Thus the major subject disciplines developed in 19th-century Europe were preserved in the curricula of secondary and tertiary institutions. This knowledge was to be applied to the many-faceted task of socialist construction, and the model for education was described as polytechnical. Substantive knowledge of the basic scientific theories underlying a wide range of technologies was to make possible an understanding of the entire cycle of production (Holmes, 1981, pp. 162–172).

We can see how these three ideal types, the Platonic, the Deweyan, and the Marxist, overlapped with Chinese ideas in distinctive ways. Plato's picture of a fixed hierarchical social order, with distinct classes having their differing functions, has some resonances with classical Chinese society in terms of the hierarchical social order. However, the Chinese had quite a different view of knowledge than that of Plato, emphasizing learning through observation and experience rather than rational deduction and theoretical understanding. They also had a different view of human persons, regarding them as having infinite potential for transformation through education and as integrally connected to family, community, and nature, rather than as individuals with innate characteristics.

We can also see the resonances between classical Chinese ways of thinking and those of Dewey and Marx. Dewey's ideas of the human person's relationship to the community, of society as changing with problems being solved collaboratively, and of knowledge as advancing experientially, are particularly close to Chinese ways of thinking (Grange, 2004). Some aspects of Marxism also appealed to Chinese thinkers: its sense of historical evolution from one type of society to another, its ability to explain the causes of imperialism in the extension of capitalist economic dynamics to a global arena, and the priority it gave to the collective over the individual good.

MODERN EDUCATIONAL DEVELOPMENT IN EAST ASIA

The term *Confucian heritage societies* is often used for East Asia, including Japan, Mainland China, Taiwan, Vietnam, Korea, Singapore, Hong Kong, and Macao. Historically, Japan was the earliest to develop a modern education system, while China followed shortly afterwards. Both Taiwan and Korea were colonized by Japan for lengthy periods of time, and Vietnam was under French colonial influence up to 1939. Hong Kong and Singapore are both essentially city states colonized by Britain. Singapore became an independent nation in 1965. Hong

Figure 2.1: Map of East Asia

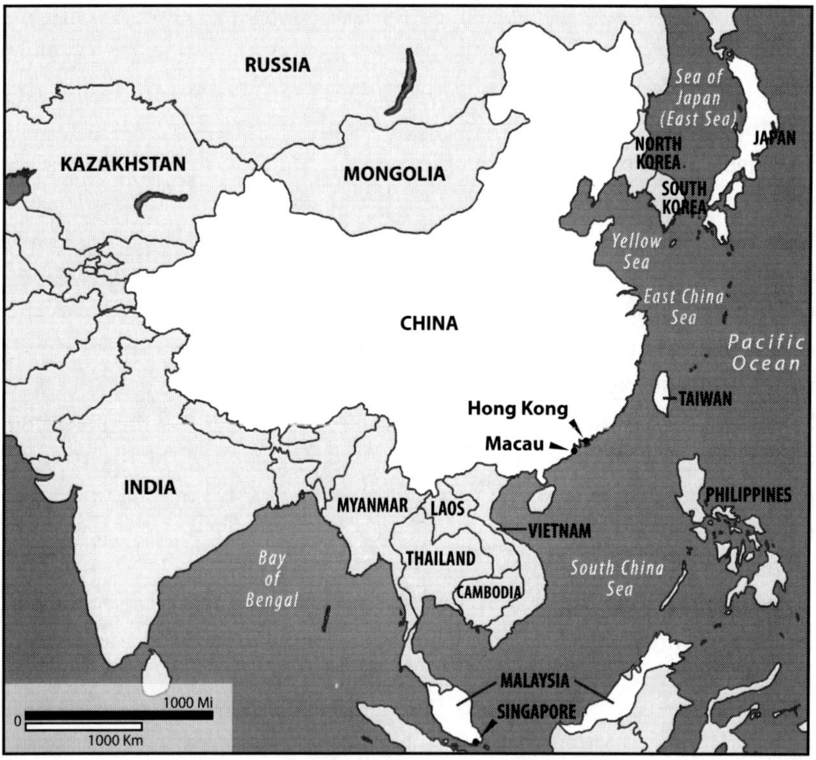

Source: Map created by Scott Wallace

CHAPTER TWO: Philosophy and Comparative Education   37

Kong's decolonization took place in 1997, when it was reunited with China under the formula of "one country, two systems." In 1999 the former Portuguese colony of Macao was reunited with China under the same formula. The whole region can thus be seen as a kind of laboratory, where European, American, and Soviet educational values interacted with shared Confucian traditions, in colonial, postcolonial, and non-colonial settings, under conditions of capitalist modernization and socialist construction.

EDUCATION IN JAPAN

Japan's written history began in about the seventh century CE, when it developed a writing system based on Chinese characters, and imported many texts of Confucianism, Daoism, and Buddhism, while developing its own religion of Shintoism. In the period known as the Meiji Enlightenment (1868–1912 CE), Japan began to selectively introduce Western educational models in an effort to achieve rapid modernization. By the late 19th century, Japan had its own modern schooling system.

School subjects were defined in similar ways to those in the curricula of European schools, and a whole new vocabulary was developed using *kanji* (Chinese characters) to name such modern subjects as physics, chemistry, mathematics, biology, and economics. Particular emphasis was given to the study of foreign languages, mainly English, French, and German, to make possible the rapid absorption of scientific knowledge from the West. Japanese was the medium of instruction, and in 1890 an imperial rescript was passed which called upon Japanese people to maintain absolute loyalty to the emperor, and preserve traditional values of family harmony and service to the public good. In this spirit they were to "pursue learning and cultivate arts, and thereby develop intellectual powers and perfect moral powers" (Horio, 1988, p. 399). Within Shintoism, the symbolism of the emperor was particularly important, since the sun goddess was seen as the ancestor of Japan's first ruler (Ching, 1996, p. 379).

Japan's success in modernizing began to be evident in the early 20th century, with a military victory over Russia in 1905, and remarkably rapid industrialization. This economic success was accompanied by increasingly aggressive behaviour toward China, however, as Japan sought to secure raw materials for its industrialization. It also copied Europe in the acquisition of colonies. Taiwan was colonized by Japan from 1895 to 1945, and Korea from 1910 to 1945.

After experiencing defeat in the Second World War, Japan was occupied by the American military for seven years. A new constitution passed in 1947 committed the country to peace, democratization, and the decentralization of education. Under American influence, the education system became more equitable, with provision made for the majority of young people to complete secondary education, and an increasingly large percentage to enter higher education. Japan was the first Asian society to achieve mass higher education, in the same time period as the United States, Canada, and the Soviet Union, and well ahead of Western Europe (Bereday, 1973).

Before 1945, the majority of teachers for primary and lower secondary education had been educated in normal training colleges that did not give degrees. After the war, most of these colleges were transformed into universities of education, and Japan became the second country in the world, after the United States, to require that all teachers hold a university degree. Professional courses for teachers are offered in both public and private universities, but certification is under the control of prefectural authorities. They select those who are most academically and professionally qualified for positions in their schools. This means that only about 20–30 percent of those who have the necessary educational qualifications for teaching are able to gain teaching positions. Teachers are civil servants, with a high social status and remuneration that is 30–40 percent higher than other public employees with equivalent qualifications (Shimihara, 1995).

The main direction of the postwar reforms in Japanese education was to reduce central control over the education system, and give greater autonomy to teachers and greater responsibility to local educational authorities. The Ministry of Education has nevertheless retained strong control over the national curriculum, with a continuing concern with moral education and education for patriotism. Some educators have been highly critical of this emphasis, wishing to emphasize children's individuality and right to learn, rather than the state's concern for shaping loyal citizens. Japan's major teachers' unions also have tended to be strongly oppositional to government, and left leaning in their orientation. There have thus been lively ongoing struggles over educational policy. Teruhisa Horio's writings give many interesting insights into these debates (Horio, 1988).

There is nevertheless widespread agreement that Japanese children learn well and have comparatively high achievement, from early

CHAPTER TWO: Philosophy and Comparative Education   39

childhood through primary and lower secondary education. The upper years of secondary education are clouded by the intense pressures of competitive examinations for entry to the top universities, with a sense that the university one enters will determine one's career chances far more than the subjects studied or the academic grades achieved. This is sometimes described as an "examination hell" and viewed as part of a widely shared Asian heritage (Miyazaki, 1971). William Cummings, one of the best-known comparative educators writing on Japan, has commented on the striking difference between Japan and the United States. Great importance is given to higher education in the United States, whereas basic education is emphasized in Japan (Cummings, 1999, p. 425).

EDUCATION IN MAINLAND CHINA AND TAIWAN

China was greatly influenced by Japan's Meiji Enlightenment reforms, which began in 1868, and shared a sense of pride in Japan's success in defeating Russia in 1905. From the 1890s to China's nationalist revolution of 1911, when the last imperial dynasty was overthrown, China's leaders emulated Japan in creating a modern education system. Hundreds of Chinese teachers studied in Japan and there was a strong belief that the Japanese model would enable China to absorb Western science and technology for national strengthening. At the same time, they could retain their Confucian identity and embrace gradual change through the establishment of a constitutional monarchy, along Japanese lines (Reynolds, 1993).

It soon became evident that this approach would not work for China. After 1911, China launched itself on a journey of change that involved radical experimentation with a range of Western models of education, and an overt rejection of its Confucian heritage as a value system then seen by many as antithetical to science and modernity. From 1912 to the early 1920s, European models were most influential in China's modern educational development, due to the leadership of scholars who had studied in Germany and France. Efforts were made to lay a foundation for basic education of five to six years, then to develop a small number of academic secondary schools and a few newly established national universities. Other specialist secondary schools offered programs in teacher education and various forms of vocational and technical education.

The May 4th Movement of 1919 was sparked by the decision of the victorious leaders of France, the United Kingdom, Italy, and the United States to give Germany's possessions on China's east coast to Japan after the First World War. Students and professors in China's major universities, led by Peking University, marched in protest against this decision. Both progressive thinkers and Marxists came to believe that China's evident weakness on the global stage was a result of its Confucian heritage, and that education for science and democracy was the only way forward. In a situation where the political leadership was weak and divided, educators and local leaders made vigorous efforts to expand basic education, and many specialist colleges were upgraded to university status.

An educational law of 1922 adopted American patterns of decentralized educational administration, and community responsibility for schools (Hayhoe, 1984, p. 38). This was shortly after John and Alice Dewey had spent two years in China, travelling throughout the country to lecture on education, science, and democracy (Keenan, 1977). An American-style schooling structure was also adopted at this time, with six years of primary education, three years of lower secondary, three years of upper secondary, and four years of tertiary education. While Dewey's ideas about education, child development, and democracy were widely appreciated by educators and scholars, China's economic conditions were such that progressive education developed in only a few relatively prosperous cities and regions. Illiteracy was widespread in most of the country, and no means were available to develop a comprehensive modern schooling system.

In 1928, the Nationalist Party came to power and established a national government with Nanjing as the capital. In the brief nine years it had before the invasion of Japan in 1937, and then the outbreak of the Second World War in 1939, great efforts were made to develop a national education system. The American structure was retained while European ideas were drawn upon to create a national curriculum and establish national standards in all the main subject areas.

The Second World War was followed by a civil war between China's Nationalist and Communist forces, with a definitive Communist victory in 1949. The Nationalist forces retreated to Taiwan, and there gained American support in developing Taiwan into a modern scientific power that built upon the infrastructure left by Japanese colonizers. Taiwan's schooling system had a structure similar to that of the United States, but conscious efforts were made to recover aspects of the Confucian heritage emphasizing family and community support for children's learning (Smith, 1991, pp. 1–98). While Taiwan was ruled by martial law under the Nationalist Party until 1987, multi-party democracy gradually emerged, and there have been several peaceful changes of government through national elections since the mid-1990s.

After the Communist revolution of 1949, China's education developed in an entirely different direction from that of Japan and Taiwan. Chinese Communist leaders felt their only recourse was to turn to the Soviet Union for assistance in the early years of the Cold War. Therefore, the Chinese education system was reformed in the early 1950s to follow Soviet patterns, with a strong emphasis on basic education for all, then a highly selective academic secondary schooling system open mainly to youth in urban areas, those academically capable, and those from the working class selected for leadership positions.

The school structure remained the same as before 1949, with six years of primary schooling, three years of lower secondary, and three years of upper secondary, followed by unified national examinations to select those who would enter higher education (Price, 1987, p. 166). The higher education system was fundamentally reformed according to Soviet patterns, with many Soviet experts helping China to design specialized institutions which would serve the planning needs of the state in such fields as engineering, agriculture, medicine, and teacher training. Most university programs required five years of study. Entrance was highly competitive and all graduates were assigned positions as state cadres in the new system (Orleans, 1987, pp. 184–195).

This system trained experts to serve the rapid development of a strong socialist economy, yet contradictions soon emerged. On the political side there was concern that the majority of young people, especially those in rural areas, had little opportunity to advance beyond basic education. On the cultural side there was a reaction against the narrow specialization and segmentation of knowledge, and the top-down centralized control. This went against China's traditions of holistic knowledge and community involvement in learning. There was thus an intense reaction against Soviet influences during the Great Leap Forward of 1958 and the Cultural Revolution of 1967. The length of schooling was shortened from twelve to nine years, five at the primary level and four at the secondary level. The curriculum was greatly broadened and access was opened up to the majority of young people to complete secondary education. While there were only 9 million students in secondary schools in 1965, by the end of the Cultural Revolution there were 58 million (Hayhoe, 1999, pp. 99–100).

Political struggle reached an extreme in the Cultural Revolution, as Mao Zedong encouraged young people to rebel against all forms of authority, and parents, elders, and teachers were subjected to violent forms of criticism. There are many interpretations of this period. The most common attributes the violence to a power struggle between the radical and conservative factions of the Chinese Communist Party. It can also be seen as a reaction against patterns imposed from the Soviet Union, which were hierarchical, centralized, and highly restrictive in the Chinese context. When Mao died in 1976, and the infamous "gang" of four leaders who had supported him fell from power shortly afterwards, a new period of development in Chinese education opened up under Deng Xiaoping.

Deng was a veteran Communist leader and also a pragmatist. He focused on providing conditions for China to modernize and open up to the world, with education as the key to successful modernization. It was a great relief for Chinese educators, teachers, and students to see increasing investment in education, greater autonomy for teachers, and educational planning focused on supporting the nation's economic and social development. At first the curricular patterns of the 1950s were restored, but they were soon broadened to respond to the changing needs of the modernization process.

Particular attention was given to respecting teachers and ensuring they had adequate academic and professional training to nurture creativity as well as academic excellence in their students. Educational research included classroom-based studies carried out by working teachers who tried to make learning more effective and more enjoyable. There were lively debates over Soviet, American, and European educational theories, and many experimental partnerships and projects. One influential educator described this period as "spring time for educational science" (Hayhoe, 2006, p. 69). It was a great relief that education was no longer a tool for class struggle, but a process of learning, growth, experimentation, and change. It was also a time for recovering some of the positive values of the Confucian tradition, which had been negated and neglected ever since the May 4th Movement of 1919 (Gu, 2001a).

EDUCATION IN VIETNAM AND KOREA
Vietnam and Korea suffered as much as China and Taiwan did from the impact of the Cold War on East Asia. For Vietnam, French colonialism ended in 1939, but the country was divided into two parts after the Second World War, with the North under Soviet influence and the South under American influence. After the end of the Vietnam War and the US

departure in 1975, Vietnam was unified under socialism and its educational patterns reflected Soviet influence. Even before the collapse of the Soviet Union, however, Vietnam began to adopt its own forms of market socialism, and education has played an important role in invigorating the economy and opening the minds of children and young people to a wider world (Dung, 2004; Hac, 1995; London, 2004).

In Korea, Japanese colonialism ended in 1945, yet the country was divided into North and South, with the South occupied by the United States until 1948 and the North under Soviet influence. The Korean War ended with an armistice that is still in place. South Korea's development parallels that of Taiwan in many ways—successful industrialization, the creation of a science-based economy, and the end of martial law in 1988. Education has been influenced by American patterns, yet there are also strong Confucian and Buddhist influences (Seth, 2002). Mass higher education was achieved in the 1980s, as a dynamic private sector responded to social demand. Teacher education was upgraded to degree level, and a number of universities of education were created to support teachers' work. For the people of Korea and Korean educators, the most painful ongoing issue is the division of the country, and the continuing poverty and isolation of the North.

EDUCATION IN SINGAPORE, HONG KONG, AND MACAO

Singapore became an independent nation in 1965, after 98 years of British colonial rule. Some elements of the British education system continue to have influence, and English has been the main medium of instruction. Yet there has been a recovery of interest in Mandarin, as well as promotion of the Tamil and Malay languages for Indian and Malay minorities. There has also been a gradual move beyond the original elitist education system to a more open one, with three universities and a large number of polytechnics providing higher education for an increasing proportion of the population (Tan, Gopinathan, & Ho, 2001). Early in the 21st century the Singapore government made the decision to become a hub for transnational education in Asia, inviting top universities from all over the world to establish branches there and attracting students from all parts of Asia (Sanderson, 2002; Lee, 2014).

Education in Hong Kong and Macao developed in completely different ways from China, due to their status as colonies of Britain and Portugal. Because they are located on the western and eastern sides of China's Pearl River Delta, decolonization could only mean a return to Mainland

China. Negotiations between China and Britain over this process began in 1984, reaching a culmination in 1997 under Deng Xiaoping's formula of "one country, two systems." Two years later, Macao returned to Chinese sovereignty under the same principle and with an education system that had already gradually adjusted to its Chinese context (Bray & Koo, 1999).

Hong Kong's return to China meant a re-emphasis on the local Cantonese dialect as the medium of instruction in schools, intense debates around citizenship education (Lee, 2004), and an increasing emphasis on learning Mandarin. It also meant a definitive move away from the British-derived structure of education, with advanced level examinations limiting university entrance to a small proportion of secondary graduates. A structural reform undertaken between 1997 and 2011 reduced examination pressures so that all students could move smoothly from primary to secondary education and face only one set of competitive examinations for university entry, as in Mainland China (Hayhoe, 2012). The other dramatic change after 1997 was the upgrading of teacher education to university level with the establishment of the Hong Kong Institute of Education as a degree-granting institution (Hayhoe, 2001).

COMPARATIVE REFLECTIONS ON EDUCATION IN EAST ASIA

Three approaches to comparative education theory were outlined in Chapter One: comparative education as a science; comparative education and imperialism/the world system; and comparative education and globalization. Each provides a distinctive framework for reflecting on the experience of educational development in East Asian societies.

If we begin with comparative education as a science, we can see how the human capital argument has played out in East Asia—with remarkable economic results for the educational investments in Japan after the Second World War, then similar patterns emerging in South Korea, Taiwan, Hong Kong, and Singapore. Given that these are all capitalist societies, this is not particularly surprising. Notably, however, China's leading comparative educator, Gu Mingyuan, argued for human capital theory being equally applicable to socialist societies (Gu, 2001b). He encouraged China's leadership to invest heavily in education after the Cultural Revolution. The resulting economic growth has been

CHAPTER TWO: Philosophy and Comparative Education   45

nothing short of remarkable. Vietnam subsequently followed a similar model with parallel success. Thus the human capital argument has been extended to include socialist societies, reflecting the flexibility of Confucian pragmatism.

Another aspect of the approach to comparative education as a science that emerges in the Asian context is the sense of the liberating power of science. In both China and Vietnam, the move away from the use of education as a tool of class struggle, and toward education as a science, signalled an end to vicious political struggles. There may be a parallel here with Jullien's early idea of educational science liberating teachers and students from the narrow rules of those controlling education on behalf of the state. While there are good reasons to critique positivistic science for its mechanical model of understanding and for legitimating the domination of the West, the East Asian experience reminds us that science may have different connotations at different times and in different socio-cultural settings.

Turning to comparative education and the world system, East Asia is a veritable laboratory of different types of imperialism. Both Japan and China developed their modern education systems in order to strengthen the nation in the face of imperialist incursions. This worked well for Japan, though it later became an imperialist power, occupying both Taiwan and Korea and invading China in conscious imitation of Europe's colonial adventures.

China was never fully colonized, yet its Nationalist leader, Sun Yat Sen, described it as a "hyper colony" because of its experience of British, French, German, Japanese, and American imperialist incursions at different times. Hong Kong became a colony of the British, Macao of the Portuguese, and Manchuria fell under Japanese control for more than a decade. China's educational policies were thus consciously selected to strengthen the nation's resistance to imperialist influences.

It is ironic, however, that China experienced education as imperialism most acutely after its successful Communist revolution. The Soviet Union's assistance in economic, political, and educational development came to be seen by the Chinese as an unacceptable form of social imperialism. China's experience can thus be better understood within Johann Galtung's structural theory of imperialism than Lenin's view of imperialism as the highest stage of capitalism.

Smaller countries of East Asia, such as Korea and Vietnam, experienced the full brunt of imperialism and the Cold War, with both countries being divided for lengthy periods of time. South Vietnam experienced American influence in education under partition, then later replaced this with Soviet influence between 1975 and the late 1980s. Nevertheless, it has found its own road to educational development, and its indigenous values have flourished under market socialism.

North Korea has experienced isolation and severe economic difficulty, in striking contrast to the affluence and success of South Korea's capitalist economy. While American educational patterns have had some influence in South Korea since the 1950s, there has also been an active anti-Americanism expressed in various popular movements. Educational development has taken its own unique forms based on indigenous traditions of Confucianism and Buddhism.

As for Singapore and Hong Kong, both are prosperous city states, though different in their political standing. The heritage of British common law, administrative systems, and educational patterns has been transformed to suit their particular development needs and interests. Macao has also done well in moving beyond the Portuguese colonial legacy.

We can see how the East Asian experience of education and development challenges a simplistic application of dependency theory or world system theory in comparative education. If taken as tentative hypotheses to be tested against the realities of the East Asian experience, the most striking failure of these theories has been an underestimation of the resilience of local cultures in the face of external political domination and economic exploitation.

It may be within the perspective of globalization and the dialogue among civilizations that we can best reflect on the lessons of the East Asian experience. In spite of the dramatic differences in political destiny experienced by each of the eight Confucian heritage societies in the geo-politics of the Cold War, there are remarkable similarities in educational processes and outcomes. Children from East Asian societies tend to have high educational achievement in international tests of mathematics, science, and language knowledge. There has also been a largely positive relationship between educational investment and economic development, within both capitalist and socialist political systems. These successes have led to considerable interest in what the West can learn from East Asian education. It seems that the most profound explanatory factors for their educational ethos and the learning achievement of their youth lie in shared views of knowledge, society, and the human person rooted in Confucian philosophy.

SO WHAT CAN WE LEARN FROM EAST ASIA?

Given the European tradition of knowledge and education, Western endeavours in schooling have tended to be diversified, individualized, and process-based; student learning activities are facilitated by teachers, who trust children to learn on their own. By contrast, the East Asian tradition is more focused, demanding, and formalized, valuing education as a critical instrument in the perfection of the individual and society. This goes back to the seventh century CE when China's civil service examination system was institutionalized; students tend to be pressured to learn by teachers who are seen as authoritative sources of knowledge.

Fundamental to the East Asian educational model is Confucian humanism, which views the purpose of education and schooling to be to let one's inborn virtue shine forth, to renew the people, and to "rest in the highest good," as stated in *The Great Learning* (Chai & Chai, 1965, p. 294). Learning, teaching, and schooling have thus been the first priority in any political agenda, as made explicit in "The Theory of Education" (Xue Ji), China's earliest essay on education (Xu & McEwan, 2016). Concomitant with the high importance given to education, teachers are usually given the most respected socio-political status. Teachers are important cultural symbols in Hong Kong, Japan, Korea, Mainland China, Macau, Singapore, Taiwan, and Vietnam, and there are very high expectations of their performance. Xun Zi (313–238 BCE) put teachers on the same level as sovereigns and made the point that teachers must be respected if the nation is to prosper (Knoblock, 1994, p. 231). Later in the Tang Dynasty, Han Yu (768–824 CE) depicted the responsibility of the teacher as encompassing the following three roles: transmitting moral values and principles (*chuandao*), delivering knowledge and skills (*shouye*), and solving the puzzles that arise in learning (*jiehuo*) (Li, 2016a). Such a concept of the teacher is deeply implanted in the East Asian model of schooling. The education and development of teaching professionals is thus recognized as the key to the success of basic education and student learning, and both normal universities and universities of education have given teacher education a high status in East Asia (Hayhoe & Li, 2010).

Confucian humanism is not merely an idealist philosophy but also a pragmatic orientation for policy action and school transformation (Li, 2015). This can be seen in the Confucian concept of the golden mean (*zhong-yong*). *Zhong* means "central, just, or right," while *yong* means "pragmatic within a norm" (Li, 2016a). This is not merely a matter of pursuing a middle course, but involves a spirit in which humaneness and rationality reach a perfect harmony (Lin, 1939). To give an example, the late Qing incrementalist Zhang Zhidong (1837–1909), founder of China's first independent normal school in 1902, put forward the idea of "Chinese learning as the essence, and Western learning for its practical utility" (Chen, 1981, p. 117). A parallel example can be found in the influential Japanese politician and educational leader, Fukuzawa Yukichi (1835–1901), who advocated national freedom and independence through personal strengths by pragmatically linking individual development to the independence and prosperity of Japan as a nation (Fukuzawa, 2012).

Institutional openness and diversity have been two core elements of the East Asian systems of teacher preparation and development. Thus Japan adopted the French and German models for its teacher education system during the Meiji Restoration to ensure teacher education would mean stability in terms of teacher supply, social development, and nation-building. China adopted the Japanese model at an early stage and then shifted to an American model that relied on comprehensive universities, within which teacher education lost its unique identity. A Soviet model influenced by France was adopted after 1949, but now the Chinese model is an open and inclusive hybrid system which continues with the French tradition but incorporates elements of the American model (Li, 2016b).

Confucian heritage values can be seen in studies done by social psychologists Harold Stevenson and James Stigler in the 1980s, at a time when Japan's economic and educational success was taken as a challenge to American education. They looked at children's learning in three East Asian cities—Sendai in Japan, Taipei in Taiwan, and Beijing in China—as well as two American cities, Minneapolis and Chicago. They made an intensive study of a large number of Grade 1 and Grade 5 children and their home, community, and school environments, taking into account the viewpoints of the children themselves, their mothers, their teachers, and their school leaders. They found that East Asian children spent many more days in school than American children, and that their school and home lives were more closely connected. Teachers tended to stay with one class for two or three years, building close links with the children's families, while parents provided their children with space to work at home, even in crowded living conditions. Children spent more time on homework, including during vacations, and their parents often purchased additional workbooks to help their children (Stevenson & Stigler, 1992).

At school, East Asian classrooms tended to have larger numbers of children than American ones, and all children learned to be responsible for classroom order. East Asian children had more opportunities for participation in group activities before and after class and in frequent recesses which allowed for vigorous play. By contrast, American children spent more time in the classroom, with less opportunity for group exercise and play during the day, and more time spent working alone at their desks. East Asian children felt very much part of a group, enjoyed learning, and gradually developed "self-direction, good study habits and motivation to do well in school" (ibid., p. 70).

The East Asian school also took considerable responsibility for the socialization of children. Role models were consistently used and upheld for children to learn from and admire. Group identification was strongly encouraged, and children became adept at an early age in group problem-solving. Children were also explicitly taught routines relating to the management of their own learning—how to keep their desks tidy, how to take notes, how to organize their clothes when change of dress was required for an outdoor class. "Asian parents regard doing well in school as the single most important task facing their children," while "American parents seek to balance academic achievement with other goals, such as developing social skills, high self-esteem and broad extracurricular interests" (ibid., p. 83).

One of the most striking differences in the attitudes of East Asian and American parents and children toward education was the importance of effort versus that of ability. East Asian teachers, mothers, and children had a strong belief that, with effort, every child could learn successfully, while American parents and children had much stronger beliefs in the innate ability of children as explaining success and failure in learning, and placed a higher priority on life adjustment and the enhancement of self-esteem than on academic achievement. They assumed that "positive self-esteem is a necessary precursor of competence and forgot that one of the most important sources of children's self-esteem is realizing that they have mastered a challenging task" (ibid., p. 111).

While East Asian countries considered a national curriculum extremely important for standard-setting, Americans emphasized the importance of individual differences, and saw the goal of education as maximizing children's differential potential. Textbooks reflected this difference, with most East Asian textbooks having to be approved by a national ministry of education before being adopted. East Asian textbooks also tended to be slimmer and less rich in illustration, but more explicit and coherent in their content.

The teaching profession also functioned differently in that American teachers had considerable freedom to decide on curricular issues and teaching approaches, while East Asian teachers worked to a national curriculum. They typically had fewer classroom hours and more time scheduled for collaborative class preparation work. Different images of the ideal teacher in Beijing and Chicago at that period give an interesting insight. Beijing teachers viewed the most important qualities of the teacher as the ability to explain things clearly, with the next most important being enthusiasm, then standards, sensitivity, and patience. Chicago teachers saw sensitivity as the most important quality, reflecting their concern with treating children as individuals. This was followed by enthusiasm, patience, standards, and last of all clarity. In East Asia, the teacher was seen as a skilled performer, striving to perfect the script in presenting each lesson, while American teachers were expected to be innovative, inventive, and original, writing their own scripts for each lesson (ibid., pp. 166–168).

More recent studies that attempt to explain the outstanding results of East Asian students in PISA tests have shown that Westerners have much to learn from East Asian values of learning and teaching. Based on PISA scores, Ho (2010) observes that East Asian students share similar strengths in terms of consistently high aspirations for learning and an orderly, disciplined climate in school; they are also high achievers in terms of problem solving, which challenges the stereotype that East Asian students are rote learners who can only drill for traditional tests (pp. 342–345). Experts at the OECD (2011) conclude that there are at least 12 important lessons Westerners can learn from such strong East Asian performers as Hong Kong, Japan, Mainland China, and Singapore. The first is to develop "a commitment to education and a conviction that all students can achieve at high levels" (OECD, 2011, pp. 231–233), key values of education that have been formed and practised over a long history in East Asian societies. More specifically, both Shanghai and Hong Kong adopt a moral approach to educational reform, seeing the whole system and the whole student body as held accountable by tough public examinations (Li, 2015; OECD, 2011, pp. 105–108). In the case of Japan, the total commitment to students is not just rhetoric but "a concrete and enduring priority, for which individuals and the nation as a whole are prepared to make real sacrifices" (OECD, 2011, p. 150). All of the East Asian societies give a high status to education and teachers, and favour centralized and standardized curricula. Their school systems have been improved by continuous and committed public funding oriented to both individual development and national strength. All East Asian societies have managed to pilot their unique pragmatic means to achieving educational success while keeping their school systems dynamic and open to learning and change.

Some of the other lessons are summarized as follows (OECD, 2011, pp. 233–254):

- establishing ambitious, focused, and coherent education standards that are shared across the system and aligned with high-stakes gateways and instructional systems;
- balancing local responsibility with a capable centre with authority and legitimacy to act;
- ensuring coherence of policies and practices, aligning policies across all aspects of the system, establishing coherence of policies over sustained periods of time, and securing consistency of implementation;
- ensuring an outward orientation of the system to keep the system evolving, and to recognize challenges and potential future threats to current success.

CONCLUSION: REFLECTING ON THE PARADOXES IN EAST ASIAN LEARNING

The main point of this chapter has been to show how important it is to learn about the religious and philosophical traditions of a society or region when seeking to understand educational policy, schools, curricula, and teaching practices. It is also important to see how the dialogue among civilizations can take us beyond national schooling systems and help us to understand ways of learning that are common to a region.

The chapter has illustrated how ideal types may be used to clarify core values about the human person, society, and knowledge; to identify contrasts; and to explore commonalities. Thus the notion of Confucian heritage societies can be fleshed out by reference to ideas of the human person as perfectible through education, of society as a macrocosm of the human family, and of knowledge as built up through a cumulative study of experience in both the social and natural worlds.

This can help us to reflect on the puzzles and paradoxes of the East Asian experience of education at a level that goes deeper than that of regional geo-politics or national educational policies. We can understand in a new way the discourses around the relative importance of ability and effort in educational achievement, the relationship between individual and collective in schooling, and the distinction between internal and external motivation in learning: these polarities can be held in balance within a flexible and dialectical thinking process. Likewise, theoretical constructs such as human capital in a socialist society, social imperialism, and market socialism are understood in relation to the lived historical experience of diverse societies that share the Confucian heritage. They take on connotations that might not be allowed in the more linear patterns of Western theoretical scholarship. Perhaps the most striking characteristic of the Confucian educational heritage is a profound and humane pragmatism that insists on the advancement of knowledge through thoughtful reflection on experience.

QUESTIONS FOR REFLECTION AND DISCUSSION
1. How do the ideal types of Platonic, Deweyan, Marxist, and Confucian values stimulate you to reflect comparatively on teaching and learning in your schools?
2. What was the most significant new fact you learned about education in East Asia in this chapter, and why?
3. Which framework for comparative education best explains East Asian schools?
4. How might you apply these East Asian educational values in your school context?

SUGGESTED AUDIO-VISUAL RESOURCES
The video clips listed below, each about 15 to 20 minutes, were made by the Pearson Foundation. They draw lessons from China, Japan, Korea, and Singapore, all Confucian heritage societies, and all of which have been superior performers among participating countries in the OECD

Programme for International Student Assessment (PISA). It provides the world's most extensive and rigorous set of international surveys assessing the knowledge and skills of secondary school students. Behind the stunning performance of their students, these superior East Asian performers all share similar Confucian values of education, though they differ from each other in educational applications.

Strong Performers and Successful Reformers in Education: China (Pearson Foundation). Available at: www.youtube.com/watch?v=yxT94FXwSPM
Strong Performers and Successful Reformers in Education: Japan (Pearson Foundation). Available at: www.youtube.com/watch?v=ygInMvH30QU
Strong Performers and Successful Reformers in Education: Korea (Pearson Foundation). Available at: www.youtube.com/watch?v=OJhzdIBUPs0
Strong Performers and Successful Reformers in Education: Singapore (Pearson Foundation). Available at: www.youtube.com/watch?v=Km25TAnPbI4

Users of this text might also find the following video material helpful:

Preschool in Three Cultures: Japan, China and the United States, by Joseph Tobin (1991).
In this film, Joseph Tobin explores the similarities and differences among the three cultures. Viewers watch preschool children go about their daily activities and hear Tobin explain how teachers from the other two cultures responded to the structure, discipline, and activities of each class. Part 1 of an updated version done in 2009 can be found at: www.youtube.com/watch?v=rz6HEcxXq2Q, while both DVDs (1991 and 2009) can be purchased from the following website: www.joetobin.net/videos.html

SUGGESTIONS FOR FURTHER READING
Chou, Prudence, & Spangler, Jonathan (Eds.). (2016). *Chinese education models in a global age*. Singapore: Springer.
Gu, Mingyuan. (2001). *Education in China and abroad: Perspectives from a lifetime in comparative education*. Hong Kong: Comparative Education Research Centre, University of Hong Kong.
Hayhoe, Ruth. (2006). *Portraits of influential Chinese educators*. Hong Kong: Comparative Education Research Centre, University of Hong Kong.

Horio, Teruhisa. (1988). *Educational thought and ideology in modern Japan: State authority and intellectual freedom*. Tokyo: University of Tokyo Press.

Kennedy, Kerry J. (2004). Searching for citizenship values in an uncertain global environment. In Wing On Lee, David L. Grossman, Kerry J. Kennedy, & Gregory P. Fairbrother (Eds.), *Citizenship education in Asia and the Pacific: Concepts and issues* (pp. 9–24). Hong Kong: Comparative Education Research Centre, University of Hong Kong.

Lee, Wing On. (1996). The cultural context for Chinese learners: Conceptions of learning in the Confucian tradition. In David A. Watkins & John B. Biggs (Eds.), *Teaching the Chinese learner: Psychological and pedagogical perspectives* (pp. 25–41). Hong Kong: Comparative Education Research Centre, University of Hong Kong.

Seth, Michael J. (2002). *Society, politics and the pursuit of schooling in South Korea*. Honolulu: University of Hawaii Press.

Smith, Douglas C. (1991). *The Confucian continuum: Educational modernization in Taiwan*. New York: Praeger Publishers.

Stevenson, Harold W., & Stigler, James W. (1992). *The learning gap: Why our schools are failing and what we can learn from Japanese and Chinese education*. New York: Simon & Schuster.

Tobin, Joseph J., Hsueh, Yeh, & Karasawa, Mayumi Dana. (2009). *Preschool in three cultures revisited: Japan, China, and the United States*. Chicago & London: University of Chicago Press.

Xu, Di, & MacEwan, Hunter (Eds.). (2016). *Universal principles for teaching and learning: Xue Ji in the twenty first century*. Albany: SUNY Press.

Zhao, Guoping, & Deng, Zongyi (Eds.). (2016). *Re-envisioning Chinese education: The meaning of person-making in a new age*. New York & London: Routledge.

REFERENCES

Ames, Roger T., & Hall, David L. (2004). *Daodejing: "Making this life significant": A philosophical translation*. New York: Ballantine Books.

Bereday, George. (1973). *Universities for all*. San Francisco: Jossey Bass.

Boyd, William, & King, Edmund J. (1975). *The history of Western education*. London: Adam & Charles Black.

Bray, Mark, & Koo, Ramsey. (1999). *Education and society in Hong Kong and Macao: Comparative perspectives on continuity and change*. Hong Kong: Comparative Education Research Centre, University of Hong Kong.

Chai, Ch'u, & Chai, Winberg (Trans. & Eds.). (1965). *The humanist way in ancient China: Essential works of Confucianism*. New York: Bantam Books.

Chen, Xuexun. (1981). *Zhongguo jindai jiaoyu dashiji [Education memorabilia of modern China]*. China: Shanghai Educational Publishing House.

Ching, Julia. (1996). East Asian religions. In Willard G. Oxtoby (Ed.), *World religions: Eastern traditions*. Toronto, New York, Oxford: Oxford University Press.

Cummings, William. (1999). The institutions of education: Compare, compare, compare! *Comparative Education Review, 43*(4), 413–437.

Dung, Doan Hue. (2004). Centralism—the dilemma of educational reforms in Vietnam. In Duncan McCargo (Ed.), *Rethinking Vietnam*. London & New York: RoutledgeCurzon (pp. 143–152).

Fukuzawa, Yukichi. (2012). *An encouragement of learning* (Trans. David A. Dilworth). Tokyo: Keio University Press.

Grange, Joseph. (2004). *John Dewey, Confucius and global philosophy*. Albany: SUNY Press.

Gu, Mingyuan. (2001a). Modernization and education in China's cultural traditions. In author, *Education in China and abroad: Perspectives from a lifetime in comparative education* (pp. 101–110). Hong Kong: Comparative Education Research Centre, University of Hong Kong.

Gu, Mingyuan. (2001b). Modern education and modern production. In author, *Education in China and abroad: Perspectives from a lifetime in comparative education* (pp. 27–51). Hong Kong: Comparative Education Research Centre, University of Hong Kong.

Hac, Pham Minh. (1995). The educational system of Vietnam. In David Sloper & Le Thac Can (Eds.), *Higher education in Vietnam* (pp. 41–61). New York: St Martin's Press.

Hayhoe, Ruth. (1984). The evolution of modern educational institutions. In author (Ed.), *Contemporary Chinese education*. New York: M. E. Sharpe.

Hayhoe, Ruth. (1999). *China's universities 1895–1995: A century of cultural conflict*. Hong Kong: Comparative Education Research Centre, University of Hong Kong.

Hayhoe, Ruth. (2001). Creating a vision for teacher education between East and West: The case of the Hong Kong Institute of Education. *Compare, 31*(3), 329–345.

Hayhoe, Ruth. (2006). *Portraits of influential Chinese educators*. Hong Kong: Comparative Education Research Centre, University of Hong Kong.

Hayhoe, Ruth. (2012). Hong Kong's potential for global educational dialogue: Retrospective and vision. In Karen Mundy and Qiang Zha (Eds.), *Education and global cultural dialogue: A tribute to Ruth Hayhoe* (pp. 265–288). New York: Palgrave MacMillan.

Hayhoe, Ruth, & Li, Jun. (2010). The idea of a normal university in the 21st century. *Frontiers of Education in China, 5*(1), 74–103.

Ho, Esther Siu-chu. (2010). Characteristics of East Asian learners: What we learned from PISA. *Educational Research Journal, 24*(2), 327–348.

Holmes, Brian. (1981). *Comparative education: Some considerations of method.* London: George Allen and Unwin.

Horio, Teruhisa. (1988). *Educational thought and ideology in modern Japan: State authority and intellectual freedom.* Tokyo: University of Tokyo Press.

Keenan, Barry. (1977). *The Dewey experiment in China.* Cambridge, MA: Harvard University Press.

Knoblock, John. (1994). *Xunzi: A translation and study of the complete works* (vol. III). Stanford, CA: Stanford University Press.

Lee, Jack. (2014). Education hubs and talent development: Policymaking and implementation challenges. *Higher Education, 68*(6), 807–823.

Lee, Wing On. (1996). The cultural context for Chinese learners: Conceptions of learning in the Confucian tradition. In David A. Watkins & John B. Biggs (Eds.), *Teaching the Chinese learner: Psychological and pedagogical perspectives* (pp. 25–41). Hong Kong: Comparative Education Research Centre, University of Hong Kong.

Lee, Wing On. (2004). Citizenship education in Hong Kong: Development and challenges. In Wing On Lee, David L. Grossman, Kerry J. Kennedy, & Gregory P. Fairbrother (Eds.), *Citizenship education in Asia and the Pacific: Concepts and issues* (pp. 59–80). Hong Kong: Comparative Education Research Centre, University of Hong Kong.

Li, Jun. (2015). When Confucianism meets Ubuntu: Rediscovering justice, morality and practicality for education and development. *International Journal of Comparative Education and Development, 17*(1), 38–45.

Li, Jun. (2016a). *Quest for world-class teacher education? A multiperspectival study on the Chinese model of policy implementation.* Singapore: Springer.

Li, Jun. (2016b). The Chinese model of teacher education: The humanist way for Chinese learners, teachers and schools. In Chuing Prudence Chou & Jonathan Spangler (Eds.), *Chinese education models in a global age: Transforming practice into theory* (pp. 249–264). Singapore: Springer.

Lin, Yutang. (1939). *My country and my people* (rev. ed.). London: Heinemann.

Llasera, Isabelle. (1987). Confucian education through European eyes. In Ruth Hayhoe & Marianne Bastid (Eds.), *China's education and the industrialized world: Studies in cultural transfer.* New York: M. E. Sharpe.

London, Jonathan. (2004). Rethinking Vietnam's mass education and health systems. In Duncan McCargo (Ed.), *Rethinking Vietnam.* London & New York: RoutledgeCurzon (pp. 127–142).

Mao, Liao-wen, & Bourgeault, Stanley E. (1991). Early childhood education and elementary education in Taiwan. In Douglas C. Smith (Ed.), *The*

CHAPTER TWO: Philosophy and Comparative Education   57

Confucian continuum: Educational modernization in Taiwan. New York: Praeger Publishers.
Miyazaki, Ichisada. (1971). *China's examination hell: The civil service examinations of imperial China*. New York & Tokyo: Weatherhill.
OECD. (2011). *Strong performers and successful reformers in education: Lessons from PISA for the United States*. Retrieved August 26, 2015, from the OECD website: www.oecd.org/pisa/46623978.pdf
Orleans, Leo A. (1987). Soviet influences on China's higher education. In Ruth Hayhoe & Marianne Bastid (Eds.), *China's education and the industrialized world: Studies in cultural transfer* (pp. 184-195). New York: M. E. Sharpe.
Price, Ronald. (1987). Convergence or copying? China and the Soviet Union. In Ruth Hayhoe & Marianne Bastid (Eds.), *China's education and the industrialized world: Studies in cultural transfer*. New York: M. E. Sharpe (pp. 158-183).
Reynolds, Douglas. (1993). *China 1898-1912: The Xinzheng Revolution and Japan*. Cambridge, MA: Council on East Asian Studies, Harvard University.
Sanderson, Gavin. (2002). International education developments in Singapore. *International Education Journal, 3*(2), 85-103.
Schwartz, Benjamin. (1985). *The world of thought in ancient China*. Cambridge, MA: Harvard University Press.
Seth, Michael J. (2002). *Society, politics and the pursuit of schooling in South Korea*. Honolulu: University of Hawaii Press.
Shimihara, Nobuo K. (1995). Teacher education reform in Japan: Ideological and control issues. In Nobuo K. Shimihara & Ivan Z. Holowinsky (Eds.), *Teacher education in industrialized nations: Issues in changing social contexts* (pp. 169-179). New York & London: Garland Publishing.
Smith, Douglas C. (1991). Foundations of modern Chinese education and the Taiwan experience. In author (Ed.), *The Confucian continuum: Educational modernization in Taiwan*. New York: Praeger Publishers.
Stevenson, Harold W., & Stigler, James W. (1992). *The learning gap: Why our schools are failing and what we can learn from Japanese and Chinese education*. New York: Simon & Schuster.
Tan, Jason, Gopinathan, S., & Ho, Wah Kam. (2001). *Challenges facing the Singapore education system today*. Singapore: Prentice Hall.
Tu, Wei-ming. (1998). Beyond the enlightenment mentality. In Mary Evelyn Tucker & John Berthrong (Eds.), *Confucianism and ecology: The harmony of heaven, earth and humans*. Cambridge, MA: Harvard University Centre for the Study of World Religions, distributed by Harvard University Press.
Vogel, Ezra. (1991). *The four little dragons: The spread of industrialization in East Asia*. Cambridge, MA: Harvard University Press.
Weber, Max. (1994). *Sociological writings*. Wolf Heydebrand (Ed.). New York: Continuum.

Weerasinghe, Henry. (1992). *Education for peace: The Buddha's way.* Ratmalana, Sri Lanka: Aarvodaya Book Publishing Services.

Xu, Di, & McEwan, Hunter. (2016). *Universal principles for teaching and learning: Xue Ji in the 21st century.* Albany: SUNY Press.

CHAPTER THREE
REINVENTING SCHOOLING: SUCCESSFUL RADICAL ALTERNATIVES FROM THE GLOBAL SOUTH

*Joseph P. Farrell, Caroline Manion,
and Santiago Rincón-Gallardo*

INTRODUCTION

As noted by Hayhoe, Manion, and Mundy in Chapter One, educational "borrowing" has long been an important strand of comparative and international education. Forms of formal schooling, originally invented in Western Europe in the early 19th century, have spread around the world for reasons introduced by Mundy and Read in Chapter Eleven. Despite the cultural and civilizational differences highlighted by Hayhoe and Li in Chapter Two, key elements of these forms have become almost universal. Unfortunately, once in place they have generally proven to be extremely difficult to change in any fundamental way, at least on a large scale. Meanwhile, starting in the late 1970s, and gaining momentum since about 1990, there has been a quiet revolution in schooling in the Global South, in many cases radically transforming those forms particularly at the primary level, but in some cases at the junior secondary level as well.

These mostly successful radical alternatives are little known and seldom remarked upon among educators and scholars of education in the Global North, and often not known, or if known not well understood, in their home nations. A small published literature about them is beginning to grow, but it consists mostly of individual case studies with few references to other cases, or comparative analyses of small sets of such cases, generally from the same geo-political region (Anderson, 2002; Reimers, 2000).

Some of these programs are still quite small, new (essentially at a pilot stage), and not well documented. Much of the information consists of lore passed informally among practitioners and scholars. Others have several decades of experience, and have grown to systems of thousands (in some cases tens of thousands) of schools, with solid research and evaluation results available. Some operate within the standard Ministry of Education administrative framework; others are operated entirely by non-governmental organizations (NGOs); still others are mixed models with various combinations of government, NGO, and civil society planning and management. In almost all cases these schools fall within what is generally referred to as "community education" or "community schools," with strong organic linkages to the communities in which the learners live. These linkages take different forms in different places, depending upon the local history and patterns of social organization, but are strong and crucial. In most cases that have been evaluated the results are very good, in terms of enrolment, retention, completion, movement to the next level of schooling, and measured academic success. Typically, students in these schools score on achievement tests at least as well as, and often better than, students in regular schools, including much more privileged youth. On-time primary completion rates range above 90 percent, and the vast majority who complete primary move on to the first post-primary level, generally with excellent results. When the focus has been middle school, a similar trend emerges: high percentages of students completing middle school and moving on to high school. Considering that the children in these schools are among the most marginalized in their own societies, and in the world overall—the "hardest to reach and hardest to teach" in traditional schooling—such results are quite spectacular.

This chapter is based upon an ongoing comparative analysis of more than 200 of these programs by an international team of scholars, graduate students, international agency officials, and program developers, co-led by the first author. This ongoing comparative analysis, best thought of as an international and comparative grounded theory exercise, is still in the early stages of development. There is much that we don't fully understand, and new questions arise regularly. But some patterns and conclusions seem to be sufficiently clear to warrant writing about them, even at this early stage. The first section of this chapter draws upon the

CHAPTER THREE: Reinventing Schooling

overall data set to present some core distinctions between the forms of formal schooling as we have come to know them and the emerging alternative model (called, respectively, the "bad news" and the "good news"). The next section provides a detailed comparative analysis of three exemplary cases that have been in existence long enough to have accumulated significant bodies of experience and evaluative research, and which collectively represent some of the major differing patterns of alternatives. While there are a wide range of questions and issues being examined in the larger comparative research program, the focus here will be on two key matters. First, the pedagogical question: how do these young people manage to learn as well as they do? What actually happens in these classrooms to produce these learning results? And second, the teacher-development question: how do the teachers/facilitators in these programs learn to successfully implement a radically different form of schooling quickly and well? In that discussion, we note some of the major lessons learned thus far. In the final section, we note two major questions, both empirical and theoretical, that remain.

The core argument here is that the best hope we have of breaking through the bad news (as outlined below) and eventually providing a better form of learning for this and future generations of young people on a large scale, in nations rich and poor, is to try to learn from those people, seemingly small in number in any one place but actually quite large in international aggregate and mostly in very poor places, who have managed to create islands of success where so many others have failed or succeeded only marginally. A subtitle of this chapter could be "Learning from Success." If we choose to try to do that, then we may help to reverse the trend of the past two centuries, in which educational ideas and patterns from the rich North have been so regularly exported to/imposed upon the poorer two-thirds of our world.

THE BAD NEWS AND THE GOOD NEWS: FORMAL SCHOOLING AS IT EXISTS AND EMERGING ALTERNATIVES

As educators we are observers of and parties to a most peculiar pattern. Over the past century or more we have come to learn much about how human beings, young and old, actually *learn* best (Bransford, Brown, & Cocking, 2000; Olson, 2003). Yet almost none of this new knowledge has penetrated into the standard practices of formal schools, which generally carry on the rituals, traditions, and conceptions of how learning occurs and what is most worth learning that were developed well over a century ago, first in Western Europe, and then spread around the world. Although this point has been made for many years, we are not the first to observe it, nor the latest (Abbott & Ryan, 2001; Caillods, 1989; Caine & Caine, 1997; Davies, 1995; Fagerlind & Sjostedt, 1990; Farrell, 1989, 1998, 2004, 2008; Polyzoi, Fullan, & Anchan, 2003). In 1995, two major books were published that chronicled and tried to understand a century of failed attempts at educational reform in the United States (Farrell, 2000; Ravitsch & Vinovskis, 1995; Tyack & Cuban, 1995). The stories told in these books of dysfunctional formal schooling and of failed reform initiatives indicated patterns that are generalizable to schooling around the world. One general lesson is that planning educational change is a far more difficult and risk-prone venture than had been imagined in the 1950s and 1960s (Farrell, 1997). Over the past two decades deliberate attempts have been made to change whole systems around the world. The knowledge on "whole system reform" was substantially advanced by the comparative study of highly successful school systems around the world in *How the World's Most Improved School Systems Keep Getting Better* (Mourshed, Chijioke, & Barber, 2010). While there is increased clarity on how to improve teaching and learning across entire systems (see, for example, Fullan & Quinn, 2015; Fullan & Rincón-Gallardo, 2016; Hargreaves & Shirley, 2012; Sahlberg, 2011; Zavadsky, 2009), there are still more examples of failure, or of minimal success, than of clear, sustainable success.

Overall, reviews of international reform experience, explored in Anderson and Sivasubramaniam's Chapter Five in this book, come to roughly the same conclusions: proposals for educational reform or change are seldom enacted. If enacted (whether via legislation, regulation, or experimental programs), they are seldom implemented well and widely. If implemented, they tend after a few years to fade away as the system slowly moves back to its normal state. If implemented well, widely, and sustainably, there is very little evidence of long-term and wide-scale impact on the primary mission of the schooling enterprise: enabling and enhancing the capacity of young people to learn deeply. What we have come to understand about human learning has almost nothing to do with how schooling continues to be conducted. The forms of formal schooling, set in the 19th century, reflect the misconceptions about human learning of the intellectual and political-economic elites of that very different time and place. But now that we have them, and have set them firmly in place, they are hard to change, at least at any large scale (see Elmore, 1996). Table 3.1 outlines key features of formal schooling, juxtaposing them with the alternative education models that are presented later in this chapter.

When looked at as a set, the list of formal schooling characteristics presented in the left-hand column illustrates the degree to which they have become taken for granted. Who would seriously question them? A striking feature of almost all of the educational reform proposals, whether for a system as a whole or school-by-school, is that they rarely if ever question the basic model, the forms of formal schooling. Typically, they aim to alter or improve one or a few bits of it, while leaving the rest unquestioned.

The existence of these forms of formal schooling and their seeming intractability to efforts at change has continued to be a source of great frustration to many individual citizens seeking a better and more productive form of organized learning for their children, to well-intentioned

Table 3.1: Key Features of Formal Schooling versus Emerging Alternative Education Models

Formal Schooling	Emerging Alternative Education Models
Teaching as the focus	Learning as the focus
Talking as dominant practice to teach	Listening as dominant strategy to enhance learning
Teacher lectures and whole group instruction as dominant form of pedagogy	Peer tutoring, individual and small group work as dominant form of pedagogy
Short responses to simple questions and exam grades as main material for evaluation	Multiple sources of evidence produced by students and captured by teachers on an ongoing basis: written work, thinking aloud, public presentations
Student evaluation as one-time event, repeated periodically	Assessment conducted on an ongoing basis accompanied by feedback in real time
Responsibility of classroom work and discipline concentrated in the teacher	Responsibility of classroom work and discipline distributed among children and adults alike

continued...

Table 3.1: Key Features of Formal Schooling versus Emerging Alternative Education Models *(continued from previous)*

Formal Schooling	Emerging Alternative Education Models
Students expected to sit in rows, mostly in silence, facing and listening to the teacher	Students move freely within and outside the classroom, to access resources (e.g., school library) and consult with adults and their peers as needed
Group to cover pre-determined content dictated by national curriculum	Flexible arrangements of curriculum to respond to the interests and/or pace of students, combining national and locally relevant curriculum
Whole group follows the same pace	Each student follows his/her own pace
School day organized in pre-set blocks of time for each subject matter	School day with flexible structure that adapts to the needs, interests, and pacing of students
Teachers and school leaders as single source of authority around instruction	Combinations of fully trained teachers, partially trained teachers, and community resources (parents and other community members) intentionally involved in children's learning and school management
School governance and management exclusively in hands of school administrators	Active student involvement in the governance and management of the school
Students organized by age groups	Multi-graded classrooms
Clear-cut separation between school and community	Free flows of children and adults between the school and the community
Teacher professional development consists mostly of one-time events, lecture-style, discussing recent theories and strategies of effective pedagogy and classroom management	Ongoing and intensive in-service peer mentoring for teachers, with multiple opportunities to experience, observe, and refine the practice they are expected to carry on in their classrooms

reformers who see their efforts fail regularly, and to scholars of learning who see their hard-won findings knocking fruitlessly on the door of the schoolhouse.

Among the first group, there has been over the past years, especially but not exclusively in North America, a small yet growing movement toward alternative schools and home-schooling (Gloeckner & Jones, 2013; Martin-Chang, Gould, & Meuse, 2011; Ray, 2013). These efforts have resulted in some cases in local alternative schools or programs. In 2005 it was estimated that there were more than 12,000 alternative schools or programs in the United States, and that at least a million parents there had opted for some form of home-schooling (Bauman, 2005); in 2010 there were an estimated two million home-school students (Ray, 2011, cited in Gloeckner & Jones, 2013, p. 310). But these efforts represent a withdrawing from the formal system among a still relatively small minority (i.e., 1–2 percent of the population), and have had no perceptible effect upon the broader formal system.

In 2003, a leading cognitive psychologist, David Olson, published a cry of desperation from the psychological researcher side:

> For some time I have been struck by the fact that whereas the psychological understanding of children's learning and development has made great strides...the impact on schooling as an institutional practice has been modest if not negligible. With most of my colleagues I had assumed that if only we knew more about how the mind works, how the brain develops, how interests form, how people differ, and, most centrally, how people learn, educational practice would take a great leap forward. But while this knowledge has grown, schools have remained remarkably unaffected. (Olson, 2003, p. ix)

The observations noted above should not lead us to conclude that there are not quite a lot of good schools and teachers out there. One finds them often, not only in well-off places but also in urban slums and poor villages, and it is like stumbling upon a beautiful blossom in the midst of desolation. The core problem is that, as Michael Fullan and many others have observed (Fullan & Watson, 1999), while we are quite good at noting a really good school, and characterizing it, we do not yet have any serious idea about how to create such schools, at least in large numbers, nor particularly how to change "traditional" schools in large numbers into places that better match what we have come to know about human learning. That is the bad news.

It is also now clear that many of the differences in the characteristics of formal and alternative education represented in Table 3.1 can best be seen not as dichotomies but as continua. As described in Niyozov's Chapter Four in this volume, forms of teaching and learning vary widely based on complex and culturally different local understandings. Successful programs can be variously close to and far away from the characteristics that seem in "pure" terms to differentiate the two core models described (see Chapter Two for a discussion of ideal types). But even in this rather generic comparison of formal and emerging alternative models of schooling there are a few points that are of great importance to consider.

First, none of the ideas undergirding these alternative programs are particularly new. They have been in the literatures of curriculum, educational psychology/pedagogy, and philosophy of education for a very long time. There are, for example, community schools even in very large cities in some places in North America and elsewhere (Melaville, Berg, & Blank, 2006). Various forms of multi-grading and continuous progress learning have been implemented, out of necessity or intentionally, in many places in the world (see, for example, the primary school policy of the Government of Quebec from 2000 (Gouvernement du Québec, Ministère de l'Éducation, 2000). Many classroom teachers and schools have implemented various aspects noted in the right-hand column of Table 3.1 (see, for example, Rodríguez, 2015). But, as suggested earlier, these have mostly remained relatively isolated examples.

The most important thing these alternative programs collectively teach us is that the traditional model can be changed, *on a large scale*. And this can clearly be done in historically marginalized places, with very limited resources, with very strong learning results. These programs demonstrate that child-centred, active pedagogy, with heavy involvement of the parents and the community in the learning of their children, works. And where this pedagogical model is implemented well, even modestly well, it is producing important learning gains among even the poorest and most disadvantaged young people. Considering the bad news outlined above, that is an extremely important finding. How to accomplish it in any particular place, rich or poor, is always a challenge, and the appropriate solution will differ from place to place, depending on local history and traditions, and socio-cultural and political-economic conditions. There is no one-size-fits-all recipe on offer

CHAPTER THREE: Reinventing Schooling 67

here. But knowing that it can and has been done even in very poor places is a learning resource available to us, if we choose to use it.

A DETAILED COMPARATIVE ANALYSIS OF ALTERNATIVE SCHOOLS IN COLOMBIA, MEXICO, AND BANGLADESH

Here we present a detailed comparative analysis of three core cases selected from a much larger database of cases: *Escuela Nueva* (New School) in Colombia; the Learning Community Project (LCP) in Mexico; and the BRAC Non-Formal Primary Education Program in Bangladesh. For the Escuela Nueva and BRAC cases we draw upon extensive and detailed case studies of these programs that were produced in 2004 (cited in the endnotes and highlighted in the suggestions for further reading at the end of this chapter), updated where appropriate with more recent research and data. The LCP case draws upon recent research undertaken by one of the co-authors. The case studies were designed to provide not only the facts of the case—for example, history, context, measured learning results, costs, teacher development programs—but also a kind of pastiche narrative account of what actually occurs in the day-to-day life of the school. These three cases were chosen for several reasons: they are well documented and evaluated, including both formal outsider evaluations and insider insights; they are exemplars of different approaches to alternative pedagogy, with a common cross-cultural core of understanding of human learning; and the authors knew the programs intimately and could thus provide the sort of day-in-the-life-of-the-school accounts we were seeking. Following is some general background on the nations/cultures in which these cases have developed, after which there are brief introductions to the cases themselves.

GENERAL BACKGROUND

All three of these nations are generally classified as poor or developing, but they are differently so in ways it is important to note. Unless you or your family originally came from one of these nations, or you have worked or travelled there or in a nearby nation, your image of them has likely been shaped by brief portrayals in the mass media, which tend to focus on natural and human-created disasters and disruptions. Table 3.2 below provides some very basic information about the three nations, with data from Canada added as a reference point.

In these figures, Gross National Income (GNI) per capita is a very rough index of how much wealth and resources are available per person in a given nation (the numbers are given in current international dollars). The next line provides rough estimates of what proportion of that total national wealth is available to and usable by the poorest 20 percent of each nation's population, and is thus an indicator of the inequality of income distribution. If one brings together those two lines and adds absolute population figures it is relatively simple, arithmetically, to calculate the average amount of wealth per year available per person, of whatever age, to members of the poorest 20 percent of the population in the nation. Those are: Bangladesh: $1,486; Colombia: $2,079; Mexico: $4,094; Canada: $15,407.

Obviously, in all of these three nations the poorer families and their children are vastly poorer than similarly placed people in a nation such as Canada, but there are important differences. Bangladesh is generally categorized as one of the poorest nations in the world, and to be poor there is vastly different than being poor in nations such as Colombia or Mexico, which are typically categorized as upper-middle-income nations in the world. This does not mean that to be poor in Colombia or Mexico is necessarily more or less difficult and desperate than to be poor in Bangladesh, but it can't be thought of as being the same either. It should also be noted that all of these nations have long traditions of advanced thought and scholarship, which have contributed much to how we together understand the world and our place within it. The adult

Table 3.2: Gross National Income per Capita in Four Nations

	Bangladesh	Colombia	Mexico	Canada
GNI per cap*	$3,340	$12,600	$16,710	$43,400
Income share held by lowest 20%**	8.9% (2000–2004)	3.3% (2010–2015)	4.9% (2010–2015)	7.1% (2000–2004)
Adult literacy rate***	62%	95%	95%	99%

Sources: *Presented in current international $ for 2010–2014. World Bank, data.worldbank.org/indicator/NY.GNP.PCAP.PP.CD/countries?display=default; **World Bank, data.worldbank.org/indicator/SI.DST.FRST.20; *** UNESCO Institute for Statistics, data.uis.unesco.org/Index.aspx?DataSetCode=EDULIT_DS&popupcustomise=true&lang=en#

literacy statistics in the table above are instructive. Even in a nation as poor as Bangladesh, more than 60 percent of adults are literate, and close to 100 percent in Colombia and Mexico. Thus, even in extremely poor places there are many people, millions indeed, who are very highly educated, having attended advanced institutions of higher education, and are the inheritors of long traditions of intellectual and spiritual culture, even though they share their national/cultural space with vast numbers of people who do not share these privileges.

The countries of Colombia and Mexico are, like most of North America, offshoots of European society. They were colonized by the Spanish in the early 1500s, with much destruction of existing Indigenous populations and their cultures, and quickly became mestizo (mixed) societies, as was the case across Latin America. By the early 1800s, they achieved their independence from their European colonial masters, like most of Latin America. This was shortly after the United States achieved independence and decades before Canada, as we now know it, managed the same thing. Colombia and Mexico are thus intellectually, culturally, and religiously (predominantly Roman Catholic, and thus Christian) inheritors historically of a long European tradition; in this case, the southern rather than the northern part of Europe. Over the two centuries since their independence, however, an intellectual tradition, including ideas about teaching and learning, developed in Latin America that is as unique and distinctive from the former European colonizers as are the intellectual and educational cultures of an offshoot society in North America, such as Canada. Over many years of living and working in Latin America, including Colombia and Mexico, the authors have come to understand that many of the common words and phrases used there to talk about teaching and learning, and about how children develop and hopefully flourish, have no easy translations into the English (or French) language and the ways we in North America think about such things.

Bangladesh is an inheritor of one of the very oldest civilizational traditions in the recorded history of humankind. Chapter Two of this book notes some of that history, in a general regional sense. Onto that long history of Confucian, Hindu, and Buddhist thought and spiritual tradition, Islam was overlaid in roughly the 12th century CE by a colonial invasion from the Central Asian and Middle Eastern Islamic heartland. A few centuries later, the British invaded and colonized the Indian subcontinent, and imposed another, European, overlay of thought and intellectual/spiritual tradition. After the Second World War, the British Raj was dismantled, with bloody and violent displacements of Hindu and Muslim peoples, leading to the establishment of two separate states in the former colony: India and Pakistan, of which Bangladesh was the eastern section. That partition did not last long, and in the late 1960s war broke out, which led to the formation of the new independent nation of Bangladesh.

The following three case descriptions from Colombia, Bangladesh, and Mexico are quite brief and introductory. Much fuller accounts are provided in the case studies to which you are referred.

ESCUELA NUEVA IN COLOMBIA

This is the oldest and perhaps best-known internationally of the programs discussed here. It started on a very small scale in the late 1970s as an alternative for primary multi-grade schools in remote rural communities in Colombia. Escuela Nueva was then carefully grown and nurtured, with constant experimentation and learning from experience. In the 1980s, Escuela Nueva was adopted as the national strategy for rural education in Colombia, and became one of the five pillars of the national plan to eradicate severe poverty. By the late 1980s, Escuela Nueva had reached 20,000 of the 34,000 rural schools in the country, with varying degrees of fidelity in implementation. In 1989, it was recognized by the World Bank as one of the three most successful public policy reforms in developing countries (Psacharopoulos, Rojas, & Velez, 1992; see also Colbert & Arboleda, 1990; Farrell, 2003; Schiefelbein, 1993; Siabato, 1997). According to an international comparative study in the late 1990s, thanks to Escuela Nueva, Colombia was the only Latin American country where, excluding the megacities, students in rural schools outperformed their counterparts in urban schools (McGinn, 1998).

In the early 1990s, a nationwide decentralization policy launched in the context of a new constitution derailed the national central plan for rural education, and from then on Escuela Nueva faded within the ministry (Benveniste & McEwan, 2001). The leaders of Escuela Nueva left the ministry and, with the support of several former ministers of education, created *Fundación Escuela Nueva* (the Escuela Nueva Foundation), with the intention of keeping the model alive in rural schools and maintaining the quality of implementation in selected regions. The model has also been adapted to serve new populations and contexts, within Colombia and internationally. The Escuela Nueva model has been adopted in at least 15 countries in Latin America, Africa, and Southeast Asia, reaching over five million students. Within Colombia, it has been adopted to serve urban regions, women's organizations, and migrant and displaced populations. In 2013, Vicky Colbert, co-creator of the Escuela Nueva education model and founding director of Fundación Escuela Nueva, received the World Innovation Summit for Education (WISE) Award in recognition for the positive impact of Escuela Nueva in the lives of millions of students worldwide (see Pitt, 2002; 2004).

LEARNING COMMUNITY PROJECT (LCP) IN MEXICO
The LCP started in 2003 as a small-scale, NGO-led pedagogical change initiative aimed at turning conventional classrooms in public rural middle schools into learning communities through a pedagogy based on tutorial relationships of dialogue and reciprocal learning among students and between students and adults. Between 2003 and 2008, the LCP pedagogy spread to over 300 schools across the country, through outreach and networking undertaken by teachers, local administrators, and project leaders. In 2009, the LCP inspired the creation of the Program for the Improvement of Educational Achievement (*Programa para la Mejora del Logro Educativo* or PEMLE), a nationwide strategy aimed at radically transforming teaching and learning in the 9,000 lowest-performing schools across the country. Between 2009 and 2012, the schools where PEMLE operated had increased the percentage of students scoring at good and excellent levels in math and language, at a faster pace than, and reaching or even surpassing, schools serving their more privileged counterparts (see Rincón-Gallardo, forthcoming).

In 2012, with the return of the political party that had historically ruled Mexico until the year 2000, a new administration at the Ministry of Education shifted priorities and asked the national team of PEMLE to leave the ministry, bringing an abrupt end to PEMLE. Several members of the PEMLE team re-organized around a small NGO called *Redes de Tutoría, S.C.* (Tutorial Networks), which currently continues to support the creation and spread of learning communities (now called tutorial networks) in a few regions and states. LCP has been featured by prominent thought leaders of the educational change field as an example of a new pedagogy for deep learning (Fullan & Langworthy, 2014) and the future of education (City, Elmore, & Lynch, 2012).

THE NON-FORMAL PRIMARY EDUCATION PROGRAM OF THE BANGLADESH RURAL ADVANCEMENT COMMITTEE (BRAC)

This program is another of the grandparents of the field. It started in the mid-1980s, has grown to involve about 37,000 rural schools in that nation, and is slowly moving into urban schools and ethnic minority regions of the nation, partly through a diffusion program with other local NGOs. It is also being adapted/adopted, with support from a variety of international and donor agencies, in nations such as Ethiopia, Sudan, Somalia, Uganda, Sierra Leone, and Afghanistan (Ahmed, 1993; Haiplik, 2004; Scott, 1996; Sweetser, 1999). Worldwide more than 900,000 students are enrolled (BRAC, 2016).

RESULTS, COSTS, AND CURRICULUM

There would not be much point in comparing and analyzing these programs and the broader set they represent, unless they can demonstrate that they are producing good learning results not just for a few young people who manage to complete the schooling process, but for most if not all of the young people involved. And the programs must be able to do this at a cost, both total and per student, that is sustainable. It is now well established that among most children in the poorer nations of the world, and among poorer population groups in rich nations, academic achievement tends to be lower, and dropout rates higher, than hoped for. As noted, all three cases have been evaluated, with Escuela Nueva and BRAC being the most extensively evaluated. The results are noted in detail in the case studies referred to above. Suffice it to say that in all of these cases extremely poor children come to school, stay in school, finish the primary cycle, learn not only the necessary academic material and skills but also develop self-confidence and self-esteem, and in large proportions carry on to the next level of formal education and do very well there. And all of this is generally at similar or superior levels to those of their compatriots in traditional schools, who are usually from more advantaged social backgrounds. Furthermore, the actual costs per successful graduate are lower than in traditional schools (DeStefano, Hartwell, Schuh Moore, & Benbow, 2005).

With reference to curriculum, all of these programs follow the standard national curriculum, if one thinks of that as a set of learning goals/objectives for a particular learning cycle or stage. What these programs do, by altering the pedagogical model fundamentally, is provide a way for children to learn that curriculum to a generally superior degree compared to traditional schools, sometimes in a considerably shorter period of time. They also provide opportunities for children to learn materials of local relevance, which are typically not included in national curricula, and also to add to the learning such matters as democratic citizenship education (Escuela Nueva is particularly strong on this), arts education (the BRAC program is particularly strong on this), or pedagogical skill as tutors of other students and adults alike (most prominently in the Learning Community Project).

PEDAGOGY

A sense of the actual pedagogy used in these programs can be obtained by reviewing Table 3.1. All of these programs have in one way or another moved away from the traditional, age-graded "egg-crate" pedagogical model. This shift both permits and encourages continuous progress learning (children advance individually or in small groups at their own pace, and at different paces in different learning areas—for example, a child may at any given age and stage be really good at reading, but not so skilled at math) and peer tutoring (older and/or more advanced children assisting younger and/or less advanced learners). All three cases presented here are multi-graded, with students of mixed ages and grade levels learning together in one classroom. The BRAC program is age-graded in a sense, as the children in any given school go together through Grade 1, Grade 2, and so forth, but these grades are not set by the calendar but by the judgment of the facilitators regarding when students are ready to move on to the next stage in a particular learning area. Thus a class may be working, for example, at Grade 3 level in reading, Grade 2 level in math, and Grade 4 level in science at any given time. The class group is composed of children of different ages, and moves together through the primary program, covering a five-year curriculum in four years, with the same teacher(s) from start to finish (which, as noted in Chapter Two, is common in many Asian school systems). This provides many opportunities for a form of continuous progress learning and peer tutoring. It is thus a locally adapted means of accomplishing the core pedagogical objectives. Escuela Nueva is fully multi-graded in the case of elementary education. It has flexible promotion mechanisms that allow students to work at their own pace. It is common in Escuela Nueva to see students working in small groups, with diverse topics being studied by different groups. Escuela Nueva Secondary is formally age-graded, and classes are divided by subject matter, reflecting the subject-content orientation and testing routines of standard secondary schooling, but they still manage to maintain much multi-grade and multi-age work and peer tutoring as part of the pedagogy. Again we see a locally adapted way of getting at the same core pedagogical changes. Mexican Learning Communities were first introduced in multi-grade public middle schools and gradually spread to schools with an age-graded structure. LCP's core pedagogy of tutorial relationships, however, is easily adaptable to multi-graded or age-graded classrooms. Students select their topics of study from a catalogue of themes formed by those topics and materials that the teacher or someone else in the group masters. They are paired up with a tutor—an adult or a peer—who supports the learning journey through tutorial dialogue. Each student follows their lines of inquiry at their own pace. The emphasis in LCP is on developing skills of independent learning, so covering the entire curriculum is not as important as ensuring that students get better at learning on their own with each inquiry project.

Within the models just described, children typically spend a large proportion of the school day working individually or in small groups, in learning centres or "corners," in some cases using learning materials that are specially designed for such self-guided learning. Standard textbooks are also often used, but only in conjunction with such specially designed materials. Not surprisingly, standard texts, which are designed for age-graded classes, do not work well as a sole learning resource for a multi-grade, multi-age school. When an individual learner, or a small group of learners, encounters a problem, they first ask older or more advanced students for assistance. If that doesn't solve the problem, they will ask the teacher/facilitator for help. Thus the adults in the classroom spend much of their time moving about, checking the progress of various learning groups, solving problems and answering questions, and recording the progress and obstacles of various individuals and groups (such as, "Jose and his group need special work in two-column multiplication" or "Tasneem is having real difficulty with verbs in the future tense, but she has just written a wonderful story which she should share with the class—perhaps as a puppet play?") for planning future work.

This does not necessarily imply that the teachers don't teach. Rather, they teach differently. They work mostly with individuals or small groups rather than the whole class, responding to learning needs as they arise. They also concentrate effort on teaching each new group of children

CHAPTER THREE: Reinventing Schooling

how to read, using a variety of teaching approaches that would be familiar to most early primary teachers in the world, until the new students have reached a level of decoding and comprehension of written text that permits them to work with self-guided materials. Teachers can concentrate their efforts on such essential learning challenges as they arise precisely because they can depend on the fact that most of the young people are engaged most of the time in their own self-guided learning. Such classrooms are busy places, with much movement and activity, and are generally rather noisy, not with the disruptive noise of children acting up or acting out but with the productive noise of young people working together on their own learning.

Figure 3.1 compares these programs on a variety of pedagogical aspects that can best be seen as continua rather than discrete categories. Two of these relate to the structuring of the school day and school year: pre-set periods—by subject and type of activity—versus time flowing freely, a standard school day/year cycle versus local adaptations. The next set of continua tries to locate these programs on now-standard categories of pedagogical difference: teacher-centred versus child-centred; passive learning versus active learning; and rote-frontal versus constructivist teaching. A caveat should be noted here: these points along the continua should be considered as approximations. All are based on informed judgments of careful observers of these programs, but they are all based on observations of a (necessarily) small set of the schools in the programs.

Moreover, in any program of modest to large scale, there will be much variation, whether intended or accidental, and these programs

Figure 3.1: Some Pedagogical Continua
Codes: ENP: Escuela Nueva Primary; ENS: Escuela Nueva Secondary;
B: BRAC NFPE program; LCP: Learning Community Project, Mexico

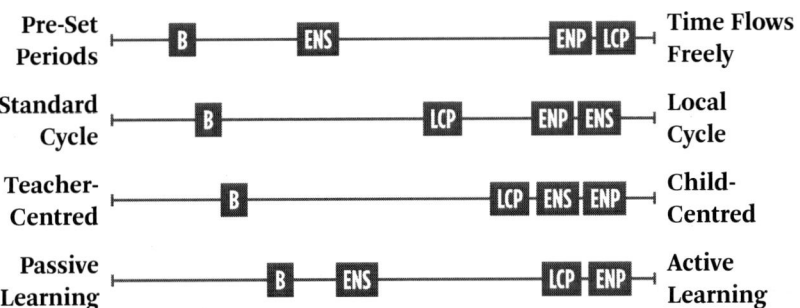

are not exceptions to that rule. Thus these locations on the continua should not be considered as exact points, but as best approximations with considerable variations around each point. With that caution in mind, the first thing to note is that on each continuum Escuela Nueva Primary (ENP) and the LCP are at or near the right-hand side. These are the examples that, in their full implementation, most completely embody the emergent model. But it is equally important to note that all other programs have moved a considerable distance away from the traditional forms of formal schooling as seen in the left-hand column of Table 3.1. Since all of these programs have achieved considerable success in improving student access, retention, and most importantly learning, this suggests that various degrees and combinations of moves away from that traditional model, suited to local conditions and traditions, can be successful. Again, the emergent model is not meant to be a one-size-fits-all recipe for school success, but rather a tool for thinking about these questions and learning from others' experience.

THE TEACHERS: WHO THEY ARE AND HOW THEY LEARN

Teachers are quite obviously the key to any successful learning enhancement system. (For more on teachers and teacher pedagogy, see Niyozov's Chapter Four.) So, who are the teachers in these alternative programs, where do they come from, and how do they learn this radically alternative form of working with children in schools? Within our overall data set, there are two distinct patterns in terms of teacher selection. In most of the programs the teachers are not formally certified according to standard systems of teacher selection and preparation (such as university-based faculties of education or normal schools). Rather, they are young people, mostly young women, who have a modest degree of formal schooling, usually junior secondary (that is, Grade 10 equivalent, which ordinarily means that they are among those in the local community with the highest level of formal school achievement available). They are locally known individuals, selected by a local school committee, and trained in the local area to teach in the locality. They are very much "of" the local community and known to that community. They are frequently called facilitators rather than teachers, so as to avoid problems with the national teacher unions or associations. The Bangladesh program exemplifies this pattern. The Colombian and Mexican programs represent the other common pattern, in which the teachers are university-educated and certified (as are all teachers in the regular formal educational system), and often move regularly from place to place under standard rules of the regional/national bureaucracy regarding fully certified teachers. This has proven to be a problem for the Colombian and Mexican programs, in that the routines of the teacher profession bureaucracy and Ministry of Education regulations often create such frequent teacher career moves that continuity of teaching in the alternative mode can be a problem, requiring a regular and constant need for teachers to learn the new mode.

What is striking, however, is that whichever model of teacher selection is implemented, whether for facilitators with no more than 10 years of formal schooling, or for teachers with up to 16 years (that is, university level) of formal education, in all of these cases the adults learn very quickly how to work in a radically alternative form of pedagogy with excellent learning results for their students. In all cases the pre-service teacher development activities are brief (a few weeks at most), but intensive and involving observation of and practice teaching in successful demonstration schools. This is followed by several years of very intensive in-service teacher-to-teacher mentoring programs and regular supervisory support. In the Escuela Nueva system and LCP teachers in a given locality are assisted to form and participate in communities of practice (called micro-centres in the case of Escuela Nueva), where they meet every one to four weeks to analyze problems and discuss results. Talking about accomplishments, sharing doubts, and thinking out loud helps teachers to progress toward specific solutions, to test them, and to share the results of these experiences. The communities of practice reduce the uncertainty and fear teachers encounter when implementing new teaching methods (Schiefelbein, 2006). The LCP established additional vehicles to consolidate its new pedagogies in classrooms, including monthly visits from a coach who spends three to five days in the school, working directly with teachers in the afternoons to model the practice of tutoring, and using the school day to model the new pedagogy with students alongside the teachers. The BRAC in-service teacher formation program is equally intensive (Haiplik, 2004) and indeed this is characteristic of almost all the cases in our broader data set.

It is important to note just how different is this approach to teacher development and learning from that typically found in North America and other developed regions, where we generally "front-end load" the process, devoting most of our teacher development resources and energy to the pre-service period. Once the new teachers are trained and hired and in their new classrooms, we essentially abandon them to their own devices. Ongoing professional learning experiences are rare, sporadic, and most commonly devised by authority levels far from the individual classroom. (There are a few exceptions, but the general pattern holds.)

The programs considered here demonstrate that, contrary to a very popular belief around the world, teachers are not obstacles to fundamental school change: one doesn't need to make reforms "teacher-proof," as believed in the "standards and accountability" movements in North American and much of European education. Rather, in these cases the teachers are the promoters and agents of such change, even when they are working in very difficult conditions, are not necessarily formally well educated, and are often very poorly paid. They, like the equally disadvantaged young people for whom they are responsible, can and do accomplish remarkable feats of learning and change in quite short periods. There is an important parallel between the young and older learners here. Just as the success for the young people seems based fundamentally on a focus on learning rather than teaching, so the changes in teachers seem based on the same shift in focus. In these systems the role of the supervisors has changed fundamentally. They are not enforcers or administrators of rules and regulations. Rather they are enablers of and promoters of teacher learning. These successful change programs generally spread or go to scale not by a centrally planned and commanded reform plan with goals and objectives set from afar, and agents or supervisors from some national or regional centre going out to teach the teachers about the latest new educational idea or theoretical scheme, but rather by an innovation-diffusion process: teachers learning from other teachers, sharing their "practical professional knowledge" (Clandinin & Connelly, 1998) and teaching skills with other teachers, and exploring together how their shared and growing knowledge and experience can help everyone, most importantly the young people in their charge.

QUESTIONS PENDING

There are in this long enterprise many questions, puzzlements, and learning challenges still before us. Here we will highlight just four of them. The first is that the literature available on these alternative

CHAPTER THREE: Reinventing Schooling

programs is generally so highly laudatory as to convey an impression that they are all paragons of pedagogical virtue. They are not. They are all very human institutions, far better on average than traditional schools, but variable among and within the programs. Among the evident successes, mistakes have been made, and in the best of cases, corrected. The people involved in these programs are learning as they go, but they are learning. A critical literature reflecting the less-than-perfect as well as the successes has not yet developed, and is much needed.

A second set of challenges concerns scaling up and sustainability. Escuela Nueva and the LCP were at some moment in their histories adopted as part of nationwide strategies to improve rural education, reaching thousands of schools (20,000 in the case of Colombia, 9,000 in the case of Mexico) and showing positive impact on student learning in a relatively short time. However, both initiatives disappeared from the national agenda in their respective countries after changes in administration resulted in shifted priorities. Both Escuela Nueva and the LCP continue to be supported by small NGOs created to keep these models alive, yet the scale has been significantly reduced. Similarly, in Bangladesh, despite considerable South-South transfer of its model, BRAC has remained unable to reach the scale necessary to meet the educational needs of rural and other marginalized communities.

A third challenge relates to the strain and tension between the global and the local, which is highlighted by Hayhoe, Manion, and Mundy in Chapter One in this book. All of these cases have drawn upon educational/pedagogical scholarship and traditions that are common, and exported, currency in the North/West of the world. Most people we have talked to and worked with who have developed/are developing these programs are well versed in the standard literature of the North/West regarding education and learning. They have studied and understood such standard icons as John Dewey, Maria Montessori, and Johann Pestalozzi, and newer pedagogical thinkers in the North/West tradition (such as Howard Gardner, Nel Noddings, and many others), and generally are well aware of the currents of critical thinking in the North/West. What they have done is taken those globalized ideas and ways of understanding education, and mixed and matched them with their own civilizational literatures and traditions of understanding teaching and learning to slowly develop very effective, locally appropriate ways of enabling effective learning among even very poor children. One thing that has struck us often as we hang around schools like these, trying to figure out how and why they actually work as well as they do, is that at some level they all feel very similar, but at another level are very different. Rural Colombia is not rural Bangladesh or rural Mexico. But there are commonalities that one can see and sense as an experienced teacher. Sorting all of that out, not in some kind of theory-driven enterprise but through careful, on-the-ground work, is a long-term field research challenge, essential if we are ever to begin to really make sense of the global-local question. For more on local and Indigenous pedagogies, see Katia Sol Madjidi and Jean-Paul Restoule's Chapter Six in this volume.

A fourth challenge is in some ways even more daunting. It has to do with the inadequacy of many of our standard terms and categories, derived from the long experience of the forms of formal schooling, to capture well what we are slowly coming to understand about these alternative programs. One such issue is the now-standard distinction between formal and non-formal education. This was introduced into the literature in the 1960s and 1970s and was very important then in denoting that education as an organized intentional enterprise could be and was provided by many means beyond formal schooling, for young people and particularly for adults (Ahmed, 1975; Coombs, 1976; Coombs & Ahmed, 1974; Evans, 1981). But what do we do with that categorization when we find, as we are, that many of these alternative programs are bringing into the walls of the schoolhouse the pedagogical models of non-formal education, including methods long advocated by adult educators? Thus our comfortable distinctions between formal and non-formal or adult and child learning seem to be broken by the people involved in these programs. We do not yet seem to have a useful practical and theoretical language to represent this reality (Rogers, 2004). This also applies to such terms as *child centred* or *active* pedagogy or *constructivist* teaching and learning (as used in Figure 3.1). As we have tried to match these many and varied programs to the terms we usually use in our discussions of schooling and pedagogy, we have found that the standard terms and categories don't fit well with what we are seeing (as in Chapter Four). They are based upon an experience of teaching and learning rooted in the long history and underlying assumptions of formal schooling as we have come to know it. Breaking out of these traditional intellectual categories and assumptions may end up being even harder than breaking out of traditional ways of practice in schools as we have come to know them. So, there is much to learn; we are in early days. But there is much already available to learn from, if we choose to do so.

QUESTIONS FOR REFLECTION AND DISCUSSION
1. In your experience as a learner, have you had learning opportunities that approximate some of the characteristics of formal and alternative education models listed in Table 3.1? What did it feel like? How did it work? Consider your formal schooling, and informal educational experiences such as a sport, music lessons, or Boy Scouts or Girl Guides. Note down your experiences and thoughts, as you understood them as a learner, and share them with your classmates.
2. The models described in this chapter suggest that multi-graded classrooms may promote better learning than age-graded classes. As a teacher you are likely to spend some of your time teaching multi-graded classes, such as split-level classes. Have you had, as part of your teacher education, any preparation for that? Why do you suppose that may be?
3. This chapter argues that the forms of formal schooling are usually very difficult to change. From your own experience as a teacher or learner, have you ever tried (successfully or not) to change some aspect of those forms of formal schooling—for example, trying to get some rule or regulation changed? If so, how did this work (or not), and what did you learn from the experience? Have you ever had much time for reflection and problem solving with other teachers/facilitators/stakeholders, as in the alternative education cases profiled in this chapter? If so, what difference did this make?

SUGGESTED AUDIO-VISUAL RESOURCES
Education through Imagination, by Antonia Antonopoulos (2002).
   Available at: www.youtube.com/watch?v=HUgLz8NQX7I
This short film (approximately 20 minutes) explains the non-formal educational programs offered by the Bangladesh Rural Advancement Committee. BRAC's creative responses to rural community learning emphasize the power of the imagination through child-friendly, gender-empowered, ethnically integrated, and community participatory

schooling. Viewers watch the daily school activities while the narrator explains the philosophies behind the many non-formal educational programs that BRAC supports.

BRAC Education Programme (2011). Available at: www.youtube.com/
    watch?v=2amWMtIJ-fk#t=19
This short (13:58) video provides a relatively recent overview of the BRAC Education Programme in Bangladesh and includes footage of BRAC classrooms and the activities of teachers and learners. Viewers can learn more about the program's history, philosophy, and objectives as well as specific details concerning the program's organization, teachers/teacher development, pedagogy, and learning materials.

Revolutionizing a School System: Vicky Colbert's Escuela Nueva
    in Colombia, by WISE (World Innovation Summit for
    Education) Channel (2014). Available at: www.youtube.com/
    watch?v=CAlMjJc6_gs
This short video (approximately five minutes) presents a brief overview of the Escuela Nueva model, including key innovations in terms of teacher training, curriculum, pedagogy, and organization. The experiences and perceptions of current and former Escuela Nueva students and teachers in Colombia are used to illustrate the value and success of the methodology.

Maravillas, by Redes de Tutoría (2013). Available at: vimeo.com/
    70279241
This 30-minute documentary presents the story of the Learning Community Project as experienced by students, teachers, and LCP leaders.

Education Innovation in the Slums, by Charles Leadbeater (2010).
    Available at: www.ted.com/talks/charles_leadbeater_on_education
In this 20-minute TED Talk, Charles Leadbeater presents some of the key lessons he learned in his exploration of over 100 education innovations across the world. He offers some examples of these innovations to argue that some of the most powerful innovation in education often takes place in emerging economies, where huge needs and unmet demands open opportunities, and even make it necessary to depart from conventional solutions, which are too costly and ineffective in serving the needs of historically marginalized populations.

SUGGESTIONS FOR FURTHER READING

Ahmed, Manzoor. (1975). *The economics of non-formal education: Resources, costs and benefits*. New York: Praeger.

Anderson, Stephen (Ed.). (2002). *School improvement in the developing world: Case studies of the Aga Khan Foundation projects*. Amsterdam: Swets and Zeitlinger.

Bransford, John D., Brown, Ann L., and Cocking, Rodney, R. (Eds.). (2000). *How people learn: Brain, mind, experience and schooling*. Washington, DC: Commission on Behavioral and Social Sciences, National Research Council, National Academy Press.

Clandinin, Jean, and Connelly, F. Michael. (1998). Stories to live by: Narrative understanding of school reform. *Curriculum Inquiry, 28*(2),149–164.

Colbert, Vicky. (2013). *Q&A with Vicky Colbert*. Lead the change series, by the AERA Educational Change Special Interest Group. Available at: www.aera.net/Portals/38/docs/Lead%20the%20Change%20series/Lead%20the%20Change%20Issue%2029%20Colbert.pdf

Colbert, Vicky. (2002). Improving the quality of education for the rural poor: Escuela Nueva in Colombia. In Claudio de Moura Castro and Aimee Verdisco (Eds.), *Making education work: Latin American ideas and Asian results* (pp. 149–167). New York: Inter-American Development Bank.

Colbert, Vicky, Arboleda, Jairo, and Chiappe, Clemencia. (1991). The New School program: More and better primary education for children in Colombia. In Henry M. Levin and Marlaine E. Lockheed (Eds.), *Effective schools in developing countries* (pp. 52–68). London and Washington, DC: Falmer Press.

Farrell, Joseph P. (1989). International lessons for school effectiveness: The view from the Third World. In Mark Holmes, Kenneth Leithwood, and Donald Mussela (Eds.), *Policy for effective schools* (pp. 131–153). New York: Teachers College Press and OISE.

Haiplik, Brenda. (2004). *BRAC's non-formal education program (NFEP)*. Washington, DC: Academy for International Development.

Olson, David. (2003). *Psychological theory and educational reform: How school remakes mind and society*. Cambridge: Cambridge University Press.

Pitt, Jennifer. (2004). *Case study for Escuela Nueva program*. Washington, DC: Academy for Educational Development.

Rincón-Gallardo, Santiago. (2015). Bringing a counter-hegemonic pedagogy to scale in Mexican public schools. *Multidisciplinary Journal of Educational Research, 5*(1), 28–54.

Rincón-Gallardo, Santiago, and Elmore, Richard F. (2012). Transforming teaching and learning through social movement in Mexican public middle schools. *Harvard Educational Review, 82*(4), 471–490.

Rogers, Alan. (2004). *Non-formal education: Flexible schooling or participatory education?* Hong Kong: Hong Kong University, Comparative Education Research Centre.

REFERENCES

Abbott, John, and Ryan, Terry. (2001). *The unfinished revolution: Learning, human behavior, communities and political paradox.* Alexandria, VA: Association for Supervision and Curriculum Development.

Ahmed, Manzoor. (1993). *Primary education for all: Learning from the BRAC experience: A case study.* Dhaka: Abel Press.

Ahmed, Manzoor. (1975). *The economics of non-formal education: Resources, costs and benefits.* New York: Praeger.

Anderson, Stephen. (Ed.). (2002). *School improvement in the developing world: Case studies of the Aga Khan Foundation projects.* Amsterdam: Swets and Zeitlinger.

Bauman, Kurt, J. (2005). One million homeschooled students. *Teachers College Record*, February 16, 2005, www.tcrecord.org/Content.asp?ContentID=11756.

Beneveniste, Patrick J., and McEwan, Luis. (2001). The politics of rural school reform: Escuela Nueva in Colombia. *Journal of Education Policy, 16*(6), 547–599.

BRAC. (2016). Education programme. Accessed April 4, 2016, from www.brac.net/education

Bransford, John D., Brown, Ann L., and Cocking, Rodney R. (Eds.). (2000). *How people learn: Brain, mind, experience and schooling.* Washington, DC: Commission on Behavioral and Social Sciences, National Research Council, National Academy Press.

Caillods, Françoise. (Ed.). (1989). *The prospects for educational planning.* Paris: International Institute for Educational Planning.

Caine, Renate, and Caine, Geoffrey. (1997). *Education on the edge of possibility.* Alexandria, VA: Association for Supervision and Curriculum Development.

City, Elizabeth A., Elmore, Richard F., and Lynch, Doug. (2012). Redefining education: The future of learning is not the future of schooling. In Jai Mehta, Robert B. Schwartz, & Frederick M. Hess (Eds.), *The futures of school reform* (pp. 151–176). Cambridge, MA: Harvard Education Press.

Clandinin, Jean, and Connelly, F. Michael. (1998). Stories to live by: Narrative understandings of school reform. *Curriculum Inquiry, 28*(2), 149–164.
Colbert, Vicky, and Arboleda, Jairo. (1990). Universalization of primary education in Colombia: The new school program. Paper presented at the World Conference on Education for All, Jomtien, Thailand.
Coombs, Philip. (1976). Non-formal education: Myths, realities and opportunities. *Comparative Education Review, 20*(3), 281–293.
Coombs, Philip, and Ahmed, Manzoor. (1974). *Attacking rural poverty: Now non-formal education can help*. Baltimore: Johns Hopkins University Press.
Davies, Lynn. (1995). The management and mismanagement of school effectiveness. In John D. Turner (Ed.), *The state and the school: An international perspective* (pp. 91–107). Washington, DC: Falmer Press.
DeStefano, Joseph, Hartwell, Ash, Schuh, Audrey-marie, and Benbow, Jane. (2005). *Meeting EFA: Cost-effectiveness of complementary approaches*. Washington, DC: Academy for Educational Development.
Elmore, Richard F. (1996). Getting to scale with good educational practice. *Harvard Educational Review, 66*(1), 1–26.
Evans, David. (1981). *The planning of non-formal education*. Paris: International Institute for Educational Planning.
Fagerlind, Ingemar, and Sjostedt, Britt. (1990). *Review and prospects of educational planning and management in Europe*. Paris: UNESCO/ International Congress on Planning and Management in Europe.
Farrell, Joseph, P. (2008). Community education in developing countries: The quiet revolution in schooling. In F. Michael Connelly, Ming Fang He, and Joanne Phillion (Eds.), *Sage international handbook on curriculum and instruction* (pp. 369–390). Thousand Oaks, CA: Sage Publications.
Farrell, Joseph P. (2004). *Alternative pedagogies and learning in alternative schooling systems in developing nations*. Paper presented at the annual meeting of the Comparative and International Education Society, Salt Lake City, Utah.
Farrell, Joseph, P. (2003). Transformación de las formas de educación en el mundo en desarrollo. La aparación de un model de educación radicalmente alternativo: El papel transformador de la "Escuela Nueva" de Colombia. In *Memorias del Primer Congreso Internacional de Escuelas Nuevas*. Armenia, Colombia: Colombia National Ministry of Education, 71–103.
Farrell, Joseph P. (2000). Why is educational reform so difficult? Similar descriptions, different prescriptions, failed explanations. *Curriculum Inquiry, 30*(1), 83–103.
Farrell, Joseph P. (1998). *Improving learning: Perspectives for primary education in rural Africa*. Comparative background paper prepared for the UNESCO/ World Bank seminar on Improving Rural Primary Education in Africa, Lusaka, Zambia.
Farrell, Joseph, P. (1997). A retrospective on educational planning in comparative education. *Comparative Education Review 41*(3), 277–313.

Farrell, Joseph P. (1989). International lessons for school effectiveness: The view from the Third World. In Mark Holmes, Kenneth Leithwood, and Donald Mussela (Eds.), *Policy for effective schools* (pp. 131–153). New York: Teachers College Press and OISE.

Fullan, Michael, and Langworthy, Maria. (2014). *A rich seam: How new pedagogies find deep learning.* London: Pearson.

Fullan, Michael, and Quinn, Joanne. (2015). *Coherence: The Right Drivers in Action for Schools, Districts, and Systems.* Thousand Oaks, CA: Corwin.

Fullan, Michael, and Rincón-Gallardo, Santiago. (2016). Developing High Quality Public Education in Canada: The Case of Ontario. In Frank Adamson, Björn Astrand, and Linda Darling-Hammond (Eds.), *Global Education Reform: How privatization and public investment influence education outcomes.* New York: Routledge, 169–193.

Fullan, Michael, and Watson, Nancy. (1999). *School-based management: Reconceptualizing to improve learning outcomes.* Paper prepared for the World Bank seminar on Improving Learning Outcomes in the Caribbean.

Gloeckner, Gene W., and Jones, Paul. (2013). Reflections on a decade of changes in homeschooling and the homeschooled into higher education. *Peabody Journal of Education, 88*(8), 309–323. doi: 10.1080/0161956X.2013.796837

Gouvernement du Québec, Ministère de l'Éducation. (2000). *Québec education program: Elementary education.* Quebec City, Canada: Ministère de l'Éducation.

Haiplik, Brenda. (2004). *BRAC's non-formal education program (NFEP).* Washington, DC: Academy for International Development.

Hargreaves, Andy, and Shirley, Dennis. (2012). *The global fourth way: The quest for educational excellence.* Thousand Oaks, CA: Corwin.

Martin-Chang, Sandra Lyn, Gould, Odette Noella, and Meuse, Reanne E. (2011). The impact of schooling on academic achievement: Evidence from homeschooled and traditionally schooled students. *Canadian Journal of Behavioural Science, 43*(3), 195–202.

McGinn, Noel F. (1998). Resistance to good ideas: Escuela Nueva in Colombia. In Lene Buchert (Ed.), *Education reform in the South in the 1990s* (pp. 29–52). Paris: UNESCO.

Melaville, Atelia, Berg, Amy C., and Blank, Martin J. (2006). *Community based learning: Engaging students for success and citizenship.* Washington, DC: Coalition for Community Schools.

Mourshed, Mona, Chijioke, Chinezi, and Barber, Michael. (2010). *How the world's most improved school systems keep getting better.* London: McKinsey and Company.

Olson, David. (2003). *Psychological theory and educational reform: How school remakes mind and society.* Cambridge: Cambridge University Press.

Pitt, Jennifer. (2004). *Case study for Escuela Nueva program.* Washington, DC: Academy for Educational Development.

Pitt, Jennifer. (2002). *Civic education and citizenship in Escuela Nueva schools in Colombia* (Unpublished master's thesis). OISE/University of Toronto.

Polyzoi, Eleoussa, Fullan, Michael, and Anchan, John P. (2003). *Change forces in post- communist Eastern Europe: Education in transition.* London: Routledge/Falmer.

Psacharopoulos, George, Rojas, Carlos, and Velez, Eduardo. (1992). *Achievement evaluation of Colombia's Escuela Nueva. Is multigrade the answer?* Policy Research Working Paper 896. Washington, DC: World Bank.

Ravitsch, Diane, and Vinovskis, Maris (Eds.). (1995). *Learning from the past: What history teaches us about school reform.* Baltimore: Johns Hopkins University Press.

Ray, Brian D. (2013). Homeschooling associated with beneficial learner and societal outcomes but educators do not promote it. *Peabody Journal of Education, 88*(3), 324–341. doi:10.1080/0161956X.2013.798508

Reimers, Fernando (Ed.). (2000). *Unequal schools, unequal chances: The challenges to equal opportunity in the Americas.* Cambridge, MA: Harvard University Press.

Rincón-Gallardo, Santiago (forthcoming). Large-Scale Pedagogical Transformation as Widespread Cultural Change in Mexican Public Schools. Accepted for publication in the *Journal of Educational Change*.

Rogers, Alan. (2004). *Non-formal education: Flexible schooling or participatory education?* Hong Kong: Comparative Education Research Centre, University of Hong Kong.

Rodríguez, Encarna. (2015). *Pedagogies and curriculums to (re)Imagine public education: Transnational tales of hope and resistance.* Singapore: Springer.

Sahlberg, P. (2011). *Finnish Lessons: What can the world learn from educational change in Finland?* New York: Teachers College Press.

Schiefelbein, Ernesto. (2006). *School performance problems in Latin America: The potential role of the Escuela Nueva system.* Paper prepared for the 2nd International New Schools Conference. Medellin, Colombia.

Schiefelbein, Ernesto. (1993). *In search of the school of the 21st century: Is Colombia's Escuela Nueva the right pathfinder?* Santiago, Chile: UNESCO Regional Office for Latin America and the Caribbean.

Scott, Suzanne. (1996). Education for child garment workers in Bangladesh (Unpublished master's thesis). OISE/University of Toronto.

Siabato, Ricardo. (1997). *Educación básica primaria en zonas rurales: La Escuela Nueva y su relación de la plan de universalación de la educación básica primaria.* Bogota: Ministerio de la Educacion Nacional.

Sweetser, Anne T. (1999). *Lessons from the BRAC non-formal primary education program.* Washington, DC: Academy for Educational Development.

Tyack, David, and Cuban, Larry. (1995). *Tinkering toward utopia: A century of public school reform.* Cambridge, MA: Harvard University Press.

Zavadsky, Heather. (2009). *Bringing school reform to scale: Five award-winning urban districts.* Cambridge, MA: Harvard Education Press.

CHAPTER FOUR

UNDERSTANDING PEDAGOGY: CROSS-CULTURAL AND COMPARATIVE INSIGHTS FROM CENTRAL ASIA

Sarfaroz Niyozov

INTRODUCTION

Teaching is a contested and complex process that cannot be encompassed in simple frameworks. This chapter begins by considering existing portrayals of teachers and teaching in the educational reform literature. Then it turns to the context of post-Soviet Central Asia, drawing primarily upon a 1999 ethnographic study of teachers' lives and work in the Republic of Tajikistan, updated through subsequent research and development activities in the region (Niyozov, 2011, 2016), and contextualized in relation to recent reports on education in Central Asia (Bulbulov, 2011; De Young & Heyneman, 2004; Silova & Steiner-Khamsi, 2008; UNESCO, 2013). The voices of teachers from Tajikistan and Kyrgyzstan illustrate the changing pressures on teachers' lives and work in this region of the world, including the interactions among education, culture, and religion (Niyozov, 2016, in press). I conclude by proposing that teaching be situated in an integrated life-work approach to understanding teachers, which helps in sustainable improvement of education in Central Asia.

IMAGES OF TEACHING AND TEACHERS

What happens in teachers' classrooms, and why, has increasingly become the central focus of educational research and professional

CHAPTER FOUR: Understanding Pedagogy

development. Ultimately, teachers and the quality of their work are central to developing particular kinds of societies and citizens, on both local and global scales (Bacchus, 1996; Dove, 1986; Hargreaves, 2003).

Teachers have been imagined in myriad complementary and contradicting ways, such as:

- transmitters of accumulated wisdom or constructors of students' knowledge;
- guardians or critics of existing moral norms (culture keepers or social reformers);
- technicians who implement others' mandates or complex professionals who as active agents decide curriculum and classroom matters;
- reflective practitioners focused on classrooms or engaged with wider educational issues;
- civil servants, reproducers of the status quo, or intellectuals who transform their social environments; and
- partners or resisters of educational and social reforms (Rust & Dalin, 1990; Larsen, 2010; Umetbaeva, 2015).

For too long, depictions of teaching were reduced to two dichotomized aspects, content and pedagogy, seen as existing independently of a teacher's mind, affect, and soul (Goodson & Hargreaves, 1996; Larsen, 2010). These reductionist conceptualizations have denigrated other important dimensions of teaching, such as teachers' purposes, emotions, visions, relationships, ethics, commitments, passions, management, and resources (Britzman, 2010). Positivist and culturally insensitive perspectives on teaching have taken products of particular social contexts, such as child-centred pedagogy, elevated them to the status of global best practices, and exported them across the various education systems. Well-intentioned progressive ideas such as whole language, cooperative learning, inquiry, critical thinking, constructivism, and child-centred teaching have been criticized as culturally or politically unsettling, socially and racially biased, intellectually superficial, or inappropriate in developing countries due to the demands they make on time and resources (Darling, 1994; Lambert & McComb, 1998). Outside of the affluent global north, such pedagogies may be viewed as Western, masculine, elitist, secular, disrespectful of traditional cultures, and "play-like" rather than "serious" (Guthrie, 1990; Henry, 1996; Kanu, 2006).

These decontextualized and dichotomous conceptualizations seem to have exacerbated educational reforms' swing from one pole to another (Alexander, 2001; Mortimore, 1990), leading to unsustainable solutions and cynicism about research, reform, and ultimately education and educators. They mask the complexity and evolving nature of the profession and the perennial question of whether advances in knowledge and professional development have led to improvement in teaching and the lives of students (see Anderson and Sivasubramaniam's Chapter Five in this volume).

By contrast, in this chapter I present rich and non-dichotomous portrayals of classrooms, schooling, and teachers' lives. The foundation is my nine months of ethnographic work, interviewing and observing five innovative teachers in their classrooms, in the mountainous Badakhshan Autonomous Province of Tajikistan. The three male and two female teachers, most of them Ismaili Muslims, but also Sovietized Tajiks, taught history, mathematics, biology, Russian language, and primary education. I interviewed them about their life histories and classroom practices, as well as about wider questions of education, culture, and society. I conducted further interviews with focus groups, school heads, other outspoken teachers, community members, representatives of the school boards and education ministry, and members of the international education community. I analyzed these data inductively and then in relation to other empirical and theoretical studies on education in Tajikistan and Kyrgyzstan, and on pedagogy in developing and industrialized societies. My subsequent qualitative work (interviews and workshops with a wider range of teachers, of multiple religious backgrounds) in Tajikistan has continued exploring teachers' life and work.

THE CONTEXT: TAJIKISTAN AND KYRGYZSTAN

Tajikistan and Kyrgyzstan are developing nation-states, framing themselves as descendants of the Silk Road's ancient civilizations (Gleason, 2004). Tajikistan claims to have been a large, flourishing state ruled by the Samanids in the ninth to tenth centuries CE. The Kyrgyz invoked a powerful *khanate* (kingdom) near the Yenisei River at around the same time. Despite claiming statehoods thousands of years ago, titular Kyrgyzstan and Tajikistan came into being recently, during the Soviet delimitations of the 1920s and 1930s (Haugen, 2003; Umetbaeva, 2015). The Russian Empire annexed both countries during its 19th-century colonization rivalry with Britain. Since then, the political, economic, cultural, and educational destinies of Tajikistan, Kyrgyzstan, and other Central Asian states of the former Soviet Union have been influenced by Russia. While Western Sovietologists and an increasing number of local nationalists have portrayed the relations between Russia and Central Asia as primarily colonial, many Central Asian development models continue to emulate Russia's education approach. Until 1991, each country had a centralized, structurally unified education system, created with Russian and Soviet help.

Despite their political independence since 1991 and some stark demographic differences (see Table 4.1), initial post-Soviet educational system restructuring, including privatization and decentralization, has also largely followed Russia's path. The Russian cultural, religious, educational, and even economic monopoly, however, is gradually withering away due to the rise of local nationalisms and globalizing influences such as the entrance of all former Soviet countries into the European education zone, the emergence of private international schools and universities, the spread of the English language, the revival of local tribal and nationalist forces, regional and global powers (China, Turkey, and the United States), bilateral and multilateral agencies

Table 4.1: Demographic, Economic, and Educational Indicators for Kyrgyzstan and Tajikistan

	Tajikistan	Kyrgyzstan
Total Population (mn) 2014	8.4	5.8
Area (thousand sq. km)	143.1	199.9
Population Growth % 2004	1.4	1.2
GNI Per Capita (US$)	1,060	1,250
Adult Literacy Rate % 2004	98	99
Life Expectancy (years) 2014	67	70
School Enrollment 0–18 (mn) 2004	1.6	1.45
Number of Students in School (Grades 1–11)	1.5 mn	58,880
Number of Teachers (Grades 1–11)	1.7 mn	93,600

Sources: Synthesized from UNESCO-UIS, 2013; UNICEF, 2014; the World Bank, 2014

(Asian Development and World Banks) (Merill, 2011), and cultural and religious movements, both Islamic (Hizb al-Tahrir, Al-Qaida affiliates such as the Islamic Movement of Uzbekistan, recently declared itself a part of the Islamic State) and pan-nationalist (pan-Turkish or pan-Irani) (McGlinchey, 2011; Roy, 2000; Heathershaw & Montgomery, 2015).

Broadly speaking, the collapse of the Soviet Union marked a series of paradigmatic shifts in Central Asia:

- from the largest unified country with a single party and state monopoly to the emergence of 15 independent nation-states, with multiple parties and political systems, struggling against the intrusion of the globalizing, state-undermining forces of financial corporations and cross-national cultural, ecological, and religious movements;

Figure 4.1: Map of Central Asia

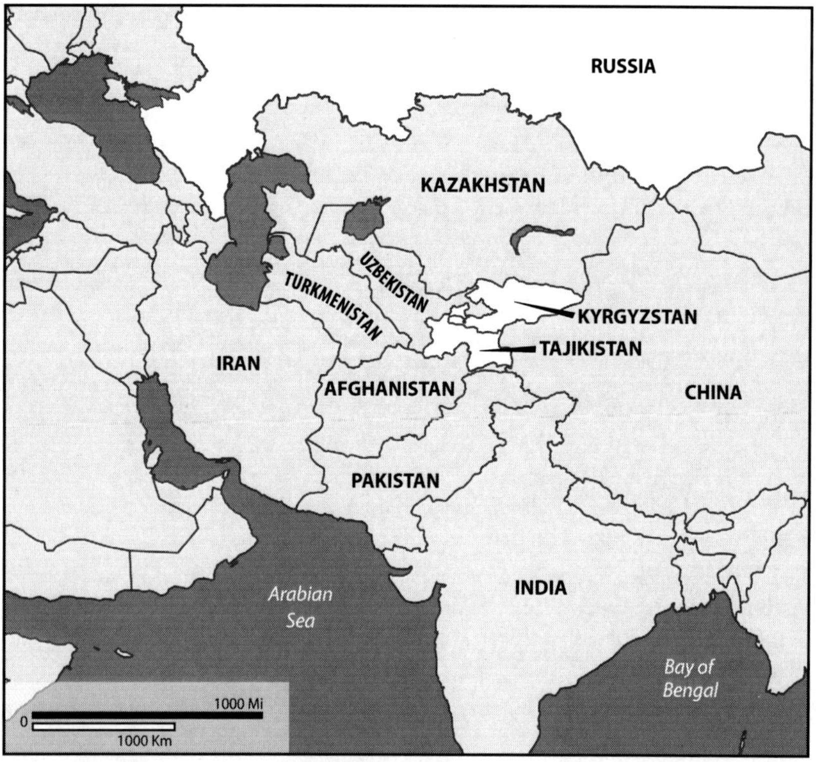

Source: Map created by Scott Wallace

CHAPTER FOUR: Understanding Pedagogy 93

- from a command planned economy to (initially "free" but now) a regulated market economy;
- from a centralized education system to one in which state control is increasingly challenged by private schools, after-school tutoring, religious instruction, and internationalization of schools and universities;
- from an atheistic and internationalist state to a space where nationalist and religious discourses shape the daily life of the citizens;
- from a single ideological-normative system to a milieu where value systems and norms clash, compete, and change, creating confusions and ambiguities.

At the same time, the two countries are heavily borrowing global structures, program models, curricula, pedagogies, and assessment tools at all education levels. These (Western) "global best practices" are at times creatively aligned with, or represented as, local ideas attributed to indigenous scholars. While this policy "talk" may appease external donors, the policy "walk" may diverge in response to local elite ambitions, historical grievances, and religious-cultural mores. For example, multiculturalism or bilingualism rhetoric may be used to encourage the countries' acceptance of European community privileges and (yet) to continue discrimination and ghettoization at home. Academic debate may be banned, because it allows students to disagree with mandated textbooks and national ideologies. Group work may be stopped simply because students could sit with their backs to the portraits of the local authorities posted on the classroom walls. Primary school English teaching may get cut because it may divert time and energy from communicating in the national languages. Religious education may be controlled or even banned because it may lead to students' religiosity or to interethnic tensions. Internet access may be limited because students would be exposed to alternative socio-political explanations. Computers may remain idle because of lack of electricity or skilled teachers. Credit systems may not work because university and school instructors lack structure or resources to implement them.

Within this local-global dialectic, Tajikistan's and Kyrgyzstan's education systems are juggling the contradictory demands of building nation-states and joining the global cultural, political, and capitalist world system. Within the nation-building project, ethno-pedagogic studies have been unearthing (or inventing) indigenous pedagogies from Tajikistan's and Kyrgyzstan's cultural histories. These studies purport to contribute to developing national consciousness, identity, and self-esteem, as well as promote tolerance, respect for other nations, and universal human values (Jalilova, 2006; Lutfulloev, 1997; Umetbaeva, 2015). In other words, post-Soviet changes and innovations are contingent on political and economic realities, cultural mores, and material and human resources (Aydarova, 2014; Niyozov & Dastambuev, 2012; Silova, 2006).

All these post-Soviet shifts and ambiguities have made the work of teachers more complex and challenging, as they face the new realities of uncertainty and intensification of their professional lives. Throughout the history of Central Asia, whether openly or otherwise, schools and teachers have always been assigned the role of the reformers of their rural societies. In pre-Soviet times, education aimed to Islamize the local populations. During the Soviet period, schools and teachers took over the role of the mosques, churches, and families in re-moralizing the community, creating Soviet human beings who were to be above ethnic and religious differences. Post-Soviet teachers are expected to instill nationalist and secularist identity in their students and communities. "During the Soviet times, we were scolded for not being socialist and atheist enough; in the post-Soviet times we are reprimanded for not being nationalist enough" (Teacher Participant in Niyozov, 2001, p. 145).

Identity and religion are major factors affecting the post-Soviet life and work of teachers. Understanding these influences requires a deep conceptual journey into the cultural mix of Central Asia, and the two countries in particular. First, both Tajikistan and Kyrgyzstan have been predominantly Muslim societies since before Russian and Soviet experiences. Soviets promoted contradictory anti-religious education policies, such as Muslim-Communist anti-imperialist cooperation in the 1920s, militant persecution of Muslims in the 1930s, co-optation in the 1940s, coexistence in the 1980s, and ultimately failure to eradicate religion from the people's consciousness (Heathershaw & Montgomery, 2014; McGlinchey, 2011). Islam is deeply rooted in the culture of Central Asians—penetrating and transforming their pre-Islamic proto-monotheistic belief systems, such as Zoroastrianism in Tajikistan and Tengrilichik in Kyrgyzstan, and affecting their customs, names, and life ceremonies in ways inseparable from their ethnic identities: "If the Soviets, instead of fighting Islam, made an alliance with it, the Soviet Union would not have collapsed,"

CHAPTER FOUR: Understanding Pedagogy

suggested a teacher in Dushanbe (Interview, June 2013). Post-Soviet emergence of religion, however, was also contested. Most Tajiks and Kyrgyz are Hanafi Sunni Muslim, a theological interpretation that emerged in the eighth century and is considered to be tolerant of local customs and other Islamic sects (Rahnamo, 2009; Turajonzoda, 2007). Tajikistan also has an indigenous minority Shi'a Ismaili community. At the end of the Soviet era (i.e., late 1980s and early 1990s), the cultural context was a mixture of pre-Islamic, Islamic, Soviet, and post-Soviet nationalist elements, often framed as not in contradiction, but in complementarity, enriching the material and spiritual life of Central Asians. Such creative synthesis was also practised in the Soviet times: Sovietized Tajik and Kyrgyz scholars creatively mined and sifted the Islamic and pre-Islamic legacies to promote a proletarian–working class worldview.

At the end of the Soviet times, anti-Russian movements, based on local languages and religious cultures, challenged this cultural construction. A perspective that frames Russians and Soviets as colonizers ebbs and flows as the geo-politics change. In 1990s Tajikistan, different perspectives on Islam vied for power: their rivalry with each other and with the Communist legacy led to a large-scale war. In Kyrgyzstan, while Islam has become a prominent force only in the last decade, the tensions have centred on Uzbek and Russian marginalization of Kyrgyz culture, ethnicity, and language.

In crafting what one might call an authentic indigenous culture, the predominant discourse in both Tajikistan and Kyrgyzstan is one of nationalism; Islam is tailored to support the nationalist discourse. To that end, the non-official interpretations of Islam, such as Salafism, Hizb al-Tahrir, and more recently, those of Al-Qaida and Islamic State, have been banned in both countries. Further, local interpretations, including those of the state, are challenged by global media and social networks, providing teachers and students with myriad potential perspectives. In the rest of this chapter, I extract from my own and others' research to illustrate how teaching has become ever more complex in post-Soviet Tajikistan and Kyrgyzstan.

TEACHING: THE USE OF CONTRADICTORY, EVOLVING, AND MIXED PEDAGOGICAL METHODS

In my 2001 ethnography, the five teacher participants practised elements of various teaching styles simultaneously. The same teachers moved between teacher-centred pedagogic modes and student-centred, democratic, collaborative pedagogies, often within the same classrooms and subjects. This shows that teaching styles observed may not reflect (and may even contradict) the teachers' espoused principles, values, and intentions. Secondly, neither teacher-centred nor student-centred styles are monolithic, but rather range by degrees from fully student-centred, to textbook- or exam-centred, to total teacher domination. Thirdly, teachers may change their teaching approaches under the influence of shifting contextual factors, such as probing by a peer or a change agent, or guidance from a religious or political figure. Fourthly, teachers' explanations of their practice may differ considerably from those of external observers. Therefore, we need to critically listen to how teachers explain their goals and ethics behind the methods they use.

Table 4.2 below illustrates the five teachers' apparently teacher-centred and authoritarian practices, in which students seem to be "passively imbibing the values, skills, and knowledge they impart" (Miller, 2000, p. 4). Selected recurring themes from interviews with the teachers are listed alongside the associated observable actions.

On the surface, Table 4.2 seems to illustrate teacher-centred transmission instruction: teacher domination of the agenda, memorization, and coercive relationships. The teachers appear to believe in a direct link between their teaching and the students' learning. They are concerned about covering the curriculum, teaching to the test, and sticking to the textbook.

To compare, Shamatov's study of teaching in Kyrgyzstan described a history teacher, Kanybek, who also appeared to favour teacher-centred practices:

> Kanybek...predominantly used the lecture method so that he could cover the material within the limited time allotted for history lessons. He commented, "I teach the most important aspects of the theme, and encourage the pupils to study the rest on their own." He dictated his conspectus to his pupils and had them copy the material to read for homework. He said, "If I lecture and have the pupils write my lectures quickly, then it will be very helpful for them when they go to university, because I learned from my university experience that writing a lecture is really tough." (Shamatov, 2005, p. 187)

Table 4.2: Teacher- and Textbook-Centred Classroom Practices

Sayings	Actions
Because there is too much information to cover in a short time, I must make it short, simple, and concrete, and lecture that to them.	Warn; stand in front; always have serious face.
Due to lack of textbooks, I have become the source of knowledge and have made them parrots.	Make sure students do not move…and follow the rules of behaviour (for example, raising hands, sitting, and standing).
Because they and I are not used to group work, I cannot switch to it right away.	Emphasize the years, dates, and names; repeat and explain the same thing more than once.
The teacher should be like an encyclopedia, [and] know everything possible.	Maintain close relationships with parents, but strict relations with students; threaten students with their parents.
How can you call it indoctrination when I tell them the good side and bad side of an issue?	Interrupt when students are off-topic.
I am more experienced and tell them so that they do not make my mistakes; I tell them the correct answer so that they do not fail; no one has become something without a teacher.	Ridicule; point out mistakes right away.

Correct the language use immediately; do not allow use of the mother tongue. |
| The younger need to listen to wise people and seek their advice. | Tell the students to move out of the classroom, stand still, or move to the corner. |
| Their language and vocabulary are too weak, and I cannot use their mother tongue—I am not allowed. | Lecture, tell, and explain.

Daily plan and develop a conspectus; ask students to copy it. |
| Due to cold-related winter break, we need to move fast to cover topics, so I have to tell them the most important points. | Evaluate students at the end of each class. |

These characterizations sound eerily familiar to earlier negative characterizations of teaching throughout much of the USSR:

> Instruction from the first grade on was characterized by a fairly rigid pattern of rote mastery of text, oral recitation by students, and teacher dominance of classroom activity...[T]he typical Soviet school was often a dreary place: a decrepit building with few textbooks, outdated equipment, alienated students, bored teachers, and authoritarian administration. Students graduated with little understanding of the concepts or principles they had studied, or with narrow, outdated occupational training that was often useless in practice. (Kerr, 1990, p. 27)

Some scholars even extended this generalization to developing countries in general:

> Most classroom activities are directed to the whole class, with the teacher appearing as a "benevolent dictator."...The children's personal experience is seldom used as a learning input....[Teachers] might "ignore" a child's response or treat a child's error as personal insult...[T]eaching of norms and rules overshadows other teaching activities... (Avalos, 1986, p. 211)

Sirotnik (1990) reports that such teaching styles prevail in most industrialized countries, including the United States:

> [A] lot of teacher talk and a lot of student listening...almost invariably closed and factual questions...all in a virtually affectless environment. It is but a short inferential leap to suggest that we are implicitly teaching dependence on authority, linear thinking, social apathy, passive involvement, and hands-off learning. (cited in Miller, 2000, p. 8)

The above portrayals, rooted in the modernist ideas of being in control, conscious, rational, and capable, have not captured the complexity and evolving nature of teaching, in Central Asia or elsewhere (Britzman, 2010).

These so-called teacher-centred practices, however, can be interpreted in more complex ways, if we engage the depth of teachers' everyday life and work. For example, warning of bad and good aspects of one's society by using living examples from recent history known to the students, or problematizing a topic in the history textbook through teachers' and students' views, represents a departure from merely delivering a "pre-cooked text." Direct instruction should not always be seen as bad or monolithic. Sometimes it may encourage critical and balanced thinking, implant doubt in students' minds, and keep them from being fooled by particular information. In sum, it may well be "a standard fallacy to presume that whole class direct instruction equates with transmission or that collective discussion respects children's capacities as thinkers" (Alexander, 2001, pp. 557–558).

In interviews, the five teacher participants in my ethnography often acknowledged that the coercive nature of their teaching, their bullying of the students, their lecturing, their use of elevated academic language, and their teaching of unrelated topics could be counterproductive and harmful. Their explanations of these contradictions illustrated their human vulnerability as well as their disempowerment in the face of the increasing intensification of their working lives:

> I become rude because life and work conditions make me get out of control, when I prepare myself and my students don't. My wife makes me angrier when, she, instead of appreciating my struggle, also curses me: "Why do you kill yourself for teaching and school, when no one cares about you and your family?" I feel she is right. (Niyozov, 2001, p. 129)

In contrast, Table 4.3 illustrates practices and attitudes that seem to represent transactive (dialogic) and/or transformative teaching, by which students reconstruct knowledge through dialogic interaction or participate in changing individuals and society. Resting on a humanistic commitment to social change, transformative teaching views a student not just in a cognitive mode, but also "in terms of his or her aesthetic, moral, physical, and spiritual needs" (Miller, 2000, p. 6).

In Table 4.3, the same five teachers appeared to believe in their students' ability to contribute, have knowledge, think, and take responsibility. They asked questions and involved their students in a series of activities. They agreed with augmenting their methods with the kind of humane and engaging activities the students suggested, such as roleplay and word guessing. Here, the students were perceived not only as knowledge receivers, but also as emulators, appliers, and even producers of

Table 4.3: Transactive and Transformative Teaching Practices

Sayings	Actions
I wanted them [11th graders] to conduct the lesson; they lived through *Perestroika* and *glasnost*, so they know about the topic.	Students discuss and provide feedback to teaching.
Once in two weeks I prepare my good students to teach the whole class.	Students dance and sing during the relevant topics, and also celebrate their talents and successes.
I agree that teachers may not know everything and students may know something that we teachers do not know. Our students travel, meet many people, and see a lot of movies.	Pose problems to do independent work; ask students to question one another.
I want the children to explain the past so as to imagine a future.	Field trips; ask them to work in large groups and arrange competition between the groups.
I expect them to create something new.	
I could have lectured, but I know you [students] all have learned a lot of poetry, so I left it to you, and you did very well.	Assign creative homework.
	Hug the smaller children when they come to the front.
I can prove to the inspector that I am doing the right thing.	Students select activities such as roleplay for some of the sessions.
I am a friend [to] my students, and they share with me more than with their parents.	Bring up social issues and let the students talk about them.
I am there for my students when they need me.	Use brainstorming and puzzles.
It is better to ask questions than tell them.	Invite the silent students to speak up.
I use Shugnani and Wakhi [local languages] from time to time to help my students understand the topics.	Relate the topics to the students' lives; ask the students to assess one another.

knowledge. The teachers allowed their students to move, recite poetry, dance, sing songs, lead the lessons, ask questions, laugh, disagree with each other and the teacher, cooperate and compete, and make noise, although to a limited degree. The teachers sat with their students, made jokes, agreed with their views, listened to their comments, and asked questions linking curricular and extracurricular topics. In interviews, the teachers mentioned the progressive theories of Pestallozi, Rousseau, Krupskaya, and Makarenko, such as belief in every student's educability, the project method, group work, socialist competition, and problem solving. They cited proponents of the Soviet-era pedagogy of cooperation, such as Shatalov, Amonashvili, Lysenko, Davidov, and their counterparts in Tajikistan and Kyrgyzstan (Lutfulloev, 1997; Akulova, 1988).

Tables 4.2 and 4.3 show some glimpses of the social construction of culture and religion. On one hand, some aspects of the traditional culture may promote passivity, obedience, and unquestioned submission and reverence to authorities, traditions, and Elders, conducive to teacher-centred instruction (Guthrie, 1990; Tabulawa, 1997). On the other hand, not all authorities and traditions are oppressive. Nor are respect and acceptance inevitably based on passivity and blind emulation. Traditional culture can (also) promote active learning, questioning, and searching (Ginsburg, 2010).

International organizations have generally ignored this complexity of instructional life. My research helps to explain why their two decades of efforts to shift Central Asian teachers into child-centred approaches have been, at best, a partial success. Even today, many teachers allow only limited use of group work, arts, interaction, or critical questioning. They generally agree that these pedagogies create confidence in the children (to present information, express their views, and overcome shyness), but teachers also want to impart what is required to be learned (and regurgitated). In my study, a school principal noted that:

> The degree and frequency of the active learning methods (*metodhoi ta'limi fa'ol*) vary: There is more of their use when teachers have just returned from professional workshops...and when the Professional Development Institute's teacher educators are still following up and inspecting the teachers. This use, however, dwindles as the visits drop, and as the teachers become complacent. The teachers justify this stoppage by saying that they achieve the same objectives through the teacher-centred methods, so there is

no need to use these child-centred (*kudakmarkaz*) methods. Some of them continue using these active methods (*metodhoi fa'ol*) when they organize debates or discussions around certain topics. But when it comes to new topics in the program (*barnoma*), the teachers use the lecture method. (Niyozov, 2001)

Active and student-centred pedagogies are not totally new in Central Asia. Rudaki and Nasir Khusraw, Ibn Sina, Omar Khayyam, and Hafiz represent Muslim traditions of active deep learning and a broad understanding of education that balance intellectual, moral, and ethical dimensions. These voices have existed across Central Asian history— sometimes becoming dominant, more often playing subordinate or oppositional roles. For instance, just before the socialist revolution, a new movement (*Jadid*) grew in Central Asia that aimed at modernizing the society through active learning, respecting the learner, and harmonizing Western and Islamic approaches to learning (Khalid, 1998; Khan, 2003). Contrary to the usual negative portrayals of education in mosques and madrasahs, several researchers have shown that even these institutions at times could serve as sites of active learning, open-mindedness, and tolerance (Boyle, 2004; Makdisi, 1981).

Similarly, Soviet educational culture, in spite of its tendency to ideological indoctrination, included: the holistic notion of harmony between instruction (*obuchenie*) and upbringing (*vospitanie*), a dialectic between collective and individual, methods of active learning, and authorities who inspired teachers and students. In 1999, the participating teachers often referred to similarities between the advice of Marx and Muhammad, or Lenin and the Aga Khan (the spiritual leader of Ismaili Muslims), in relation to learning and humanistic values. One teacher summed this up:

> During Perestroika and Independence, I was worried about the excess of talk about Islam, but then I realised that the major principles of the ethical code of the constructor of communism are similar to those of *javonmardi* (manliness) in Islam. The problem is how to apply them in practice. I don't see that happening with either of them. (Niyozov, 2001, p. 276)

In sum, based on the particularities of the teaching moments, teachers make decisions about what methods to use, switching between teacher-, student-, textbook-, and exam-centred pedagogies and drawing upon various cultural traditions.

SUBJECT MATTER: MORE THAN FACTS AND INERT IDEAS

Teaching is more than methods and more than facts, formulas, propositions, definitions, rules, and textbook information. The five teachers in my ethnography deeply cared about knowing and imparting all the above in their daily instruction. Like elsewhere, a certain status hierarchy existed among the school subjects: the devaluation of Russian (an elite subject in the Soviet Union) and rewriting of history (also important for the ruling Communist Party) as a result of the collapse of the USSR created tough emotional, epistemological, and ethical crises for teachers of these subjects. As facts, concepts, and principles that had been "universal truths" during Soviet times turned out to be ideological and political "lies," these teachers experienced a sense of betrayal, guilt, and burnout. Debates arose about the educational relevance of these subjects to the mountainous regions of Central Asia. "What happened to the Soviet Union? What went wrong with socialism?" were among the questions raised to teachers, especially the history teachers. In the last 20 years, Russian and history (and their teachers) have lost and then recovered their status: in the 2010s, history teachers are once again propped up because they are to impart Tajik and Kyrgyz histories, central to the project of the new nation-states. According to the history teacher, the Soviet "lies" have been replaced with new "truths," with similar nature and purpose. With the recent decline of trust in the West and migration of millions of Central Asian labourers to Russia, Russian language has revived as the medium of interethnic communication and as a defence mechanism against westernization. Russian—unlike English, French, or even Arabic—is rarely viewed as a "foreign" language by Central Asians. Most local elites in Dushanbe and Bishkek use Russian in their informal and formal conversations. This Russian presence, together with the earlier forceful intrusion of English and weak material investment, have delayed the recovery, development, and representation of local languages and cultures in school curricula.

Such ideological tension also occurred in science subjects. The biology teacher in my ethnography had his belief in evolution challenged by a student's assertion of divine creation. In response, the student's conservative parents (the father was an active mujahideen leader) warned the teacher not to teach any atheistic or anti-Islamic topics. "Now, I do not become emotional in such situations. I say evolution and creationism are two options. You can choose the one you want" (Niyozov, 2001, p. 321). The re-emergence in the region of political and religious discourses (including aggressive nationalism) has created tensions for these teachers' internationalist visions of education and citizenship in Central Asia. In order to address these tensions, local scholars and policy-makers have aligned the national with "universal" and humanistic values (Lutfulloev, 1997; Niyozov, 2016, forthcoming; Umetbaeva, 2015) and religious values (e.g., Turajonzoda, 2006). Teaching "extremist" views, whether national or religious, is now officially banned in Tajikistan. Thus, school subject matters and their teachers have undergone the journeys of loss and gain, which have affected their lives and work, identities, and professional status.

TEACHING AS RELATIONSHIP

Changing times and complex tensions were also reflected in the relationships among teachers and students. One teacher explained:

> Ten years ago I was more strict and demanding with my students....In the Soviet times, I knew the students were fed and clothed. That's why I not only asked the students to study harder but also watched that they did not get spoiled and involved in bad activities. Now, if I am too strict, things get worse. If a child has not eaten bread for a while and I "twist his ears," he may kill himself because of too much pressure here and at home. Two students from our Tajik and Kyrgyz schools have tried this already. That is why my expectations have gone down. (Niyozov, 2001, p. 163)

Box 4.1 illustrates the complex relationships and the forms of caring in (rural, traditional, and transitioning) Tajikistan society.

Relationships are central to the success of any pedagogy. In the rural Tajikistan context of my study, most of the teachers had a personal rapport with their students.

A teacher in Shamatov's related study in Kyrgyzstan, like her Tajik colleagues, focused on social principles, important to her, that she felt were in decline: respecting Elders, helping others, preserving family and community values, caring, doing what is right, and avoiding wrong. She commented, "As teachers, we should have ethical sessions or informal conversations with our pupils more often. And we should also be models for them" (Shamatov, 2005, 186–187). Clearly, such caring is complex; it extends to students' families, communities, and the teachers' own need to be cared for (Noddings, 1992).

However, contemporary teacher-student relationships in Tajikistan and Kyrgyzstan have been affected by the rise of private tutoring, corruption, consumerism, and the decline of teachers' professional status. While some parents and students continue to treat teachers with respect out of tradition or empathy, others perceive teachers as corrupt (believe they sell grades, drink alcohol, use school to lure students into their private sessions) and lack knowledge and courage to challenge social and political problems. Public school teachers, especially, are now seen as beggars expecting gifts and money for taking better care of particular children. This has created an asymmetry in teachers' relations toward the children of high-status parents versus those whose parents are unable to afford gifts and bribes. Thus, teachers' relationships with

Box 4.1: Teachers' Expressions about Student-Teacher Relationships

- In the Soviet times, our respect was contrived by the Party. Now we need to work hard to earn respect.
- Too much kindness makes students lazy and weak, and too much cruelty makes them stubborn and passive.
- Sometimes I scold the students, other times shout at them, yet other times I joke, but they know I care for them. I do that for their benefit and that is why they do not get angry.
- I defend the students from abusive parents when needed.
- We have decided to treat children as human beings. We decided to fight those who pull our students into drugs and guns.
- I feel hurt when someone has become rich and disrespects his teacher; nowadays people respect only the rich, the mafia, and the merchants.
- When I see parents avoiding me, I feel something went wrong in my work with their children. Here, if things go bad, they may go so between families and for generations.
- Nowadays, if you don't give the students good grades, their parents won't say *salom* [hello].

students and communities have strong effects on the success of their teaching, the quality of the students' learning, and the teachers' position in the community.

TEACHERS' MORAL COMMITMENT, INTEGRITY, AND VISION IN CONTEXT

Teaching included commitment and moral responsibility, yet in the context of the decline in teachers' status, their fragile economic situation, and the increase in pressure (for unpaid service) by state and civil society. A teacher in my ethnography explained how commitment and responsibility were interconnected with his teacher identity, vision, purpose, and ethical stance.

> Materially this teaching does not give me even 5% of what I would do in my farm. I could collect wood for winter and look after my cattle. But I prepare myself and come to teach. I feel I have to care for them and for my community. No one can do that except teachers. The authorities and parents do not appreciate this, which makes me very angry, so much that I cannot sometimes control myself and unleash my anger on my students. (Niyozov, 2001, pp. 102–103)

Since 2000, hundreds of teachers have left teaching for other jobs, within or outside Tajikistan. Some who have stayed have been spending minimum energy on teaching, using it as a safety net but doing other jobs to make money for paying rent, getting their children admitted to universities, and financing their children's marriages. However, there are still teachers in Central Asia who do not compromise on their commitment to serve all students regardless of their wealth, gender, or ethnic background. For example, a school principal at the sociology seminar I facilitated in Dushanbe supported such commitment with institutional expectations: "In our school we have warned the teachers that whether someone takes a gift or not, we should not penalize those students whose parents cannot afford giving such gifts with low-quality teaching" (Interview, June 2013).

Reflecting their multiple roles and coping with dramatic post-Soviet changes, the participants in my ethnography, and in subsequent studies, emerged as responsible citizens, whose zone of praxis went beyond

CHAPTER FOUR: Understanding Pedagogy 107

school walls. They were concerned about where society was heading—its lack of care for the poor and their neighbours, and the lack of accountability to the rule of law or social norms. One teacher explained:

> The children witness in the street how modesty, honesty, hard work, and knowledge fail. Once I talked about Tajikistan being socialist; now we criticize that. Once we talked against religion, capitalism, and private ownership; now we praise all of them. Once I said Uzbeks were our brothers; now some people view them as occupiers of Samarqand and Bokhara. If I talk today about Russians as brothers and friends, the youth of the village and my students do not like it. How can I state that we have a law-abiding, democratic, and secular society, when there are drugs, guns, corruption, religious imposition, and nepotism? I do not want to be a liar again. (Niyozov, 2001, p. 242)

The teachers in the ethnography had envisaged and worked for a society based on pluralism, cooperation, sharing, and caring for each other and the poor. One teacher expressed it this way:

> You noticed how many nationalities and ethnicities we have got here in [a study site]. We should...promote education that teaches respect, justice, and internationalism. By internationalism, I mean the equality of people despite their geographical locations, languages, races, and religions. I like when there is pluralism of thinking, instead of having an ideology of a party or a clan. (Niyozov, 2001, p. 159)

These teachers worked for a Tajikistan that would be free from drugs, guns, and corruption, which had spread due to bureaucratic mismanagement and incompetence. The teachers joined their school's effort to save their society: talking with parents about people who had strayed into drugs and guns, avoiding drugs and guns themselves, and mobilizing the sayings of the president, figures from literature, and the Aga Khan. Another teacher in Tajikistan summed up:

> Teachers are a source of spirituality, culture, education, and the future of the society. We work so that the children live better and our community does not fall back to the level of Afghanistan. In

the 70 Soviet years we have moved so much ahead, and we do not want our people to become ignorant again, get involved in drugs and wars. (Niyozov, 2001, p. 187)

TEACHING AS CONTEXTUAL RELEVANCE AMID A MULTIPLICITY OF GOALS

While teachers I worked with were aware of the mandated Soviet-era curriculum's failure to provide real, relevant, and meaningful learning, they did not consider it useless. A history teacher suggested that researchers and policy-makers should learn from the Soviet period:

> We knew nearly nothing about ourselves, [or] our neighbours, Afghanistan and China. Ultimately, we came to teach our Tajik history. But...I would include the view of mountains, the traditions of the people of Badakhshan, the needs of Badakhshan and the problems we face today. I have nothing against the Romans and Russians, nothing against the Soghdians and the Bactrians [ancient peoples of Central Asia], but I want to know about ourselves first and how are we connected to them....We in the school conduct extracurricular activities to teach more about our prominent figures and our [locality], bring in a veteran of the war or a local scholar, arrange a visit to the Ethnographic Museum. On our own efforts, time, energy, and expenses. No one pays us for these. No one thanks us. (Niyozov, 2001, pp. 102–103)

Relevance also involved pedagogically linking content to students' needs and experiences. For instance, a teacher of Russian in my study decided to adapt his implemented curriculum:

> I said, "To hell with the 'parts of speech' [in the mandated program]." I will do everything to enable these students to read and write first, if not to speak. When they start reading and writing, we can move to grammar. I knew that I was violating the directives. In the journal, I would write that I am covering grammar, but in reality I was intensively teaching them reading. (Niyozov, 2001, p. 187)

National priorities had taken over curriculum content. Due to scarcity of skills and resources, as well as tightening control of teachers' work by the state, teachers rarely considered as important their own and students' experiences and ideas about curricular topics. For example, while the history curricula have in recent years tilted toward national histories in both Tajikistan and Kyrgyzstan, the portrayal of historical events tends to be nationalist and sterilized. Recent conflicts, such as the civil war in Tajikistan (1992–97), the 1990s and 2010 Uzbek-Kyrgyz conflicts, the overthrows of the two governments (2005, 2010), and labour migration, corruption and religious strife are either avoided or presented simplistically as foreign plots, individual politicians' mistakes, or anomalies to be avoided through patriotic endurance and rallying around existing leadership. Making learning relevant to students' experiences may once again become a risky endeavour in the resurgent centralized and authoritarian political systems in Central Asia (Umetbaeva, 2015).

Teaching has multiple purposes and goals—such as enabling students to access higher education, and to become knowledgeable and ethical, creative and internationalist, and even famous. Teachers in my research had subject-pertinent goals, such as helping students learn to speak Russian, English, and Chinese; to value consensus and national unity; to be wary of politicians; and to use biological knowledge in their daily lives. There were also topic-related goals, such as explaining the causes and outcomes of Perestroika, the reasons for the rise and fall of the Samainds, and the names of fruits and vegetables in Russian and Tajik. There were social and ethical goals, such as teaching children to avoid bad habits involving alcohol, drugs, and guns; encouraging love for the motherland, the president, and the imam; developing pride in the village's contribution to the development of Tajikistan; and fostering friendship with the neighbouring Kyrgyz. There were logistical and organizational goals, such as attending class regularly and observing hygiene, bringing peers and younger children to school, and carrying wood to heat the classrooms. Also, the teachers had goals for individual students, such as fostering freedom of expression and instilling confidence.

All five teacher participants in my ethnography, at the time, supported continuing Soviet educational traditions reflecting the moral and ethical aims of education. The teachers considered social and moral goals more important, and harder to achieve, than academic ones. They worried about the ineffectiveness of the newly introduced subjects of ethics, morality, conflict resolution, and peacemaking. Comments like "[T]he more we teach ethics, the less ethical we are becoming. The street has a stronger influence on students than we do.... With dollars in hand, you can buy any kind of education and position" are signs of this frustration. Despite the spread of these societal ills—such as corruption, violence, and drugs—a teacher participant argued that they needed to emphasize and practise the humanistic values of care and honest work, which in their view crossed various ideological positions and withstood the trials of history.

Yet, their classrooms mostly remained focused on covering the formal curriculum. This concern often made them teacher-and-textbook-centred, and coercive in their relationships. The rural post-Soviet realities in Tajikistan, in which (due to cold and scarce resources) the academic year was reduced to six or seven months instead of nine, coupled with the demands of disciplining and grading, created a panic situation. They felt their educational goals and societal visions were doomed to fail within the current conditions of work, which included widespread corruption. The nationally prescribed curriculum demanded that teachers promote ethnic nationalism. History teachers found this intrusion of religion and nationalism unacceptable. They were uncomfortable with the government's reinterpretation of the Basmachis (Islamic guerrillas of the 1920s) as freedom fighters and with presenting Russians as colonialists. They continued to have sympathy for aspects of socialism that had by now disappeared.

The teachers argued that being a good human (in terms of character, ethics, and values) was actually the same as being a good Muslim, a good Communist, or a good democrat. Some schools displayed the pictures and sayings of Lenin and Marx alongside those of their national president and religious authorities, to show the continuity in perennial values such as hard work, honesty, justice, and caring. A teacher observed that—as theories—socialism, democracy, and Islam were great, whereas at the level of practice, the teachers were wearied by competing ideas they faced in the contemporary confusing, chaotic, and unjust environment.

The teachers' practices embodied some disagreements with the values and perspectives of their traditional communities, particularly in relation to citizenship education. At the same time, the teachers had stopped idealizing the West as the beacon of democracy and progress. Currently Tajik and Kyrgyz teachers are servants of states that (ostensibly) promote inclusive nationalism. While patriotism and national consciousness are favoured, they are aligned with the values of tolerance and respect for other nations and religions. As elsewhere, elites, through nation-states, used schools and teachers to perpetuate whatever was presumed to be the best social order (Apple, 1982).

PEDAGOGY, IDENTITY, AND RELIGION

The five teachers in my ethnography drew upon various cultural authorities pragmatically to promote their students' development, often quoting 9th-century poet Rudaki, 11th-century thinker Nasir Khusraw, and the Aga Khan. Khusraw's life epitomized active inquiry: knowledge, reasoning, quality evidence, and active interpretation were used in a search for truth, social justice, and ethical conduct (Hunsberger, 2000). Khusraw modelled learning upon diverse Islamic and non-Islamic perspectives, represented in the following poem:

> I began to ask questions from thinking people of their opinions:
> From the Shafi'I, Maliki, Hanafi, I asked of what they said.
> I began to search for the guidance of the Chosen One of God
> But when I asked (my teachers) about the reasons for injunctions of the religion, or the verses of Qur'an on which they were based.
> None proved to be helpful, one resembling the blind and the other deaf.
> Then I rose from my place and started my journey,
> Abandoning without regret my house, my garden, those whom I was accustomed to see.
> From Persian and Arab, Indian and Turk,
> From inhabitants of Sind, Byzantium and Jew, from every one,
> From the philosophers, Manichee, Sabean, from an atheist,
> Did I inquire as to what interested me with much persistence.
> (quoted in Ivanow, 1948, pp. 22–23)

Culture and religion are richly complex and dynamic constructs that can be used for different purposes. As Tajikistan and Kyrgyzstan further assert their identities, religion, language, and local history will become more visibly important factors in teachers' professional lives. These will, however, be challenged by interpretations coming down from the state and from international movements.

Both states have been debating whether religion should be taught in schools. In both countries, youth radicalizing and joining pan-Islamist groups (such as the Taliban, Salafiya, Hizb al-Tahrir, and Islamic State) have led to increasing consensus that avoiding religious education would lead to religious illiteracy, or rather to students' seeking (perhaps intolerant) religious understandings from the internet and other global sources. In Tajikistan, a new secondary school course called History of Religion, a comparative presentation of world religions, is expected soon.

Similarly, history and language are important in the creation of the new nations. Although inevitably sources of tensions and conflicts, these subjects also can provide hope and opportunities for renewal, empowerment, active learning, justice, tolerance, and humane education. Which way this goes is dependent on teachers' values, knowledge, skills, commitment to local and global justice, and empowerment as professionals (Hayhoe & Pan, 2001).

CONCLUSIONS AND IMPLICATIONS

Teachers are as important as ever in their work with and against the challenges of the 21st century. In post-Soviet Central Asia, the proliferation of multiple local (e.g., Pamirism and Shugnanism in Tajikistan) and national (Kyrgyz, Tajik, Pan-Turkic, Pan-Persian) discourses and religious perspectives (Hanafism, Salafism, Ismailism), and the emergence of market capitalist economies, have complicated the meaning, purpose, and vision of teaching and have extended and intensified teachers' responsibilities. Compounded by decreasing resources and support and declining status and remuneration, this post-Soviet condition has led to the demoralization of teachers. Reforms in teacher education and school improvement have remained fragmented, outside-in, top-down, and technical effectiveness–oriented. Reform efforts have tended to treat the local cultural, structural, political, and religious factors in monolithic and dichotomous terms, as either all-progressive or totally inhibiting. These efforts have also ignored the growing complexities of teachers' work in the rapidly changing world and increasing demands and labour intensification. They are based on limited portrayals and quick-fix solutions that lack sustainability. This has given people the feeling that education reform rhetoric is less about improved teaching and learning, community, and global justice than about making money, exercising power, and reproducing inequalities (Silova, 2006). When policy-makers perceive teachers as deficient, overly didactic, and coercive, the solution is to replace their practice with externally developed "effective" methods, objectified and separated from the complex and contradictory features of the teachers' contexts.

The alternative to the above bureaucratic approach is to reflect on research and development as a professional and ethical endeavour, with implications at individual and societal levels. Listening to teachers' voices makes it clear that teaching entails a plurality of evolving goals, content, and methods. It is a lived experience. Each pedagogical style embodies complementary and conflicting principles and practices.

> Teaching is situated in relationship to one's life story, present circumstances, deep commitments, affective investments, social contexts, and conflicting discourses. Teaching concerns being, acting, and living in a setting characterized by contradictory realities, negotiation, and dependency and struggle. (Britzman, 1991, p. 8)

Engagement with teachers' ideas and experiences can facilitate innovation from within, and at the same time prevent falling into dogmatic and arrogant idealization of traditions, rejecting learning from the present and from the outside world. The challenge is to set up a process by which new learning influenced by internal and external sources can become real, meaningful, and relevant for local teachers and students in Central Asia—not based on "ours versus theirs" polemics, but on the quality of an idea, its validity, effectiveness, and ethical implications at personal, communal, and global levels.

QUESTIONS FOR REFLECTION AND DISCUSSION

1. How does this chapter complexify the understanding of teaching/pedagogy? Is this portrayal of teaching and learning relevant in educational and cultural contexts familiar to you?
2. How do you view the author's approaches to educational reform and teacher development? In what ways might they be (in)applicable to the context of an industrialized country?
3. This chapter suggests that, despite knowledge of active learning pedagogies, many Tajik teachers did not use interactive practices while teaching the prescribed curriculum. Why do you think this occurs in those contexts? How is this similar or dissimilar to your experience?
4. The chapter suggests that culture, religion, history, and languages are becoming critical factors in the post-Soviet education

landscape. What are the implications of such revival, and what approaches should be employed to engage local and global cultures and ideas in the business of teaching and learning?

SUGGESTED AUDIO-VISUAL RESOURCES
Almaz, directed by Elnura Osmonalieva (2010). Available at vimeo.com/33583714
This documentary film reflects rural aspirations and life in Kyrgyzstan by following the story of Almaz, a boy who was forced to leave school in order to work to help support his family after they moved from a rural area into the city. However, despite many hardships, Almaz does not give up and is able to return to school, ultimately participating in an exchange that takes him to the Netherlands. This inspiring story destroys stereotypes and presents a new hero of our time.

SUGGESTIONS FOR FURTHER READING
De Young, Alan, Reeves, Madeleine, & Valyaeva, Galina. (2006). *Surviving the transition? Case studies of schools and schooling in the Kyrgyz Republic since Independence.* Greenwich, CT: Information Age Publishing.
Heathershaw, John, & Montgomery, David. (2015). *The myth of post-Soviet Muslim radicalization in the Central Asian Republics.* London: Chatham House. The Royal Institute of International Affairs.
Khan, Sarfraz. (2003). *Muslim reformist political thought: Revivalists, modernists, and free will.* London and New York: Routledge Curzon.
Niyozov, Sarfaroz. (2011). Revisiting the teacher professionalism discourse via teachers' lives and works in Tajikistan. In I. Silova (Ed.), *Globalization on the margins. Education and post-Socialist transformations in Central Asia* (pp. 145 169). Charlotte, NC: Information Age Publishing.
Niyozov, Sarfaroz. (forthcoming, 2016). Islamic education in Tajikistan: Ceasing the potential of a contested field. In D. Ashraf, M. Tajik, & A. De Young (Eds.), *Contested terrain: 21st century fights over purposes and policies of schooling in the mountains of Pakistan, Afghanistan and Tajikistan.* Greenwich, CT: Information Age Publishing.
Niyozov, Sarfaroz, & Dastambuev, Nazarkhudo. (2012). Exploiting globalization while being exploited by it: Insights from post-Soviet education reforms in Central Asia. *Canadian and International Education, 41*(3), 5–37.

Niyozov, Sarfaroz, & Qobilova, Gulchehra. (2013). *Sociology of education in Central Asia, part 2: A report on the course offered in Dushanbe, Tajikistan in June 2013*. Available with the Open Society Institute. Dushanbe, Tajikistan.

Silova, Iveta. (2006). *From sites of occupation to symbols of multiculturalism: Reconceptualizing minority education in post-Soviet Latvia*. Greenwich, CT: Information Age Publishing.

Silova, Iveta. (Ed.). (2011). *Globalization on the margins: Education and post-Socialist transformations in Central Asia*. Charlotte, NC: Information Age Publishing.

Silova, Iveta, & Steiner-Khamsi, Gita. (Eds.). (2008). *How NGOs react: Globalization and education reform in the Caucasus, Central Asia and Mongolia*. Bloomfield, CT: Kumarian Press.

Teleshaliyev, Nurbek. (2012). *An exploration of teacher professionalism in Kyrgyzstan*. (Unpublished MPhil thesis.) University of Cambridge.

Umetbaeva, Damira. (2015). Paradoxes of hegemonic discourse in post-Soviet Kyrgyzstan: History textbooks' and history teachers' attitudes toward the Soviet past. *Central Asian Affairs, 2*, 287–306.

REFERENCES

Akulova, Ainura. (1988). *Anthology of pedagogical thoughts in Kyrgyz SSR* (in Russian). Moscow: Prosveshenie.

Alexander, Robin. (2001). *Culture and pedagogy: International comparisons in primary education*. Maiden, MA: Blackwell.

Apple, Michael. (Ed.).(1982). *Cultural and economic reproduction in education*. London: Routledge & Kegan Paul.

Avalos, Beatrice. (1986). Training for better teaching in the third world: Lessons from research. *Teaching and Teacher Education, 1*(4), 289–299.

Aydarova, Olena. (2014). Universal principles transform national priorities: Bologna process and Russian teacher education. *Teaching and Teacher Education, 37*(1), 64–75.

Bacchus, Mohammed Kazim. (1996). The role of teacher education in the development of southern countries. *The Alberta Journal of Educational Research, 42*(2), 77–86.

Boyle, Helen. (2004). *Quranic Schools: Agents of preservation and change*. New York/London: Routledge Falmer.

Britzman, Deborah P. (1991). *Practice makes practice: A critical study of learning to teach*. Albany: SUNY Press.

Britzman, Deborah P. (2010). *The very thought of education: Psychoanalysis and the impossible professions*. Albany: SUNY Press.

Bulbulov, Juma. (2011). *Teachers' qualifications' improvement: Reality, specificity, and reflections* (in Tajik). Dushanbe: Irfon Publishing House.

Darling, John. (1994). *Child-centred education and its critics*. London: Paul Chapman Publishing.

De Young, Alan, & Heyneman, Stephen. (Eds.). (2004). *The challenges of education in Central Asia*. Greenwich, CT: Information Age Publishing.

Dove, Linda. (1986). *Teachers and teacher education in developing countries*. London: Croom Helm.

Ginsburg, Mark. (2010). Improving educational quality through active-learning pedagogies: A comparison of five case studies. *Educational Researcher, 1*, 62–74.

Gleason, Gregory. (2004). Introduction to Central Asia: Ancient societies and the new millennium. In A. De Young & S. Heyneman (Eds.), *The challenges of education in Central Asia* (pp. 11–20). Greenwich, CT: Information Age Publishing.

Goodson, Ivor, & Hargreaves, Andy. (Eds.). (1996). *Teachers' professional lives: Aspirations and actualities*. New York: Falmer Press.

Guthrie, Gerard. (1990). To the defense of traditional teaching in lesser-developed countries. In V. Rust & P. Dalin (Eds.), *Teachers and teaching in the developing world* (pp. 119–232). New York: Garland Publishing.

Hargreaves, Andy. (2003). *Teaching in the knowledge society: Education in the age of insecurity*. New York: Teachers College Press.

Haugen, Arne. (2003). *The establishment of national republics in Soviet Central Asia*. New York and Hampshire: Macmillan.

Hayhoe, Ruth, & Pan, Julia. (Eds.). (2001). *Knowledge across cultures: A contribution to dialogue among civilizations*. Hong Kong: Comparative Education Research Institute, University of Hong Kong.

Heathershaw, John, & Montgomery, David. (2014). *The myth of post-Soviet Muslim radicalization in the Central Asian republics*. London: Chatham House. The Royal Institute of International Affairs.

Henry, Annette. (1996). Five black women teachers critique child-centred pedagogy: Possibilities and limitations of opposing standpoints. *Curriculum Inquiry, 26*(4), 363–384.

Hunsberger, Alice. (2000). *Nasir Khusraw, The Ruby of Badakhshan: A Portrait of a Persian Poet, Traveler, and Philosopher*. London: I.B. Tauris.

Ivanow, Wladimir. (1948). *Nasir-i Khusraw and Ismailism*. Bombay: Ismaili Association Publications.

Jalilova, Jamila. (2006). *Islamic socio-cultural tradition in the context of ethno-pedagogy*. Dushanbe: Irfon Publishing House.

Jonbekova, Dilrabo. (2010). *Understanding faculty motivation in relation to retention at universities in post-Soviet Tajikistan*. (Unpublished master's thesis.) University of Cambridge.

Kanu, Yatta. (2006). Tensions and dilemmas of cross-cultural transfer of knowledge: Post-structural/postcolonial reflections on an innovative teacher education in Pakistan. *International Journal of Educational Development, 25*(5), 493–513.

Kerr, Stephen. (1990). Will Glasnost lead to Perestroika? Directions of educational reform in the USSR. *Educational Researcher, 19*(7), 27–39.

Khalid, Adeeb. (1998). *The politics of Muslim cultural reform: Jadidism in Central Asia.* Berkeley: University of California Press.

Khan, Sarfraz. (2003). *Muslim reformist political thought: Revivalists, modernists, and free will.* London and New York: Routledge Curzon.

Lambert, Nadine, & McComb, Barbara. (Eds.). (1998). *How students learn: Reforming schools through learner-centred education.* Washington, DC: American Psychological Association.

Larsen, Marianne. (2010). Troubling the discourse of teacher centrality: A comparative perspective. *Journal of Education Policy, 25*(2), 207–231.

Lutfulloev, Mahmadullo. (1997). *Revival of the persiana te pedagogy* (in Tajik). Dushanbe: Donish.

Makdisi, George. (1981). *The rise of colleges: institutions of learning in Islam and the West.* Edinburgh: Edinburgh University Press.

McGlinchey, Eric. (2011). *Chaos, violence, dynasty: Politics and Islam in Central Asia.* Pittsburgh: University of Pittsburgh Press.

Merrill, Martha. (2011). Kasha and quality in Kyrgyzstan: Donors, diversity, and disintegration in higher education. *European Education, 43*(4), 5–25.

Miller, John. (2000). *The holistic curriculum.* Toronto: University of Toronto Press.

Mortimore, Peter. (Ed.). (1999). *Understanding pedagogy and its impact on learning.* London: Paul Chapman Publishing.

Niyozov, Sarfaroz. (2001). *Understanding teaching in post-Soviet, rural, mountainous Tajikistan: Case studies of teachers' life and work* (PhD dissertation). University of Toronto.

Niyozov, Sarfaroz. (2011). Revisiting the teacher professionalism discourse via teachers' lives and works in Tajikistan. In I. Silova (Ed.), *Globalization on the margins: Education and post-Socialist transformations in Central Asia* (pp. 145–169). Charlotte, NC: Information Age Publishing.

Niyozov, Sarfaroz. (2016, forthcoming). Islamic education in Tajikistan: Ceasing the potential of a contested field. In D. Ashraf, M. Tajik, & A. De Young (Eds.), *Contested terrain: 21st century fights over purposes and policies of schooling in the mountains of Pakistan, Afghanistan and Tajikistan.* Greenwich, CT: Information Age Publishing.

Niyozov, Sarfaroz, & Dastambuev, Nazarkhudo. (2012). Exploiting globalization while being exploited by it: Insights from post-Soviet education reforms in Central Asia. *Canadian and International Education, 41*(3), 5–37.

Noddings, Nel. (1992). *The challenge to care in schools: An alternative approach to education.* New York: Teachers college Press.

Rahnamo, Abdullo. (2009). *Islamic Ulama in Tajikistan, Book 1* (in Tajik). Dushanbe: Irfon Publishing House.

Roy, Olivier. (2000). *The new Central Asia: The creation of nations.* London: I.B. Tauris.

Rust, Val, & Dalin, Peter. (Eds.). (1990). *Teachers and teaching in the developing world.* New York: Garland Publishing.

Shamatov, Duishon. (2005). *Beginning teachers' professional socialization in post-Soviet Kyrgyzstan: Challenges and coping strategies* (PhD dissertation). University of Toronto.

Silova, Iveta. (2006). *From sites of occupation to symbols of multiculturalism: Reconceptualizing minority education in post-Soviet Latvia.* Greenwich, CT: Information Age Publishing.

Silova, Iveta, & Steiner-Khamsi, Gita. (Eds.). (2008). *How NGOs react: Globalization and education reform in the Caucasus, Central Asia and Mongolia.* Bloomfield, CT: Kumarian Press.

Sirotnik, Kenneth A. (1990). On the eroding foundations of teacher education. *Phi Delta Kappan, 71*(9), 710–716.

Tabulawa, Richard. (1997). *Pedagogical classroom practice and the social context: The case of Botswana.* International Journal of Educational Development, 17(2): 189-204.

Turajonzoda, Akbar. (2006). *Shari'a and Society* (2nd ed., in Tajik). Dushanbe: Nodir Publishing House.

Umetbaeva, Damira. (2015). Paradoxes of hegemonic discourse in post-Soviet Kyrgyzstan: History textbooks' and history teachers' attitudes toward the Soviet past. *Central Asian Affairs, 2*, 287–306.

UNESCO. (2013). *Tajikistan: Country study.* Available at www.uis.unesco.org/Library/Documents/out-of-school-children-tajikistan-country-study-2013-en.pdf

UNECSO-UIS. (2013). *Adult and youth literacy: National, regional and global trends, 1985–2015.* Available at www.uis.unesco.org/Education/Documents/literacy-statistics-trends-1985-2015.pdf

UNICEF. (2014). *Tajikistan. Overview of basic education.* Available at www.unicef.org/tajikistan/overview_27465.html

The World Bank. (2014). *Data: Tajikistan.* Available at data.worldbank.org/country/tajikistan

CHAPTER FIVE
COMPARATIVE PERSPECTIVES ON SCHOOL IMPROVEMENT

Stephen Anderson and Malini Sivasubramaniam

The impetus to "improve" schools is as old as the existence of public schools. Teachers working in the public school system can take it for granted that they will practise their profession under persistent public scrutiny and pressure not only to do their job and do it well, but to constantly strive to do it better. For years, the conventional approach to improving schools emphasized the development and provision of good curriculum and learning materials; investment in the initial and continuing professional education of teachers and school administrators; and inspection to ensure compliance with externally prescribed education policies. Since the mid-1970s, the focus of responsibility and accountability for the quality of public education has shifted away from individual teachers to the collective actions and outcomes of educators at the school level. The shift has been marked by education policies, practices, and research that target "school improvement" as a focus for education quality development and accountability. This chapter reviews the history of school improvement trends internationally over the past quarter of a century.

INNOVATION ADOPTION AND IMPLEMENTATION

Education change researchers (e.g., Michael Fullan, 2001) characterize the 1960s and 1970s as the innovation adoption and implementation era of change. School personnel were expected to adopt and put into practice new instructional programs, materials, and methods, typically developed by external experts (government agencies, university professors, textbook publishers, etc.). In theory, the quality of education in schools would cumulatively improve as a result of implementing a new math program here, a new social studies program there, new teaching methods now, new instructional arrangements (e.g., open classrooms, team teaching) then, and so on.

Researchers who set out to document the effects of this idiosyncratic and uncoordinated innovation activity soon burst the bubble of optimism for this approach. They repeatedly discovered that change is an implementation-dominant process (e.g., Berman, 1981). The formal adoption of new programs and practices, whether mandated or voluntary, simply did not mean that school personnel would actually change what they were already doing. Some innovations were never implemented. Others were put into practice, but in the process of implementation local educators made modifications that virtually assured little change in existing practices and student learning outcomes. "Improvement" was equated with the mere fact of getting new programs and practices into place, rather than with the innovations' impact on the quality of teaching and learning. Researchers found that even when innovations were implemented, there was no guarantee that their use would be "institutionalized" or sustained over time.

Notwithstanding recurrent tales of failure, researchers also reported some cases of successful implementation of new programs and practices in schools and classrooms. The "lessons" from these positive experiences are well reported (e.g., Fullan, 2001; Hall & Hord, 2014), but are not necessarily picked up and skillfully applied by education policy-makers and practitioners. Strategically, however, the idea that the quality of teaching and learning in schools would improve overall and continuously through the incremental and uncoordinated adoption and implementation of multiple innovations targeting specific subjects, students, teaching methods, or management practices was not supported by reliable evidence. While the adoption and implementation of discrete new programs and practices continues unabated, at least in schools within the developed countries of the world, the attention (and resources) of school improvement advocates and researchers has shifted to other, more systemic change strategies, as reviewed later in this chapter.

COMPARATIVE RESEARCH

A distinct history of educational innovation in the developing world began in the 1970s (e.g., Havelock & Huberman, 1978). Educational improvement initiatives in the developing world in the 1970s and 1980s often exemplified the innovation adoption and implementation approach to change previously described (e.g., Lewin with Stuart, 1991; Rust & Dalin, 1990). Verspoor (1989), for example, conducted a multi-case analysis of the process and results of 21 high-outcome education improvement projects selected from a sample of 282 World Bank–funded projects between 1963 and 1984 in Africa, Latin America, South Asia, and Asia. Many of the findings from that study echoed findings on innovation implementation elsewhere in the world. In-service teacher training, for example, was a key element in the successful implementation of change. The most effective teacher training designs provided local training (at school or school cluster level) to support implementation of change programs, with regular classroom visits, support, and assistance from supervisors and program staff. Initial and ongoing access to in-service training and support contributed to the development of teacher expertise and motivation to change.

Some of Verspoor's findings highlight differences in the experiences of innovation-focused change initiatives in the developing world. For example, the most successful projects combined project-specific assistance with interventions designed to develop the capacity of education systems to plan and support innovation on a continuous basis. Policymakers and researchers in the developed world tended to take the organizational capacity to manage change in public education systems for granted at the state, national, or even school district levels. Verspoor found that change projects that focused primarily on a single component of education provision (e.g., curriculum, teacher training, school management, material resources) had lower outcomes than projects that addressed multiple components in a coordinated approach over time. The relative power of comprehensive change was only recognized later in the history of school improvement in the developed world. Finally, Verspoor described four "pathways to change": progressive innovation (multiple linked innovations introduced over a period of time); incremental expansion (innovation introduced in a small number of settings with a gradual planned increase in the scope of use); discrete change (isolated projects implemented in limited settings, uncoordinated with other projects); and permanent pilot (experimental change program that never gains political support and resources for broader use). Critics of the innovation adoption and implementation approach to school improvement in the developed world point to the frequency of

Verspoor's discrete change approach, and the failure to plan for scaling up of successful small-scale changes to the larger system (Elmore, 1996).

EFFECTIVE SCHOOLS AND SCHOOL EFFECTIVENESS

A significant shift in thinking and practice about how to improve the quality of public schools developed through comparative education research in North America and England during the 1980s (reviewed in Levine & Lezotte, 1990). Education researchers in the United States and England compared successful and ineffective schools serving traditionally low-achieving pupils in order to determine what differentiated the successful from unsuccessful schools. From this research, a common list of the characteristics of "effective schools" was identified, including instructional leadership, clear and focused mission, safe and orderly environment, climate of high expectations for success, frequent monitoring of student progress, positive home-school relations, and student opportunity to learn and time on task in the classroom. The point was not that schooling wholly determines students' academic success, but that what happens in schools does significantly influence learning outcomes. Failure cannot simply be attributed to student abilities and social background.

Critics of this research cautioned against overgeneralization of findings that were based on comparisons of small numbers of exceptionally good and bad schools, mostly at the elementary level, mostly in low-income urban settings, narrowly focused on basic skills performance, and sorted by performance differences at a single point in time, rather than over a sustained period of time (Purkey & Smith, 1983). They also noted that the research did not reveal how the good schools got that way, nor did it provide much insight into teacher and administrator actions underlying the effective schools' correlates. The original effective schools research contributed to the evolution of a strand of inquiry known as "school effectiveness research." Initially, school effectiveness researchers distinguished themselves from school improvement researchers, arguing that while they were concerned with quality and outcomes, school improvement research was more concerned with the processes of planned change in schools and school systems. Eventually, these two strands of inquiry converged in a common search for understanding not only the ingredients of effective schools, but how to develop and sustain school effectiveness at the school system level (e.g., Reynolds et al., 2000).

CHAPTER FIVE: Comparative Perspectives on School Improvement 123

COMPARATIVE RESEARCH

During the 1980s and 1990s a separate tradition of research on school effectiveness developed among researchers studying education in developing countries (e.g., Avalos, 1980; Fuller, 1987). Comparative research on school effectiveness across developed and developing countries reveals differences, but also some similarities (e.g., Reynolds et al., 2002; Teddlie & Reynolds, 2000; Levin & Lockheed, 1993). Some of the differences are obvious. In comparatively wealthy countries, variations in school effectiveness are not associated with differences in the provision and quality of material inputs (e.g., textbooks, facilities, well-educated teachers), because national and state governments have the capacity to assure that all schools have the basic human and material resources. In developing countries, however, variations in the provision and quality of essential resources is often an enduring challenge for government budgets and education authorities, and thus a key factor in discriminating more and less effective schools (Fuller, 1987; Levin & Lockheed, 1993). The influence of school inputs on student achievement is greater in schools in developing countries (e.g., statistical analysis of school effects in Third World countries attribute up to 25 percent of the variation in student performance to school inputs, while estimates of school effects in North American and European schools are in the neighbourhood of 9–14 percent [cited in Reynolds et al., 2000]).

Many developing-world countries are still struggling to make free public schooling accessible at the primary school level. Due to endemic basic funding and resource problems, fundamental issues of the quality of education provision in schools persist. Unfortunately, this situation was exacerbated by the international goal of achieving universal access to free quality primary education by the year 2015 (see Mundy and Read's Chapter Eleven in this book). In Malawi and Uganda, for example, the effect of implementing free primary education policies was a dramatic increase in public school enrolment that far exceeded the current resource capacity of local governments (Task Force, 2006). In Malawi, primary school enrolment rose from 1.9 million to 2.9 million pupils following the announcement of free primary education by the government in 1994, resulting in class sizes ranging from 60 to 140 pupils per teacher (often inadequately trained) according to one study (Chimbombo, 2005). In Uganda, after the government adopted its Universal Primary Education policy, primary school enrolment increased from less than 3 million in 1996 to 7.3 million in 2002, with similarly dramatic effects on class size and school resource capacities (Higgins & Rwanyange, 2005). Notwithstanding reported improvements in access to school (especially for girls), major education quality issues at the primary school level in the developing world persist, including high dropout rates, grade repetition, and failure on school-leaving exams.

Comparative effective schools research also exposes and challenges some fundamental beliefs and assumptions about student learning and about the organizational conditions that best support it. Reynolds et al. (2002) observe, for example, that in Western countries there is a strong emphasis on shifting the responsibility for learning to the student, on the presumption that students' capacity to learn on their own is an essential employability skill. One consequence of this emphasis is to privilege students whose social and cultural capital (related to family background and support) enables this kind of behaviour. In Pacific Rim Asian school systems, however, greater emphasis is placed on the role of the teacher in directing student learning. Research shows less evidence of variation in student performance by family background. Schools in some Asian countries also provide more time and support for teachers to engage in collaborative professional work during the work day (e.g., joint lesson planning, mutual observation, sharing and problem solving) than is typical in most North American and European schools, where teachers spend most of their day teaching, perhaps with a period of individual time for preparation and planning (Stigler & Hiebert, 1999; Hayhoe and Li, Chapter Two in this volume). These kinds of findings highlight the potential for comparative research to question taken-for-granted assumptions about school effectiveness structures and processes.

The effective schools research has had a profound impact on ideas, policies, and practices oriented toward improvement. One such impact is the idea that school effectiveness is more a function of school-wide norms and processes that affect the quality of student learning than of human and material resource inputs, or of the aggregated efforts of well-intentioned teachers and principals acting independently of one another. Second is the idea that school effectiveness can be assessed and acted upon using measures and indicators of student results and progress aggregated to the school level (e.g., standardized test scores, retention rates). Third is the belief that if some schools are capable of creating productive learning environments for all students, then it is reasonable to expect all schools to do the same.

CHAPTER FIVE: Comparative Perspectives on School Improvement 125

Finally, findings from the effective schools research have contributed to the development of models and projects aimed at replicating the characteristics of effective schools. Typically, effective schools projects involve self-assessments by school personnel of their "needs" vis-à-vis the effective schools correlates, the development of school improvement plans that address perceived weaknesses, and the temporary funding and assistance to implement the plans (e.g., Stoll & Fink, 1996).

Unfortunately, research on the impact of effective schools projects has failed to produce consistent evidence that needs assessments and action plans tailored to the effective schools characteristics make schools better. A common finding is that school personnel tend to focus their plans on factors with weak links to teaching and learning in the classroom and that the best-laid plans often do not play out as imagined in the process of implementation, leaving the results unpredictable. Ultimately, the effective schools correlates provide useful hints for what to look for in effective schools, but little practical guidance in how to (re)create those conditions.

The practice of cyclical school improvement planning, however, has become institutionalized in school systems around the world. Virtually every provincial and state government in North America, for example, requires school personnel to submit school improvement plans to school system authorities on a regular basis (e.g., three-year cycles with annual updates). Sponsoring agencies for school improvement initiatives in developing countries now routinely include school improvement planning in training programs for school management and in accountability reporting for project activities.

The effective schools and school effectiveness research crystallized the focus of efforts to improve educational quality on the school as the "unit of change." Other approaches to school improvement, however, were developed during the 1990s in North America and Europe. The remainder of this chapter reviews five alternative approaches that have exerted a strong influence on efforts to improve the quality of education in schools around the world:

1. Decentralization and school-based management
2. Comprehensive school reform
3. School choice and privatization
4. Standards and accountability-driven improvement
5. Professional learning communities and networks

DECENTRALIZATION AND SCHOOL-BASED MANAGEMENT

The effective schools practice of school improvement planning coincided with the decentralization and school-based management (SBM) approach to school improvement. Proponents of this approach, often referred to as "restructuring" in the 1980s and 1990s, argued that the needs and circumstances of schools were too varied to mandate a single solution and plan for improvement, and that schools were constrained from introducing change by education bureaucracies and policies that required standardization in structure and practice (see Murphy & Hallinger, 1993, for review of the restructuring phenomenon). The solution was to allow school personnel greater freedom to determine their needs for improvement, as well as greater control over the use of resources (e.g., money, staffing, time) and organizational arrangements (e.g., roles, decision-making processes, grouping of students and teachers). Decentralization and SBM advocates argue that this approach honours the professional expertise of those working closest to the problems of teaching and learning to determine what and how to improve. In their commonest form, SBM initiatives in North America amounted to little more than requiring (often on a voluntary basis) schools to establish school teams of administrators, teachers, and parents to produce school improvement plans.

Government policies mandating the establishment of school councils whose membership is dominated by parent and community representatives, not by teachers and principals, are another common school-based management approach to school improvement. In theory, this strategy shifts greater power and authority over school decision-making to school clients. In practice, many of these policies only assign an advisory role to the school councils, reserving important management decisions (e.g., hiring and dismissal of principals and teachers, allocating school budget) and educational decisions (e.g., school goals, program change) to professional educators at the school and school system levels.

Although there was a lot of talk about SBM as the new strategy for improving schools in the developed world in the 1990s, the practical reality was that the education bureaucracies and the overlay of external policies and laws regulating funding, equality of educational opportunities, and virtually all other aspects of public school operations were too entrenched to permit dramatic changes in public control and resource allocation. A decade of experimentation with school restructuring in North American schools yielded little evidence that school-based management strategies in and of themselves had made any significant difference in school effectiveness where enacted (Leithwood & Menzies, 1998). There are, of course, some reported exceptions. In the United States, the Chicago school district is the most widely acclaimed example of "successful" decentralization. Notably, decentralization in Chicago involved a significant transfer of power over school decisions (e.g., principal hiring) to parent-dominated school councils (not simply increased control by principals and teachers); it was system-wide (not a voluntary option for schools), and occurred in a context of mandatory accountability for school performance results (conditions absent or weakly present in many SBM strategies during the restructuring era). However, analysts of the Chicago experience note that evidence of school improvement on a wide scale only materialized when the school district reasserted its role in providing guidance, pressure, and support for school quality and improvement (e.g., Eason-Watkins, 2005). The mere act of decentralization and school-based management did not lead to school improvement without a shift and reorganization of direction, authority, and support at the district level.

COMPARATIVE RESEARCH
The World Bank has been an active advocate for decentralization of educational management in developing countries, and a critical observer and funder of research on the effects of decentralization policies and strategies on education quality (for syntheses of this research see Task Force, 2006). Typically, this takes the form of school councils or management committees formally empowered with considerable decision-making authority over staffing (hiring and firing of principals and teachers), teacher supervision, school finances, school maintenance, and, to a lesser degree, curriculum and instruction.

School-based management initiatives in the developing world tend to place more emphasis on parent and community influence on school decision-making than on expanding the scope of authority of school personnel. The arguments for increased local control centre on strengthening parent and community pressure on school personnel to carry out their duties in a professional manner; enhancing parental commitment to sending their children to school; and increasing parental involvement in managing and perhaps supplementing school funding. Teacher and student absenteeism, and lack of accountability for use of school funds, for example, are commonly reported problems in public schools in the developing world. When the right to hire and fire teachers (and principals) shifts from education authorities to local school parents, research on decentralization effects shows improvements in teacher attendance. When parents take on increased responsibility for the management and upkeep of their children's school, they are more likely to make sure that the kids attend regularly. Use of funds for the purchase of needed school resources is more likely to happen when parents have ways to ensure that principals are accountable for spending. It stands to reason that student achievement is likely to improve if teachers are consistently on-the-job teaching, if students regularly attend classes, and if school funds are efficiently spent on essential resources for teaching and learning.

Some words of caution are needed about the relationship of decentralized school management to "school improvement." First, schools operating under local SBM systems can be run just as ineffectively as schools operating under more centralized policies and systems. It is not the act of decentralization that improves schools, but the quality of implementation at the local level, including the quality of supports such as management training for school committees. The best research (see Task Force, 2006) indicates that decentralized management of schools (both primary and secondary), when effectively implemented, does not harm the academic achievement of students, and may be correlated with slightly better results than for comparable students in traditional schools on standardized tests of basic skills (e.g., reading, mathematics). There is little research on the impact that decentralization through school-based management has on school quality and improvement over time. Local parent/community management may help raise the baseline level of school performance, but does not guarantee ongoing improvement unless combined with measures that directly affect the quality of teaching.

COMPREHENSIVE SCHOOL REFORM

The comprehensive school reform (CSR) movement emerged in the United States in the 1980s and 1990s (see Murphy & Datnow, 2003, for an overview of the CSR movement). The basic idea is that change has to be "whole school," involving all participants, and the improvement process needs to encompass a comprehensive array of related factors (e.g., curriculum, materials, teaching methods, school management and leadership, teacher development, funding, parent involvement, performance monitoring and evaluation). A comprehensive school reform "model" provides a blueprint, process, and support for school development across multiple components of school operations, teaching, and learning.

In the United States, the CSR movement evolved out of a number of university-based whole school improvement initiatives in the 1980s, including the Coalition of Essential Schools (Brown University), Success for All (Johns Hopkins University), Accelerated Schools (originally associated with Stanford University), and the Comer School Development Program (Yale University). In the CSR approach to school improvement, individual schools voluntarily choose a CSR model. The school pays a fee for the right to implement the model. In return, school personnel receive training, on-site assistance, and program materials from the model developers. CSR schools join networks of schools using the same model, and the model developers facilitate information sharing and mutual assistance across the network.

Overall, the CSR approach to school improvement fares better than the innovation adoption, effective schools, or site-based management approaches to school improvement in terms of demonstrating measurable benefits for student learning and for growth in teachers' professional skills. As a strategy for system-wide improvement, however, the CSR approach is problematic. Expertise to support implementation rests with the model developers, not the local education authority (i.e., school district), and the proliferation of different CSR models in the same school system inhibits school participation in common system-wide initiatives.

COMPARATIVE RESEARCH

The CSR school improvement models received a lot of positive attention in the United States, but these school designs have not spread far beyond the US borders. Interestingly, however, similar programs of comprehensive school reform with similar tales of success have evolved independently in various regions of the developing world. Several of these are described by Farrell, Manion, and Rincón-Gallardo in Chapter Three of this textbook. The two best known are *Escuela Nueva*, which began as a pilot project in Colombia in the 1970s and eventually spread to over 20,000 rural schools (Colbert, 2002), and BRAC in Bangladesh.

The BRAC system has grown to over 30,000 schools. The network is now supported by its own post-secondary education institute, and is being implemented in other countries, such as Afghanistan. Other comprehensive school reform models have emerged elsewhere in the developing world. Anderson describes the evolution of a whole school development approach to school improvement through a series of school improvement initiatives sponsored by the Aga Khan Foundation in Kenya, Tanzania, and Uganda (Anderson, 2002). As the school improvement program matured, it encompassed an increasing array of organizational factors that affect the quality of teaching and learning, including: teacher learning, school and school district management, teaching and learning resources, parental and community involvement, funding for school and teacher development, change agent development, assessment and evaluation, and teacher working conditions. In northern Pakistan, faculty from the Professional Development Centre–North of the Aga Khan University Institute for Educational Development created a Whole School Improvement Program (WSIP) that operates in a growing network of government and NGO-sponsored independent schools in predominately rural and remote mountain communities (Kanji & Ali, 2006; Shafa, Karim, & Alam, 2011).

As an approach to school improvement, the CSR strategy seems to work and to be replicable on a wide scale. However, comprehensive reform programs tend to depend on external support networks, rather than on support from the school systems in which participating schools are located. Coordination between school systems and the CSR networks can be politically, financially, and logistically problematic.

Corporate Actors

The emergence of corporate investment in the education sector targeting low-income households through for-profit schools in low-income countries is a recent development. Some are partnerships between the private and public sectors; others are for-profit enterprises that may be in competition with the state sector. While these corporate interventions relate to school choice and privatization (see next section), they also exemplify commercialization of the idea of comprehensive school reform programs.

Pakistan is often held up as the model for international donor initiatives to support private provision and is the most significant exemplar of World Bank support for privatization in the K–12 sector (Menashy,

Mundy, & Afridi, 2014). In addition to the World Bank, Britain's Department for International Development is also funding private education reforms in Punjab. The money is channelled through the Punjab Education Foundation (PEF), an independent body with large private sector involvement that is spearheading Punjab's educational reforms. In fact, PEF educates more school children than the state school system itself, with almost one-fourth of all school-going children enrolled in private schools.

The corporate sector is emerging as a key player in the provision of for-profit, market-based education in many low-income countries. Pearson Education, one of the more influential players in the field of education, with operations in more than 70 countries, established its affordable learning fund (PALF) in 2012. According to Pearson, this initiative uses capital investment "to help millions of children in the world access a quality education in a cost effective, profitable and scalable manner" (Pearson Affordable Learning Fund, n.d.). Two of the larger chains that Pearson has invested in are Bridge International Academies and Omega Schools. Bridge oversees around 400 schools in Kenya and Uganda, with plans for expansion into Nigeria and India, whereas Omega Schools Franchise operates 20 schools in Ghana, with plans for expansion into Sierra Leone, Liberia, Nigeria, and the Gambia.

These low-cost school chains operate on market-oriented principles of efficiency of cost. Many of these low-cost schools often report lower per-student cost compared to public schools (Tooley et al., 2011). While many of these schools offer fee-subsidies, one of the more controversial ways in which they reduce costs is by employing a large pool of non-formally trained contract teachers who are paid lower salaries than their counterparts in public schools. Those hired are trained in short teacher-training programs to deliver the school's own scripted curriculum. These hiring practices bring to the fore several problematic issues around teacher training and professionalism, including the recruitment and hiring of predominantly young local women. In Pakistan, Andrabi, Das, and Khwaja (2008) suggest that these young women are well-suited for these teaching positions because they provide a steady source of inexpensive labour. The growth of low-cost, for-profit private school chains in urban centres in Africa and South Asia continues to be an area where there is still a lack of much evidence-based research, and one that raises several important equity considerations.

SCHOOL CHOICE AND PRIVATIZATION

School choice is a cover term that encompasses an array of strategies and policies based on the premise that competition for clients (students, families) among schools would compel school personnel to find ways to get better at what they do (see Godwin & Kemerer, 2002, for a review of school choice in the United States). The literature on school choice identifies two policy strategies (Levin, 1991). *Public choice* refers to the provision of greater choice among different schools within the public sector through such mechanisms as open enrolment among schools within or between school districts; access to alternative schools or programs serving students with special needs or interests (e.g., arts, technology, French immersion); and parallel publicly funded school systems based on religious preferences or language of instruction (e.g., secular public and Catholic school districts in Ontario; French and English medium districts in Quebec). *Market choice* refers to the use of funding mechanisms such as educational vouchers, scholarships, and tuition tax credits to create competition between private and public schools for students and government funding. Of these, "voucher programs" are the most widely known, implemented, and debated. The basic idea is that a government provides parents of school-age children with a voucher worth X amount of dollars per child, the parents choose where to send their children from an open market of public and private schools, and government funding follows the child to the chosen school. In theory, a voucher system would lead schools to compete for students and dollars in order to survive and thrive in the education marketplace. School personnel would be motivated to innovate and improve. School choice policies are silent, however, on what strategies and knowledge schools might use to respond to the pressures to improve.

Although voucher programs have been widely debated in the United States, they have not been widely implemented. During the 1990s a few school districts (e.g., Milwaukee, Cleveland, and San Antonio) implemented small-scale voucher programs that targeted poor inner-city children in schools where students scored persistently below minimum state and district standards of acceptable performance on standardized tests in basic skills. An alternative version of choice in the form of "charter schools" began to emerge in the United States in the late 1990s and continues to grow with non-partisan political support in the new millennium. Essentially, a charter school is a kind of publicly subsidized private school that operates within the administrative jurisdiction of the public school system. The developers and managers of a charter school could be a group of educators (e.g., teachers) or external agents (individual entrepreneurs or organizations). They negotiate a formal agreement with a local school district authority to establish a school (typically within an existing facility). Waivers are granted so that the school can operate free of some of the policy conditions that regular public schools must adhere to—most notably, contractual policies regulating requirements for teacher employment and teacher compensation. They remain subject, however, to government (state and federal) accountability policies and processes (e.g., curriculum standards, state-mandated standardized testing requirements). In principle, because they are publicly subsidized, they cannot charge tuition and are supposed to be inclusive in the admission of students with varying personal and academic backgrounds. The number of charter schools in the United States continues to grow (about six thousand as of 2012), despite the lack of consistent evidence that student learning outcomes are significantly better on state and national standardized assessments of student learning when viewed overall.

COMPARATIVE RESEARCH
School choice policies and options have been implemented on a wider scale in some countries (see Plank & Sykes, 2003, for comparative analysis of choice policies in Chile, New Zealand, Australia, England and Wales, Sweden, South Africa, China, the Czech Republic, and Hungary). These policies merge with the phenomenon of government subsidies for private school provision, similar to the US charter school described above. In Chile, for example, the government funds a national voucher program whereby a set amount of money is allocated per pupil, and students can elect to attend either public schools or private schools (except those that charge tuition). In New Zealand, the government eliminated school districts, making all schools self-governing entities responsible directly to the central government, and established open enrolment boundaries to create full choice (and competition) among public schools for students and funds. In these two examples, the move toward greater choice was linked to political beliefs that a market-like approach to education provision would lead to higher-quality teaching and better learning outcomes. State subsidies for private school provision in high-income countries can also be found in countries like

Australia, Germany, Norway, Sweden, and England. In other contexts, particularly in low-income countries, a lack of financial resources has led governments to encourage the expansion of private schools. In Tanzania, for example, about 60 percent of secondary schools are private schools run by non-governmental organizations or by for-profit entrepreneurs (Anderson, 2002). In Pakistan and Bangladesh literally thousands of schools are independently financed and operated by community and other non-governmental organizations with minimal governmental regulation.

Findings from research on the implementation and outcomes of strategies for school choice (e.g., vouchers, open boundaries, subsidized private schools) in the United States and internationally do not generally support the claim that increased choice leads to greater competition and more effective schools (Godwin & Kemerer, 2002; Plank & Sykes, 2003). In fact, the effects of greater choice have been found to exacerbate the problems of low-performing schools. More academically motivated students (whose parents tend to be more educated and to have higher aspirations for their children) are most likely to exercise choice options, leaving the source schools with an even greater proportion of hard-to-serve students, with fewer funds to do it, and with reputations guaranteed to deter recruitment of quality teachers. Inter-school competition for students (and resources) may lead to reduced cooperation across schools, thereby diminishing the potential for school personnel to learn from each other about effective practices, and lowering the commitment of school personnel and parents to the right to quality education as a common public good. Finally, choice research in multiple countries has demonstrated that given an option, parents do not choose schools solely on the basis of academic quality. They are equally if not more concerned about how their child will fit (racially, socio-economically) with other children, or about the implications of having their children associate with students that represent the majority in a particular school. The capacity to exercise choice beyond the neighbourhood school is also highly dependent on family resources (e.g., access to transportation, child care arrangements).

In sum, available research does not support political arguments that increased school choice leads to school improvement, though there are other valid reasons for advocating for increased choice in educational programs and schools. Across Canada, arguments about increased choice are framed more in terms of parental rights to choose the kind of education they want for their child and to have their tax dollars support that choice, rather than on choice as a quality-improvement mechanism.

Low-Fee Private Schools

The burgeoning growth of what has now come to be termed as *low-fee private schools*, *low-cost private schools*, *budget schools*, or *private schools for the poor* as an alternative to government-run schools in a number of developing countries has been the focus of much recent research and debate (see, for instance, Akaguri [2013] for Ghana; Andrabi, Das, & Khwaja [2008] for Pakistan; Cameron [2010] for Bangladesh; Härmä [2010] and Srivastava [2013] for India; Stern & Heyneman [2013] and Oketch & Ngware [2010] for Kenya; and Rose & Adelabu [2007] for Nigeria).

While the term *low-fee private schools* was originally coined by Srivastava (2006) referring to unregulated, unregistered, and unrecognized private schools in India, the term has gained much currency and is widely used interchangeably with *low-cost private schools* to loosely describe these private schools that charge minimal fees; target poorer, low-income households; and are run by private entrepreneurs, non-governmental organizations, or faith-based providers. Some attribute this mushrooming of private schools for the poor to the low quality of government schools in many low-income countries, including problems with teacher absenteeism and a lack of teacher commitment (Tooley & Dixon, 2005, 2007). Others point to factors such as high hidden costs of government schooling (Oketch & Ngware, 2010), covert exclusion from state schooling as well as lower private tuition costs because of fee subsidies, and choice of language of instruction (Phillipson, 2008) as driving the market demand for these low-fee schools.

The growth of low-fee private schools is controversial. Evidence concerning their impact on access to education and on the quality of teaching and learning is mixed and strongly polarized along ideological grounds. There is very limited research on school leadership and school improvement in low-fee schools (Anderson & Mundy, 2014).

One of the more vociferous advocates for these low-fee private schools, James Tooley, extols the superior cost efficiency of these private schools over state-run schools, and the potential of market mechanisms such as choice, competition, and deregulation to improve the provision of educational services (Tooley & Dixon, 2005). In his original study examining low-fee private schools in Kenya, China, India, Nigeria, and Ghana, he concludes that "private education is good for the poor" as these schools are serving the needs of low-income households better than the state schools that are failing them. However, other researchers point out that households in the lower quintiles are often excluded from private schooling (Lewin, 2007) and are not able to access these schools; low-fee schools still remain unaffordable to them (Akaguri, 2013; Cameron, 2010; Härmä, 2010; Srivastava, 2013). Srivastava's research (2006) on low-fee schools in India also suggests that girls may be more disadvantaged by these schools.

There has been sharp debate around the quality of schooling that low-fee schools provide. Several empirical studies demonstrate that performance is better in private schools than in public schools (Muralidharan & Kremer, 2009; Kingdon, 1996; Tooley & Dixon, 2007). Other studies (Akaguri, 2013; Srivastava, 2013) report that differences in the performance of government school students and low-fee school students are not significant or yield minimal differences in student performance. These studies show that when discussing questions of quality of teaching and learning it is difficult to generalize the results given variability in school, household, and individual characteristics. Government schools may outperform low-fee private schools in some aspects, and vice-versa. Perhaps, as Srivastava (2013) suggests, it is more important to reframe the question as "not whether low-fee private schools are uniformly better, but in what instances, under what circumstances, and owing to which background characteristics do students in different school types achieve higher results" (p. 25).

STANDARDS AND ACCOUNTABILITY-DRIVEN IMPROVEMENT

The imposition by government agencies of standards for curriculum and for student performance, coupled with mandatory testing and public reporting of student results, is key to the standards and accountability approach to school improvement. Government policies mandating this approach emerged concurrently in the United States, England, Canada, and other regions of the developed world in the 1990s (Sahlberg, 2010).

The logic of this approach to school improvement is straightforward. Government education agencies prescribe core curriculum content standards, specified in terms of outcomes that all students should achieve by subject area and grade level. Aligned to the curriculum, the government prescribes student achievement standards (often the standards differentiate minimum levels of acceptability from unacceptable and advanced levels of performance). All students are expected to achieve at least the minimum levels of acceptable performance. The government then mandates standardized testing of student achievement in core subjects (reading, writing, and mathematics are most common) at designated intervals (e.g., Grades 3, 6, and 9; annually in some parts of the United States).

Accountability is not just about student testing, but also about the reporting and use of test results. Ideally, school personnel examine assessment results to identify which students (individuals and groups) are having difficulty achieving acceptable performance levels in the tested curriculum areas, and use this information to plan and implement interventions intended to assist those students in raising their performance in those areas.

Standards and accountability-driven school improvement does not begin with a particular "solution" (i.e., curriculum program, instructional arrangement, or teaching practice) for identified student learning needs relative to the targeted outcomes. The premise is that school personnel have the professional expertise to discern what works for the particular students being taught, and to find or create alternative strategies to replace or supplement practices that are not working. Thus standardized testing tends to lead to a preoccupation with discovering "best practices"—in other words, instructional strategies that are correlated with evidence of student success in achieving expected performance standards under similar conditions (e.g., students with similar educational profiles; schools with similar characteristics, such as size and resources; schools serving similar communities in terms of student and family socio-economic indicators). Government agencies and school district authorities often try to facilitate networking between classrooms, between schools, and across school districts in order to enable sharing and diffusion of experiences about what practices work best with which students for particular curriculum and performance expectations (e.g., Fullan, Bertani, & Quinn, 2004), as explained in "Professional Learning Communities and Networks" below.

Government agencies do not typically rely on the professionalism of school system personnel to do all this without additional pressure and, perhaps, support. The pressure can come in several ways. One way is to require schools and school districts to submit school improvement plans that are justified partly in terms of their test results. A second way is to make the school-level test results publicly available. In some jurisdictions, schools are ranked according to their performance, and even officially labelled (e.g., in Texas, where one of the authors has done research, schools are labelled each year as Exemplary, Recognized, Academically Acceptable, or Academically Unacceptable in terms of state test results). In theory, school personnel, concerned about the status of their school's academic standing and responding to parental concerns, will be motivated to try to improve where needs for improvement are indicated, and to try to sustain already high performance where that is in evidence. The pressure on school personnel to ensure adequate student performance increases when test results are high stakes for students, as well. In some jurisdictions student promotion (from one grade to another) or student graduation (from high school) is dependent upon the results of their performance on these tests. Finally, additional pressure on schools to perform and improve can be applied through the proclamation of government targets for student performance. For example, in 2004, the Liberal government of Ontario set a provincial target for 75 percent of all students to achieve acceptable performance on elementary school test results by 2007. In the United States, federal government policy under the Bush Republican administration set the highest target of all: No Child Left Behind, where the official goal is for all students to be at or above performance standards established by each state. By setting these targets (whether practically attainable or not), government agencies increase the pressure on underperforming schools to improve, and on high-performing schools to sustain if not improve upon their already satisfactory results.

Beyond the reputational and emotional effects of ranking and labelling, government agencies may mandate school "consequences" based on test results. The harshest scenarios require the dismissal or replacement of principals, or even the closing and reconstitution of persistently "failing" schools with a new crew of teachers and principals. Normally, drastic measures are only taken after a period of intensive assistance by local district or government school-improvement teams to try to turn the failing school results around. A central feature of the standards and accountability movement is that schools as organizational units are held accountable for the quality of student learning, that consequences are tied to this accountability, and that schools are expected to improve where student results are below par. It is in that sense that the standards and accountability movement represents an approach to school improvement.

CHAPTER FIVE: Comparative Perspectives on School Improvement 139

The standards and accountability approach to school improvement is controversial, and space will not permit us to do more than highlight some key points of contention. Does it force teachers to "teach to the test" (the answer is "yes"), and is this an undesirable effect? The answer to the latter part of that question is debatable. If you agree with the curriculum, and the tests are well aligned with the curriculum, then teaching to the test is really just teaching the curriculum and not necessarily a bad effect. If you do not like the curriculum, and think that preoccupation with the tested curriculum diverts teaching and learning time and energy away from other important focuses of student development (e.g., the arts, social skills, civic and values education, maybe more complex or higher-order cognitive skill development), or that prescribed standards for curriculum, learning, and assessment are an affront to teachers' professional autonomy, then you are less likely to regard teaching to the test in a positive light. Is it fair to expect all students to be able to attain the same levels of performance in a limited range of subject areas? Some will argue that this denies the pragmatic reality of students' differing abilities, interests, and strengths as learners. Others will argue that setting minimum standards for all students in core curriculum areas (e.g., reading, writing, mathematics), and holding school personnel responsible and accountable for student performance, provides not only a guarantee of quality, but also a guarantee of equity. Ultimately, the standards movement could be interpreted as an expression of confidence, not a lack of confidence, in the professionalism of school system personnel to find solutions to student learning problems. On the downside, advocates of high standards and accountability seem to have forgotten that even the best statistical analyses of school effects on student achievement from comparative studies in developed countries attribute only 9–14 percent of student academic results to school effects. To hold schools solely accountable for those results and the improvement of results seems unfair.

COMPARATIVE RESEARCH
Finnish education system improvement scholar Pasi Sahlberg (2010) characterizes the proliferation of the standards and accountability approach to school improvement as the Global Education Reform Movement (GERM). The short answer to the question of whether standards and accountability systems have led to improvements in student achievement (as reflected in standardized test results) is "yes, but yes with limitations."

Michael Fullan, a prominent analyst of educational change movements, cites analyses of student test scores over time in both England and Ontario that show overall gains in student performance in basic skills areas (reading, writing, mathematics), and reductions in the gaps between lower- and higher-performing students (which suggests a reduction of the traditional inequities in student outcomes for socio-economically disadvantaged students, who tend to be overrepresented in the ranks of low achievers). On the other hand, Fullan (2005) observes that after a few years the improvements in student achievement results tend to plateau; they do not get worse, but stop getting better. Skeptics might argue that commonly reported improvements in the first few years are little more than a reflection of school personnel aligning and adjusting what they do in the classroom to new curriculum and testing regimes (not really getting better at what they do). Fullan contends that continuing improvement beyond this plateau requires new kinds of interventions, in particular interventions that enable school personnel to collaboratively investigate gaps in student learning in their particular contexts, and to find ways and learn to solve those problems through interaction with educators in other classrooms and schools facing similar problems of practice (see "Professional Learning Communities and Networks" below).

National curricula and standardized testing programs in the developing world are common and are frequently maligned as impediments to, not stimuli for, change and improvement. The curricula are criticized for overemphasizing the content to be covered, as opposed to the knowledge and skills outcomes to be achieved. The tests are criticized for rewarding lower-level learning (rote memorization and factual recall, use of standard procedures such as mathematical formulas), as opposed to more complex and demanding learning objectives that require open-ended problem solving, application, and synthesis of knowledge in authentic "real world" (not just textbook) contexts. National testing programs in the developing world are often more high stakes for students than for schools. That is, the tests and test results are used mainly as gate-keeping devices to control access to further education (primary to secondary school, lower to higher secondary school, university entrance) and to stream students into education tracks (e.g., sciences, general education, vocational education). Schools may use student test results as marketing tools (e.g., advertising the number of pupils scoring high on the tests), particularly in school systems

CHAPTER FIVE: Comparative Perspectives on School Improvement 141

where school boundaries are open and where private school options are common. The public school systems, however, are not typically organized around the use of test results at the school level as a basis for and indicator of school quality and improvement. Results-based school improvement plans are not required. School system authorities at the national or local levels do not invest in developing the capacity of school personnel to use assessment data as a basis for school improvement planning, and do not provide funding, technical assistance, or other forms of intervention (e.g., dissemination networks) strategically linked to data-based accountability and improvement. Comparative research on the implications and effects of government-mandated external standards and accountability policies and systems on school-level improvement is lacking. International comparative assessments of educational quality, however, constitute another stream of the educational standards and accountability movement, and are the focus of Chapter Thirteen in this textbook.

PROFESSIONAL LEARNING COMMUNITIES AND NETWORKS

In the mid-1990s a new research-based image of the organizational and professional characteristics of effective schools took shape around the concept and practice of schools in which teachers work and learn collaboratively on solving problems of teaching and learning (Little, 1982; Rosenholtz, 1989; Hord, 1997; DuFour, Eaker, & DuFour, 2005). As the concept of professional learning communities, or PLCs as they are now typically known, took hold, school improvement promoters and policymakers introduced interventions intended to promote and support the practice of PLCs in schools.

Professional learning networks (PLNs) are being introduced internationally as an innovative strategy for both in-service teacher development and school leader development, with an emphasis on supporting the implementation of more effective methods of teaching and learning and of school management (e.g., Katz, Earl, & Ben Jaafar, 2009). The idea of PLNs is similar to that of PLCs except that the scope of professional collaboration extends across multiple school sites. PLNs typically involve participating teachers and head teachers in inter-school communication and collaborative activities that are aimed at supporting and improving continuous professional learning and school improvement. PLNs address four fundamental challenges to continuous professional learning:

1. How to motivate and sustain ongoing professional learning in the work of practising teachers and school leaders;
2. How to support the implementation of knowledge that educators are exposed to in professional development experiences outside the classroom and school into skillful ongoing practice;
3. How to adapt external knowledge to local contexts and needs; and
4. How to mobilize practice-based experiences and knowledge of teachers and head teachers into shared continuous improvement efforts.

Prominent experts in the field of school improvement such as Fullan (2005) and Stoll (2010) emphasize the value of lateral capacity-building through networks that reduce school-based educators' isolation and reliance on external expertise for solutions to the problems and challenges they experience in their professional work in classrooms and schools, and that help focus ongoing learning and improvement efforts on locally relevant problems of practice. Hargreaves and Fullan (2012) extend the idea of teachers working collectively in professional learning communities toward school improvement through the concept of professional capital. They emphasize the importance of developing and integrating three dimensions of professional capital in teachers' work in schools:

1. Human capital (professional knowledge and skill)
2. Social capital (interactions and relationships that increase access to knowledge and skill)
3. Decisional capital (the authority and collective discretion to make judgments about problems of professional practices)

COMPARATIVE RESEARCH

Cross-cultural and comparative research on the practice of professional community in schools is scarce, except for Japanese Lesson Study (Stigler & Hiebert, 1999). In the Lesson Study approach, Japanese teachers working in grade, division, or special topic teams determine focuses for lesson development based on evidence of problems in student learning. The teacher teams investigate the selected problem and possible solutions, and design a lesson. Team members pilot the lesson while others observe. They debrief and refine the lesson. The process is repeated until the lesson achieves the intended results. Successful "research lessons" are shared across the school and with educators from other schools. While Lesson Study is not the only model of how teachers can work together to address collectively identified problems of student learning, it is the most widely known. Within the education sector of the Aga Khan Development Network, efforts have been made to promote educational communities of practice as a school-based strategy for school improvement (Shamim & Farah, 2005). This approach to teacher collaboration resembles what is elsewhere referred to as PLCs.

The investigation of professional networks as a strategy for continuous professional learning and school improvement has been largely limited to the developed-world context, such as the United States (Elmore, 2007; Leiberman & Grolnick, 1996), England (Bell et al., 2006), and New Zealand (Annan, 2015). Jita & Mokhele (2014) argue that "while the utility of such collaborative structures for teacher learning is fairly well established in many developed countries, we still know very little about how the intended beneficiaries (the teachers) experience these non-traditional structures of professional development" (p. 1). The use of PLNs in low- and middle-income country contexts is a promising focus for professional development practice and for research to explore the experiences, challenges, and benefits of this innovation for participants, their schools, and student learning (e.g., Jita & Mokhele, 2014; Ali Baber et al., 2005).

In many countries, government education policies, and the policies of professional organizations that govern teacher licensure and professional learning, only recognize and reward educator participation in traditional professional development activities (i.e., courses, workshops, and conferences). The impact of a sole focus on these traditional professional development activities has been widely critiqued (e.g., Timperley et al., 2007). Professional learning communities within schools and networked learning communities across schools are actively being promoted and supported to enable peer support for implementation of professional knowledge from outside the school, as well as to stimulate knowledge sharing and production grounded in the practical problems and knowledge arising from interaction among professionals within and between schools.

SCHOOL IMPROVEMENT: THE WAY FORWARD

This chapter provides an introduction to seven major approaches to school improvement: (1) innovation adoption and implementation; (2) replication of the effective schools characteristics; (3) decentralization and school-based management; (4) comprehensive school reform; (5) school choice and privatization; (6) standards and accountability-driven improvement; and (7) professional learning communities and networks. While different approaches have dominated education policy, practice, and research at different times over the past half century, they are not mutually exclusive. The adoption and implementation of "best practices," for example, is integral to the standards and accountability-driven approach to improvement. Decentralization and school choice policies often converge together in system-wide approaches to school improvement. The adoption of a comprehensive school reform model is an example of school choice, and school-based management and instructional innovations are integral to many CSR models.

Ultimately, it is not so hard to find schools where a majority of students are succeeding academically, and it is possible to find schools where student results have progressively improved over time. The challenge is to take local knowledge of what makes schools effective and how to make schools more effective, and then replicate those characteristics and processes across many schools—to move beyond "islands of excellence" to develop excellence in all schools in a school system (Togneri & Anderson, 2003). Therein lies the fundamental challenge of school improvement. As if that were not enough, there is the further challenge of how to sustain improvement and positive outcomes in instructional practice and student learning over time despite ongoing turnover in school leadership, teaching staff, education system policies, and school community demographics. Comparative research is helpful in sorting out that which is common to school effectiveness and school improvement, regardless of differences in context, from that which is relatively unique to specific organizational, political, and cultural contexts. And finally, comparative research is an essential tool in the search for and sharing of education policies and practices that work best for meeting particular educational needs.

QUESTIONS FOR REFLECTION & DISCUSSION
1. What do teachers and administrators in schools that you know say about current needs for improvement?
2. What organizational processes are school personnel using to try to improve the schools that you know? How are these processes expected to result in change?
3. What are the major influences, both internal and external to your school, that contribute to the identification of and plans for improvement in the school?
4. How do school improvement needs and processes reported by teachers in today's schools relate to the major approaches to school improvement described in this chapter?

SUGGESTED AUDIO-VISUAL RESOURCES
To complement this chapter we are recommending some video resources that feature two leading scholars in the field of educational change and school improvement talking about what is known from research and their own professional experience on effective and less effective approaches to school improvement at the school and system levels. Both Michael Fullan and Andy Hargreaves are recognized internationally for their research, consulting, and publications.

Choosing the Wrong and Right Educational Drivers, by Michael Fullan (2012). Available at: www.michaelfullan.ca/choose-the-wrong-and-right-educational-drivers/

Park Manor Public School, by Michael Fullan (2014). Available at: www.michaelfullan.ca/ontario-park-manor/

Michael Fullan is Professor Emeritus from the Ontario Institute for Studies in Education, University of Toronto. Professor Fullan's website, www.michaelfullan.ca, contains an archive of short (e.g., three-minute) videos that are accessible for use at no cost on many topics related to educational change. Two videos that we recommend for starters are the three-minute *Choosing the Wrong and Right Educational Drivers* for productive change, and the 13-minute *Park Manor Public School*, which features the story of a school in Waterloo, Ontario, that successfully transformed itself from a low-performing to a high-performing school.

RSA Replay: Building a Teacher-Powered Education System, by Andy Hargreaves (2016). Available at: www.youtube.com/watch?v=qT_MYgDAsa8
Andy Hargreaves is the Thomas Moore Brennan Chair in Education currently with the Lynch School of Education, Boston College. From Professor Hargreaves we suggest listening to and discussing a thought-provoking 30-minute video of a presentation for the Royal Society for Arts that focuses on improving schools through investing in teachers' professional capital and collective autonomy as key drivers in promoting educational reform.

SUGGESTIONS FOR FURTHER READING

American Educational Research Association (AERA) Educational Change Special Interest Group. *Lead the Change Series*. Available at: www.aera.net/SIG155/NewsAnnouncements/tabid/12194/Default.aspx
The Lead the Change Series features renowned educational change experts from around the globe, highlights promising research and practice, and offers expert insight on small- and large-scale educational change.

Chapman, Christopher, Muijis, Daniel, Reynolds, David, Sammons, Pam, & Teddlie, Charles (Eds.). (2015). *The Routledge International Handbook of Educational Effectiveness and Improvement: Research, Policy, and Practice*. London & New York: Routledge.

Datnow, Amanda, Hubbard, Lea, & Mehan, Hugh. (2002). *Extending Educational Reform: From One School to Many* (Educational change and development series). London: RoutledgeFalmer.

Fuhrman, Susan (Ed.). (2001). *From the Capitol to the Classroom: Standards-Based Reform in the States—One Hundredth Yearbook of the National Society for the Study of Education*. Chicago: University of Chicago Press.

Fullan, Michael. (2007). *The New Meaning of Educational Change* (4th ed.). New York: Teachers College Press.

Macpherson, Ian, Robertson, Susan, & Walford, Geoffrey (Eds.). (2014). *Education, Privatization and Social Justice: Case Studies from Africa, South Asia and South East Asia*. Oxford: Symposium Books.

Stoll, Louise, & Fink, Dean. (1996). *Changing Our Schools*. Buckingham, UK: Open University Press.

Teddlie, Charles, & Reynolds, David (Eds.). (2000). *The International Handbook of School Effectiveness Research*. New York: Falmer Press.

REFERENCES

Akaguri, Luke. (2013). Fee-free public or low-fee private basic education in rural Ghana: How does the cost influence the choice of the poor? *Compare, 44*(2), 140–161.

Ali Baber, Sikunder, Sarwar, Zakia, & Safdar, Qamar. (2005). Networks for Learning: Professional Associations and the Continuing Education of Teachers. In J. Rettalick & I. Farah (Eds.), *Transforming Schools in Pakistan* (pp. 215–245). Oxford: Oxford University Press.

Anderson, Stephen (Ed.). (2002). *Improving Schools through Teacher Development: Case Studies of the Aga Khan Foundation Projects in East Africa*. Lisse, the Netherlands: Swets & Zeitlinger.

Anderson, Stephen, & Mundy, Karen. (2014). *School Improvement in Developing Countries: Experiences and Lessons Learned*. Report prepared for the Aga Khan Foundation, Canada. Available at www.oise.utoronto.ca/cidec/Research/index.html

Andrabi, Tahir, Das, Jishnu, & Khwaja, Asim Ijaz. (2008). A Dime a Day: The Possibilities and Limits of Private Schooling in Pakistan. *Comparative Education Review, 52*(3), 329–355.

Annan, Brian. (2015). *Learning and Change Networks: Milestone 5*. Auckland: University of Auckland.

Avalos, Beatrice. (1980). Teacher effectiveness: Research in the Third World, Highlights of a Review. *Comparative Education, 16*(1), pp. 45–54.

Bell, Miranda, Jopling, Michael, Cordingley, Philippa, Firth, Antonia, King, Emma, & Mitchell, Holly. (2006). *What Is the Impact on Pupils of Networks That Include at Least Three Schools? What Additional Benefits Are There for Practitioners, Organisations, and the Communities They Serve?* National College for School Leadership.

Berman, Paul. (1981). Educational Change: An Implementation Paradigm. In R. Lehming & M. Kane (Eds.), *Improving Schools: Using What We Know* (pp. 253–286). Beverly Hills: Sage Publications.

Cameron, Stuart. (2010). *Access and Exclusion from Primary Education in Slums of Dhaka, Bangladesh*. CREATE Pathways to Access Research Monograph No. 43. Available at: r4d.dfid.gov.uk/pdf/outputs/impaccess_rpc/pta45.pdf

Chimbombo, Joseph Patrick Godson. (2005). Quantity versus Quality in Education: Case Studies in Malawi. *International Review of Education 51*, 155–172.

Colbert, Vicky. (2002). Improving the Quality of Education for the Rural Poor: Escuela Nueva in Colombia. In C. de Moura Castro & A. Verdisco (Eds.), *Making Education Work: Latin American Ideas and Asian Results*. New York: Inter-American Development Bank.

DuFour, Richard, Eaker, Robert, & DuFour, Rebecca (Eds.). (2005). *On Common Ground: The Power of Professional Learning Communities*. Bloomington, IN: National Education Service.

Eason-Watkins, Barbara. (2005). Implementing PLCs in the Chicago Public Schools. In R. DuFour, R. Eaker, & R. DuFour (Eds.), *On Common Ground: The Power of Professional Learning Communities* (pp. 193–207). Bloomington, IN: National Education Service.

Elmore, Richard F. (1996). Getting to Scale with Good Educational Practice. *Harvard Educational Review, 66*(1), 1–26.

Elmore, Richard F. (2007). Professional Networks and School Improvement. *School Administrator, 64*(4), 20–24.

Fullan, Michael. (2001). *The New Meaning of Educational Change* (3rd ed.). New York: Teachers College Press.

Fullan, Michael. (2005). *Leadership & Sustainability: System Thinkers in Action.* Thousand Oaks, CA: Corwin Press.

Fullan, Michael, Bertani, Al, & Quinn, Joanne. (2004). New Lessons for Districtwide Reform. *Educational Leadership, 61*(6), 42–46.

Fuller, Bruce. (1987). School Effects in the Third World. *Review of Educational Research 57*(3), 255–292.

Godwin, R. Kenneth, & Kemerer, Frank. (2002). *School Choice Tradeoffs: Liberty, Equity, and Diversity.* Austin: University of Texas Press.

Hall, Gene, & Hord, Shirley. (2014). *Implementing Change: Patterns, Principles, and Potholes* (4th ed.). Boston: Pearson Education.

Hargreaves, Andy, & Fullan, Michael. (2012). *Professional Capital: Transforming Teaching in Every School.* New York: Teachers College Press.

Härmä, Joanna. (2010). *School Choice for the Poor? The Limits of Marketisation of Primary Education in Rural India.* CREATE Pathways to Access Monograph No. 23. Brighton, University of Sussex. Available at: www.create-rpc.org/pdf_documents/PTA23.pdf

Havelock, R. G., & Huberman, A. M. (1978). *Solving Educational Problems: The Theory and Reality of Innovation in Developing Countries.* Paris: UNESCO.

Higgins, Liz, & Rwanyange, Rosemary. (2005). Ownership in the Education Reform Process in Uganda. *Compare 15*(1), 7–26.

Hord, Shirley. (1997). *Professional Learning Communities: Communities of Continuous Inquiry and Improvement.* Austin: Southwest Educational Development Laboratory.

Jita, Loyiso C., & Mokhele, Matseliso L. (2014). When Teacher Clusters Work: Selected Experiences of South African Teachers with the Cluster Approach to Professional Development. *South African Journal of Education, 34*(2), 1–15.

Kanji, Gulzar, & Ali, Takbir. (2006). School Improvement: A Case from the Northern Areas in Pakistan. In I. Farah & B. Jaworksi (Eds.), *Partnerships in Educational Development* (pp. 193–206). Oxford: Symposium Books.

Katz, Steven, Earl, Lorna, & Ben Jaafar, Sonia. (2009). *Building and Connecting Learning Communities: The Power of Networks for School Improvement.* Thousand Oaks, CA: Sage.

Kingdon, Geeta. (1996). The Quality and Efficiency of Private and Public Education: A Case Study of Urban India. *Oxford Bulletin of Economics and Statistics, 58*(1), 57–82.

Leiberman, Ann, & Grolnick, Maureen. (1996). Networks and Reform in American Education. *Teachers College Record, 98*(1), 7–45.

Leithwood, Ken, & Menzies, Teresa. (1998). A Review of Research Concerning the Implementation of School-Based Management. *School Effectiveness and School Improvement 9*(3), 233–285.

Levin, Henry. (1991). The Economics of Educational Choice. *Economics of Education Review, 10*(2), 137–158.

Levin, Henry M., & Lockheed, Marlaine E. (Eds.). (1993). *Effective Schools in Developing Countries*. London: Falmer Press.

Levine, Daniel, & Lezotte, Lawrence. (1990). *Unusually Effective Schools: A Review and Analysis of Research and Practice*. Madison, WI: The National Center for Effective Schools Research and Development.

Lewin, Keith, with Stuart, Janet. (1991). *Educational Innovation in Developing Countries: Case Studies of Changemakers*. London: MacMillan Press.

Lewin, Keith. (2007). The Limits in Growth of Non-government Private Schooling in Sub-Saharan Africa. CREATE Pathways to Access Research Monograph No. 5. London: Department for International Development (DFID). Available at: r4d.dfid.gov.uk/PDF/Outputs/ImpAccess_RPC/PTA5.pdf

Little, Judith Warren. (1982). Norms of Collegiality and Experimentation: Workplace Conditions of School Success. *American Educational Research Journal, 19*, 325–340.

Menashy, Francine, Mundy, Karen, & Afridi, Momina. (2014). The Role of the World Bank in the Private Provision of Schooling in Pakistan. In I. Macpherson, S. Roberston, & G. Walford (Eds.), *Education, Privatisation and Social Justice: Case Studies from Africa, South Asia and South East Asia* (pp. 239–257). Oxford: Symposium Books.

Muralidharan, Karthik, & Kremer, Michael. (2009). Public-Private Schools in Rural India. In R. Chakrabarti & P. Peterson (Eds.), *School Choice International: Exploring Public-Private Partnerships* (pp. 91–109). Cambridge, MA: MIT Press.

Murphy, Joseph, & Datnow, Amanda. (2003). *Leadership Lessons for Comprehensive School Reform*. Thousand Oaks, CA: Corwin Press.

Murphy, Joseph, & Hallinger, Philip. (1993). *Restructuring Schooling: Learning from Ongoing Efforts*. Newbury Park, CA: Corwin Press.

Oketch, Moses, & Ngware, Moses. (2010). Free Primary Education Still Excludes the Poorest of the Poor in Urban Kenya. *Development in Practice, 20*(4–5), 603–610.

Pearson Affordable Learning Fund. (n.d.). *About Pearson Affordable Learning Fund*. Available at: https://www.affordable-learning.com/about/vision.html

Phillipson, Bob. (Ed.). (2008). *Low-Cost Private Education: Impacts on Achieving Universal Primary Education*. London: Commonwealth Secretariat.

Plank, David, & Sykes, Gary. (2003). *Choosing Choice: School Choice in International Perspective*. New York: Teachers College Press.

Purkey, Stewart. C., & Smith, Marshall. (1983). Effective Schools: A Review. *The Elementary School Journal, 83*(4), 427–452.

Reynolds, David, Creemers, Bert, Stringfield, Sam, Teddlie, Charles, & Schaffer, Gene. (2002). *World Class Schools: International Perspectives on School Effectiveness*. London and New York: RoutledgeFalmer.

Reynolds, David, & Teddlie, Charles, with Hopkins, David, & Stringfield, Sam. (2000). Linking School Effectiveness and School Improvement. In C. Teddlie & D. Reynolds (Eds.), *The International Handbook of School Effectiveness Research* (pp. 206–231). New York: Falmer Press.

Rose, Pauline, & Adelabu, Modupe. (2007). Private Sector Contributions to Education for All in Nigeria. In P. Srivastava & G. Walford (Eds.), *Private Schooling in Less Economically Developed Countries: Asian and African Perspectives* (pp. 67–87). Oxford: Symposium Books.

Rosenholtz, Susan. (1989). *Teachers' Workplace: The Social Organization of Schools*. New York: Longman.

Rust, Val, & Dalin, Per. (1990). *Teachers and Teaching in the Developing World*. New York: Garland.

Sahlberg, Pasi. (2010). *Finnish Lessons: What Can the World Learn from Change in Finland*. New York: Teachers College Press.

Shafa, Mola Dad, Karim, Darvesh, & Alam, Sultan. (2011). What Works in Education in Pakistan and Why? The Case of PDCN's Whole School Improvement Program in Gilgit-Baltistan of Pakistan. *International Journal of Business and Social Science, 2*(16), 132–145.

Shamim, Fauzia, & Farah, Iffat. (2005). Building Communities of Practice in Pakistani Schools. In J. Retallick & I. Farah (Eds.), *Transforming Schools in Pakistan* (pp. 199–214). Oxford: Oxford University Press.

Srivastava, Prachi. (2006). Private Schooling and Mental Models about Girls' Schooling in India. *Compare, 36*(4), 497–514.

Srivastava, Prachi. (2013). Low-Fee Private Schooling: Issues and Evidence. In P. Srivastava (Ed.), *Low-Fee Private Schooling: Aggravating Equity or Mitigating Disadvantage* (pp. 7–35). Oxford: Symposium Books.

Stern, James, & Heyneman, Stephen. (2013). Low-Fee Private Schooling: The Case of Kenya. In P. Srivastava (Ed.), *Low-Fee Private Schooling: Aggravating Equity or Mitigating Disadvantage* (pp. 1051–28). Oxford: Symposium Books.

Stigler, James, & Hiebert, James. (1999). *The Teaching Gap*. New York: The Free Press.

Stoll, Louise. (2010). Connecting Learning Communities: Capacity Building for Systemic Change. In A. Hargreaves, A. Lieberman, M. Fullan, & D. Hopkins

(Eds.), *Second International Handbook of Educational Change* (pp. 469–484). Dordrecht: Springer.

Stoll, Louise & Fink, Dean. (1996). *Changing Our Schools*. Buckingham, UK: Open University Press.

Task Force on Education and Gender Equity. (2006). *Towards Universal Primary Education: Investments, Incentives and Institutions. A United Nations Millenium Project Report*. New York: United Nations Millennium Project.

Teddlie, Charles, & Reynolds, David (Eds.). (2000). *The International Handbook of School Effectiveness Research*. New York: Falmer Press.

Timperley, Helen, Wilson, Aaron, Barrar, Heather, & Fung, Irene. (2007). *Teacher Professional Learning and Development: Best Evidence Synthesis Iteration*. Wellington, New Zealand: Ministry of Education. Available at: educationcounts.edcentre.govt.nz/goto/BES

Togneri, Wendy, & Anderson, Stephen. (2003). Beyond Islands of Excellence: What Districts Can Do to Improve Instruction and Achievement in All Schools. Washington, DC: The Learning First Alliance.

Tooley, James, & Dixon, Pauline. (2005). *Private Education Is Good for the Poor: A Study of Private Schools Serving the Poor in Low-Income Countries*. Washington: Cato Institute.

Tooley, James, Bao, Yong, Dixon, Pauline, & Merrifield, John. (2011). School Choice and Academic Performance: Some Evidence from Developing Countries. *Journal of School Choice, 5*(1), 1–39.

Tooley, James, & Dixon, Pauline. (2007) Private Education for Low-Income Families: Results From a Global Research Project. In: P. Srivastava & G. Walford (Eds.), *Private Schooling in Less Economically Developed Countries*. Oxford: Symposium Books.

Verspoor, Adrian. (1989). *Pathways to Change: Improving the Quality of Education in Developing Countries*. World Bank Discussion Papers #53. Washington, DC: the World Bank.

SECTION II

JUSTICE, KNOWLEDGES FOR CHANGE, AND SOCIAL INCLUSION

CHAPTER SIX

COMPARATIVE INDIGENOUS WAYS OF KNOWING AND LEARNING

Katia Sol Madjidi and Jean-Paul Restoule

INTRODUCTION

Comparative education has tended to focus primarily on dominant national systems of education. These systems are often colonial models superimposed on the earlier inhabitants of the country, although that point is not always made explicit by the comparativist (Masemann, 1994, pp. 1848–1852). Indigenous epistemologies and pedagogies have garnered little attention in comparative education theory and practice. However, Indigenous peoples have maintained and honoured their distinct ways of knowing for generations, even while experiencing intense colonial pressure. In a time when many are recognizing the limitations of Eurocentric, mono-cultural education systems, Indigenous ways of knowing and learning provide a rich basis for comparative education study. As this chapter illustrates, these worldviews have much to offer today's Indigenous and non-Indigenous students and educators as we seek sustainable, peaceful ways to live.

This chapter highlights key areas for the comparative study of Indigenous ways of knowing and learning. We begin by demonstrating that an opportunity for comparative education presents itself transcending nation-state borders, through the study of Eurocentric (dominant) and Indigenous (locally contextual) worldviews. We then discuss the representation of Indigenous knowledge in comparative education, and introduce four areas for further comparative study: the reclaiming of Indigenous ways of knowing, comparative Indigenous-to-Indigenous exchange, Indigenous knowledge and international educational policy, and the relevance of Indigenous ways of knowing for reform of dominant educational systems and curricula. We conclude by discussing some implications of Indigenous ways of knowing and learning for teachers, and offer suggestions for practical ways to incorporate these into today's classrooms.

In this chapter, the terms *Indigenous* and *Indigenous peoples* refer to the original or prior inhabitants of a particular geographic territory, as well as collectively to Indigenous peoples internationally.[1] The capitalized term *Aboriginal* refers specifically to the Métis, Inuit, and First Nations peoples in Canada or to original peoples of Australia,[2] whereas *American Indian* or *Native American* usually refers to Indigenous peoples in the United States. *Eurocentric* refers to a perspective that centres or privileges thought, customs, and ideas originating from European worldviews to the exclusion or marginalization of others. The curriculum and values of schools in countries with majority populations of European descendants (such as Canada, the United States, and Australia) tend to represent a Eurocentric perspective. When referring to views and values originating from and privileging Indigenous thought and traditions, we use the word *Indigenist*. Wherever possible, the specific name for a particular cultural group will be used (e.g., Anishinaabe, Innu, Swedish), to honour the specific tribal or nation-state affiliation (SABAR, 2015; Simpson, 2000, pp. 165–185). Eurocentric and Indigenist are broad monolithic generalizations, as both categories are comprised of diverse national and cultural groups, each with their own unique traditions, perspectives, and approaches to knowing and learning. However, as Hayhoe and Li do in Chapter Two, we use general categories as a basis for drawing out points of comparison between two distinct sets of worldviews and approaches to knowing and learning. We also name the specific affiliation of the author or tribe, wherever possible, to help distinguish and honour the specific cultural roots of each contribution.

CONFLICTED ROOTS

The clash of Eurocentric and Indigenist epistemologies can be traced back to "first contact," meaning the moments in which colonial and Aboriginal cultures collided. Although it was usually assumed by colonizers that the Indigenous populations were "primitive" cultures without sophisticated social systems, each Indigenous group had its own developed worldview and corresponding approaches for the socialization and

CHAPTER SIX: Comparative Indigenous Ways of Knowing and Learning   157

education of its people (Stiffarm, 1998; Ermine, 1995; Cajete, 1994). For example, Wendy Brady (Aborigine) states that her Australian Aboriginal ancestors had systems of education in place for 40,000 years before these were destroyed by 208 years of colonialism (Brady, 1997, p. 421).

Further conflict occurred as the colonizers attempted to assimilate, subjugate, or "save" Indigenous people by indoctrinating them in Eurocentric educational systems. Having realized that direct annihilation was no longer acceptable, the Canadian and US governments shifted their approach to assimilation, in an overt attempt to "educate the Indian out of them." Carried out in Canada and the United States through the residential/boarding schools, this systematic effort to instill Eurocentric knowledge and values, and to simultaneously erase Indigenous cultural ways of knowing and learning, is at the root of many of the challenges troubling Indigenous populations in North America today.³ The Carlisle Indian Industrial School, founded by US Army officer Richard Henry Pratt in 1879 at a former military installation, became a model for others established by the Bureau of Indian Affairs (BIA) in the United States. Pratt said in a speech in 1892, "A great general has said that the only good Indian is a dead one. In a sense, I agree with the sentiment, but only in this: that all the Indian there is in the race should be dead. Kill the Indian in him and save the man" (Bear, 2008). Over 30 percent of Indigenous children were removed forcibly from their families, made to cut their hair and wear uniforms, forbidden to speak their language or practise their cultural traditions, and in many cases subjected to physical, mental, emotional, and sexual abuse and even sterilization. The last residential school in Canada did not close until 1996. The impact of this systemic violence is well documented in numerous studies, perhaps most comprehensively by Canada's recent Truth and Reconciliation Commission (2015). In the United States, President Obama signed a Native American Apology Resolution in 2009, but no resulting amends have been made.

In the face of this attack on their cultural fabric of knowledge, Indigenous communities persisted in maintaining their ways of knowing and learning. In many places going underground, they continued to sustain their languages, ceremonies, knowledge bodies, and practices. There has since been a resurgence of Indigenous communities reclaiming and rediscovering their traditions and ways of knowing. The "Rediscovery" movement, started in Haida Gwaii in the late 1970s, is an example of one such reclamation, which has spread to many places and communities in the United States and Canada since that time (Henley, 1996). Also related to Indigenous education are the cultural resurgence movements of survival schools, tribal colleges, and numerous examples of language revitalization across the Americas (see Reyhner, 2015; also CulturalSurvival.org).

As Canadian and American Indigenous peoples continue to struggle in and be failed by the dominant Eurocentric educational systems (see Statistics Canada, 2013; DeVoe & Darling-Churchill, 2008), the resurgence of Indigenous-controlled and culturally sourced models of education is gaining attention and importance. Indigenist academic scholarship is also rising, as individuals learn to successfully navigate both worlds of their Indigenous ways of knowing and the Eurocentric educational system. In addition, more and more people from European backgrounds are turning to Indigenous peoples for ceremony and guidance, indicating that Indigenous knowledge is relevant not only for Indigenous peoples but for all peoples.

With this background in place, we turn to our exploration of the comparison of Eurocentric and Indigenist ways of knowing and learning, in an attempt to elaborate and name the main distinctions between the two. Given that this chapter falls primarily into the context of a Eurocentric knowledge paradigm, we focus primarily on Indigenous ways of knowing and learning as our way of centralizing that knowledge in this comparative analysis.

COMPARATIVE EUROCENTRIC AND INDIGENOUS WAYS OF KNOWING AND LEARNING

Eurocentric and Indigenist models of education are each framed by worldviews that inform their epistemologies and pedagogies. Epistemology, from a Eurocentric standpoint, is the theory of knowledge, and pedagogy, the processes by which people come to learn or know (Battiste, 2002). The essential conflict between Indigenous and "imported" educational systems arises, as Vandra Masemann describes, "from a basic epistemological difference in the path to knowledge itself; that is, a basic disagreement about how people come to know what they know and why they believe it to be true" (Masemann, 1994, p. 1849).

As the primary basis for most colonially imposed systems of education, Eurocentric methods are currently accepted as the dominant approach to education in most countries. This model emerged relatively

CHAPTER SIX: Comparative Indigenous Ways of Knowing and Learning   159

recently from its own comparative background across Eurocentric cultures; for example, we learned in Chapter One that the United States borrowed from the Prussians in developing free and compulsory education in the mid-1800s. This system of schooling has not always been widely accepted or implemented, as we learn from Mundy and Read in Chapter Eleven. However, Eurocentric educational models have converged today to comprise what is commonly thought of as "schooling" or "education," and generally include formal school settings, age- and grade-segregated classrooms, separation of learning into disciplines, concepts of a linear and objective pursuit of truth, and a focus on relatively narrow approaches to science, numeracy, and literacy as primary areas for basic education.

Common generalizations comparing Eurocentric and Indigenous epistemologies include binary classifications such as linear versus cyclical, objective versus subjective, secular versus spiritual, industrial versus nature- and context-based, and fragmentary versus integrated and holistic (Little Bear, 2000; Hampton, 1995; Masemann, 1994). To construct a more in-depth comparative picture, the following aspects of ways of knowing and learning can be explored: What are learning and knowledge? Where do people come to learn and know? How do people come to learn and know? From whom do they learn? And, why/for what purpose do they learn? Given the wealth of literature on Eurocentric models of education, and the Eurocentric educational paradigm in which this chapter is being written, this section will focus on Indigenous approaches and perspectives from Indigenous scholars. Through an analysis of this literature, we draw out comparisons between Eurocentric and Indigenous ways of knowing and learning.

WHAT ARE LEARNING AND KNOWLEDGE?
Mi'kmaq scholar Marie Battiste describes Aboriginal epistemology as including theories, philosophies, histories, ceremonies, and stories as ways of knowing. She offers the following commonly used understanding of Indigenous knowledge: "Indigenous knowledge comprises all knowledge pertaining to a particular people and its territory, the nature or use of which has been transmitted from generation to generation" (Battiste, 2002, p. 6). However, she also claims that, rather than being diametrically opposed to Eurocentric education, Indigenous knowledge in fact reveals Eurocentric limitations by presenting a more holistic, developed form of knowledge that "fills the ethical and knowledge gaps

in Eurocentric education, research and scholarship" (ibid., p. 4). She provides a fuller definition of Indigenous knowledge, explaining that it

> embodies a web of relationships within a specific ecological context; contains linguistic categories, rules and relationships unique to each knowledge system; has localized content and meaning; has established customs with respect to acquiring and sharing of knowledge...and implies responsibilities for possessing various kinds of knowledge. (Battiste, 2002, p. 13)

Several Indigenous scholars identify two central themes underlying Indigenous worldviews: all things are animate and all things are interconnected. Joseph Couture (Cree) writes, "There are only two things you have to remember about being Indian. One is that everything is alive, and the second is that we are all related" (Couture, 1991, pp. 201–217). Willie Ermine (Cree) articulates the two key concepts in Aboriginal philosophy as power and place, "power being the living energy that inhibits and/or composes the universe, and place being the relationship of things to each other" (Ermine, 1995, p. 107). In this worldview, human beings are seen as one element in a greater circle of unity with all Creation. Understanding this relationship is foundational to learning one's place in the world.

The notion of spiritual reality is also central to Indigenous epistemology (Hampton, 1995, p. 19). Battiste (Mi'kmaq) explains, "Knowledge is not secular. It is a process derived from creation, and as such, it has a sacred purpose. It is inherent in and connected to all of nature, to its creatures, and to human existence" (Battiste, 2002, p. 13). Leroy Little Bear (Blackfoot) states, "In Aboriginal philosophy...all things are animate, imbued with spirit, and in constant motion. In this realm of energy and spirit, interrelationships between all entities are of paramount importance, and space is a more important referent than time" (Little Bear, 2000, p. 77). From an Indigenous perspective, it is through the spiritual or metaphysical worlds that one can construct meaning in the physical world (Ermine, 1995, p. 107). This contrasts sharply with the modern-day secularity of Eurocentric education. Although many colonial schools have been associated with the church, Eurocentric religious practices in the school are primarily externally imposed, prescriptive, and treated as separate subject matter within the disciplinary pursuit of knowledge. Indigenous spirituality is largely personal, sacred, and integrated throughout one's interaction with and interpretation of the world (ibid., p. 101).

The importance of spiritual development is represented in the framework known as the medicine wheel. While there is some debate about the true origins of the medicine wheel, many Indigenous peoples have claimed this teaching symbol and made it their own so that it is a significant contemporary expression of Indigenous knowledge today. Depictions of the medicine wheel are usually divided into four quadrants, representing the four cardinal directions as well as the four areas of human development (physical, emotional, mental, and spiritual). Each of these directions is associated with multiple meanings, such as stages of life, seasons, animals, gifts, or qualities. Some cultures include additional dimensions, such as placing the self at the centre of the wheel to mark balance and the spiritual relationships between all things (Hampton, 1995, p. 19), or two additional directions above and below to represent the sky world and the Mother Earth. Although its use is primarily associated with North American Plains cultures (such as Cree, Dakota, and Blackfoot), similar concepts are used by Indigenous groups throughout the world, such as the Maori "Nga hau e wha" (four winds) and other models based upon the circle and the idea of four or six directions (Moeke-Pickering et al., 2006). Marlene Brant Castellano (Mohawk) writes that the medicine wheel "is not a model of rigid categorization...rather it is a model of balance....The medicine wheel teaches us to seek ways of incorporating the gifts of the other quadrants....Through the sharing of diverse gifts, balance is created in individual lives and in society as a whole" (Castellano, 2000, pp. 21–36).

The medicine wheel offers a clear basis for Indigenous epistemological frameworks and the development of related pedagogy. The Sacred Tree describes the four directions as each holding particular gifts, which an individual has the potential to develop throughout a lifelong journey of learning. Rather than viewing education as the development of intellectual capacity, as is primarily the case in Eurocentric education, the medicine wheel frames human development holistically. With developmental capacities falling in each area of the medicine wheel, corresponding pedagogical practices and educational objectives can be constructed (Bopp et al., 1989).

WHERE DO PEOPLE LEARN?

For Indigenous peoples, knowledge is firmly grounded in a particular sense of place. Little Bear writes, "The Earth cannot be separated from the actual being of Indians" (Little Bear, 2000, p. 78). This relationship with the earth as Mother, and with a traditional territory as the basis for and source of life, is central to all processes of learning and knowing for Indigenous peoples. Tewa Pueblo educator and scholar Gregory Cajete explains, "Indigenous education is, in its truest form, about learning relationships in context" (Cajete, 2000, p. 183). African scholar George Dei also emphasizes the importance of place as the basis for Indigenous spirituality and knowledge (Dei, 2000, pp. 70–86), as we learn in Chapter Eleven. Therefore, for Indigenous people to be educated in Eurocentric school buildings, separate from their traditional

Figure 6.1: Medicine Wheel

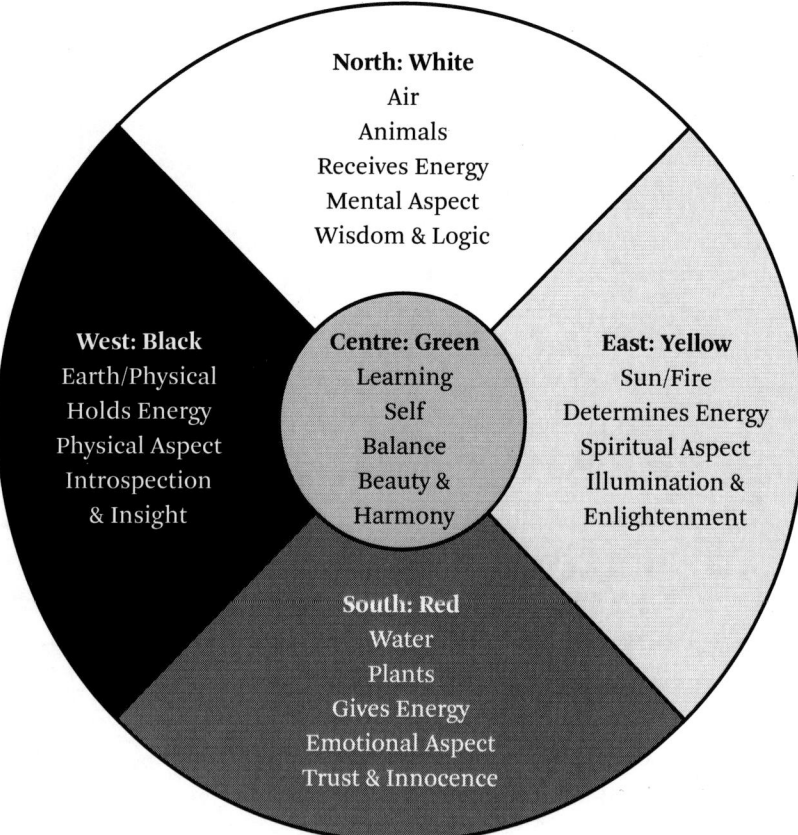

Note: Interpretations of the medicine wheel vary widely according to each Indigenous culture and tradition; for example, in some cultures black is not used as one of the four colours since in those cultures it represents death.
Source: Crystal Links, n.d.

CHAPTER SIX: Comparative Indigenous Ways of Knowing and Learning   163

land, is to decontextualize their learning and disconnect learners from their base of experience.

The Canadian Royal Commission on Aboriginal Peoples (RCAP) describes the importance to Indigenous peoples of learning from the land:

> The need to walk on the land in order to know it is a different approach to knowledge than the one-dimensional, literate approach to knowing. Persons schooled in a literate culture are accustomed to having all the context they need to understand...embedded in the text before them....Persons taught to use all their senses—to interpret a complex, dynamic reality—may well smile at the illusion that words alone, stripped of complementary sound and colour and texture, can convey meaning adequately. (RCAP, 1996a, pp. 622–623)

In this context, Eurocentric educational superiority is questioned, and claiming to understand through words alone is exposed as a rather limited experience of knowing.

Another point of contrast between Eurocentric and Indigenous cultures is the relationship of human beings to the earth and other beings. Eurocentric, monotheistic religious perspectives place "man" as dominant over all Creation, a concept that has been applied to humanity's search for domination over the earth and its resources. This belief has also been translated to a search for domination over knowledge itself. In contrast, many Indigenous nations view humans as the last beings to be created and therefore the most humble and dependent in relation to the natural world (Deloria, 1997; Smith, 1995). Similarly, knowledge is viewed not as an area to be dominated but rather as an ongoing contextual experience of understanding one's relationship to the land, community, and all created beings.

In an Indigenous worldview, education is based upon the requirements of everyday life. In this way, education is "an experience in context, a subjective experience that, for the knower, becomes knowledge in itself. The experience is knowledge" (Ermine, 1995, p. 104). Thus, the "where" of learning defines one's experience and happens everywhere. The idea that learning should take place only within the four walls of a school, through the prescription of a fixed written curriculum, is diametrically opposed to the idea that learning is dynamic, experiential, and grounded in the place where one lives.

Indigenous epistemology conceptualizes education and learning as both life-wide (happening across formal, non-formal, and informal settings) and lifelong (Lanigan, 1998, p. 106). Traditionally, education from an Indigenous perspective was not conducted through a formal, age- and grade-segregated system. The importance of different life stages was recognized, represented in the medicine wheel by childhood, adolescence, adulthood, and old age. In Anishinaabe teachings, seven-year cycles mark significant moments in a person's life. The first seven years are the good life and the main responsibility is only to be loved. The next seven years are considered the fast life, the next seven after that the wandering life, and so on. Different learning would take place at different points in time. The period of adolescence has been marked in many Indigenous cultures by rites of passage and initiation. These rites of passage are important for a healthy transition from childhood to adulthood. David Lertzman (Jewish) ties some of Aboriginal youth's social struggles today to the loss of these cultural practices (2002). Fhulu Nekhwevha (South African) describes similar cultural practices that are central to Indigenous education in African contexts (1999, pp. 491–506). However, this recognition of learning through different stages is distinct from current Eurocentric systems, which place learning within a formal, age-graded schooling structure from ages 5 to 18, with higher education expected after age 18. In Eurocentric cultures, education is often considered synonymous with schooling. Although this is changing as more emphasis is placed in Eurocentric cultures on lifelong learning, the expectation still is that one must first learn through the intensive accumulation of knowledge over several years, and then "do" once he or she graduates from the formal system. In contrast, in Indigenous cultures, learning has always been viewed as "a life-long responsibility" (Battiste, 2002, p. 13) for each individual, taking place in a variety of contexts.

HOW DO PEOPLE LEARN?
Indigenous worldviews on the origin of knowledge inform how one learns in an Indigenous epistemological framework. Castellano presents three categories of Indigenous knowledge, each with a particular origin. The first, traditional knowledge, includes the histories, Creation stories, genealogies, rights, and relationships that are passed on from generation to generation. This knowledge is often considered sacred to a particular Indigenous nation, and is passed on through storytelling, apprenticeship, and elaborate ceremonies and rituals to ensure

CHAPTER SIX: Comparative Indigenous Ways of Knowing and Learning   165

its preservation. The second category, empirical knowledge (such as the healing properties of a particular plant), is most easily related to Eurocentric means of obtaining knowledge as it is acquired through testing and observation. However, in Indigenous epistemology this is not considered a linear process in which a particular truth is hypothesized, tested, and then proven as true, as in the "scientific method." Rather, empirical knowledge is viewed as cyclical, dynamic, and evolving over time through the collaborative observations and inputs of many individuals. The third category Castellano calls revealed knowledge. This kind of knowledge comes from the spirit world, and is acquired through dreams, visions, and intuitions. Whereas revealed knowledge in the Eurocentric world is reserved exclusively for prophets of God and miracles, in the Indigenous world each individual has the responsibility to make his or her own inner journey into the metaphysical (Castellano, 2000, pp. 23–24). Great significance is attributed to dreams, and intentional visioning is viewed as the way in which an individual finds his or her purpose of life. Castellano explains, "Sometimes knowledge is received as a gift at a moment of need; sometimes it manifests itself as a sense that the 'time is right' to hunt or counsel or to make a decisive turn in one's life path" (ibid.). This multi-faceted understanding of the origins of knowledge makes how one learns a dynamic process, going far beyond the limits of an approved curriculum, textbook, or schoolteacher's personal knowledge base.

A commonly cited difference between Eurocentric and Indigenous modes of education is of primarily literate versus primarily oral cultures. In Indigenous societies, great emphasis has been placed on the oral transmission of knowledge through storytelling, traditionally used to convey Aboriginal knowledge, customs, and values (Castellano, 2000, p. 31; Little Bear, 2000, p. 81). Cajete (1994) says that "stories [teach] people who they are so they can become all they were meant to be" (p. 112). Storytelling is described as the oldest form of the arts and thus the basis for the other arts, such as drama, dance, and music (Lanigan, 1998, p. 113). Whereas Eurocentric cultures often view storytelling as an activity to entertain small children, in Indigenous pedagogy it is a central tool for teaching and learning (Cajete, 1994, p. 68).

Equally important to Indigenous pedagogy are the various modes of experiential learning, such as modelling, observation, in-context learning, apprenticeships, learning games, and tag-along teaching as methods for "learning by doing" (Simpson, 2000, p. 257). "Through observation, experience, and practice children learned the skills, beliefs, values, and norms of their culture" (Swan, 1998, pp. 51–52). These practices are not exclusive to Indigenous cultures, and were central to most cultures prior to industrialization. However, the introduction of Eurocentric schooling marked the separation of children from the community as a base of experience and learning. Lertzman describes the Indigenous context for learning: "Within a community, extended family supplies the social context, along with teachers and individual specialists for these important tasks. Mother Earth provides everything else: classroom, science lab, playground, athletics facility, church, grocery, hardware store, and drug store" (Lertzman, 2002, p. 4).

Another important aspect of Aboriginal pedagogy is language, which "embodies the way a society thinks" (Little Bear, 2000, p. 78). Ermine (1995) calls language a "touchstone" for Aboriginal cultures, saying, "It is imperative that our children take up the cause of our languages and cultures, because therein lies Aboriginal epistemology, which speaks of holism" (p. 107). As has been well documented by anthropologists, language is central to cultural worldviews. For example, in Mi'kmaq culture, languages are verb rich; they are process and action oriented, describing "happenings" rather than objects (Ermine, 1995). James (Sákéj) Youngblood Henderson (Chickasaw) explains that the use of fewer verb tenses in some Indigenous languages does not imply a more simplistic language structure but rather a view of time and space as continuous rather than fragmented (Henderson, 2000, p. 263).

Other language differences include a varying cadence of speech, commonly known as "wait-time." From an Indigenous perspective, when in dialogue, one should take time to internalize and process the other's remarks before responding. Eber Hampton (Chickasaw) terms this "reflective thinking" (Hampton, 1995, p. 2). When Indigenous students do not respond immediately to a question in the classroom, the Eurocentric teacher might consider them slow or disrespectful, whereas for the Indigenous student this may be a sign of their thoughtfulness and respect for the other's ideas.

Sacred cultural practices embody ways for knowing and learning that often fall under the "spiritual education" quadrant of the medicine wheel. Ceremonies help create the conditions necessary for the inward journey toward metaphysical knowledge (Henderson, 2000, p. 263), "instilling the attitude of expectant stillness that opens the door to full awareness" (Castellano, 2000, citing Cardinal, 1990, p. 29).

CHAPTER SIX: Comparative Indigenous Ways of Knowing and Learning   167

Ceremonies are also considered opportunities for educational reward, praise, and recognition.[4] Through honouring ceremonies, such as conferral of a name or holding of a potlatch, the community recognizes the individual's movement through the life stages and/or development of certain capacities. Rather than conforming to external rules, as in Eurocentric society, within Indigenous ways one is responsible to the group. Ceremonies therefore also confer responsibilities and authority upon wisdom keepers in the community to hold knowledge in service to others. Sacred practices thus serve as educational markers, points of recognition or "graduation," and to award a greater level of responsibility in the community.

Eurocentric evaluation of knowledge contrasts with the sacred practices and educational measures of Indigenous people:

> Educational philosophy in contemporary education has focused on information to the masses, leading to standardized tests...and those who can extract information are called educated and intelligent. What this approach ignores is the knowledge that comes from introspection, reflection, meditation, prayer, and other kinds of self-directed learning. (Battiste, 2002, p. 15)

The subjective, such as the experience of participating in ceremonies and cultural practices, is central to Indigenous epistemology and access to truth. This stands in opposition to the Eurocentric value of objectivity (Ermine, 1995, p. 110). This notion of Indigenous knowledge as personal and sacred leads us into the next discussion, of who teaches or confers knowledge.

FROM WHOM DO PEOPLE LEARN?
In Eurocentric educational contexts, the authority of those who confer knowledge is clearly established. Through formal certification, an individual receives the designation "teacher," carrying the defined role of educating his or her students. Other sources for knowledge in the classroom include the approved curriculum and pedagogical materials the teacher may draw upon.

In an Indigenous context, the question of who may teach and from whom one learns is much more complex. As described above, Indigenous knowledge is grounded in the land; therefore, Mother Earth is considered by many as the supreme teacher. Equally important is the spirit world, which includes all Creation and the ancestors who have passed on. As all Creation is considered animate, all beings are imbued with Spirit and are therefore potential teachers. Animals or transformative spirit beings, such as the "trickster," are characters used to teach children what to do and especially (through their mistakes) what not to do (Lanigan, 1998, p. 112). Rocks are referred to as "grandmothers and grandfathers" and are considered the oldest living teachers.

In Indigenous epistemology, the self is the ultimate teacher. Ermine describes the meeting of Eurocentric and Indigenous peoples in 1492 as a clash between peoples destined for two different journeys of discovery—one toward the physical, or "outer space," and the other toward the metaphysical, or "inner space." He writes, "Aboriginal epistemology is grounded in the self, the spirit, the unknown....[It] speaks of pondering great mysteries that lie no further than the self" (Ermine, 1995, p. 108). Ways of knowing and learning in an Indigenous paradigm are therefore profoundly personal and spiritual, based upon a journey into the inner metaphysical and spiritual worlds of the self.

Indigenous pedagogy assumes personal authority in the search for knowledge, and "values a person's ability to learn independently by observing, listening, and participating with a minimum of intervention or instruction" (Battiste, 2002, p. 14). The Indigenous educational principle of noninterference sets forth the idea of respect for others' wholeness and their independent ability to understand and access knowledge. Although Eurocentric educational theorists such as Johann Pestalozzi, Hans Frochel, Maria Montessori, and more recently Paulo Freire have argued for the inherent capacity of the individual and for child/learner-centred dialogic education, dominant Eurocentric education has viewed the teacher (and the text) as the authority who holds the knowledge and who has the right to deposit this knowledge in the minds of students. These contrasting values have been a source of conflict between Eurocentric teachers and Indigenous students in the classroom, leading some Indigenous students to rebel when they feel they have been disrespected through the teacher's interference in their personal learning processes.

Conflicts also arise in relation to questions of authority. On the one hand, all beings are teachers in an Indigenous paradigm. Education is considered a collective responsibility that is taken on by the whole community (Little Bear, 2000, p. 81). On the other hand, the right to hold and transfer knowledge is a responsibility endowed by the community

CHAPTER SIX: Comparative Indigenous Ways of Knowing and Learning   169

based on an individual's having earned it, as well as by familial and ancestral relationships. Particular individuals are designated as educators in specific contexts; for example, an uncle or aunt is typically chosen to lead a child through his or her rites of passage. Therefore, an Indigenous child entering a Eurocentric classroom may question the authority of the teacher, since he or she has no context to value that teacher's authority.

In Indigenous communities, positions of knowledge or respect in the community, such as Pipe Holders, Bundle Holders, or Wisdom Keepers, are obtained through ancestral rights or personal worth, as well as through an elaborate process of apprenticeship training. These are viewed as positions of service and responsibility rather than of hierarchical superiority. For example, most Indigenous cultures identify Elders within the community who hold a central role in teaching and guiding children and the community. The designation of Elder (in contrast to "senior citizens") implies gifts of experience and knowledge. Most Elders do not seek status, and position themselves with humility, understanding themselves as still learning (RCAP, 1996b). One Elder stated, "I am just one day old" (Hampton, 1995, p. 19). Elders traditionally are treated with ultimate respect—if an Elder is speaking, he or she will not be interrupted. This value of respect can create confusion for Indigenous students in a Eurocentric context, when they are encouraged to think critically and to question those in authority.

Deborah McGregor, an Anishinaabe educator, argues that Indigenous knowledge is governed by rules, inextricable from Indigenous peoples' traditional relationships to personal and historical identity, experience, land, and ancestral or earned rights. Therefore, it not a subject that can be studied and then mastered: "just because someone has studied [Traditional Ecological Knowledge] does not mean that one now has it" (McGregor, 2004, pp. 385–410). In contrast, in Eurocentric science, the objective is to obtain or "possess" knowledge by studying it, with increasing amount of study time qualifying one as an "expert" in a field (Battiste, 2002). From an Indigenous perspective, "Knowledge is not a commodity that can be possessed or controlled by educational institutions, but is a living process to be absorbed and understood" (ibid., p. 14).

FOR WHAT PURPOSE DO PEOPLE LEARN?
The question of why we learn, or the purpose of knowledge, is best understood within the Indigenous worldview that all things are related.

The survival of each life form is dependent on the survival of the others. A common Indigenous saying is: "The honour of one is the honour of all; the hurt of one is the hurt of all."

The Eurocentric concept of education as a means for individual advancement contrasts with the Indigenist idea that education is a means for the individual to serve the group. According to Hampton, "Education is to serve the people....The competitive success of the individual is an implicit value of Eurocentric schools and, as such, is in direct conflict with the Indian value of group success through individual achievement" (Hampton, 1995, p. 21). In a study conducted on the student experiences in the American Indian Program at Harvard, Hampton found that the majority of Native American students went there with the intention of using their education to help their communities.

The goal of Indigenous education is not individual prosperity or success, but dignity and responsibility to the community. The ultimate purpose of learning is to understand one's place in relation to the web of life, and to gain the skills and knowledge needed to contribute to the advancement of all beings. In this context, the greater one's knowledge, the greater the responsibility that one holds.

THE FOURTH WAY

Could aspects of Indigenous ways of knowing and learning be incorporated in dominant educational reform, not just for Indigenous peoples but for all people? Is there value in this? Could it be done while respecting the rights to and sacredness of that knowledge? What would a curriculum incorporating Indigenous knowledge look like? These questions set the stage for our final discussion.

In her presidential address to the Comparative and International Education Society in 1990, Masemann proposed that forms of Indigenous knowledge were not only valid, but also potentially instructive for widespread educational reform. Referring to the rise of alternative paradigms for knowing, she argued, "What these paradigms have in common is that they are holistic, context dependent, and integrative. They propose ways in which society might be knit together again, not sundered apart" (Masemann, 1990, p. 471).

Although world culture theory (discussed in Chapter One) suggests that education systems around the world are moving toward a uniform, standardized education model based upon a Eurocentric, graded, formal system, there is strong evidence that this model does not work for many of the world's peoples. For example, demand is swelling in North America for alternative schooling options like Montessori and Waldorf, which promote holistic child-centred pedagogy, and for home-schooling. There is also a growing openness to Indigenous practices, as individuals become increasingly dissatisfied with the current trend of world affairs, and with the failed mission of modernity as the elixir for the progress of humanity. Evidence of this shift has emerged in several arenas, notably in health and environmental sciences, as the world looks to Indigenous peoples to share their traditional knowledge in a time of crisis.

The postmodern debate merely reflects the Eurocentric world's emerging recognition of paradigms that Indigenous peoples have lived and known for thousands of years. Despite years of oppression, scholars, leaders, and Elders from within the Indigenous world are also reaching out to their non-Indigenous brothers and sisters, offering once again to share their wisdom where the dominant paradigm has fallen short. For most Indigenous peoples, this is the only choice. If education is service, and the hurt of one is the hurt of all, then the sharing of Indigenous wisdom at a time of need is the fulfillment of prophecy and our responsibility as part of the circle.

A leading example of this kind of scholarship is *The Fourth Way: An Indigenous Contribution for Building Sustainable and Harmonious Prosperity in the Americas*. This document, written by Four Worlds International and the United Indians of All Tribes Foundation (2006), originates from nine years of consultation with Indigenous leaders and communities across the Americas. *The Fourth Way* proposes that the time has come for humanity to adopt new ways of learning that will prepare us for a sustainable global future, and that we need to look toward an Aboriginal, holistic education model to lead the way toward the establishment of world peace. The Fourth Way movement is not alone in this call—organizations such as Global Elders are also offering to share models of Aboriginal pedagogy and teachings (Castellano, 2000, p. 87). Another excellent reference for this is the work of Arkan Lushwala (2012), an Indigenous Peruvian ceremonialist and teacher who was also adopted by a Lakota medicine man, and thus bridges the worlds of the "condor and the eagle" and the Indigenous traditions of South and North America. Lushwala's book, *The Time of the Black Jaguar: An Offering of Indigenous Wisdom for the Continuity of Life on Earth*, directly relates Indigenous teachings to the needs of our time, applying them to topics such as economic models, the environment, the healing of masculine and feminine, and education. As Couture writes, "There are those who say that the Native Way holds a key, if not the key, to the future survival of mankind" (Couture, 1991, p. 202).

INDIGENOUS INFUSION EFFORTS: THE DEEPENING KNOWLEDGE PROJECT

Since 2007, OISE's teacher education program at the University of Toronto has attempted to increase awareness and understanding of Indigenous issues, histories, perspectives, and knowledges among teachers in training, and encourages them to take these up in their work after graduating. The effort is known as Deepening Knowledge, Enhancing Instruction, more commonly referred to as the Deepening Knowledge Project. In its earliest days, this group sought to understand why most instructors were not including Indigenous topics and perspectives. They carried out a needs assessment, finding that instructors reported no time to create lessons or to develop the expertise needed to adequately teach the topics under consideration, and inability to locate resources that were accurate or fit these topics. In its second year, the Deepening Knowledge Project received support from the Ontario government to hire a consultant to analyze all the required components of OISE's largest pre-service program, to find spaces where new lessons could easily be adapted and inserted. Our consultant created class-period-length lessons, with all resources, readings, and activities included to reduce the burden and effort needed on the part of an instructor to design or find them independently.

The next year, we followed up with instructors to find out how the lessons were working. While some had taken up the lessons, many had not. Of the instructors who tried them, the majority had been already teaching some Indigenous content. They used the new resources to supplement their teaching. The minority who were trying the resources as the first or only inclusion of Indigenous material in their repertoire reported some hesitation to use these materials a second time. They had found follow-up conversations, or facilitating discussions they were less prepared for, to be difficult. For the instructors who had not even tried to use the resources or admitted they were unaware of them, our survey brought attention to where to find them and encouraged them to try using the material. A follow-up later in the year found that most of the instructors who hadn't tried to incorporate the lessons continued

CHAPTER SIX: Comparative Indigenous Ways of Knowing and Learning   173

to express anxiety about using them. They felt ill-prepared to handle the directions in which conversations might go and the questions that might come from teacher candidates. Similar fears and anxieties have been reported even among teacher candidates who are keen to incorporate Indigenous perspectives in their teaching (Nardozi et al., 2014).

Angela Nardozi, Manager of Deepening Knowledge from 2010 to 2016, has studied the impact of the project and found that teacher candidates who reported being "willing" to take up Indigenous issues often felt "unready" to do so. Teacher candidates in a cohort within the OISE program of approximately 70 teacher candidates, whose lead instructors had opted to focus on Indigenous infusion in addition to arts, drama, and restorative justice between 2011 and 2014, were surveyed at three points in their degree program. Before their classes began they reported feeling willing but unknowledgeable to teach Indigenous material. Midway through the program they reported being much more knowledgeable and maintaining the same motivation or willingness to teach Indigenous material. By the end of the program they almost all felt more knowledgeable than at the beginning of their program, but reported more hesitance than at the midpoint. Nardozi and her co-authors have surmised that the candidates may have adopted the humility associated with Indigenous ways of teaching and learning and thus indicated in the survey that, although they knew more about Indigenous ways than when they started, they realized just how much they still didn't know and how far they had to go. As resources and time scarcity were continually reported as barriers to taking up Indigenous topics in classrooms, Deepening Knowledge adapted and disseminated online a resource kit for novice teachers (see resources at end of chapter). Over the years, it has evolved to become a portal to resources for teaching, organized the way teachers typically search for support: by age and grade level and by subject. Knowing the importance of building networks and relationships, Deepening Knowledge also developed a social media presence to share information about local events, news, and gatherings, to connect teachers with the Indigenous communities near where they live. An essential principle learned from this project, and others cited in Nardozi's work, is that the best way to deepen knowledge is to make connections in the community and form relationships with Indigenous people, parents, children, and families. Ultimately, the Deepening Knowledge team hopes that our education efforts help to lift the Indigenous community and to improve relations between Indigenous peoples and settlers.

IMPLICATIONS FOR TEACHERS

It is not difficult to imagine that all people might thrive in environments that value wholeness, spirituality, and diverse modes and means of learning. Aboriginal pedagogical methods present a "valuable addition to the present systems of education in any teaching topic, not only when teaching Aboriginal people. By incorporating observation, experience, introspection, and inquiry during the education process, we will begin to create linkages from the experiences of human beings and transmit them wholly to students in the classroom" (Wheaton, 2000, pp. 151–166).

Note that the shift required is not to adopt the "cultural" or "exotic" elements of Indigenous ways. As demonstrated in this chapter, the foundations of Indigenous epistemology are much deeper than this. Investigations of the relevance of Indigenous knowledge for Eurocentric or global comparative education must consider the values and philosophical underpinnings informing Indigenous pedagogy:

> Indigenous knowledge presents several goals for educational reform: acknowledging the sacredness of life and experiences; generating the spirit of hope based on experience as a connection with others in creating a new and equitable future; generating the meaning of work as a vocation and as a mission in life; and developing the capacity to do everything to open a new cognitive space in which a community can discover itself and affirm its heritage and knowledge in order to flourish for everyone. (Battiste, 2002, pp. 28–29)

It is indisputable that any investigations of how Indigenous ways of knowing and learning could be applied to dominant efforts *must* involve Indigenous peoples in their research, design, and implementation. Otherwise, despite the best of intentions, they risk becoming yet another example of colonization, co-optation, and exploitation of Indigenous peoples. As this chapter has explained, Indigenous knowledge is intimately connected to the historical, ecological, social, spiritual, and ceremonial fabric of Indigenous societies and to the Indigenous peoples themselves. It cannot be understood outside of those contexts. In encouraging respectful, collaborative, comparative scholarship between non-Indigenous and Indigenous peoples, and among diverse Indigenous peoples, lies the potential for discerning the path forward for education.

CHAPTER SIX: Comparative Indigenous Ways of Knowing and Learning   175

Figure 6.2: Ideas for Incorporating Indigenous Ways of Knowing and Learning in Your Classroom

Find out who the traditional inhabitants are of the land on which your school stands. Using proper protocols, invite an Elder to come to your classroom and share some of his of her teachings. Make a field trip to visit that Elder at home or at a local teaching facility, such as a Friendship Centre.

Make space for prayer and the expression of spirituality in your classroom. Create a "spirit spot"—a quiet time that students can use for personal reflection, journaling, art, prayer, meditation, etc., each day.

Reinforce respect among students for one another and the world around them. Demonstrate that same respect toward them.

Post Indigenous teachings in the classroom, such as the Seven Sacred Teachings or the medicine wheel.

Use circles and interactive modes of sharing, such as a weekly or daily "sharing circle" in which you pass around a special object and all students have the opportunity to have a voice and share their emotions.

Incorporate music, art, and storytelling integrally in the classroom as valid ways of sharing and learning. Invite Aboriginal artists to the class to share these traditions and guide the class in participating.

Have your class explore Indigenous languages through place names on the map. Words like Toronto, Ottawa, Ontario, and Canada all have surprising and interesting stories behind them.

When studying history, ask students how these events would affect Aboriginal people. Assign a local oral history project where students interview community elders (of all backgrounds) to tell the history not represented in textbooks. Assign groups to research Aboriginal perspectives on all topics covered in a year.

When studying biology, take your students outside to learn the names of the plants around your school. Have students bring to class examples of Indigenous foods or medicines. Seek out opportunities for your students to learn through apprenticeship, observation, and experience from people in your community.

Create an environment conducive to sharing and cooperation. Promote a sense of knowledge as responsibility and learning as a means for service to the greater community.

Use the world as your classroom, and all of its beings as teachers.

For teachers searching for practical ways to incorporate Indigenous ways of knowing and learning in the classroom, there are many curricular and online resources available. In Figure 6.2, we summarize some ideas for beginning to incorporate Indigenous ways of knowing and learning in teaching practice. The way in which you incorporate these suggestions will vary based on your personal interests, relationships, and expertise, and your classroom and school context. Consider teaching in ways that value every learning style in the medicine wheel: the spiritual, emotional, physical, and mental. In other words: for each topic, find a way to intuit, feel, act, and think about it.

A common question from teachers, both Indigenous and non-Indigenous, is, "Do I have the right to teach from Aboriginal cultural worldviews and perspectives?"[5] An Aboriginal Studies scholar at the University of British Columbia has advised reframing this question to ask, "What is our responsibility?" (Justice, 2004). At a time of spiritual, ecological, and social crisis, the opportunity exists to turn toward Aboriginal holistic frameworks for knowing and learning, to help humanity develop a sense of respect and relationship with all Creation. In this age of rapid globalization and increased interaction and interdependence across cultures, the need to take into consideration Indigenous ways of knowing and learning has never been more relevant.

QUESTIONS FOR REFLECTION AND DISCUSSION
1. How might you use Indigenous Knowledge and Pedagogy in your teaching? Which characteristics or examples of Indigenous knowledge and pedagogy strike you as most consonant or dissonant with typical educational practices in your teaching context?
2. How do you think the need to incorporate/recognize Indigenous worldviews in the classroom can be reconciled with the need to respect the context, rights, and responsibilities associated with that knowledge?
3. Thinking about your own practical needs and interests, explore some resources on oise.utoronto.ca/deepeningknowledge. Did you find any that are useful to your own practice? What further skills or knowledge do you require to adopt them? How will you develop the skills or knowledge you've identified?

CHAPTER SIX: Comparative Indigenous Ways of Knowing and Learning   177

SUGGESTED AUDIO-VISUAL RESOURCES
Hi-Ho Mistahey! by Alanis Obomsawin (2013). Available at: www.nfb.ca/film/hi-ho_mistahey_en
This documentary tells the story of Shannen's Dream, a national campaign to provide equitable access to education in safe and suitable schools for First Nations children, which eventually brings Shannen's Dream all the way to the United Nations in Geneva.

It's Not an Opinion, It's a Fact: Aboriginal Education in Canada, produced by MyNVIT (2012). Available at: www.youtube.com/watch?v=tswVV2YkjKA
This YouTube video highlights the impacts of gaps in Aboriginal education and the opportunities to improve the quality of life for all Canadians.

Deepening Knowledge Project OISE's Aboriginal Peoples Curricula Database. Available at http://www.oise.utoronto.ca/deepeningknowledge/
The Deepening Knowledge Project seeks to infuse Aboriginal peoples' histories, knowledges and pedagogies into all levels of education in Canada. The project is a part of the Ontario Institute for Studies in Education, University of Toronto, which is located on the territories of Anishinaabe and Onkwehonwe peoples.
On this site you'll find information about the history and traditions of First Nations, Métis, Inuit and Native American cultures, information about the challenges facing Aboriginal communities today, and curricula for incorporating this information into your teaching practice.

SUGGESTIONS FOR FURTHER READING
Battiste, Marie. (2013). *Decolonizing Education: Nourishing the Learning Spirit.* Saskatoon: Purich Publishing.
Bell, Nicole. (2014). Teaching by the Medicine Wheel: An Anishinaabe Framework for Indigenous Education. *Education Canada* (June 2014). Available at www.cea-ace.ca/education-canada/article/teaching-medicine-wheel
Bopp, Judie, Bopp, Michael, Brown, Lee, and Lane, Phil. (1989). *The Sacred Tree* (3rd ed.). Twin Lakes, WI: Lotus Light Publications.
Cajete, Gregory. (1994). *Look to the Mountain: An Ecology of Indigenous Education.* Durango, CO: Kivaki Press.
Cajete, Gregory. (2000). Indigenous Knowledge: The Pueblo Metaphor of Indigenous Education. In *Reclaiming Indigenous Voice and Vision,*

edited by Marie Battiste. Vancouver: University of British Columbia Press. 181–191.

Castellano, Marlene Brant. (2000). Updating Aboriginal Traditions of Knowledge. In *Indigenous Knowledges in Global Contexts: Multiple Readings of our World*, edited by George. J. Sefa Dei, Budd L. Hall, and Dorothy Goldin Rosenberg. Toronto: OISE/University of Toronto Press. 21–36.

Colorado, Pam. (1988). Bridging Native and Western Science. *Convergence, 21*(2–3), 49–68.

Ermine, Willie. (1995). Aboriginal Epistemology. In *First Nations Education in Canada: The Circle Unfolds*, edited by Marie Battiste and Jean Barman. Vancouver: University of British Columbia Press. 101–112.

Four Arrows. (2013). *Teaching Truly: A Curriculum to Indigenize Mainstream Education*. New York: Peter Lang Publishing.

Four Worlds International and United Indians of All Tribes Foundation. (2006). *The Fourth Way: An Indigenous Contribution for Building Sustainable and Harmonious Prosperity in the Americas*. Seattle: United Indians.

Hampton, Eber. (1995). Towards a Redefinition of Indian Education. In *First Nations Education in Canada: The Circle Unfolds*, edited by Marie Battiste and Jean Barman. Vancouver: University of British Columbia Press. 5–46.

Lertzman, David. A. (2002). Rediscovering Rites of Passage: Education, Transformation, and the Transition to Sustainability. *Conservation Ecology, 5*(2), 30. Available at: www.consecol.org/vol5/iss2/art30/

Little Bear, Leroy. (2000). Jagged Worldviews Colliding. In *Reclaiming Indigenous Voice and Vision*, edited by Marie Battiste. Vancouver: University of British Columbia Press, 77–85.

Lushwala, Arkan. (2012). *The Time of the Black Jaguar: An Offering of Indigenous Wisdom for the Continuity of Life on Earth*. Ribera, NM: Arkan Lushwala.

Masemann, Vandra. (1990). Ways of Knowing: Implications for Comparative Education. *Comparative Education Review, 34*(4), 465–473.

McGregor, Deborah. (2004). Coming Full Circle: Indigenous Knowledge, Environment and Our Future. *American Indian Quarterly, 28*(3–4), 385–410.

Strategic Alliance of Broadcasters for Aboriginal Reflection (SABAR). (2015). *Key Terms*. Available at: sabar.ca/key-terms

Stronger Smarter. (n.d.). *Home page*. Available at: strongersmarter.
com.au/

Toulouse, Pamela. (2016). What Matters in Indigenous Education:
Implementing a Vision Committed to Holism, Diversity and
Engagement. In M*easuring What Matters, People for Education*.
Toronto: People for Education. Available at peopleforeducation.ca/
measuring-what-matters/wp-content/uploads/2016/04/P4E-MWM-
What-Matters-in-Indigenous-Education.pdf

NOTES

1. As per the Royal Commission on Aboriginal Peoples, *Indigenous* and other such terms are capitalized in this chapter wherever they are used as proper names for a collective group of people, such as would be used in identifying the French or Chinese, as well as when used as a modifier for those groups (for example, French cuisine; Aboriginal traditions).
2. Although the scope of this chapter encompasses Indigenous peoples worldwide, it primarily focuses on the Indigenous peoples of Canada, the United States, Australia, and New Zealand. This is due in part to the concentration of scholarship that has emerged from those countries on Indigenous topics and by Indigenous scholars, as well as to the background and experience base of the authors.
3. There is wide documentation on the negative impacts of colonization and practices such as enforced residential schooling on Aboriginal peoples. Challenges such as breakdown in family structures, family violence, alcoholism, and high suicide rates are often linked to ruptures caused by the residential schooling experience. See, for example, the reports of the Truth and Reconciliation Commission: nctr.ca/reports.php
4. The potlatch is a complex ceremony practised primarily by Northwest coastal peoples in North America (such as Haida, Haisla, Coast Salish, and Kwakiutl). A form of political, economic, and social exchange, it is a vital part of these cultures' way of life. Although protocol differs among the Indigenous nations, the potlatch could involve a feast, with music, dance, and spiritual ceremonies. Gifts are given by the host to establish or uphold status positions in society; gifting also serves to redistribute resources throughout the community. Potlatches often mark a significant event, such as the celebration of births, rites of passage, weddings, funerals, puberty, and honouring of the deceased. Potlatches are also the venue in which ownership to economic and ceremonial privileges is asserted, displayed, and formally transferred to heirs.
5. We suggest Henley, Thom. (1996). *Rediscovery: Ancient Pathways—New Directions: A Guidebook to Outdoor Education*. Calgary: Lone Pine Publishing.

REFERENCES

Battiste, Marie. (2002). *Indigenous Knowledge and Pedagogy in First Nations Education: A Literature Review with Recommendations*. Report Commissioned by the Minister's National Working Group on Education. Ottawa: Indian and Northern Affairs Canada.

Bear, Charla. (2008, May 12). American Indian Boarding Schools Haunt Many, Part 1. *NPR*. Available at: www.npr.org/templates/story/story.php?storyId=16516865

Bopp, Judie, Bopp, Michael, Brown, Lee, and Lane, Phil. (1989). *The Sacred Tree* (3rd ed.). Twin Lakes, WI: Lotus Light Publications.

Brady, Wendy. (1997). Indigenous Australian Education and Globalisation. In *Tradition, Modernity and Post-Modernity in Comparative Education*, edited by Vandra Masemann and Anthony Welch. Dordrecht, the Netherlands: Kluwer Academic Publishers. 421.

Cajete, Gregory. (1994). *Look to the Mountain: An Ecology of Indigenous Education*. Durango, CO: Kivaki Press.

Cajete, Gregory. (2000). Indigenous Knowledge: The Pueblo Metaphor of Indigenous Education. In *Reclaiming Indigenous Voice and Vision*, edited by Marie Battiste. Vancouver: University of British Columbia Press. 183.

Cardinal, Douglas. (1993). Dancing with Chaos: An Interview with Douglas Cardinal. Quoted in Dennis H. McPherson and J. Douglas Rabb, Indian from the Inside: A Study in Ethno-Metaphysics. *Occasional paper 14*. Thunder Bay, ON: Lakehead University Centre for Northern Studies.

Castellano, Marlene Brant. (2000). Updating Aboriginal Traditions of Knowledge. In *Indigenous Knowledges in Global Contexts: Multiple Readings of Our World*, edited by George J. Sefa Dei, Budd L. Hall, and Dorothy Goldin Rosenberg. Toronto: OISE/University of Toronto Press. 21–36.

Couture, Joseph. (1991). The Role of Native Elders: Emergent Issues. In *The Cultural Maze: Complex Questions on Native Destiny in Western Canada*, edited by John W. Friesen. Calgary: Detselig Enterprises Ltd. 201–217.

Crystal Links. (no date). *Hopi*. Retrieved from: www.crystalinks.com/hopi.html

Dei, George J. Sefa. (2000). African Development: The Relevance and Implications of "Indigenousness." In *Indigenous Knowledges in Global Contexts: Multiple Readings of Our World*, edited by George J. Sefa Dei, Budd L. Hall, and Dorothy Goldin Rosenberg. Toronto: OISE/University of Toronto Press.

Deloria, Jr., Vine. (1997). *Red Earth, White Lies: Native Americans and the Myth of Scientific Fact*. Golden, BC: Fulcrum Publishing.

DeVoe, Jill Fleury, and Darling-Churchill, Kristen E. (2008). *Status and Trends in the Education of American Indians and Alaska Natives: 2008*. NCES 2008-084. National Center for Education Statistics.

Ermine, Willie. (1995). Aboriginal Epistemology. In *First Nations Education in Canada: The Circle Unfolds*, edited by Marie Battiste and Jean Barman. Vancouver: University of British Columbia Press. 101–112.

Four Worlds International and United Indians of All Tribes Foundation. (2006). *The Fourth Way: An Indigenous Contribution for Building Sustainable and Harmonious Prosperity in the Americas*. Seattle: United Indians.

Hampton, Eber. (1995). Toward a Redefinition of Indian Education. In *First Nations Education in Canada: The Circle Unfolds*, edited by Marie Battiste and Jean Barman. Vancouver: University of British Columbia Press. 5–46.

Henderson, James Sakej Youngblood. (2000). Ayukpachi: Empowering Aboriginal Thought. In *Reclaiming Indigenous Voice and Vision*, edited by Marie Battiste. Vancouver: University of British Columbia Press. 248–263.

Henley, Thom. (1996). *Rediscovery: Ancient Pathways, New Directions*. Calgary: Lone Pine Publishing.

Justice, Daniel. (2004, November 26). *Bringing Great Minds Together as One: How Aboriginal Worldviews Can Enhance Learning in the Academy*. Panel presentation for workshop held at Emmanuel College, University of Toronto.

Lanigan, Mary-Anne. (1998). Aboriginal Pedagogy: Storytelling. In *As We See: Aboriginal Pedagogy*, edited by Lenore A. Stiffarm. Regina: University of Saskatchewan. 106.

Lertzman, David. (2002). Rediscovering Rites of Passage: Education, Transformation, and the Transition to Sustainability. *Conservation Ecology*, 5(2). Retrieved from: www.consecol.org/vol5/iss2/art30

Little Bear, Leroy. (2000). Jagged Worldviews Colliding. In *Reclaiming Indigenous Voice and Vision*, edited by Marie Battiste. Vancouver: University of British Columbia Press. 77–85.

Lushwala, Arkan. (2012). *The Time of the Black Jaguar: An Offering of Indigenous Wisdom for the Continuity of Life on Earth*. Ribera, NM: Arkan Lushwala.

Masemann, Vandra. (1990). Ways of Knowing: Implications for Comparative Education. *Comparative Education Review*, 34(4), 465–473.

Masemann, Vandra. (1994). Educational Reform: Impact of Indigenous Knowledge. In *Encyclopedia of International Education* (2nd ed.), edited by Torsten Husén and T. Neville Postlewaite. Oxford: Pergamon. 1848–1852.

McGregor, Deborah. (2004). Coming Full Circle: Indigenous Knowledge, Environment and Our Future. *American Indian Quarterly*, 28(3–4), 385–410.

Moeke-Pickering, T., et al. (2006). Keeping Our Fire Alive: Towards Decolonising Research in the Academic Setting. *World Indigenous Nations Higher Education Consortium Journal*, 5. Available at: http://multiworldindia.org/wp-content/uploads/2009/12/Keeping-Our-Fire-Alive.pdf

Nardozi, Angela, Restoule, Jean-Paul, Broad, Kathy, Steele, Nancy, and James, Usha. (2014). Deepening Knowledge to Inspire Action: Including Aboriginal Perspectives in Teaching Practice. *Education*, 19(3), 106–122.

Nekhwevha, Fhulu. (1999). No Matter How Long the Night, the Day Is Sure to Come: Culture and Educational Transformation in Post-Colonial Namibia and Post-Apartheid South Africa. In *Education, Equity, and Transformation*, edited by Crain Soudien and Peter Kallaway. Dordrecht, the Netherlands: Kluwer Academic Publishers. 491–506.

Reyhner, Jon. (2015). *Teaching Indigenous Languages*. Available at: jan.ucc.nau.edu/~jar/TIL.html

Royal Commission on Aboriginal Peoples (RCAP). (1996a). *Report of the Royal Commission on Aboriginal Peoples* (vol. 1). Ottawa: Government of Canada.

Royal Commission on Aboriginal Peoples (RCAP). (1996b). Elders' Perspectives. In *Report of the Royal Commission on Aboriginal Peoples* (vol. 4). Ottawa: Government of Canada. Available at: http://www.collectionscanada.gc.ca/webarchives/20071115053257/http://www.ainc-inac.gc.ca/ch/rcap/sg/sgmm_e.html

SABAR. (2015). *Key terms*. Available at: www.sabar.ca/key-terms/

Simpson, Leanne. (2000). Anishinaabe Ways of Knowing. In *Aboriginal Health, Identity, and Resources*, edited by Jill Oakes, and others. Winnipeg: Aboriginal Issues Press, University of Manitoba. 165–185.

Smith, Theresa. (1995). *The Island of the Anishnaabeg: Thunderers and Water Monsters in the Traditional Ojibwe Life-World*. Toronto: University of Toronto Press.

Statistics Canada. (2013). *The Educational Attainment of Aboriginal Peoples in Canada*. Catalogue no. 99-0120X2011003.

Stiffarm, Lenore A. (1998). *As We See: Aboriginal Pedagogy*. Regina: University of Saskatchewan Press

Swan, Ida. (1998). Modelling: An Aboriginal Approach. In *As We See: Aboriginal Pedagogy*, edited by Lenore A. Stiffarm. Regina: University of Saskatchewan Press. 51–52.

Truth and Reconciliation Committee of Canada. (2015). Available at: www.trc.ca/websites/trcinstitution/index.php?p=905

Wheaton, Cathy. (2000). An Aboriginal Pedagogical Model: Recovering an Aboriginal Pedagogy from the Woodlands Cree. In *Voice of the Drum*, edited by Roger Neil. Brandon, MB: Kingfisher Publications. 151–166.

CHAPTER SEVEN
GENDER AND EDUCATION

Kara Janigan and Vandra Lea Masemann

INTRODUCTION

Wherever we look in educational systems, we find boys and girls, men and women, in unequal numbers. Of all the inequalities that exist within and across different educational systems, gender inequality has attracted perhaps the most sustained concern and attention within the field of comparative education over the last 30 years.

The term *gender* refers to the ways that male and female roles are socially defined in any given society. Gender has two dimensions. In popular usage and in many administrative settings, the term *gender* is used to refer to biological sex (i.e., whether one is male or female). In the field of comparative education and across the social sciences, the term *gender* is used in a more nuanced manner, referring to the specific roles, treatment, and expectations that accompany one's biological sex. This meaning of gender refers not only to power dynamics between men and women but also to the ways concepts of gender are socially constructed and historically changing.

Gender relationships are fundamentally rooted in the historical division of labour between women and men in society. The closer a person is to the physical, emotional, and social care of young children, the more likely that person is to be a woman (mother or grandmother) or girl (sister), and the less likely that person is to earn money or receive other tangible rewards for doing so. Intangibles, such as respect, love, honour, and other forms of emotional rewards, are heavily favoured. Worldwide, mothers carry their children in pregnancy, give birth to them or adopt them, feed them, physically care for them, and provide them with the rudiments of education before they go to school, if they go to school. These universal aspects of human reproduction and child socialization influence the ways education separates boys and girls into categories, often deepening gender inequalities. Since notions of gender are socially constructed, relationships between gender and education differ within different cultural, political, and economic contexts. This process makes issues of gender and education of particular interest to comparative educators.

In this chapter, we use a comparative and international lens in several ways to explore the complex relationships between gender and education. We begin by looking at different ways of conceptualizing gender equality in education and explore four theoretical approaches to the study of gender and education. Then, we delineate how large-scale statistical surveys of educational issues such as access, attainment, and achievement provide comparative educators with valuable insights into the educational circumstances of girls and boys nationally, regionally, and globally. However, we suggest that it is only through qualitative research, such as small-scale ethnographic studies of schooling, that insights can be gained as to the lived reality of gender discrimination in education. To illustrate, we present two case studies set in two very different former colonies: the experiences of secondary school girls in rural Eritrea, in the Horn of Africa, and the historical evolution of gender equality in Canadian schooling (specifically, in Ontario). Both cases highlight persistent aspects of gender inequality and evolving gender dynamics. From these examples, we see that beyond the overarching issues of outright discrimination and gender stereotyping in education, other important dimensions include the intersection of gender inequalities with inequalities perpetuated on the basis of class, race, and ethnicity, in two postcolonial contexts that vary in time and place.

WAYS OF LOOKING AT GENDER EQUALITY

When researchers explore issues of gender and education, the terms *gender parity*, *gender equity*, and *gender equality* are often used. Gender parity refers to the actual number of girls and boys, women and men participating within an institution (sameness), whereas gender equity refers to the treatment of girls and boys, women and men within that institution (fairness).

The term *gender equality* is used in different ways. In its more narrow usage, the term refers to equal numbers—whether referring to girls' and boys' relative levels of participation or to levels of resource allocation

CHAPTER SEVEN: Gender and Education

by sex. When used more broadly, the term refers to equity/fairness. For example, the United Nations Educational, Scientific and Cultural Organization (UNESCO) uses *gender equality* to mean that "all girls and boys, all women and men, have equal opportunity to enjoy education of high quality, achieve at equal levels and enjoy equal benefits from education" (UNESCO, 2015a, p. 9). A broad definition of gender equality was enshrined in the United Nations Universal Declaration of Human Rights in 1948 and, more comprehensively, in the 1979 Convention on the Elimination of All Forms of Discrimination against Women (CEDAW):

> Parties shall take all appropriate measures to eliminate discrimination against women in order to ensure to them equal rights with men in the field of education and in particular to ensure, on a basis of equality of men and women:
> a. The same conditions for career and vocational guidance, for access to studies and for the achievement of diplomas in educational establishments of all categories in rural as well as in urban areas; this equality shall be ensured in pre-school, general, technical, professional and higher technical education, as well as in all types of vocational training;
> b. Access to the same curricula, the same examinations, teaching staff with qualifications of the same standard and school premises and equipment of the same quality;
> c. The elimination of any stereotyped concept of the roles of men and women at all levels and in all forms of education by encouraging coeducation and other types of education which will help to achieve this aim and, in particular, by the revision of textbooks and school programs and the adaptation of teaching methods;
> d. The same opportunities to benefit from scholarships and other study grants;
> e. The same opportunities for access to programmes of continuing education, including adult and functional literacy programmes, particularly those aimed at reducing, at the earliest possible time, any gap in education existing between men and women;
> f. The reduction of female student drop-out rates and the organization of programmes for girls and women who have left school prematurely;

g. The same opportunities to participate actively in sports and physical education;

h. Access to specific educational information to help to ensure the health and well-being of families, including information and advice on family planning.

—Article 10, Convention on the Elimination of All Forms of Discrimination against Women (UNHCHR [United Nations High Commissioner for Human Rights], 1981)

Different notions of gender equality have also developed from competing theoretical and conceptual frames for studying gender. Four different theoretical frames have been particularly influential: equalitarianism; feminism and feminist standpoint theories; conflict theories; and postmodernism. Each approach attempts to explain the existence of gender inequalities and provide possible solutions to reduce or eliminate these inequalities.

The first approach, equalitarianism, is based on the assumption that all human beings are (or should be) essentially equal. Its proponents, including many national and international educational campaigns, frame their educational goal as equal enrolment of girls and boys in schools at every level of schooling and in all areas of study. Equalitarianism is based on a liberal democratic philosophy, in which all citizens have equal rights to social participation and government services, including education at public expense (Lewis & Lockheed, 2006). This approach is ultimately related to theories of social functionalism, which suggest that all parts of society work in harmony or at least in complementarity (Merton, 1957). Proponents of equalitarianism assume that equal enrolment of females and males in educational and other institutions will result in increased female participation and, inevitably, gender equality in terms of educational and life outcomes.

A central aim of many educational systems has been to increase the numbers of girls in classrooms. The enormous amount of statistical information that has been and is being gathered on school enrolment is used to monitor and evaluate efforts to increase female enrolment, among many other things. Sociological survey methods are used to handle large amounts of numerical data. Countries submitting enrolment figures to international organizations, such as UNESCO, are required to gather information in this way, no matter what their prevailing political philosophy.

CHAPTER SEVEN: Gender and Education

Equalitarianism is linked to human capital theory, in which human beings and governments are understood to invest in themselves through education. According to human capital theory, educated mothers will have better-educated sons and daughters, who will in turn be more economically productive (see Chapter Eleven). The writing of Nobel Prize winner Theodore Schultz (1971) on human capital reflects the male-oriented language and embedded assumptions of the 1970s:

> The distinctive part of human capital is that it is a part of man. It is human because it is embodied in man, and it is capital because it is a source of future satisfactions, or of future earnings, or of both. Where men are free agents, human capital is not a negotiable asset in the sense that it can be sold. It can, of course, be acquired not as an asset that is purchased in the market but by means of investing in oneself. (As cited in Unterhalter, 2007, p. 40)

A second approach to understanding gender is feminist standpoint theory, which "rejects the notion of an unmediated truth, maintaining that knowledge is always mediated by the individual's position and identity according to race, class, and gender in a particular socio-political formation and a certain point in time" (Braidotti, Charkiewicz, Hausler, & Wieringa, 1994, p. 44). Feminist standpoint theory is based on people's perceptions of their place in society and their path to progress, rather than those of policy-makers and/or bureaucrats. Feminist theory has its roots in the female suffrage movement in the late 19th century in North America and Europe. Suffragists sought to gain the legal definition of women as persons, rather than as chattels of their husbands. They also fought for women's right to vote in public elections, seeing this as key to gender equality. Later waves of the women's movement in North America have also been based on participants' analysis of their diverse situations as married women; partners in civil unions; lesbians; mothers; caregivers; artists; union workers; racial, linguistic, and other minorities; professionals; elected officials; and many others.

Educational literature based on standpoint theory problematizes women's relationship to curriculum in schools, to modes of educational administration and decision-making, and to the ways people respond to or create knowledge itself (Shepherd, 1993). In contrast to research based on equalitarianism, studies based on feminist standpoint theory require a more anthropological approach. For example, in the Eritrean case that follows, students were asked about factors that helped or hindered them in their efforts to finish secondary school. Anthropological research methods also may be used in pilot studies to ascertain relevant research questions or to clarify sources of cultural bias, before resources and personnel are invested in large-scale data-collecting based on the equalitarian model. Sometimes qualitative research is used to respond to quantitative findings. For example, in response to Foster's (1965) general survey of Ghanaian secondary schools, Masemann (1972) conducted a two-year ethnographic study of the life of a girls' boarding school in Ghana to investigate questions regarding girls' schooling and women's lives.

Conflict theory offers a third approach to gender. Conflict theory may be based either on a neo-Marxist analysis of women's relationship to the means of production—women can be shown to perform some two-thirds of the world's work, including their private and public labour, but receive a much smaller proportion of the world's monetary remuneration for that work—or on an analysis of the nature of patriarchal domination of women by men. The underlying assumption of conflict theory is that the relationship between women and men is not ultimately harmonious but is a constant struggle of two classes of people with contradictory interests (Sarup, 1978). According to this view, merely adjusting the numbers of females and males in schools is not a solution to this power imbalance. Much broader forms of social transformation are needed, and can only be achieved through direct efforts to organize and mobilize women. The relationship between feminism and Marxism is very much unresolved, however. The feminist critique of Marxism, as it existed historically, is that its political movements subjugated women.

A fourth approach to gender is postmodernist. Here, the narratives of women's and men's lives are read as text, and the very categories people use to describe themselves and their lives are up for interpretation. Even the categories of male and female are seen as socially constructed, with their respective boundaries and implications open to challenge. "The central tenet of the post-modern radical epistemology is that the self-legitimation of the One (the male) rests on and is nourished by the exclusion of the Other [the female]" (Braidotti, Charkiewicz, Hausler, & Wieringa, 1994, p. 48). Postmodern approaches question the dichotomous views of human sexual identity and sexuality. In postmodern research, the very tenets of the "scientific canon" are questioned, including the traditional distanced relationship of the so-called objective researcher. Notions of subjectivity and objectivity are reconfigured, and the researcher finds it necessary to identify her or his personal biographical relationship (point of view) to the research question and/or the study's participants. The researcher may formulate research questions collaboratively with the study's participants, rather than without consideration of their views. When conducting the study, the researcher may play a more participatory role, and the traditional line between subjectivity and objectivity may be deemed irrelevant. When analyzing data and writing up the study, such a researcher will attempt to make the participants' "voices" heard and not impose her or his views over those of the participants. Postmodern approaches to gender equity suggest that true social transformation requires more than getting women into positions of power previously occupied by men: "what matters is that women as newcomers into these places be allowed to redefine the structures in such a way as to make them less discriminatory not only for women but ultimately for all people" (ibid., pp. 48–49).

These four approaches help to shape different conceptualizations of gender equity, offering different solutions to its challenges. More recently, approaches to gender inequity have become more complex, by acknowledging context and intersectionality (the linkages among factors of gender, race, and social class) (McCall, 2005). Even within each of these major approaches, there is a confluence of critical perspectives such as world systems theory, dependency theory, queer theory, critical race theory, postcolonial theory, critical pedagogy theory, and social reproduction theory (Klees, 2015).

CURRENT EDUCATIONAL STATISTICS

The present moment in the history of comparative education is greatly influenced by the Education For All movement (see Chapter Eleven), with its emphasis on increasing girls' enrolment in schools. National and regional statistics collected and reported by governments and international organizations such as UNESCO, UNICEF (United Nations Children's Fund), and the World Bank provide comparative educators with data to compare and contrast what is happening in different countries and regions worldwide. Educational data disaggregated by sex enable us to compare the situation for girls and boys, and women and men, broadly and quantitatively. Efforts of this type draw upon equalitarian approaches to gender equity.

Current education statistics help us to compare the educational experiences of girls and boys in various regions. Fifty-nine million primary school-age children are out of school worldwide, meaning those of primary age, typically from 6 to 11 years old, who are not enrolled in school (UNESCO Institute for Statistics, 2016). Thirty-four million of these children live in sub-Saharan Africa, while 11 million live in South and West Asia (ibid.). Thirty-two million (53 percent) of all out-of-school children are girls (ibid.). Thirty-five percent of out-of-school children live in conflict-affected countries. One-half of all out-of-school children live in just 19 countries (ibid.). At least one million children are out of school in India, Indonesia, Kenya, Niger, Nigeria, Pakistan, South Sudan, Sudan, and the United Republic of Tanzania (ibid.). An estimated one-third of all out-of-school children have a disability (UNESCO, 2016). The 61 million out-of-school children includes children who had enrolled in school and later dropped out (20 percent), children who are likely to enrol in the future (39 percent), and children who will never go to school (41 percent) (UNESCO Institute for Statistics, 2016). Of the out-of-school children who are expected to never enrol in school, roughly 17 million (two-thirds) are girls and 8 million are boys (UNESCO, 2016). In sub-Saharan Africa, 9 million girls and 6 million boys will never attend school whereas in Southern Asia roughly 5 million girls and 2 million boys will never attend school (UNESCO Institute for Statistics, 2016). Girls from the poorest families are the most likely of all children to never have attended school (UNESCO, 2015b). Once enrolled, girls are more likely to drop out of school than boys (ibid.).

The number of out-of-school children has decreased from 106 million in 1999 to 61 million in 2014 (ibid.), largely due to the expansion of access to primary education that occurred after many developing countries eliminated primary school fees. This policy change has been of particular benefit to girls in developing countries, as evidenced by the steady reduction in the gender gap favouring boys in terms of primary school enrolment. Global initiatives such as the EFA goals, Millennium Development Goals, and Sustainable Development Goals emphasize gender parity and equity in schools worldwide, including universal primary education.

When examining enrolment figures, we need to consider certain realities that can negatively affect statistical accuracy. First, in some countries, a child can be registered at two or more schools and attend only one of them, or a child can be registered at a school even if she

CHAPTER SEVEN: Gender and Education

or he does not attend classes (UNESCO Institute for Statistics, 2015b). Second, one-half of out-of-school children live in countries affected by conflict, where sufficient or consistent (or sometimes any) statistical data collection is impossible (UNESCO, 2007) (see Chapter Ten).

When examining primary school statistics through a gender lens worldwide, we find that gender parity has been achieved by 69 percent of the 154 countries from which UNESCO was able to collect data in 2012 (UNESCO, 2015b). At the primary level, there were 97 girls in school for every 100 boys; this is the threshold for gender parity (ibid.). Regionally, the greatest gender disparities were found in sub-Saharan Africa and the Arab States, where 92 and 93 girls were enrolled for every 100 boys, respectively (ibid.). At the country level, 16 countries have fewer than 90 girls enrolled in primary school for every 100 boys. Thirteen of these countries are in sub-Saharan Africa (ibid.). The poorest countries have the widest gender gaps, with these gaps commonly favouring boys (King & Winthrop, 2015).

In some countries, such as Gambia, Nepal, and Senegal, gender gaps have been reversed, with a slight advantage in girls' primary enrolment compared to boys' (UNESCO, 2015b). In some cases, such as Senegal, changes in gender parity are as a result of an increase in boys' dropout rates (113 boys dropped out for every 100 girls) (ibid.).

> "There are various barriers to girls' education throughout the world, ranging from supply-side constraints to negative social norms. Some include school fees; strong cultural norms favouring boys' education when a family has limited resources; inadequate sanitation facilities in schools[,] such as lack of private and separate latrines; and negative classroom environments, where girls may face violence, exploitation or corporal punishment. Additionally, schools often lack sufficient numbers of female teachers."
> —UNICEF (2015)

While issues of access to education are important, it is also very important to examine how the girls and boys who do go to school progress through the educational systems. Educational statistics show that once girls are enrolled in primary school they are as likely, or sometimes more likely, than boys to complete school (UNESCO, 2015b). Countries such as Bangladesh, Myanmar, and the United Republic of Tanzania have achieved gender parity in primary enrolment. However, boys are more likely than girls to leave school before completing their primary education (ibid.).

Gender disparities grow wider at the secondary school level in many developing countries. Only slightly more than one-third of all the countries from which UNESCO collected data in 2012 reached gender parity at the secondary level (ibid.). At this level, an equal number of countries had gender disparities favouring girls as had gender disparities favouring boys, revealing regional differences.

Fewer girls than boys are enrolled in secondary school in sub-Saharan Africa and South and West Asia. In 2012, in sub-Saharan Africa, 84 girls were enrolled in secondary school for every 100 boys, whereas in South and West Asia there were 93 girls for every 100 boys (ibid.). In contrast, in countries in Latin America and the Caribbean there were, on average, 93 boys enrolled for every 100 girls (ibid.). However, "the most extreme cases of disparity are still at girls' expense" (ibid.). For example, in 13 countries fewer than 80 girls were enrolled in secondary school for every 100 boys enrolled (ibid.).

Adult literacy statistics reveal similar patterns to those just presented. Women comprise 63 percent (477 million) of the 757 million adults (age 15 and older) worldwide who currently do not have basic literacy skills (UNESCO Institute for Statistics, 2015a). According to UNESCO (2015b), a literate person "can read and write with understanding a simple short statement related to his/her everyday life" (p. 409). Regionally, adult literacy rates are lowest in sub-Saharan Africa (60 percent), South and West Asia (68 percent), and the Arab States (78 percent), all with fewer literate women than men (UNESCO Institute for Statistics, 2015a).

As illustrated in this section, the collection and reporting of sex-disaggregated educational statistics provides critical information enabling comparative educators to better understand certain aspects of educational access and achievement nationally, regionally, and globally. Annual publications, such as UNESCO's *EFA Global Monitoring Report* (renamed *Global Education Monitoring Report* in 2016) and UNICEF's *State of the World's Children*, enable us to compare statistics over time. However, without contextual meaning, these statistics can be easily misinterpreted. For example, some might consider the problem of gender inequality "solved" once a country reaches parity in access at the primary level, despite other issues at play causing gender inequalities within and beyond the education system that need to be addressed. Qualitative research helps to bridge this gap in understanding, by

CHAPTER SEVEN: Gender and Education

providing valuable insights into the often-unheard voices and lived experiences of girls and women. We now examine such a lived reality, in a case study of female students in Eritrea, Africa.

CASE STUDY: EXPERIENCES AND PERCEPTIONS OF SUCCESSFUL FEMALE GRADE 11 STUDENTS IN ERITREA

The findings presented in this section are from a study conducted by Kara Janigan in 2001 on factors that enabled some girls to succeed, against great odds, in graduating from secondary school in rural Eritrea (Janigan, 2002). Eritrea is a small country in the Horn of Africa. After a 30-year liberation struggle, Eritrea gained its independence from Ethiopia in 1991. Tensions that led to war between Eritrea and Ethiopia from 1998 to 2000 persist. Eritrea has some of the lowest social and economic indicators in the world. In 2005, Eritrea's Gross National Income per capita was US$200 (World Bank, 2007).

Educational statistics, appropriate to the time of the research, reveal how few female students were able to move up through the Eritrean educational system. According to UNICEF (1996), "for every 100 girls starting Grade 1, only 40 will graduate from Grade 5" (p. 35). Even fewer graduate from secondary school. According to Eritrean Ministry of Education statistics (1999), in 1998–99, the senior secondary school gross enrolment ratio (GER) for girls was 13.4 percent compared to 21.2 percent for boys. In that same year, a female student was twice as likely as a male student to repeat a grade in secondary school. GER refers to the "total enrolment in a specific level of education, regardless of age, expressed as a percentage of the population in the official age group corresponding to this level of education" (UNESCO, 2015b, p. 408).

While these statistics are telling, qualitative research is needed to provide insight into the reasons why so few girls are able to complete primary and secondary school successfully. In individual interviews in the Eritrean study, female students in Grade 11 shared their perceptions of the obstacles they faced, as well as the factors that enabled them to complete their secondary schooling. By listening to these students and better understanding their lived experiences, we gain valuable insights that can be used by educators to improve educational opportunities not only for Eritrean girls but also for girls facing similar situations in other countries.

The research was conducted at school in Debarwa, a rural village 29 kilometres south of the capital, Asmara. The students interviewed—roughly half of all Grade 11 female students there—ranged in age from 16 to 20, averaging age 19. All were Christian except one Muslim. All were from the dominant ethnic group, Tigrinya. Seventeen students were single, one was married with a child, and one had been engaged since she was 14. Nine students were from Debarwa, while ten came from smaller neighbouring or distant villages. Two students, from a neighbouring village, walked to and from school daily; the others stayed in Debarwa, two with relatives, three in rented rooms, and three in the local convent.

The students came from relatively similar socio-economic backgrounds, with two-thirds from farming families. The heads of the other students' families worked for the government or were local traders. Just under half of the students' mothers (nine) never attended school; six

Figure 7.1: Map of Eritrea and Surrounding Countries

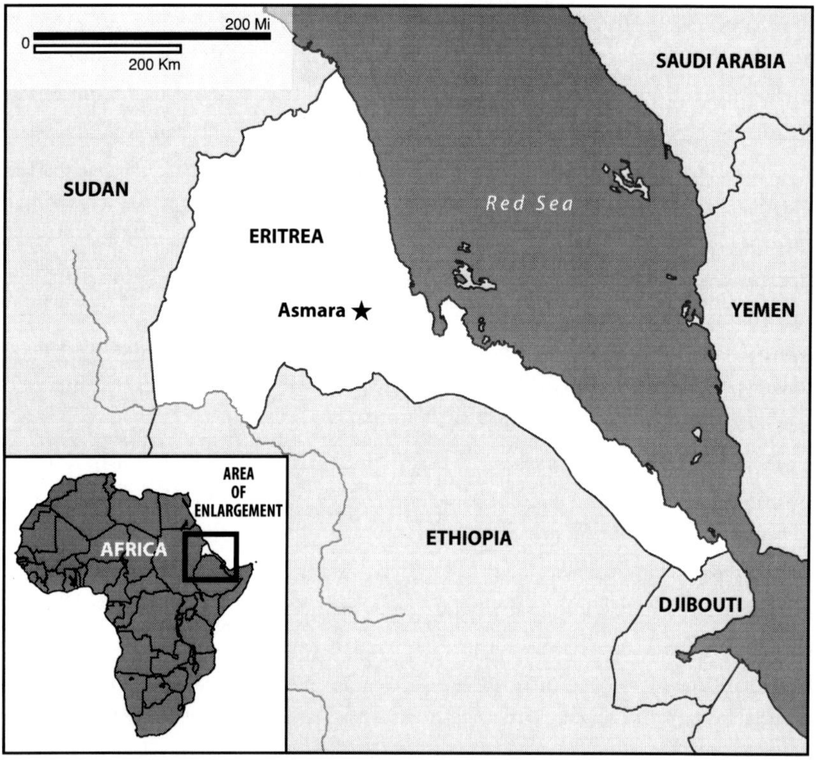

Source: Map created by Scott Wallace

had received some primary education (Grade 3, 4, or 5), while two had completed Grade 6 or 7 (junior secondary education). Of the students' fathers, just over one-quarter (five) had never attended school, while six had completed Grade 3, 4, or 5. Unlike any of these students' mothers, four fathers had received some senior secondary school education; two of these had completed this cycle, one of whom had obtained a postsecondary education degree. Ten students came from a family with five children or fewer, while the largest family had nine children.

This study showed the complexity of the students' lives and decision-making processes, and uncovered supports for and barriers to girls' education. When discussing their experiences, the students identified several issues related to the ways they received support from their mothers and fathers to enable them to be successful students. Economic support, attributed to the father, was predominantly mentioned. Another of the most critical factors mentioned by the students was their fathers' and mothers' attitudes regarding the age at which their daughters should marry. These attitudes are intricately linked to their perceptions of the value of education for their daughters. Also of significance to these daughters were the ways their parents, directly and indirectly, had expressed their belief in their daughters' academic capability and potential.

PARENTS' ECONOMIC SUPPORT FOR GIRLS' EDUCATION

Despite the fact that primary education is compulsory in Eritrea, parents decide whether or not to send their daughter(s) or son(s) to school, and often at what grade their child will stop attending school. For poor families, economic factors related to schooling are often the most important considerations. These factors include the direct costs of schooling (such as fees, uniforms, textbooks, and the number of children in the family) and indirect costs (such as time allocation which otherwise could have been used for labour).

Several students noted how difficult it was for their families to cover school costs. The greatest economic sacrifices appeared to be made by the families of the three students renting a room in Debarwa. Each student came from a village located one and a half to two and a half hours' walk from school. Their parents had chosen to undergo economic sacrifices to enable their daughters to have a better chance at academic success by eliminating the difficulties inherent in walking several kilometres daily to and from school. All three students attributed this decision to their fathers, all of whom were farmers. They spoke of their fathers' anger at having been unable to receive more than just a few years of schooling. Despite the economic struggles, all nineteen students came from families who sent all their children, girls and boys, to school, though not every sibling progressed as far in school as had these students. For example, one student's sister got married at 18 after completing Grade 7.

REJECTION OF EARLY MARRIAGE
Parents play a critical role in the decision-making process regarding the life choices of their children, especially as many marriages are arranged. The age considered suitable for a girl to be married varies among communities in Eritrea. In some areas, marriages are arranged for girls as young as nine (Eritrean Ministry of Education, 1997). Students in this study spoke of female friends and peers who, as one student stated, were "married by force" when they were fourteen or fifteen. Another noted that "fathers that live outside town, they think a girl should be married at eighth grade." It is extremely rare that a married girl or boy continues to attend primary or secondary school: marriage effectively closes the door on a student's further education. Since, on average, males get married at a later age than females in Eritrea, they often have greater educational opportunities.

When speaking of the support they had received, the vast majority of the students noted the importance of their father's and/or mother's rejection of early marriage for their daughter, enabling her to continue her schooling. The married student who participated in this research said she had been encouraged by both her parents and her husband, a teacher, to complete her secondary school education. One-quarter of the students mentioned that the head of their family, which in some cases was their mother, had explicitly rejected early marriage for her or his daughter. Several students spoke of how their father had refused marriage offers by telling the prospective husband that their daughter must finish school before getting married. Other parents urged their daughter to finish school, thus implicitly rejecting marriage at that time. One student, whose mother had been married when she was 11 or 12, recalled her mother saying, "At that time I was a child."

The student who had been engaged since she was 14 was allowed by her family to delay her marriage until she completed Grade 11. This student described how, if she were accepted into a post-secondary institution once she was married, her husband would then decide whether she might continue her studies. Another form of rejecting early marriage can be seen in the families who allowed their daughters to live at the convent; two of the three students living at the convent expressed their plans to become Catholic Sisters.

Four students said their mother and/or father had told them to decide for themselves who they would marry. One student stated, "My mother says, 'Don't marry. Complete your school. After that you will do whatever you like.'" Another said, "[My father] is always encourag[ing] me to finish my school. [He says] after that, by selection [of a husband] yourself, you will do the marriage."

PARENTAL ENCOURAGEMENT

When speaking of the support they received, the students spoke predominantly about their fathers having enabled them to continue their schooling. As one student stated, "My mother help[s] me but not more than my father." This perspective is likely due to the traditional role of the father as the negotiator when marriages are arranged. Also the fathers, as often the main or only wage earners, were seen by the students as suppliers of the funds to cover the direct costs of their schooling. According to the students' comments, their fathers appeared to be the ultimate decision-makers in the family, with the mothers having a voice in the decision-making process, particularly regarding certain issues, such as their children's marriage. While the fathers were most often the first to be mentioned, many of the students later said that their mothers shared the same views and attitudes on these issues of marriage and schooling as their fathers.

Integrally linked to parental attitudes regarding age of marriage are parental attitudes about the value of education and their aspirations for their daughters. Through their words and actions, the research participants' fathers and/or mothers demonstrated that they believed education was of value for their daughter and, most importantly, that she was capable of succeeding academically. Furthermore, one-quarter of the students noted explicitly that their parents were motivated by the belief that, once educated, their daughter would be able to get paid employment. When speaking about other girls in her very small village, one student said, "Parents [think that], for the girls, marriage is useful. They think education is not useful for girls. That is the problem, [the] main problem."

Thus parental educational decisions intersect with economic issues, with parents' perceptions of appropriate age for marriage and of the value of education in relation to aspirations for their child, as well as with the child's academic performance.

ACADEMIC EXCELLENCE

These girls were exceptional students: the majority of them had never repeated a grade, whereas Eritrean Ministry of Education statistics (1999) show that, on average, it took a student up to eight or nine years to obtain five years of primary education. Students may do poorly in school for any number of reasons, including absenteeism, lack of adequate nutrition, and/or inability to complete their homework. Repeating a grade or grades can have a particularly negative effect on the educational opportunities of female students, when considered in relation to marriage norms for girls. A girl who begins Grade 1 at age seven and takes eight years to complete primary school will be fifteen when she finishes. As evidenced by the students' comments, this is considered by many in rural Eritrea to be a suitable age for a girl to marry and to stop going to school. This calculation helps to explain why, although the average age of both female and male students was 19, only 15 percent of Grade 11 female students at the Debarwa Senior Secondary School were 20 years old or older, compared with 37.5 percent of all Grade 11 male students (Janigan, 2002).

STUDENTS' OWN ATTITUDES TO SCHOOLING, HIGHER EDUCATION, AND WORK

All the participating students were adamant about not wanting to marry until they had completed their schooling and had obtained a job, except the student who was already married, and the students living at the convent who, after finishing school, intended to become Sisters. The vast majority of the students stressed a strong connection between education and employment: they believed that only by receiving a high level of education would they have a chance of obtaining paid employment in the future. In a typical statement, one student said, "I'm thinking I do not like to get married at this age but after I finished my school and I get a special job. And especially my husband he have to get a job. After that, it is life." Another student expressed her aspirations by stating, "I hope...to enter university. It's the only thing I hope with my thinking. I always think when I sleep to go to university only. After I get to university...I can work."

CHAPTER SEVEN: Gender and Education

Twelve of the students spoke explicitly of their hope to score high enough in their matriculation exams to gain admittance to either the University of Asmara or the Teacher Training Institute. A few mentioned the desire to become a doctor, a teacher, or an engineer. One student said, "in the future, I want to go to the university and I want to be a doctor. I want to help many people to cure." While a few students were very specific about their aspirations, most were not. They spoke about getting a job, any job. One stated, "If you learn or if you study very well you will get any work, because in the world there is learning only."

As one student said, "I don't want marriage. I finish school. I get a job. Then I [will be] helping country and family." This desire to give back to their family was commonly expressed.

The aspiration to get paid employment was also influenced by the desire of some students to remain in the public sphere. These students linked early marriage and a lack of education to young women's being restricted to staying primarily in their home. As one student put it, "If finishing school, I can get job, I can working. I can get money by myself. If I not finishing school, only my husband is get job, only staying in the house. That's not good."

LACK OF TIME TO STUDY

Another critical factor was parents' allocation of their daughters' time. The availability of time to study is important throughout schooling years, but most critical for Grade 11 students because their matriculation exam results are the sole determinant of admittance to a post-secondary institution. In addition, high marks ensure greater likelihood of a student being admitted into a program of their choosing. Although many students throughout Eritrea write the matriculation exams each year, only a very small percentage are able to contine their studies.

For the majority of the students in this study, a shortage in available time to study was identified as the greatest difficulty they faced. This was attributed particularly to household responsibilities. Students living at home with their families described daily routines that included cooking, cleaning, washing clothes, and fetching water and wood. In Eritrea, these tasks are traditionally considered "girls' work." In a typical comment, one student noted:

> The work in their house [is] totally finished by the girls. Boys [do] not work in the house. That is the problem. For example, my

brother in my house, I am working anything in the house, cooking, but he studies only your books, only his books. You do not help me with the work. [She laughs.] I am all, the work is finished by me.

Many students pointed out that, although girls' work is usually in the house, during harvest time girls also may be needed to help with the family farming. One student explained, "[T]here are some girls who are as clever as boys. But mostly girls are not good [students]...more work is for girls, especially in the harvest time, all boys and girls are working together, but during other free times [when we are] working in the house, boys are playing or studying."

Many students said their mothers supported them by allocating their time, lessening their household responsibilities. For instance: "I am in the school. My mother helping me in the house," or, "[S]he gives me time to read in the house." Several of the students' mothers had told them explicitly to study and not to work at all in the house.

Despite their mothers' urging, several students spoke of their personal sense of obligation to work in their home. Even when these students appeared to have the possibility of extra study time, their sense of familial obligation did not allow them to take advantage of this opportunity: there was a strong sense that it was wrong not to help. When describing the work her family was doing at harvest time, one student said, "Always we are working all the day, because we should help our parents, because we are their children. Even when they say 'don't work,' how can we, as they are working?"

Seven of the 19 students described a daily routine that allowed for study time at night after completing household work, such as, "After helping my mother, I study." Some also mentioned waking up early in the morning, especially during exam times, to study before helping their mothers with housework. A few spoke of waking up in the middle of the night for an hour or two of quiet, uninterrupted study time. One student, who set her alarm clock to wake her at 1 a.m. so that she could study for a couple of hours before going back to sleep, reflected, "I like to study in night. There is no...noise." Similarly, another student described how, at 2 a.m., "That time is very nice, not noisy." She read her notes and books for about an hour and a half before going back to sleep. "If I tired, I sleep, but always I wake up."

One student described her seemingly exceptional circumstances. Being the eldest and only girl in her family, she said her younger brothers

CHAPTER SEVEN: Gender and Education

were required to take on work, such as fetching water and wood, even though this is considered girls' work. This allowed her more time and energy to devote to her studies.

Students living at the convent and those who lived in a neighbouring village also spoke of a shortage of time to study. Students living at the convent mentioned similar household responsibilities, along with the responsibility to attend various church services, leaving them little time to study. A shortage of time to study was most acute for students living in neighbouring villages, who had household responsibilities as well as having to walk long distances (up to two and a half hours each way) to and from school daily.

In contrast to the students living at home or at the convent, the four students living on their own had no difficulty finding time to study. Three of these students were renting a room and one was living on her own, in a traditional house inherited by her family from her grandparents. All four of these students only had to take care of themselves. One of these students spoke of how her life differed greatly from when she had lived at home while attending the junior secondary school in her village. She described how, when living at home, there was "no time to study." When asked what difficulties she faced at the time of the interview, she replied, "no difficulties."

This case study demonstrates many difficulties that female students must overcome in order to graduate from secondary school in an environment such as rural Eritrea. Factors such as distance from school, place of residence, and other domestic obligations played a strong role. Parental encouragement and financial help were important supports to enable girls to complete their education.

The key variable in this study was the fact that most of the families lived in rural areas, where human labour was needed to farm to produce food and to perform domestic duties. In this context, girls' and women's work is necessary for survival. Families need to make a calculation as to what labour they can forfeit in order for their children to remain in school and to eventually obtain employment in the urban sector. These factors are not unique to Africa. They were also salient in the earlier, more rural history of industrial countries within the last century or two, as we will see when we look at the history of gender and education in Canada.

GENDER INEQUALITY IN EDUCATION IN CANADA

The historical evolution of gender equality in Canada (and more specifically in Ontario) illustrates both persistent aspects of gender inequality in education and the fact that gendered practices evolve and change over time, and vary significantly across cultural settings. In this section, we review two histories of education in the 18th to 20th centuries that have shaped gender (in)equality in Canadian education. We also look briefly at issues of gender equality in Canadian schools today.

An important dimension of gender (in)equality in Canada grew out of the colonial education of Canada's First Peoples during the 19th and 20th centuries. In contrast to the dynamics of gender and class in the education of European-descended Canadians, it is here that the intersection of gender, colonialism, and ethnicity has produced and reinforced gender inequality.

Upon the arrival of the Europeans in what is now Canada, the First Nations of that land had already developed a great diversity of gender-specific cultural practices and beliefs, passed down through many generations. These practices differed according to each Indigenous nation; for example, many of the Eastern and West Coast First Nations (e.g., Mohawk, Haida, Kwakiutl) had matriarchal societies, in which women held the decision-making power and rights of ownership. A man could act as chief, but only if chosen by the "clan mothers," and he could similarly be removed from power if the women disagreed with his politics. Plains cultures (e.g., Blackfoot, Nakoda, Cree) tended to be more patriarchal. However, a close sense of gender interdependence was prevalent, as the survival of a society depended intimately on the participation of both men and women in their respective roles (such as hunting and raising children) (Masemann, 1999). Beginning in the early 1600s, formal (colonial) education was introduced to the First Nations through missionary activity. At the end of the 19th century, public authorities in both English and French Canada launched efforts to school their First Nations populations (see Chapter Six). This process had multiple effects on Indigenous concepts of gender roles, values, and practices, as well as on other aspects of First Nations life. Girls and boys were taken away from their parents to live in residential schools, where European gender-role constructs were imposed through lessons of domestic servitude for girls and manual labour for boys (Haig-Brown, 1988). Federal legislation, enacted after 1869, institutionalized gender inequalities

CHAPTER SEVEN: Gender and Education   203

by introducing patriarchal rules for determining Indian status, band membership, and rights to reserve residency ("Women in First Nations politics," 2005). Schooling and the laws meant to "modernize" First Nations communities had the paradoxical impact of eroding important aspects of female authority and leadership that had characterized earlier eras in Canadian Aboriginal societies.

For residents of European origin, gendered educational experiences can be traced back to the voluntary provision of schooling in the early years of British colonialism. European settler children learned, from their parents or other adults in the community, in a mainly agrarian and extractive economy (Prentice, 1977, p. 15). Some children had tutors, learned in church or mission settings, or attended small private schools. However, by 1807, government-funded district grammar schools were established in Upper Canada (Ontario), while local common schools emerged in 1816. These common schools were attended by both girls and boys. The grammar schools (forerunners of high schools) were considered more elite institutions: by the 1850s and 1860s, there was an attempt to curtail the attendance of girls there, since it was thought that attendance at grammar schools "ought to be tied to [boys'] academic ambition and ability rather than to [girls'] social status or wealth" (ibid., p. 143). In 1871, after Canadian Confederation in 1867, Upper Canada became the province of Ontario and passed the School Act, under which each municipality had to provide free common schooling for girls and boys. All non-Aboriginal Ontario children between seven and twelve were required to attend school for at least four months of any school year. The common school was then called the public school, and was funded with public money to achieve public goals (ibid., pp. 16–17).

Although girls were admitted to common and grammar schools, the design of these schools indicated a grave mistrust of the idea of educating girls and boys together.

> Common school architecture and pedagogy as well as Education Office advice throughout the period insisted on separate entrances, separate playgrounds, separate seating and even separate recitations for boys and girls "except in the primary department and there too when practicable." And where most of the students were adolescents, as increasingly seems to have been the case in the grammar schools, segregation seems more important still. (Prentice, 1977, p. 112)

The greatest barrier to higher education for girls was a Council of Public Instruction regulation passed in 1865 that allowed the admission of girls into the grammar schools on passing the appropriate examinations, but excluded them from taking the classical course that was the prerequisite for entry into university or professions. As Prentice explained, it was not envisaged that a "lady" would be pursuing higher education or indeed any form of paid employment. "Significantly, education and power were masculine. The intellectual student grew up into 'masculine maturity and vigour'; the college graduate appeared as '*a man*'; and the purpose of educating boys was to impart to them a 'manly and Christian energy'" (ibid., p. 115). The intersection of social class and gender bias meant that upper-class girls were seen as not needing higher education or employment, because they were going to marry wealthy men and were, in any case, "ill-adapted for the various professions open to young gentlemen, to the rough games of boys, or even to higher education" (ibid., p. 113). On the other hand, girls of the lower classes, who had to work for a living, were seen as "low and vulgar"; it was considered "better that grammar school boys not know that girls could be 'pert and bold'" (ibid., p. 113). "The occupations of employed women who were not ladies, or even of employed ladies, were rarely if ever discussed by leading Upper Canadian school promoters. The education of girls in the public system, if referred to at all, was most frequently discussed in very negative terms" (ibid., pp. 113–114). By 1869, however, the Education Department had to rescind this discriminatory provision in order to qualify for the provincial grant to education (ibid., p. 111).

Notions of gender difference also shaped teacher training institutions (called normal schools) between the 1800s and 1930. Strict rules were enforced concerning respectable behaviour for future teachers. "At the Normal School in Toronto, male and female students were not permitted to address each other in the school, let alone meet outside" (ibid., p. 153). After graduation, the careers of male and female teachers took different trajectories, with male teachers being much better paid and in positions of administration, while female teachers were relegated to less lucrative positions with less chance for promotion and with stringent rules that forced them to give up their jobs if they married. As late as the 1950s, women were expected to retire from teaching upon marriage. Reflecting the entrenched differentiation of male and female teachers, elementary school teachers' unions in Ontario were divided by gender

CHAPTER SEVEN: Gender and Education   205

until 1998, when the Ontario Public School Teachers Federation (for men) and the Federation of Women Teachers' Association of Ontario (for women) amalgamated to create the Elementary Teachers' Federation of Ontario. After secondary schools began to employ women, the Ontario Secondary School Teachers Federation included both genders, although it remained male-dominated until recent years. The history of schooling and the teaching profession in Ontario is inextricably linked to issues of gender, and many of these issues are still salient in the schools and classrooms of today (Coulter, 1996).

How have gender inequality, and efforts to deal with it, changed in Canada over the past century? As in many rich, industrialized countries, girls' and women's access to education has steadily improved in Canada. Today, Canada's federal government reports that women are achieving higher levels of educational attainment than men: they are more likely than men to be high school graduates; they make up the majority of full-time students in most university departments; 25- to 29-year-old women are more likely than men in the same age range to have university degrees. In keeping with equalitarian notions of gender, Status of Women Canada (2003) proudly noted that "this is a reversal of historic trends and indicates that policies aimed at improving women's educational outcomes have achieved a degree of success."

These gains have been hard won. They are the result of active organizing and advocacy among women's organizations, teachers' unions, and academic researchers, especially from the late 1960s to the early 1980s. Educational systems across Canada expanded rapidly in this period, and a second wave of feminist organizing swept across North America. During this period, the focus was not only on expanding female access to higher levels of education, but also on changing the content of the school curriculum: efforts to remove sex-role stereotyping from textbooks and courses of study multiplied rapidly. Since the 1970s, sex-role stereotyping has been repeatedly identified as a key educational issue contributing to woman's inequality in Canada—for instance, in reports by the Royal Commission on the Status of Women in Canada in 1970 and the Royal Commission on Learning in Ontario in 1995 (Coulter, 1996). At the same time, scholarship and training programs to encourage women to enter higher levels of education proliferated. Teachers' unions have also fought to improve the position of women in the higher administrative levels of education and in school board employment-equity policies and practices (ibid.).

Nonetheless, many of the earlier dimensions of gender inequality have persisted in Canadian education, and feminist scholars continue to raise questions about best approaches for achieving greater gender equity in Canadian schools. An enormous gap persists in wages earned between men and women with equal levels of educational attainment; women have only slowly made inroads in male-dominated fields of study. Gender inequality in educational attainment is also heavily apparent in today's First Nations communities.

Many critics have argued that the Canadian "gender equality" approach has focused too much on the attitudes and aspirations of the *individual* girl or woman as the key factor in her opportunity and capacity to compete for the educational and occupational rewards in capitalist society. This approach, based on liberal equalitarian (individualist) assumptions, claims to be "non-sexist": it focuses on adding relevant curricular content about non-traditional jobs to redress the imbalance caused by the omission of material relevant to girls' lives. In reality, this approach holds the male model of achievement as the standard. Its influence is still prevalent today (Coulter, 1996). Feminist scholars in Canada take a more structural conflict approach to issues of gender inequity in Canadian schools: they argue that changes in education need to be matched by broader social transformation. Frustration with equalitarianism has led to the development of "anti-sexist" philosophies and initiatives, which focus on building an awareness of the systemic nature of sexism. For example, workshops and conferences for students may teach a critical approach to schooling and pedagogy, not only in relation to gender but also to race, ethnicity, and social class (ibid.).

CONCLUSION

In this chapter, we illustrated how a comparative and international approach to issues of gender and education can be useful for educators. We reviewed how *gender* and *gender equality* have been conceptualized and used in quantitative and qualitative research, and showed how sex-disaggregated statistics enable us to compare educational access, attainment, and achievement of girls and boys, worldwide. The two cases presented, of girls' experiences in 21st-century rural Eritrea and of the history of gender equality in Ontario, illustrate some social factors that support and impede girls' diverse educational opportunities. By comparing these cases, we can see similarities and differences in beliefs about gender roles and education in different cultural contexts. From a comparative perspective, some would see the question of gender equality in education as "solved" in the wealthier countries, but not in the poorer ones, based on enrolment statistics. Many in the Western world probably believe that opportunities for females and males to enter the educational institutions of their choice are no longer restricted on the basis of gender. However, there is much evidence that widespread gender-based harassment and violence in education still exists (Leach, Dunne, & Salvi, 2014). A comparative and international approach to gender and education helps us, as educators, think more broadly about gendered norms and practices; how these play out within our classrooms, educational systems, and wider society; and how they affect our teaching philosophy and practice.

QUESTIONS FOR REFLECTION AND DISCUSSION
1. Describe your own educational background, and trace your parents' and grandparents' experiences of education in their lifetimes. What role did gender play in the educational experiences of the three generations of your family? (For example, discuss access to education, reasons for attending and/or dropping out, gender roles, academic ambitions or frustrations, and economic considerations.)
2. Compare the educational experiences of the female students in the Eritrean and Canadian examples presented in this chapter. What factors were similar in shaping their education, and what factors were different? How do you think some of those factors operate in your local school system today?
3. Compare this chapter's international perspectives on gender and education with some present-day gender issues that may affect: your life as a teacher, the experiences of your various students (e.g., wealthier and poorer, young and old, culturally diverse), interactions in your classroom, and your future career trajectory.

SUGGESTED AUDIO-VISUAL RESOURCES
Girl Rising, directed by Richard E. Robbins (2013). Available at: girlrising.com/
Directed by Academy Award–nominated director Richard E. Robbins, this documentary on girls' education highlights the experiences of

schooling of nine girls from a wide range of developing country contexts (Sierra Leone, Haiti, Ethiopia, Afghanistan, Peru, Egypt, Nepal, India, and Cambodia) within the global discussions of the topic.

SUGGESTIONS FOR FURTHER READING
Coulter, Rebecca P. (1996). Gender equity and schooling: Linking research and policy. *Canadian Journal of Education, 21*(4), 433–452.
Sperling, Gene, & Winthrop, Rebecca. (2016). *What works in girls' education: Evidence for the world's best investment.* Washington, DC: Brookings Institution Press.
Stromquist, Nelly P. (2013). Women's education in the twenty-first century. In Robert F. Arnove & Carlos Alberto Torres (Eds.), *Comparative education: The dialectic of the global and the local* (4th ed.) (pp. 175–200). Lanham, MD: Rowman & Littlefield.

REFERENCES
Braidotti, Rosi, Charkiewicz, Ewa, Hausler, Sabine, & Wieringa, Saskia. (1994). *Women, the environment and sustainable development: Towards a theoretical synthesis.* London: Zed Books with INSTRAW. p. 44.
Coulter, Rebecca Priegert. (1996). Gender equity and schooling: Linking research and policy. *Canadian Journal of Education, 21*(4), 433–452.
Eritrean Ministry of Education. (1997). *Girls' education in Eritrea.* Asmara, Eritrea: Ministry of Education. p. 65.
Eritrean Ministry of Education. (1999). *Eritrea: Essential education indicators 1998/99.* Asmara, Eritrea: Ministry of Education.
Foster, Philip. (1965). *Education and social change in Ghana.* London: Routledge & Kegan Paul.
Haig-Brown, Celia. (1988). *Resistance and renewal: Surviving the Indian residential school.* Vancouver: Tillacum Library.
Janigan, Kara. (2002). *Defying the odds: A study of female students in grade 11 in Eritrea* (Unpublished master's thesis). Ontario Studies in Education/ University of Toronto.
King, Elizabeth M., & Winthrop, Rebecca. (2015). *Today's challenges for girls' education.* Washington, DC: Brookings.
Klees, Steven. (2015). *Gender and education committee symposium report*, CIES Meeting, Washington DC, March 2015.
Leach, Fiona, Dunne, Máiréad, and Salvi, Francesca. (2014). *School-related gender-based violence: A global review of current issues and approaches in policy, programming and implementation responses to School-Related Gender-Based Violence (SRGBV) for the education sector.* Paris: UNESCO Education Sector.

CHAPTER SEVEN: Gender and Education

Lewis, Maureen, & Lockheed, Marlaine. (2006). *Inexcusable absence: Why 60 million girls still aren't in school and what to do about it.* Baltimore: United Book Press.
McCall, Linda. (2005). The complexity of intersectionality. *Signs, 30*(3), 1771–1800.
Masemann, Vandra. (1972). Motivation and aspirations in a West African girls' secondary school (Unpublished doctoral thesis). University of Toronto.
Masemann, Vandra Lea. (1999). Culture and education. In Robert F. Arnove & Carlos Alberto Torres (Eds.), *Comparative education: The dialectic of the global and the local.* Lanham, MD: Rowman & Littlefield. pp. 115–133.
Merton, Robert King. (1957). *Social theory and social structure.* Toronto, ON: Collier-Macmillan Canada Ltd.
Prentice, Alison. (1977). *The school promoters: Education and social class in mid-nineteenth century Upper Canada.* Toronto: McClelland and Stewart.
Sarup, Madan. (1978). *Marxism and education.* London & Boston: Routledge & Kegan Paul.
Schultz, Theodore W. (1971). *Investment in human capital: The role of education and of research.* New York: The Free Press. pp. 48–49, as cited in Unterhalter, Elaine. (2007). *Gender, schooling and global social justice.* London & New York: Routledge.
Shepherd, Linda Jean. (1993). *Lifting the veil: The feminine face of science.* Boston: Shambhala Publications Inc.
Status of Women Canada. (2003). *Canada and the United Nations General Assembly: Special Session: Beijing +5: Factsheets.* Ottawa: Status of Women.
UNESCO. (2007). *Education for All Global Monitoring Report 2007.* Paris: UNESCO.
UNESCO. (2015a). *Framework for Action Education 2030: Towards inclusive and equitable quality education and lifelong learning for all (DRAFT).* Paris: UNESCO.
UNESCO. (2015b). *Education for All global monitoring report 2015: Education for All 2000–2015.* Paris: UNESCO.
UNESCO. (2016). *Global eduation monitoring report 2016: Education for people and the planet.* Paris: UNESCO.
UNESCO Institute for Statistics. (2015a, September). *Adult and youth literacy: Fact sheet.* No. 32. Montreal: UNESCO Institute for Statistics.
UNESCO Institute for Statistics. (2015b). *Fixing the broken promise of Education for All: Findings from the global initiative on out-of-school children.* Montreal: UNESCO Institute for Statistics.
UNESCO Institute for Statistics. (2016, July). *The challenge of getting all children and youth into school is immense.* Policy paper 27/Fact sheet 37. Montreal: UNESCO Institute for Statistics.
UNHCHR. (1981). *Convention on the elimination of all forms of discrimination against women.* Geneva: UNHCHR. Retrieved from www.unhchr.ch/html/menu3/b/e1cedaw.htm

UNICEF. (1996). *Eritrea: Frontlines of a different struggle.* Namibia: UNICEF.
UNICEF. (2015, July 23). *Girls' education and gender equality.* Retrieved August 30, 2015, from www.unicef.org/education/bege_70640.html
Unterhalter, E. (2007). *Gender, schooling and global social justice.* Abingdon, UK: Routledge.
Women in First Nations politics. (2005, November 22). *CBC.* Retrieved from www.cbc.ca/news2/background/aboriginals/roleofwomen.html
World Bank. (2007). *Eritrea country brief.* Washington, DC: World Bank.

CHAPTER EIGHT

HUMAN RIGHTS EDUCATION FOR SOCIAL CHANGE: EXPERIENCES FROM SOUTH ASIA[1]

Monisha Bajaj

> Human rights education (HRE) has created a lot of change in the school itself. Earlier, there was this big tree behind my school and if you take a stick from that tree, and hit someone on the hand or anywhere, the place will swell up a lot. We used to get beaten black and blue with those sticks before human rights education. Once we got the book and HRE started, our teachers came and told us, "hereafter, we are not going to touch the stick." That really took us aback and we were shocked, in fact. That increased our interest and curiosity about the entire [HRE] book because they became so different.... The teachers became so friendly that we could go and even stand close to them, which we couldn't do earlier because you would not know what kind of mood they are in, and if they were just going to hit you and take it out on you. Now we even go into the staff room and ask any questions we have.... So we really like school now.
> —Madhu, eighth-grade student respondent from India, as cited in Bajaj, 2012, p. 116

Mukul Jaan completed the HRLE [human rights and legal education] course successfully...and became inspired by the idea of upholding human rights and dignity of destitute people. After she became equipped with theoretical human rights and legal awareness from the HRLE course, nothing could stand in her path from applying this intelligence in vital real life situations....On 31 October 2012, Mukul and her fellow [community Rights Implementation Committee] members, Monwara and Afela, demonstrated their ingenuity in preventing a child marriage from

> *taking place in their community. A student of Class 5 named Rizwana was being forced by her family to marry. On hearing this startling news, these [committee] members...reached Rizwana's house. During their visit, Mukul Jaan spoke out about child marriage being a punishable offense. She explained how this crime had dangerous consequences on a girl child in terms of health risks, she spoke of the pitfalls of stopping Rizwana's education, and how [it would] inflict grave psychological trauma on Rizwana....In the end, this collaborative attempt proved to be successful. [Rizwana] has resumed her formal education due to her family's newly acquired social awareness against this injustice.*
> —*Story from BRAC's HRLE program, Bangladesh, as cited in BRAC, 2013, pp. 58–59*

INTRODUCTION

Since the Second World War, increasing commitment to global human rights frameworks has advanced the vision of respect for the basic rights and dignity of all people. Correspondingly, human rights have greatly influenced the field of education in a variety of areas, including in discussions of access, equity, quality, curriculum, pedagogy, and accountability. Human rights have been differentially incorporated in educational policy discussions, textbook revisions, teacher education, and the everyday life of schools. This chapter addresses the question, "How are educators and community-based organizations in South Asia utilizing human rights education in seeking to transform the unequal social conditions faced by marginalized groups?"

The South Asian region, comprised of the diverse nations of Afghanistan, Bangladesh, Bhutan, India, Maldives, Nepal, Pakistan, and Sri Lanka, is home to one-fifth of the world's population. Educational realities differ widely across the region: for example, 65 percent of girls in Bangladesh are married before age 18 (HRW, 2015), while, at the same time, each year approximately two hundred thousand students from affluent Indian families pursue higher education in North America, Europe, and Australia (Clark, 2013). Widening social inequalities within and across nations further distinguish the educational experiences of youth throughout the region (World Bank, 2014), including their ability to enjoy the rights enshrined in international documents.

There is a long history of commitment to human rights in the South Asian region, although gaps exist between human rights policies and

CHAPTER EIGHT: Human Rights Education for Social Change   213

actual practices on the ground. Anti-colonial movements espoused (at that time, radical) goals of equality, non-discrimination, and dignity—pillars of international human rights. The adoption in 1948 of the United Nations (UN) Universal Declaration of Human Rights (UDHR), arguably the cornerstone document of the global rights framework, occurred around the same time as the independence of many South Asian nations from British rule (Bajaj & Kidwai, 2016). Indeed, three of South Asia's eight nations (Afghanistan, India, and Pakistan) were among the original 48 votes in favour of the UDHR, and were among the few independent nations at that time in the global South.

From 1948 to the present day, there has been a rise in attention to education as a core component of human development, dignity, and basic rights. Article 26 of the Universal Declaration of Human Rights guarantees a right to education, and one that "strengthens respect for human rights and fundamental freedoms." Children's right to education was further codified through the Education for All conferences (1990 and 2000), the Millennium and Sustainable Development Goals (2000 and 2015, respectively), and other global commitments, as is further discussed by Mundy and Read in Chapter Eleven of this book. Among other evidence of global support for education, in 2014, two advocates for the right to education—both from South Asia—were awarded the Nobel Peace Prize: Malala Yousafzai, a Pakistani adolescent shot for advocating for girls' right to go to school, and Indian activist Kailash Satyarthi, who has long campaigned for an end to child labour and is the co-founder of the Global Campaign for Education.

Less than a century ago, education was seen in many places as a privilege rather than a right. For instance, at India and Pakistan's independence in 1947, a mere 16 percent of the populace was literate (Rana & Sugden, 2013). The 2014 Nobel Peace Prize signalled the ongoing evolution within global consciousness that the right to education is an aspect of comprehensive and sustainable peace, and its denial a grave social injustice. This chapter focuses on a less-discussed component of the international human rights framework: the right to an education that fosters and promotes human rights and that prepares active participants for democratic life; in other words, "human rights education."

This chapter explores how human rights education (HRE) as a global educational movement is taken up locally by educators, activists, and non-governmental organizations (NGOs) in South Asia. Human rights education assumes various forms, depending on context, ideologies, and location (Bajaj, 2012; Tibbitts, 2002; Tsolakis, 2013). Transformative human rights education—rooted in critical analyses of power and social inequalities—has been developed by non-state actors more than by government school systems, specifically by NGOs, social movements, and community-based educators. As a result, this chapter zooms in on two examples of transformative human rights education in the South Asian context that seek—in different locally contextualized ways—to interrogate power asymmetries and offer members of marginalized groups the opportunity to envision and demand equal rights. The first example is a school-based program designed by a human rights organization (People's Watch) that trains teachers to offer a weekly human rights course in Grades 6 through 8 across India. The second example is a human rights education and legal empowerment program for poor women in Bangladesh, offered by the world's largest non-governmental organization, BRAC (formerly the Bangladesh Rural Advancement Committee). The two cases presented in this chapter differ in approach, population, and context, but—as will be seen—both programs rely on well-trained teachers/facilitators who use innovative curriculum, effective participatory pedagogies, and strong relationships with learners to assist them in recognizing and confronting the injustices that surround their lives.

Human rights education has been discussed by some international and comparative education scholars as a product of growing educational convergence (Ramirez et al., 2007; Meyer et al., 2010; Suarez, 2007): a process through which systems look "strikingly similar" when looking downward from North to South (as cited in Krücken & Drori, 2010, p. 125). This, indeed, proves true at the level of global discourse, national policies, and textbook revisions (Meyer et al., 2010). Research on HRE in South Asia and elsewhere, however, has shown that examining grassroots human rights education closely offers a more dynamic glimpse into how such global discourses and policies are strategically utilized and galvanized in securing support and legitimacy for radical educational projects that seek to empower marginalized communities (Bajaj, 2012).

Thus, this chapter provides a window into the complex ways in which NGOs localize human rights, based on the population and context, to cultivate a critical consciousness (Freire, 1970) among learners and to equip them with a globally recognizable language—that of human rights. While convergence (world culture) theorists bring distinct, overlapping

CHAPTER EIGHT: Human Rights Education for Social Change 215

realities into focus through the singular gaze of a telescope, my approach starts with a kaleidoscopic examination of local activists and educators that brings into view how constellations of actors in diverse settings connect human rights education to locally meaningful traditions of critical education to enhance the pursuit of equity and justice.

HUMAN RIGHTS EDUCATION

While human rights education had mention in the 1948 Universal Declaration of Human Rights, there was little corresponding global action by governments or NGOs to address and encourage HRE. In 1993, soon after the end of the Cold War, the UN held a World Conference on Human Rights in Vienna. The conference marked a turning point for HRE, since it created the post of the United Nations High Commissioner for Human Rights, an office charged with education and public information related to human rights (Bajaj, 2014). Further, the Vienna Conference Declaration and Program of Action (adopted by consensus by the representatives of the 171 countries present) exhorted "all States and institutions to include human rights, humanitarian law, democracy and rule of law as subjects in the curricula of all learning institutions in formal and non-formal settings" (United Nations, 2013, para 1).

Given growing momentum for realizing the vision of the Vienna Conference, the United Nations declared 1995 to 2004 the UN Decade for Human Rights Education, resulting in various publications and initiatives, and the opportunity for nation-states to develop plans of action to implement HRE. In 2005, the UN Office of the High Commissioner for Human Rights (OHCHR) in Geneva created the (still ongoing) World Programme for Human Rights Education to "promote a common understanding of basic principles and methodologies of human rights education, to provide a concrete framework for action and to strengthen partnerships and cooperation from the international level down to the grass roots" (OHCHR, n.d.). International advocacy also led to the adoption of the 2011 Declaration on Human Rights Education and Training by the UN General Assembly. The declaration highlights the need for HRE at all educational levels—primary, secondary, vocational, tertiary—as well as in the professional training of teachers, law enforcement, state officials, et cetera.

Over the past three decades, various definitions have emerged for what human rights education is; most HRE scholars, however, would argue that words in a policy document or textbook revisions, absent of any other components, are a superficial form of HRE (Bajaj, 2012; Tibbitts, 2017). While there are many versions of HRE, there is general agreement about certain core pieces. First, most scholars and practitioners agree that HRE should include both *content* and *processes* related to human rights (Flowers, 2003; Tibbitts, 2002). Further, scholars often include three components for a program or initiative to qualify as HRE: (1) cognitive components and content related to human rights and struggles to achieve them; (2) affective dimensions that foster attitudes and behaviours in line with respect for rights and dignity; and (3) action-oriented strategies to have learners connect the classroom with the community (Flowers, 2003; Tibbitts, 2005).

Scholars have increasingly advocated for "critical" (Keet, 2007) and "transformative" (Bajaj, 2011, 2012; Bajaj et al., 2016; Tibbitts, 2005) forms of human rights education that take into consideration the distinct social locations and forms of marginalization faced by different groups in order for educational strategies to be more relevant and effective. The two cases presented in this chapter highlight two examples of transformative HRE from South Asia for marginalized groups whose rights have been trampled and denied, often for centuries, with long-standing forms of caste, ethnic, and gender exclusion.

TRANSFORMATIVE HUMAN RIGHTS EDUCATION IN SOUTH ASIA

> *Education either functions as an instrument which is used to facilitate integration of the younger generation into the logic of the present system and bring about conformity or it becomes the practice of freedom, the means by which men and women deal critically and creatively with reality and discover how to participate in the transformation of their world.*
> —Paulo Freire, 1970, p. 34

In South Asian educational systems, set up under British colonial rule, rote learning and what educational philosopher Paulo Freire (1970) referred to as "banking education" dominate; in this approach, children are seen as (passive) empty vessels to be filled with content by authoritarian teachers. Formal education was set up in colonial India (which then included the majority of the countries that now make up the South Asian subcontinent) to produce small cadres of "Anglicized

CHAPTER EIGHT: Human Rights Education for Social Change 217

Indians...[meaning] a class of persons Indian in blood and colour, but English in tastes, in opinions, in morals and in intellect" (Lord Macaulay, as cited in Evans, 2002, p. 271), as intermediaries between the colonialists and the masses. Thus, Western education in South Asia was designed to reach a small proportion of the population: mostly young men of the (small) middle class. Unsurprisingly, in 1900, less than 6 percent of the population of colonial India and less than 1 percent of women and girls were literate (Chaudhary, 2007). Despite independence from the British and the creation of various new nation-states in the mid-1900s, certain legacies lingered: the higher status afforded to English education, the predominance of rote learning, and a distinction between elite and mass education. In contrast, non-formal and alternative education has been conceived of as a site for resistance to unequal social conditions in South Asia. For example, independence leader Mahatma Gandhi's vision for education was to reorient education toward village life and the realities of the rural majority in order to "spearhead a silent revolution" (as cited in Bajaj, 2010, p. 47).

Paulo Freire's theories of individual and collective empowerment through education for critical consciousness have travelled far and wide from South America (Freire was Brazilian and wrote *Pedagogy of the Oppressed* while in exile in Chile), to find resonance on the South Asian subcontinent. In South Asia, where Freire's work has been translated into multiple regional languages, progressive educators have been engaged with ideas of education for critical consciousness for many decades, preceding the recent rise of human rights education. For example, the adult literacy campaign in the Indian state of Kerala in the 1980s and 1990s, resulting in the state's near-universal literacy rates for men and women—far exceeding national levels—drew from Paulo Freire's ideas about literacy and popular education (Mayfield, 2012). Both the Indian and Bangladeshi NGOs profiled in this chapter were also heavily influenced by Paulo Freire's writings.

Human rights education scholars and practitioners globally have drawn on Paulo Freire's seminal writings (though he was not a human rights education scholar per se) to inform *how* the field approaches the teaching and learning of material related to human rights. By raising the "critical human rights consciousness" of learners (Meintjes, 1997, p. 78) with analyses of social inequalities and historical forms of oppression, South Asian educators, such as those working for organizations like People's Watch and BRAC (both profiled in this chapter), seek to offer learners the ability to transform their own realities. It is important to note the specific influence Freire had on the founders of each of the organizations discussed in this chapter, though their specific approaches will be discussed in the following section. One of the founders of People's Watch (India), who oversaw the writing of the human rights education textbooks, taught (and helped translate into Tamil) Paulo Freire's works for decades. Further, posters with Freire's image and quotes written in local languages hang in the thousands of schools where the organization operates its HRE program.

Many of Freire's books can also be found in BRAC's offices in Dhaka, Bangladesh, and the founders of the organization have noted the influence of his theory on their establishment of the organization. According to one of BRAC's early staff members, "In 1973, [BRAC's founder, Fazle Hasan] Abed started reading Freire. His reading was quite revolutionary, and he made me read *Wretched of the Earth* and Ivan Illich. And then we all got hooked on Freire, and we thought about how to use Freire's methods in our literacy work" (as cited in Smillie, 2009, p. 154). Fazle Hasan Abed has further stated that poverty is a result of powerlessness and that BRAC's work is to enable poor people to "organise themselves so that they may change their lives" (BRAC, 2014). Freire's ideas and theories undergird these transformative human rights education efforts in South Asia and beyond as BRAC has expanded globally (Bajaj, 2012; Tsolakis, 2013; Flowers, 2003).

The two cases of human rights education initiatives presented in this chapter have been selected for a variety of reasons in two domains: national context and organizational strategies. In terms of the national contexts of their work, the two nations occupy different sizes and locations in South Asia: India is the largest regional economy (yet still classified as a lower-middle-income country) with a population of 1.2 billion, and an average literacy rate of 74 percent; Bangladesh is a low-income nation plagued by natural disasters, with 150 million residents and an average literacy rate of 58 percent (UNICEF, 2013; World Bank, 2015). Further, while both countries have constitutional guarantees for the right to primary education, there is little in government policy requiring human rights education per the vision of the UDHR and subsequent international agreements.

In terms of organizational strategies and the scope of their operations, People's Watch and BRAC offer points of similarity and difference that make putting their human rights education efforts in conversation

CHAPTER EIGHT: Human Rights Education for Social Change 219

fruitful. First, both People's Watch (India) and BRAC (Bangladesh) have a national scope of operations that transcends one particular region. Second, both have been the subject of scholarly attention to examine their approaches (Bajaj, 2012; Smillie, 2009). Third, each case offers a different glimpse into transformative human rights education—People's Watch has a three-year-long course in human rights for middle school–level children, developed by an NGO that works in formal government-run schools; BRAC has a non-formal education program that utilizes "barefoot lawyers" to educate women through clear and accessible curriculum on their rights and how to access justice. Lastly, while there are over two million non-governmental organizations in South Asia, and countless programs and movements using education to raise awareness about and transform social conditions, the two presented here explicitly call what they do "human rights education." While this nomenclature is certainly not a measure of success or legitimacy, these two organizations were chosen because they provide insights into how those deliberately using the framework of human rights education are localizing it, making it contextually relevant, and reimagining its purpose and function in distinct locales.

FROM STICKS TO STUDENTS' RIGHTS: SCHOOL-BASED HRE IN INDIA

After attending the HRE training, I could understand the students from their point of view. For example, when I go to class, if I see a boy sleeping on the desk, I used to have the tendency to beat him or be harsh on him, without knowing if he may be hungry, without knowing anything about his family background. Maybe he is sleeping because he is having some problems in the family; maybe his father was drunk at night and beating his mother. So after attending this training, I have come to ask the children their problems instead of beating them; I try to understand the children, be friendly, and respect them. The students have started moving more freely and talking to me more also, so the distance [between us] is much reduced. If anything happens in their homes, if they have any family problems, they are sharing them with us. Even the District Education Officer has noticed these changes...because a lot of teachers have attended the training in human rights.
—*HRE teacher focus group, as cited in Bajaj, 2012, p. 123*

People's Watch is a human rights organization that was founded in 1995 in the southern Indian state of Tamil Nadu. The organization has pioneered HRE in India nationwide through its Institute for Human Rights Education (IHRE), which has complemented the organization's legal and advocacy work. Starting as an experiment in a handful of schools, HRE now operates in four thousand schools in more than 18 states of India (Bajaj, 2012). The organization has developed textbooks, delivered trainings for teachers, and expanded their human rights work (initially primarily on caste discrimination and police abuse) into a broad-based educational program. As connections were made with the United Nations Decade for Human Rights Education (1995–2004), IHRE was able to gain support by aligning with international efforts to promote human rights education and translating these interests into funding for their work.

Table 8.1: Content and Pedagogy of the IHRE Textbooks

Topics *(In order of frequency, from highest to lowest)*	Methods *(In order of frequency, from highest to lowest)*
1. Poverty/underdevelopment/class inequalities	1. Reflective/participatory in-class exercise
2. Gender discrimination/need for equal treatment	2. Illustrated dialogue or story
3. Child labour/children's rights	3. Community interviews and/or investigation and research
4. Caste discrimination/untouchability/need for equality	4. Small group work and discussion
5. Social movements/examples of leaders and activists	5. Creative artistic expression (drawing, poetry, etc.)
6. Religious intolerance/need for harmony and pluralism	6. Class presentation
7. Rights of Indigenous/Adivasi communities	7. Inquiry questions & essay writing
8. Rights of the disabled and mentally ill	8. Role play, dramatization, song-writing
9. Democracy	9. Letter writing to officials
10. Environmental rights	10. School or community campaign

Source: Bajaj, 2012, p. 79. Used by permission of Bloomsbury Publishing Inc.

CHAPTER EIGHT: Human Rights Education for Social Change   221

Cooperation and collaboration with government officials has also been essential since most of the four thousand schools IHRE operates in are government-run (Bajaj, 2012). Textbooks have been developed in multiple regional languages, and an estimated five hundred thousand Indian students have participated thus far in a three-year course in human rights. Year one introduces students to human rights; year two focuses on children's rights; and year three addresses discrimination and inequality. The data from this chapter come from 13 months of data collection in India (2009–10) as well as follow-up interviews and communications with the organization (for more information on the larger study, see Bajaj, 2012).

IHRE's model aims to introduce students in primarily government schools and those from marginalized communities (those from the lowest castes, Indigenous groups, and others) to human rights concepts and principles. The course is taught by teachers from these schools who attend trainings to offer two human rights classes per week for three school years (Grades 6, 7, and 8). Teachers either volunteer to be their school's representative for this program or are assigned by their headmasters; in practice, those attending the trainings tended to be teachers with a pre-existing interest in the subject or younger teachers who were "volunteered" by their administrators.[2] Both men and women teachers were active human rights teachers in the IHRE program.

Officials from the Institute of Human Rights Education maintained contact with teachers over the phone and through in-person visits; there were also refresher trainings and opportunities for human rights educators to get together throughout the school year, sponsored by the organization. The textbooks developed by IHRE and trainings included concepts related to general human rights guarantees; corporal punishment and other forms of violence; children's rights; and issues of discrimination based on caste, gender, religion, ability, skin colour, and ethnicity, among others.

After the HRE lessons began, many students reported (as in the quote at the beginning of this section) that teachers were more attentive to students' rights, particularly with regard to the illegal but commonly utilized practice of corporal punishment. While students discussed attempting to intervene in social injustices they found in their communities (as I have discussed extensively elsewhere; see Bajaj, 2012), what are equally interesting are the responses that teachers had to learning about and teaching human rights.

While teachers are often discussed in human rights education literature as messengers who simply transmit human rights instruction, IHRE focuses on teachers as correspondingly important *agents* of human rights education who can go through transformative processes as well as take action, rooted in knowledge and skills, in their own lives as well as those of students and community members. Many human rights abuses that take place in Indian government schools (which primarily serve relatively poor children)—including gender discrimination, caste discrimination, and corporal punishment—are often perpetuated by teachers or allowed to occur among students without any intervention. For example, during my research, respondents discussed multiple cases of teachers who verbally and physically abused students based on their caste backgrounds or poor academic performance, and mentioned several examples of sexual abuse. Given teachers' relatively respected status in rural areas as part of a minority of literate professionals, their potential transformation through human rights education to become allies and advocates of human rights can result in effective interventions on behalf of victims, whether the victims are their students or not (Bajaj, 2012).

HRE created an opportunity for teachers to exert their agency in a large bureaucracy that often dehumanized both educators and students. Most teachers (nearly all of the 118 interviewed in this study) sent their children to private, English-medium schools that their middle-class salaries permitted; many reported that prior to HRE, they regarded the low-caste, Indigenous, and poor students that comprised their government school classrooms as "other people's children," to borrow US educational scholar Lisa Delpit's term for the mismatch between students and teachers (Delpit, 2006). A core part of the training on the HRE textbooks developed by People's Watch included participatory activities for students to identify and analyze human rights and social inequalities in their own communities. When teachers learned more about their students, and as students shared more with teachers, perhaps with less fear of getting beaten, it allowed for close relationships to form. One teacher, Mr. Kumar, discussed buying prizes with his own money for students to speak publicly and sing songs about human rights at a local festival. He also talked about how the HRE program helped foster relationships in his classroom so that he began to see his students like his own son who attended a nearby private school.

As teachers and students formed close-knit and reciprocal bonds, many came to see challenges in the community as a collective project

CHAPTER EIGHT: Human Rights Education for Social Change   223

for them to address. Numerous teachers I interviewed discussed taking some form of action to address problems they saw in their lives, their communities, or those of the children and families. These examples ranged from trying to convince family members not to pull children out of school to work or to marry off girls at a young age, to reporting abuse they learned about in schools and homes. Mr. Gopal, a teacher from the state of Tamil Nadu, related the following incident, emblematic of several other instances wherein teachers had reported an abuse:

> In the first year of human rights education, my student, Kuruvamma, overheard from a neighbour that if their child was born a girl, they would kill it since they already had three female children. The child was born a girl and what they planned to do was make the baby lie down on the ground without...any bed sheets, and put the pedestal fan on high speed in front of her. The baby...would not be able to breathe and then she would automatically die. Kuruvamma told me and together we gave a complaint in the police station. The family got scared and didn't kill the baby. Now that girl is even studying in first standard. My student Kuruvamma is now in high school. (as cited in Bajaj, 2012, p. 127)

In many communities where the HRE program was offered, female infanticide was a common practice, although it is illegal in India. It is estimated that three million girls have gone missing in India through sex-selective abortions (after a fetus is determined to be a girl) and infanticide, in poor and rich communities alike ("The Hindu," 2012). Students and teachers reported encountering evidence of infanticide, including young students happening upon dead (female) babies or overhearing stories such as the one above.

Of course, the introduction of HRE overlays existing socio-economic realities, like those that drive practices like infanticide. Even amidst adverse material conditions, students identifying abuses—and having teachers willing to help report or intervene—were noted by both students and teachers as critical components of making human rights come alive. A key by-product of the transformative education offered by IHRE is that it gave meaning to the educational process by deeply engaging the educators (Bajaj, 2012). Mrs. Mohanta, a retired teacher from Orissa who taught human rights education for many years, continued going to the trainings and visiting her former school to help with classes even after her retirement because of the satisfaction she derived from being involved.

While the IHRE program in India has been operating for two decades, more than 30 years ago, a Bangladeshi NGO began offering non-formal education through trainers, also known as "barefoot lawyers," seeking to empower poor women who were unable to access justice.

"BAREFOOT LAWYERS" AS HUMAN RIGHTS EDUCATORS IN BANGLADESH

BRAC's human rights and legal aid services programme is dedicated to protecting and promoting human rights of the poor and marginalized through legal empowerment. The blend of legal literacy initiatives with comprehensive legal aid services throughout the country helps spread awareness needed to mobilize communities to raise their voices against injustices, discrimination and exploitation—whether at the individual or collective level.... Our "Barefoot Lawyers" impart legal literacy and spur sustainable social change by raising awareness and informing people of their rights. They operate on a 3P model of "Prevent-Protest-Protect" and are usually the initial contact points in their communities when human rights violations occur.
—BRAC, n.d.

BRAC is the largest NGO focused on development in the world. It emerged just after Bangladesh's war for independence from Pakistan in 1972. The organization was founded by Fazle Hasan Abed as a relief organization, but now, in its fifth decade of operation, BRAC has programs in education, health, economic development, and women's empowerment across Bangladesh and internationally in various countries such as Afghanistan, South Sudan, the Philippines, and Uganda. In order to mitigate reliance on donor funding, BRAC—unlike most NGOs—also operates various income-generating enterprises such as a dairy business, handicraft stores, and a university (Smillie, 2009). BRAC is referred to as the largest NGO because it has a staff of more than a hundred thousand people (mostly women) and serves over a hundred million people. Its non-formal education program has received commendation for its tremendous efficacy in providing culturally relevant and locally tailored education for marginalized children who lack access to government schools due to poverty (see also Chapter Three in this

CHAPTER EIGHT: Human Rights Education for Social Change   225

volume, by Farrell, Manion, and Rincón-Gallardo); over three million children have been enrolled, and the program boasts an extremely low dropout rate as compared to government education (Smillie, 2009). While children are one recipient of BRAC's educational efforts, youth and women also receive education about their rights through the women's empowerment program.

BRAC's Human Rights and Legal Services (HRLS) program,[3] started in 1985, has multiple components, of which human rights education is just one. In the school-based HRE example from India (above), students were taught about human rights, and action often ensued of their own accord or with teachers' help. In BRAC's program, action and redress for violations are central to the human rights and legal services program. According to BRAC, HRLS (1) provides "legal and human rights education and awareness to rural poor[,] in particular women, and to local community leaders"; (2) provides "legal services, in particular alternative dispute resolution and court oriented legal aid"; and (3) "creates and activates social catalysts drawn from among the village elite to respond to human rights violations" (Islam et al., 2012, p. 6). Core to BRAC's approach is human rights education as the foundation for the legal, advocacy, and community mobilization approaches that build on top of this awareness for marginalized women.

Through the HRLS program, non-formal educators provide adolescent girls and women with a foundational 14-day human rights and legal education (HRLE) course as the first step in the program. The HRLE course draws from the approaches in BRAC's other educational initiatives as well as the organization's original grounding in participatory approaches to development. For example, a report profiling the HRLS program noted that methodological approaches included "workshops, committees, popular theater shows, and courtyard sessions to bring local leaders together and effectively engage the entire community in preventing and addressing human rights violations" (Kolisetty, 2014, p. 41). A BRAC senior staff member noted that the pedagogical approach and curriculum are tailored to the realities of poor rural women in Bangladesh: "This might be the only time we have access to this household or to this woman, so we would like to have a sustainable impact on this person's life. One of the ways I believe we do that is by making the methodologies interactive in such a way that it becomes a personal journey rather than just a class" (interview, July 12, 2015). As a result, the HRLE course starts with situating learners in an analysis of their own lives the first few days, and further offers basic knowledge about the legal system and human rights more broadly.

The HRLE course—taught by *shebikas*, or "barefoot lawyers"—emphasizes laws related to common problems encountered by women, namely: dowry, mistreatment and abuse from spouses, child marriage, divorce, and right to land and inheritance, among other topics (see Table 8.2). Since there are different laws in Bangladesh for individuals of different religions, these trainings also elucidate distinct rules and norms under the customary laws that apply to particular women related to the issues they face.

All of the training materials for the courses are pictorial given that many rural women are illiterate (women's literacy in Bangladesh is 55 percent, and largely skewed toward urban women) (World Bank, 2015). Many of the materials interrogate common gender stereotypes, utilizing drawings of real-life situations as a starting point (akin to Paulo Freire's approach of using a generative theme to spark discussion of broader injustices) (Freire, 1970).

Table 8.2: Content of HRLE 14-Day Course

Day	Topics
1	Myself and my community
2	Family and social analysis
3	Social discrimination and gender
4	Abuse
5	Basic rights and entitlements
6	International rights mechanisms (CEDAW, UNCRC, CAT, etc.)
7	Marriage
8	Dowry
9	Divorce, separation, guardianship and custody, post-nuptial rights
10	Police duties and jurisdiction
11	Hindu, Muslim, and Christian women's right to land
12	Opportunities for women to own and control land
13	Land mutation, tax, and state-owned land
14	Closing

Sources: BRAC, 2013; and from interview with a BRAC staff member

CHAPTER EIGHT: Human Rights Education for Social Change   227

After each 14-day course, the three most vocal and participatory women are selected to participate in the training to become *shebikas*, or "barefoot lawyers," who help women access justice and who also facilitate future trainings and courses. Ongoing training is provided both to participants in the 14-day courses and to trainers, who undergo longer trainings and "refreshers" for professional development. BRAC notes, "The refreshers are an effective way of standardizing the quality of the shebikas' performance and of keeping them updated on current laws" (BRAC, 2013, p. 55).

The HRLE course, as embedded as one piece of the larger HRLS program that includes education, legal aid services, and community mobilization, offers a holistic approach to addressing the challenges faced by poor rural women in Bangladesh. Many of them, unaware of their rights, are subject to abuses by husbands, and by corrupt officials who may accept bribes rather than enforce laws that are meant to protect poor women. In reflecting on the overall vision of the HRLS program, a senior staff member of BRAC noted:

> We try to bring about a level of conscientization [related to] the inter-linkages between oneself and one's community and then the larger political structure. So instead of going into the law and the rights first, we start with a bit of a social analysis; understanding and asking questions and getting towards knowing one's own self and one's environment....What is very important is to understand the *agency* of the person. Most people are not aware of their own agency in their own lives. They feel like there's a predestined karma, like I was born to be poor or I was meant to die poor. But if one can understand, *who am I* really, apart from being the wife of so-and-so, or the mother of so-and-so, [one can ask oneself,] "What do I want to do with my day, if not my life?" (interview, July 12, 2015)

Agency and empowerment for poor rural women is at the core of the human rights and legal education courses offered by BRAC. The entire design of the courses vis-à-vis structure, content, and pedagogy, coupled with the mechanisms to allow women to seek justice, offers a way to combat marginalization in a highly stratified social context. Transformative human rights education in this case includes knowledge of oneself and one's role in society in order to counter internalized forms of oppression that limit poor women from even believing they have rights; once this social analysis is sparked, information about domestic and international rights that apply to all and about one's own inherent dignity can serve as meaningful for the women in BRAC's programs.

DISCUSSION AND CONCLUDING THOUGHTS

In a region known for rote learning in schools and strict hierarchies—based on age, gender, class, and/or caste—transformative human rights education occurs in countless classrooms and community centres, spearheaded by innovative non-governmental organizations. Policy-makers in India and Bangladesh, while perhaps engaging in international discussions about the right to education and human rights education, are not, by and large, drawing on Freire's notions of empowering the marginalized through learning about social inequalities and ways to redress them. Transformative human rights education espouses a "globalization from below" ethic where global ideas, such as Freire's, that offer techniques and methods for inculcating a critical consciousness about processes of exclusion can offer learners the chance to question unequal social relations. Both People's Watch and BRAC draw on these legacies in order to infuse their human rights education programs with meaning and relevance for the marginalized children, youth, and women that participate in them.

Facilitators and teachers in these programs, whether community- or school-based, are essential to the efficacy of teaching about rights because they are the primary catalysts for participants' transformation. Educators worldwide seek to offer students knowledge and skills to permit them to effectively respond to their current and future realities. In the case of the two examples from South Asia offered above, trainers and teachers draw from their own personal understandings of human rights to offer learners a chance to analyze and take action based on the social conditions that surround them: gender violence, caste inequalities, discriminatory laws, child labour, and corruption.

Transformative human rights education in South Asia offers a way to draw upon the visions of Paulo Freire (1970) and leaders like Mahatma Gandhi (Bajaj, 2010) that learning spaces not just be laboratories for future citizenship, but be integrally embedded in the formation of active participants in democratic life. Learning about human rights guarantees—along with observations of the gap between promises and actual realities, paired with information about effective forms of activism—can provide learners important analyses and lenses with which to understand and engage with the world.

For teachers in classrooms across the globe, integrating human rights and examples of organizations like People's Watch and BRAC that seek to empower marginalized communities by spreading human rights literacy can be a way to connect across borders, building empathy and solidarity. The role of the educator and facilitator in transformative human rights education efforts is not only to impart information, but also to build the capacity for learners to believe that they are worthy of rights when their communities may have been marginalized for generations, as well as to nurture the social action that may result from learning about deep-seated inequalities. Ultimately, human rights education, if locally tailored and well designed, has the potential to foster teaching and learning for individual and social transformation, as the cases in this chapter have demonstrated.

QUESTIONS FOR REFLECTION AND DISCUSSION
1. Consider a transformative educational experience you have had inside or outside of a school context. What factors made that experience meaningful?
2. What kind of content, pedagogy, and approach would facilitate transformative education in the context in which you work or plan to work in the future?
3. How can transformative education be incorporated into schools in your context? What role could policy play to support such an integration?
4. What skills do teachers need to foster meaningful education for students?

SUGGESTED AUDIO-VISUAL RESOURCES
Path to Dignity: The Power of Human Rights Education, directed by Ellen Bruno (2012). Available at: www.path-to-dignity.org
This open-access film offers a global picture of human rights education and offers three case studies, one of which is on the Institute of Human Rights Education/People's Watch.

The Revolutionary Optimists, directed by Nicole Newnham and Maren Grainger-Monsen (2013). Available at: revolutionaryoptimists.org Learn about non-formal education efforts that seek to empower young people as agents of change in Kolkata's slums.

He Named Me Malala, directed by Davis Guggenheim (2015). Available at: www.henamedmemalalamovie.com/
This film profiles the courageous young Nobel Peace Prize winner Malala Yousafzai, who was shot by the Taliban for advocating for girls' right to education in Pakistan.

SUGGESTIONS FOR FURTHER READING

Amnesty International. (1999). *Siniko: Towards a Human Rights Culture in Africa*. London: Amnesty International. Available at: www.amnestymena.org/Documents/AFR%2001/AFR%20010031999en.pdf

Amnesty International. (2012). *Becoming a Human Rights Friendly School: A Guide for Schools around the World*. London: Amnesty International. Available at: www.amnesty.org/en/human-rights-education/human-rights-friendly-schools/

Andreopoulos, George, & Claude, Richard Pierre. (1997). *Human Rights Education for the Twenty-First Century*. Philadelphia: University of Pennsylvania Press.

Bajaj, Monisha. (Ed.). (2017). *Human Rights Education: Theory, Research, Praxis*. Philadelphia: University of Pennsylvania Press.

Benedek, Wolfgang. (2012). *Understanding Human Rights: Manual on Human Rights Education*, 3rd edition. Graz, Austria: European Training and Research Centre for Human Rights and Democracy. Available at: www.etc-graz.at/typo3/fileadmin/user_upload/ETC-Hauptseite/manual/versionen/english_3rd_edition/Manual_2012_FINAL.pdf

Flowers, Nancy. (2000). *The Human Rights Education Handbook: Effective Practices for Learning, Action, and Change*. Minneapolis: Human Rights Resource Center, University of Minnesota. Available at: www1.umn.edu/humanrts/edumat/hreduseries/hrhandbook/toc.html

Flowers, Nancy (Ed.). (2009). *Compasito: Manual on Human Rights Education for Children*, 2nd edition. Budapest: Council of Europe. Available at: www.eycb.coe.int/compasito/pdf/Compasito%20EN.pdf

Holland, Tracey, & Martin, John Paul. (2014). *Human Rights Education and Peacebuilding*. New York: Routledge.

Human Rights Education Associates (HREA). (2016). *Learn*. Available at: hrea.org/index.php?base_id=102

Katz, Susan, & Spero, Andrea. (2015). *Bringing Human Rights Education to US Classrooms*. New York: Palgrave.

Tibbitts, Felisa, & Fritzsche, Peter (Eds.). (2006). International Perspectives of Human Rights Education (HRE) [Special issue]. *Journal of Social Science Education, 5*(1). Available online and open-access at: www.jsse.org/2006-1/index.html

United Nations. (2011, December 19). *United Nations Declaration on Human Rights Education and Training*. Available at: documents-dds-ny.un.org/doc/UNDOC/GEN/N11/467/04/PDF/N1146704.pdf?OpenElement

NOTES

1. Thank you to Lydia Evans and Eli Jacobs-Fantauzzi for their assistance with this chapter.
2. While the requirements differ by state in India, teachers have generally completed a multi-year teacher training course on top of their high school diplomas.
3. Data for this section were gathered from an extensive review of documents written about the HRLS program as well as an hour-long interview and email correspondence with a senior staff member at BRAC.

REFERENCES

Bajaj, Monisha. (2010). Conjectures on Peace Education and Gandhian Studies: Method, Institutional Development, and Globalization. *Journal of Peace Education, 7*(1), 47–63.

Bajaj, Monisha. (2011). Human Rights Education: Ideology, Location, and Approaches. *Human Rights Quarterly, 33*, 481–508.

Bajaj, Monisha. (2012). *Schooling for Social Change: The Rise and Impact of Human Rights Education in India*. New York: Continuum International Publishing Group/Bloomsbury Publishing.

Bajaj, Monisha. (2014). The Productive Plasticity of Rights: Globalization, Education and Human Rights. In N. Stromquist & K. Monkman (Eds.), *Globalization and Education: Integration and Contestation across Cultures*, 2nd edition (pp. 51–66). Lanham, MD: Rowman & Littlefield.

Bajaj, Monisha, & Kidwai, Huma. (2016). Human Rights and Education Policy in South Asia. In K. Mundy, A. Green, R. Lingard, & A. Verger (Eds.), *Handbook of Global Policy and Policy-Making in Education*. Hoboken, NJ: Wiley-Blackwell.

Bajaj, Monisha, Cislaghi, Beniamino, & Mackie, Gerry. (2016). Advancing Transformative Human Rights Education. Annex to G. Brown (Ed.),

The Global Citizenship Commission Report: The Universal Declaration of Human Rights in the Twenty-First Century; A Living Document in a Changing World. Cambridge, UK: Open Book Publishers. Available at: https://www.openbookpublishers.com/shopimages/The-UDHR-21st-C-AppendixD.pdf

BRAC. (2013). The Lantern of Legal Literacy. In *Human Rights Education in Asia-Pacific: Volume Four* (pp. 51–60). Osaka: HuRights Osaka.

BRAC. (2014). "Paulo Freire and Subaltern Consciousness"—a discussion by Dr. Laurence Simon. Retrieved July 28, 2015, from www.brac.net/content/'paulo-freire-and-subaltern-consciousness'-discussion-dr-laurence-simon#.VbgJVYtQr8E

BRAC. (n.d.). *BRAC Overview*. Retrieved July 28, 2015, from hrls.brac.net/overview

Chaudhary, Latika. (2007). *An Economic History of Education in Colonial India*. Retrieved July 28, 2015, from economics.ucr.edu/seminars_colloquia/2007/political_economy_development/LatikaChaudhary5-6-07.pdf

Clark, Nick. (2013). *Indian Study Abroad Trends: Past, Present and Future*. Retrieved July 28, 2015, from wenr.wes.org/2013/12/indian-study-abroad-trends-past-present-and-future/

Delpit, Lisa. (2006). *Other People's Children: Cultural Conflict in the Classroom*. New York: New Press.

Evans, Stephen. (2002). Macaulay's Minute Revisited: Colonial Language Policy in Nineteenth-Century India. *Journal of Multilingual and Multicultural Development, 23*(4), 260–281.

Flowers, Nancy. (2003). *What Is Human Rights Education? A Survey of Human Rights Education*. Retrieved from www.hrea.org/erc/Library/curriculum_methodology/flowers03.pdf

Freire, Paulo. (1970). *Pedagogy of the Oppressed*. New York: Continuum.

HRW. (2015). *Marry before Your House Is Swept Away: Child Marriage in Bangladesh*. New York: Human Rights Watch.

Islam, Md. Akramul, Khan, Ashrafuzzaman, Chodhuary, Shuburna, & Samadder, Mrinmoy. (2012). *Exploring Legal Aid Services of BRAC HRLS Programme in Cox's Bazar*. Dhaka, Bangladesh: BRAC.

Keet, André. (2007). Human Rights Education or Human Rights in Education: A Conceptual Analysis (PhD dissertation). University of Pretoria.

Kolisetty, Akhila. (2014). *Examining the Effectiveness of Legal Empowerment as a Pathway out of Poverty: A Case Study of BRAC*. Justice & Development Working Paper Series. Washington, DC: World Bank.

Krücken, Georg, & Drori, Gili S. (Eds.). (2010). *World Society: The Writings of John W. Meyer*. Oxford: Oxford University Press.

Mayfield, James B. (2012). *Field of Reeds: Social, Economic and Political Change in Rural Egypt: In Search of Civil Society and Good Governance*. Bloomington, IN: AuthorHouse.

Meintjes, Garth. (1997). Human Rights Education as Empowerment: Reflections on Pedagogy. In G. Andreopoulos & R. P. Claude (Eds.), *Human*

Rights Education for the Twenty First Century (pp. 64–79). Philadelphia: University of Pennsylvania Press.

Meyer, John, Bromley-Martin, Patricia, & Ramirez, Francisco. (2010). Human Rights in Social Science Textbooks: Cross-National Analyses, 1970–2008. *Sociology of Education, 83*(2), 111–134.

OHCHR. (n.d.). *World Programme for Human Rights Education* (2005–ongoing). Retrieved July 28, 2015, from www.ohchr.org/EN/Issues/Education/Training/Pages/Programme.aspx

Ramirez, Francisco, Suarez, David, & Meyer, John (2007). The Worldwide Rise of Human Rights Education. In A. Benavot, C. Braslavsky, & N. Truong (Eds.), *School Knowledge in Comparative and Historical Perspective* (pp. 35–52). Netherlands: Springer.

Rana, Preetika, & Sugden, Joanna. (2013). India's Record Since Independence. Retrieved July 28, 2015, from blogs.wsj.com/indiarealtime/2013/08/15/indias-record-since-independence/

Smillie, Ian. (2009). *Freedom from Want: The Remarkable Success Story of BRAC, the Global Grassroots Organization That's Winning the Fight Against Poverty*. Boulder, CO: Kumarian Press.

Suarez, David. (2007). Education Professionals and the Construction of Human Rights Education. *Comparative Education Review, 51*(1), 48–70.

"The Hindu" Editorial. (2012). India loses 3 million girls in infanticide. Retrieved July 28, 2015, from www.thehindu.com/news/national/india-loses-3-million-girls-in-infanticide/article3981575.ece

Tibbitts, Felisa. (2002). Understanding What We Do: Emerging Models for Human Rights Education. *International Review of Education, 48*(3–4), 159–171.

Tibbitts, Felisa. (2005). Transformative Learning and Human Rights Education: Taking a Closer Look. *Intercultural Education, 16*(2), 107–113.

Tibbitts, Felisa. (2017, pp. 69–95). Evolution of Human Rights Education Models. In M. Bajaj (Ed.), *Human Rights Education: Theory, Research, Praxis*. Philadelphia: University of Pennsylvania Press.

Tsolakis, Marika. (2013). Citizenship and Transformative Human Rights Education: Surveys as "Praxis" in the São Paulo Periphery. *Journal of Social Science Education, 12*(3), 39–50.

UNICEF. (2013). *Bangladesh-Statistics*. Retrieved July 28, 2015, from www.unicef.org/infobycountry/bangladesh_bangladesh_statistics.html

United Nations. (2013). *Outcomes of Human Rights*. United Nations. Retrieved July 28, 2015, from www.un.org/en/development/devagenda/humanrights.shtml

World Bank. (2014). Addressing Inequality in South Asia: Policy Reforms as Important as Economic Growth. Retrieved July 28, 2015, from www.worldbank.org/en/news/feature/2014/12/04/addressing-inequality-policy-reforms-important-economic-growth

World Bank. (2015). *Bangladesh Data*. Retrieved July 28, 2015, from data.worldbank.org/country/bangladesh

CHAPTER NINE

GLOBAL CITIZENSHIP EDUCATION IN SCHOOLS: EVOLVING UNDERSTANDINGS, CONSTRUCTING PRACTICES

Mark Evans and Dina Kiwan

INTRODUCTION

Shifting economic, cultural, political, environmental, technological, and ideological forces are reshaping the transnational landscape. These forces, increasingly diverse, conflictual, and global in scope, transcend formal local boundaries and national borders and are creating tensions and conditions that require collaborative and integrated responses. Not surprisingly, educational systems worldwide are carefully considering what kinds of education are needed to respond to these changing circumstances and how schooling can strengthen global understanding and civic literacy among youth, to prepare them to meaningfully engage as citizens in today's world.

Global citizenship education (GCE) is an important part of these deliberations. While GCE is a relatively new area of educational research, it has experienced enormous momentum in recent years, accentuated by a number of local, national, and international policy and curriculum initiatives, including Ban Ki-moon's announcement (September 26, 2012) that global citizenship education would become a core pillar of the United Nations' Education First initiative.

In this chapter, we explore and examine GCE in today's evolving educational milieu from a comparative perspective. Particular attention is given to:

CHAPTER NINE: Global Citizenship Education in Schools   235

- current characterizations of global citizenship education;
- educational approaches in Canada, the Arab world, and UNESCO; and
- contrasting perspectives, challenges, and concluding reflections.

This chapter—intended primarily for teachers, non-formal educators, teacher candidates, curriculum developers, and teacher educators—presents recent work undertaken by researchers and educational practitioners.

CURRENT CHARACTERIZATIONS OF GLOBAL CITIZENSHIP EDUCATION

Citizenship has been an important theme in public education over the last century and more. Different perspectives, policies, and practices have developed worldwide, the result of ongoing theoretical inquiry, practical experience, and political deliberation and debate. As such, attempting to characterize citizenship or citizenship education has been an ongoing, contested process. Historically, citizenship was understood rather narrowly and seen as a privilege. At first, only certain categories of men were included; women, the very young, the old, those who did not own property, and those of certain occupations were excluded. Over time, as noted in British sociologist T.H. Marshall's well-known analysis of citizenship (1950), there has been a gradual movement toward more inclusive understandings of citizenship with the development of civil, political, and social rights. More recent understandings of citizenship have continued to expand, today embodying a range of contrasting perspectives (e.g., civic republican, liberal, communitarian, social democratic, multicultural, postcolonial) (Arthur, Davies, & Hahn, 2008; Ichilov, 1998; Isin & Turner, 2003; Parker, 1996).

Today, most countries include citizenship education as an important explicit and implicit feature of their education systems. Such educational purposes and approaches vary across and within differing contexts, ranging from those that aim to reproduce existing social conditions to those that embody a more transformative intent. Scholars offer diverse conceptions of citizenship education, its learning goals and practices, and the implications of these varying approaches (Banks, 2004, 2008; McLaughlin, 1992; Stevick & Levinson, 2007; Westheimer, 2015). Four main conceptions of citizenship—moral, legal, identity-based, and participatory—are typically drawn upon in educational policy and curriculum formulations (Kiwan, 2008).

Whilst the idea of conceptualizing citizenship beyond one's national borders is not new, recent shifting and deepening global forces have led to what David Held et al. (1999) refer to as "a transformation in the organization of human affairs by linking together and expanding human activity across regions and continents" (p. 15). Increased attention to various issues that transcend borders (e.g., international migration, global health, multilingualism, economic neoliberalism, global democracy, new technologies, disparities of wealth, global justice and inequality, etc.) has prompted questions related to rights, responsibilities, diverse identities and allegiances to community, culture, nation, and an evolving global civic culture. These citizenship (education) issues are being explored and debated with increased intensity and scrutiny.

Existing understandings of citizenship, grounded in the modern nation-state, are increasingly being critiqued and extended, to blend and juxtapose a broader range of perspectives and practices (e.g., cosmopolitanism, transnationalism, multiculturalism, planetary). There has been growing concern that educational systems worldwide need to do more to strengthen and deepen global understanding and civic literacy among youth in this shifting transnational landscape. Students, who find themselves implicated in a web of global networks and pressures in their day-to-day lives, have shown interest in learning more about global themes and issues. Policy-makers, curriculum developers, researchers, and educators are attempting to understand the intricate knowledge, skills, and processes of teaching and learning needed to become informed and meaningfully engaged citizens, including in global civic contexts and issues (Aleinikoff & Klusmeyer, 2001; Cogan & Grossman, 2009; Harshman, Augustine, & Merryfield, 2015).

The roots of GCE can be traced to various educational movements: peace education, multicultural education, human rights education, education for sustainable development, development education, education for intercultural awareness. Early characterizations of GCE connected core themes of citizenship education and global education (see Table 9.1).

British scholar Lynn Davies (2006) notes, however, that GCE presents a heightened sense of obligation to act for social justice in transnational contexts, compared with previous conceptions of either citizenship education or global education. Today, GCE is viewed as an important medium through which, for example, to raise learners' critical global

CHAPTER NINE: Global Citizenship Education in Schools 237

awareness, enhance civic literacy (including critical thinking, media literacy, collaboration skills, conflict management), ethic of care, responsibility and appreciation for diversity, and inclusive and responsible engagement in global issues in their local-to-global communities. Predictably, these goals are being taken up in different ways, reflecting

Table 9.1: Core Themes in Citizenship Education and Global Education

Core Themes Associated with Citizenship Education	Core Themes Associated with Global Education
An understanding of concepts, structures, and processes necessary for informed civic decision-making and involvement (for example, rule of law, local and national governance structures and processes)	An understanding of concepts and the workings of the wider world (for example, interdependence, international legal principles, global systems, sustainable development, peace and conflict)
Sense of membership or identity with one's varied communities that extend from the local to the national to the global	Worldmindedness, a sense of membership or kinship with all of humanity
An understanding of rights and corresponding duties and responsibilities, usually within the national context (Charter of Rights and Freedoms)	An understanding of rights and responsibilities within the global context (Human Rights Act, Rights of the Child)
An understanding of civic conflict and decisions, personal values, and perspectives that guide citizen thinking and action, and the challenges of governing communities in which contrasting values and perspectives coexist	An understanding of global conflict and decisions, respect for diverse perspectives, cross-cultural understanding, and a commitment to global social justice and equity
The development of a set of virtues and capacities that enable someone to critically explore, reflect upon, and participate in civic questions and issues, mostly of local and national interest and importance	The development of a set of virtues and capacities that enable someone to critically analyze and actively engage in questions and issues of global interest and concern, in relation to local and national circumstances

diverse and contending conceptual lenses through which GCE is understood and practised. Below, we overview learning goals, practices, and orientations evident in current GCE literature.

LEARNING GOALS

Global citizenship learning goals, at first glance, might seem potentially infinite. One review of recent GCE literature (Evans, Ingram, MacDonald, & Weber, 2009, pp. 20–21) showed that learning goals highlighted included opportunities to:

- deepen understanding of global themes, structures, and systems (e.g., interdependence, peace and conflict, sustainable development);
- explore and reflect upon one's identity and membership through a lens of worldmindedness (e.g., Indigenous, local, national);
- examine diverse beliefs, values, and worldviews (e.g. cultural, religious, political) that guide civic thinking and action within and across varied contexts;
- learn about rights and responsibilities within the context of civil society and varying governance systems, from the local to the global (e.g., human rights, Rights of the Child, corporate social responsibility);
- deepen understandings of power, privilege, equity, and social justice within governing structures and processes (e.g., personal/global inequities, power relations/power sharing);
- investigate global issues and ways to manage and deliberate conflict (e.g., health, ecological, terrorism/security);
- develop critical civic literacy capacities (e.g., critical inquiry, decision-making, conflict management); and
- learn about and engage in informed and purposeful civic action (e.g., community involvement and service, involvement with non-governmental organizations [NGOs], development of civic engagement capacities).

Many of these goals have to do with developing deep, critical understandings of the world we live in, forms of governance, cooperation and managing conflict, identities and memberships in the world community, notions of fairness and justice, forms of engagement in issues of global concern, and learner capacities that ought to be nurtured.

TEACHING PRACTICES

Teaching practices highlighted in the same review of literature underscore GCE's transformative intent toward a more inclusive, peaceful, and just world, recognizing and valuing diverse and marginalized learners' knowledge and real-world experiences. Participatory, learner-centred, cooperative, and inclusive practices are often emphasized. Also evident is attention to the learning environment, clear and manageable learning expectations, and suitable ways of assessing results. The literature reviewed generally advocates practices that:

- nurture a respectful, inclusive, and interactive classroom/school ethos (e.g., shared classroom norms, student voice, inclusive seating arrangements and use of wall/visual space, global citizenship imagery);
- infuse learner-centred, culturally responsive, independent, and interactive pedagogical approaches that align with learning goals (e.g., independent and collaborative learning structures, deliberative dialogue, media literacy);
- embed authentic performance tasks (e.g., creating displays on children's rights, peacebuilding programs, student newspaper addressing global issues);
- draw on globally oriented learning resources that assist students in understanding a "larger picture" of themselves in the world, in relation to their local circumstances (e.g., variety of sources and media, comparing diverse perspectives);
- use assessment and evaluation strategies that align with the learning goals and forms of instruction used to support learning (e.g., reflection and self-assessment, peer feedback, teacher assessment, journals, portfolios);
- offer opportunities for students to experience learning activities in varied contexts, including classroom, whole school, and local to global community participation (e.g., municipal, virtual, and international exchanges); and
- foreground the teacher as a role model (e.g., up to date on current events, community-involved, practising environmental and equity values).

Many of these practices emphasize active strategies that nurture students' capacity-building (e.g., to become informed, to think critically, to recognize diverse perspectives, to manage conflict, to analyze global issues). In addition, they emphasize presenting opportunities for critical and active reflection through practices such as cooperative learning, deliberative dialogue, democratic decision-making, and experiential learning. Teaching for transformative learning entails intellectual, emotional, and practical changes—both personal and community-level processes. American philosopher John Dewey (1933) described transformative learning as when participants come to see some aspect of the world in a new way. In a similar vein, in Brazilian educator Paulo Freire's (1970) approach to dialogic education, the knowledge, experiences, and perspectives of both educators and learners are valued. In these pedagogic models, reflection and dialogue are important in raising critical consciousness, coupled with context-specific action. Drawing on learners' lived experiences in and beyond the classroom facilitates a cyclical learning process of reflection, dialogue, and action (see also Kolb, 1984). This triad of intellectual/cognitive development, affective/emotional engagement, and engaged action has been referred to as a "head, hands, and heart" organizing principle (Sipos, Battisti, & Grimm, 2008). Such an approach "enables marginalized perspectives to be heard, recognizing the power dynamics involved in the production of knowledge. This is not to promote unchallenged relativism, but rather is a starting point for critical inquiry in relation to real-world problems" (Kiwan, 2014, p. 3). Increasingly, GCE literature also emphasizes building capacities for communication at multiple levels, through new technologies and social media, and asking difficult questions about what and whose knowledge counts.

Various GCE curriculum delivery approaches are used. Some schools have developed school-wide extracurricular activities revolving around GCE themes and/or issues, explicitly expressed in school-wide priorities that become part of the school ethos. Discrete course approaches, while rare, provide focused attention to particular aspects of GCE learning. Most often, it is delivered as an integrated component of existing curricula, connecting student learning in subject areas (e.g., civics, social studies, environmental studies, world geography, religious education, music, science). Also, non-formal global citizenship education—outside established formal school contexts—is sometimes established by community groups and other organizations (e.g., *Activate* from South Africa; Forum by Luiz Carlos Guides, Youth Leader, Lute Sem Fronteiras, Brazil; Inter-Agency Network for Education in Emergencies Conflict-Sensitive Education Pack in post-armed-conflict settings). Learning within these

CHAPTER NINE: Global Citizenship Education in Schools 241

NGO contexts is often self-governing, characterized by flexibility in organization and method.

VARIED ORIENTATIONS

GCE learning theories, policies, and practices reflect diverse, multifaceted and contending conceptual lenses (Faour, 2012; Oxley & Morris, 2013; Peters, Britton, & Blee, 2008; Schattle, 2008; Westheimer, 2015). Each orientation underscores an emphasis on distinctive goals and practices, and raises questions about what kinds of citizen(s) are being proposed. Early orientations foregrounded the acquisition of knowledge, the examination of diverse attitudes and values, and the application of relevant skills in ways that contributed to learners' sense of "worldmindedness" (Merryfield, 1998; Pike & Selby, 1988, 2000). Some GCE emphasizes relatively instrumentalist, neoliberal orientations that foreground knowledge and competencies to be skilled workers in the competitive global marketplace, to fit into the world "as it is" (O'Sullivan, 1999; Portelli & Solomon, 2001). Others represent cosmopolitan orientations that emphasize identity and citizenship, human rights, and ways of addressing local, national, regional, and global issues in order to live together in increasingly diverse local communities and an interdependent world (Heater, 2002; Osler & Starkey, 2003, 2006). Some GCE has a more critical and transformative orientation, concerned with issues of social justice and human rights whereby learners develop capacity to critically reflect upon their own social positions and backgrounds and to act in relation to local and global injustices and inequalities (Andreotti, 2006; Davies, 2006; Shultz, 2007). These orientations provide "multiple entry points for taking a more 'radical' approach in curriculum," but "more impactful outcomes rely heavily on the actual capacity of schools and teachers" (Davies, 2006, p. 22). Note that most of these orientations rest on Western ideas of citizenship and education. Nevertheless, this breadth of "ways in" to educating for the global dimensions of citizenship point to its possibility, and to the need to prepare teachers, students, policy-makers, and educational researchers.

EDUCATIONAL APPROACHES IN CANADA, THE ARAB WORLD, AND UNESCO

Both formal and non-formal educational contexts in various parts of the world have shown interest in enhancing and deepening learners' global understanding and opportunities to contribute to addressing global civic questions in local, national, regional, and international communities. Below are three vignettes—one national, one regional, one supra-national—that illustrate ways in which GCE is being approached in differing formal education contexts:

- Canada
- the Arab world
- internationally, through UNESCO

In the vignette about each context, the following questions are considered:

1. How is citizenship education understood? How is it defined in curriculum policy, and what delivery approaches are being suggested?
2. What explicit learning goals are emphasized in school curriculum in relation to global citizenship education, and why? How is it being taught, using what resources? What types of professional learning are provided for teachers?
3. What key challenges are associated with GCE? What types of scholarly inquiry are underway?

EDUCATING FOR CITIZENSHIP IN CANADIAN SCHOOLS

Education in Canada is the responsibility of provincial and territorial governments operating within a federal system. Each of the ten provinces and three territories administers its own curricula and programs, although a degree of commonality exists across them and some regions share policy development. Educating for citizenship has been a curricular theme throughout the history of K–12 public education in all provinces and territories (Sears, 2004). Approaches to educating for citizenship that emerged in the early 20th century—and continue today—encourage social and political assimilation, foregrounding the study of public institutions and the ascribed roles and responsibilities of citizens. Interest in international and global perspectives in education became more apparent in the early 20th century. Church groups, adult educators, and international organizations like the Red Cross undertook much of this work. In school curricula, international and global perspectives were most evident in geography, history, and social studies. Internal and external factors fostered increased interest in the

CHAPTER NINE: Global Citizenship Education in Schools   243

global dimensions of citizenship education within Canadian schools during the second half of the 20th century.

Since the Second World War, expanded notions of citizenship education's purposes and practices have been advanced. The Quiet Revolution in Quebec, the United States' increasing influence on the Canadian economy, changing immigration patterns, Canada's growing military involvement in international peacekeeping initiatives, and Aboriginal land claims, for example, have challenged existing understandings and goals for citizenship education, prompting increased attention to Canada's national civic identity, social cohesion, and cultural diversity. As Canada struggled with its persisting questions of self-definition, the country's first large-scale assessment of civic education was undertaken (Hodgetts, 1968). Hodgetts' results portrayed a largely pessimistic picture of Canadian citizenship education, and advanced a new vision of an increasingly multidimensional, culturally diverse, and pluralistic Canadian civic identity and an emerging global dimension, prompting a rethinking of citizenship along critical and reformist lines.

In the final decades of the 20th century, significant legislation (Multiculturalism Policy, 1971; Canadian Charter of Rights and Freedoms, 1982; Canadian Multiculturalism Act, 1988) signalled broadened understandings of national identity and Canada's position in the world. Canadian Studies curricula were developed, creating new opportunities for teachers and students to explore Canada's cultural diversity, the complex dynamics of French/English relations and Canadian/American relations, and Canada's emerging role in the global community. Academics, teachers, curriculum developers, government development agencies, charities, and educational movements (e.g., peace education, development education, environmental education) were proposing new constructs of citizenship education, seeking to deepen understandings of diversity, global and transnational themes, and civic engagement. During this period, global education was gaining momentum, influencing priorities of Ministries of Education, school boards, and Faculties of Education. Substantial discussion about the scope and breadth of citizenship education was underway. Theoretical perspectives—such as Sears' (1996) "Conceptions of Citizenship Education" model, Strong-Boag's (1996) "pluralist" orientation, and Osborne's (2001) "12 Cs" framework—acknowledged citizenship education's developing global dimension. The Canadian International Development Agency funded a number of Global Education Centres across Canada to assist teachers in exploring and developing classroom materials and pedagogies for the study of global themes and issues (Holland, 2004). A report from South House Exchange (2001) for the Council of Ministers described various ways that themes of citizenship and global understanding had been included in the curricula across Canada in the previous two decades. Importantly, these movements also pushed for pedagogical practices congruent with citizenship education's shifting goals, moving beyond "knowing about" to focus purposefully on "thinking about" and "engaging in" citizenship.

While changing educational priorities and funding cuts have slowed down some of this work in recent years, interest and attention to global citizenship education persists across the Canadian educational landscape. Discussion is underway about the scope and breadth of GCE (Abdi, Shultz, & Pillay, 2015; Harshman, Augustine, & Merryfield, 2015; O'Sullivan & Pashby, 2008; Peters, Britton, & Blee, 2008). Provincial mandates reveal infusion and deepening of GCE themes in official curricula.[1] A range of new resource materials are being developed, designed to guide teachers' work in various aspects of teaching and learning. Increased attention to GCE has also been evident in teacher education.[2] Today, civic literacy, equity and inclusion, the exploration of civic conflict issues, the infusion of local through global perspectives, and active civic engagement are evident in the current rhetoric of citizenship education (Abdi & Shultz, 2008; Hébert & Sears, 2002; Osborne, 2001). Questions of social cohesion and diversity, in particular, continue to occupy a critical space in these characterizations, given Canada's unique mix of peoples, cultures, languages, and geography (Bickmore, 2007, 2009, 2014; Joshee, 2004; Kymlicka, 1998).

As the global dimension of citizenship evolves in schools in Canada, however, a variety of questions and concerns have been noted in recent GCE literature. For example, implementation is often uneven and fragmented such that it is unclear what learning opportunities students are actually experiencing in schools—various learning goals and various types of teaching and learning practices are privileged (Evans, 2004; Evans et al., 2013; Mundy & Manion, 2008; Rapoport, 2015). Scholars are challenging what and whose knowledge counts, concerned that GCE is often narrowly conceptualized as "a matter of national self-interest, and almost exclusively tied to the civic structures of the nation state" (Richardson, 2004, p. 145; see Pike, 2000; Richardson & Abbott, 2009). Others express concern about insufficient criticality, calling for

CHAPTER NINE: Global Citizenship Education in Schools   245

new educational resources and pedagogical practices to deconstruct stereotypes and problematic representations (Abdi, Shultz, & Pillay, 2015; Bickmore, 2014; Eidoo et al., 2011). Still others challenge the adequacy of teacher education to support the conceptual and instructional complexities and sophistication associated with GCE (Cook, 2014; Guo, 2013, 2014; Larsen & Faden, 2008; McLean, Cook, & Crowe, 2006; McLean & Ng-A-Fook, 2013; Schweisfurth, 2006). Support is needed for additional research, and for curriculum, instructional, and professional development work, to better understand the theoretical and practical complexities associated with this emerging and important dimension of education.

EDUCATING FOR GLOBAL CITIZENSHIP IN THE ARAB WORLD
Contemporary conceptualizations of citizenship in the Arab Middle East are evolving in the context of the ongoing "Arab Spring" uprisings (Kiwan, 2014). These revolts were typically preceded by the "explosive" combination of severe economic and political conditions under authoritarian regimes—in which populations have suffered for many years from high levels of unemployment, poor living conditions, and denial of political and civil rights. Since the unfolding of Arab Spring events starting in December 2010, academic and policy interest in the domain of education for citizenship has gained significant attention in the Arab world. In addition, there is interest in the role of (social) media networks in the Arab revolutions, whereby the "digital citizen," using various information technologies, actively participates in the politics of the public sphere. It has been argued that such technologies, though not themselves causing the uprisings, have played an important role in mobilizing participation by bringing together otherwise disparate groups and also by circumventing traditional state control of the media (Hansard Society, 2011). A recent report from the Pew Research Center's Global Attitudes Project found that Arab citizens' most favoured social networking subjects included politics, community issues, and religion. In particular, in Egypt and Tunisia, 60 percent of those engaged in social networking shared their views about politics online, compared with only 34 percent in 18 other countries[3] in the study (Pew Research Center, 2012).

Education as a site for socio-political transformation is particularly significant in contexts of large youth populations in the Arab world, with over 40 percent of the population being under the age of 18 (Faour &

Muasher, 2012). Empirical findings in a report published by Carnegie Middle East Center suggest that school ethos across the Arab world is quite negative, with students reporting that they do not feel safe physically, socially, or emotionally. Teachers are not sufficiently trained, their pedagogical approaches tend to be didactic and rely on memorization, and there are limited resources (ibid.). Policy-makers and academics in the Arab world are calling for recognition of the importance of civic education, and also for a new democratic pedagogy (Faour, 2012; Faour & Muasher, 2012; UNDP, 2008a; UNDP, 2008b). There are mixed views regarding whether global citizenship education approaches are appropriate, or effective in dealing with pressing local, national, and regional concerns, in Arab formal education systems.[4] However, recent informal communication[5] suggests that the UNESCO GCE Curriculum guiding framework was well received by many Arab states. Particular Arab Gulf states have commissioned work to look into incorporating GCE into the school civics curricula.

One initiative, the Middle East Network on Innovative Teaching and Learning (MENIT), was launched in March 2011 on behalf of the German Federal Ministry for Economic Cooperation.[6] This regional platform of more than 300 experts and practitioners of innovation and education covers Palestine, Jordan, Syria, and Lebanon. It aims to facilitate regional educational dialogue and exchange of good practice, as well as the implementation of joint research projects. MENIT is a member of the Arab Campaign for Education for All and the regional Initiative to Promote Adult Education. In 2011, a research project was conducted on supporting active citizenship education using a legal (human rights) framework. A survey study evaluated indicators for various pedagogical approaches to promoting active, intercultural, inclusive citizenship, and for measuring various cognitive competencies, skills, values, and behaviours, including indicators of knowledge (e.g., democracy, human rights, responsibility, participation); values (e.g., transparency, tolerance, human dignity); and skills (e.g., analysis, making decisions) (Kiwan, forthcoming).

Another example is a partnership called the British Council's Connecting Classrooms. This initiative connects learners online in different parts of the world, giving them the opportunity to learn about different country contexts and to develop skills of global citizenship in particular, using online and social media. It also provides teachers with an opportunity to develop their skills in teaching global citizenship. For example, a British Council partnership between a primary school in

CHAPTER NINE: Global Citizenship Education in Schools 247

Beirut and a primary school in Lincolnshire, England,[7] introduces students in the United Kingdom to the ongoing crisis in Syria and its impact on Lebanon—both in that many students in Lebanon schools are themselves Syrian refugees, and Lebanese children experience the effects of the large-scale demographic change in Lebanese society. The theme of living together is introduced, with sub-themes of conflict and peace, and identity and belonging. Lebanese and Syrian children are also taught about life in the United Kingdom: through personal stories, they see that children in other parts of the world also face different sorts of daily challenges of adversity, conflict, and living together amidst diversity.

Key challenges for implementing GCE in the Arab region include:

- conceptual challenges: the appropriateness of global focus in contexts of civil, national, and regional conflict;
- demographic changes and conflict: introducing change is a challenge in a socio-political context where educational systems are operating in emergency mode with large numbers of refugees, and many children are not even enrolled in formal education;
- pedagogical challenges: in a context of heavy reliance on rote learning and didactic pedagogies, introducing transformative approaches will be a challenge conceptually and in terms of resources;
- resources: securing political will and resources for teacher training will be critically important in order to implement such change (Kiwan, forthcoming).

EDUCATING FOR GLOBAL CITIZENSHIP ACROSS THE WORLD, THROUGH UNESCO

Global citizenship education has become an important priority for UNESCO, particularly since the launch of UN Secretary-General Ban Ki-moon's Global Education First Initiative in 2012. GCE is identified as one of three core pillars, accentuating the importance of strengthening global understanding and civic literacy among youth, and a key objective from 2014 to 2021. GCE builds on the "Learning to Live Together" work, which is central to UNESCO's mission: "recognizing and appreciating diversity, developing an understanding of others through dialogue, and acknowledging interdependence and shared futures." It also builds on UNESCO' s long-standing work in human rights education, peace education, and education for sustainable development (see Chapters Eight and Ten in this volume).

Global Citizenship Education: Preparing Learners for the Challenges of the Twenty-First Century (UNESCO, 2014) and *Global Citizenship Education: Topics and Learning Objectives* (UNESCO, 2015) overview UNESCO's intentions, rationale, and suggested practices, drawing on various understandings and approaches to global citizenship education, and are intended for use by policy-makers, curriculum planners, and other educators in formal and non-formal sectors.

In *Global Citizenship Education: Preparing Learners for the Challenges of the Twenty-First Century* (2014), UNESCO defines GCE as

> a framing paradigm which encapsulates how education can develop the knowledge, skills, values and attitudes learners need for securing a world which is more just, peaceful, tolerant, inclusive, secure and sustainable....It represents a conceptual shift in that it recognizes the relevance of education in understanding and resolving global issues in their social, political, cultural, economic and environmental dimensions. It also acknowledges the role of education in moving beyond the development of knowledge and cognitive skills to build values, soft skills and attitudes among learners that can facilitate international cooperation and promote social transformation. (UNESCO, 2014, p. 9)

It highlights five dimensions:

- an attitude supported by an understanding of multiple levels of identity, and the potential for a "collective identity" that transcends individual cultural, religious, ethnic, or other differences;
- a deep knowledge of global issues and universal values such as justice, equality, dignity, and respect;
- cognitive skills to think critically, systemically, and creatively, including adopting a multi-perspective approach that recognizes the different dimensions, perspectives, and angles of issues;
- social skills such as empathy and conflict resolution, communication skills, and aptitudes for networking and interacting with people of different backgrounds, origins, cultures, and perspectives; and

- behavioural capacities to act collaboratively and responsibly to find global solutions for global challenges, and to strive for the collective good.

UNESCO notes that the above dimensions take on varying orientations in different contexts, regions, and communities:

> Interpretations and focus often vary, and there is no "one size fits all" model for implementation. For example, where there are intensified conflicts or in post-conflict settings, GCE is often considered within the rubric of peace education, as has been...the case in parts of Africa. In countries experiencing transitions in government regimes, including those in Latin America and more recently in the Middle East, civic education has been an entry point to reinforce principles of democratic participation and other universal values embodied in GCE. Regional integration and the establishment of regional cooperation mechanisms (such as the Southern African Development Community or the Association of Southeast Asian Nations), have also led to an increased emphasis on civics and citizenship, democracy and good governance, and peace and tolerance—all critical elements of GCE. (UNESCO, 2014, p. 17)

The resource discusses the shifting context of globalization and GCE's connections to formal and non-formal education, enabling conditions for implementation and some persisting tensions (e.g., global solidarity versus competition, reconciling local and global identities and interests, the role of education in challenging the status quo). Particular attention is given to GCE implications for education content, pedagogies, and practices. Implementation of transformative pedagogies, "a wide range of active and participatory learning methods that engage the learner in critical thinking about complex global issues, and in developing skills such as communication, co-operation and conflict resolution to resolve these issues," is presented as central to effective GCE. These pedagogies help increase the "relevance of education in and out of classrooms by engaging stakeholders of the wider community who are also part of the learning environment and process" (UNESCO, 2014, p. 21).

Global Citizenship Education: Topics and Learning Objectives (UNESCO, 2015) outlines UNESCO's first round of pedagogical guidance on GCE, to assist member states in integrating GCE into their education systems and to form part of the Education for All post-2015 development goals. This resource looks at the subject matter contents of GCE, questions of implementation, and a sampling of promising practices and resources that can be adapted to different national and local contexts. Detailed guidance is provided through elaborated learning objectives at different ages and levels of preparedness. This resource is flexible, encouraging consultation, adaptation, and contextualization at country level: it is not intended to be prescriptive. Three core dimensions (ibid., p. 15) are identified:

- acquisition of knowledge, understanding, and critical thinking about global, regional, national, and local issues and the interconnectedness and interdependency of different countries and populations;
- a sense of belonging to a common humanity, sharing values and responsibilities, empathy, solidarity, and respect for differences and diversity; and
- acting effectively and responsibly at local, national, and global levels for a more peaceful and sustainable world.

Learning domains and outcomes, learner attributes, and topics and objectives are more fully delineated and interwoven throughout the resource.

UNESCO offers a multi-faceted approach to GCE with a range of core learning goals and practices and a distinctive transformative intent. Some instrumentalist intentions regarding the acquisition of knowledge and deep understanding of the world we live in are evident. At the same time, opportunities to inquire into questions of identity and citizenship, human rights, living together in increasingly diverse and interdependent communities, conflict and power dynamics, and social injustices are evidence of its more critical and transformative elements. There is a clear assumption across the UNESCO documents that there should be opportunities to develop capacities for community engagement, to contribute "to a better world through informed, ethical and peaceful action" (ibid., p. 24). The document makes it clear that teachers are central to GCE's success in the formal (school) sector: its complex makeup requires skilled educators with a good understanding of transformative and participatory forms of teaching and learning, who are able to guide, facilitate, and encourage learners "to engage in critical inquiry and supporting the development of knowledge, skills, values and attitudes that promote positive personal and social change" (ibid., p. 51). It is noted, however, that

CHAPTER NINE: Global Citizenship Education in Schools 251

suitable preparation and ongoing professional learning will be critical to ensure that teachers (many of whom have limited background knowledge and/or experience) are prepared to offer quality GCE.

Table 9.2: Citizenship Education: Topics and Elaborated Learning Objectives

	Learning Objectives		
Pre-primary & lower primary (5–9 years)	Upper primary (9–12 years)	Lower secondary (12–15 years)	Upper secondary (15–18+ years)
Topic 1. Local, national and global systems and structures			
Describe how the local environment is organized and how it relates to the wider world, and introduce the concept of citizenship	Identify governance structures, decision-making processes and dimensions of citizenship	Discuss how global governance structures interact with national and local structures and explore global citizenship	Critically analyse global governance systems, structures and processes and assess implications for global citizenship
Topic 2. Issues affecting interaction and connectedness of communities at local, national and global levels			
List key local, national and global issues and explore how these may be connected	Investigate the reasons behind major common global concerns and their impact at national and local levels	Assess the root causes of major local, national and global issues and the interconnectedness of local and global factors	Critically examine local, national and global issues, responsibilities and consequences of decision-making, examine and propose appropriate responses
Topic 3. Underlying assumptions and power dynamics			
Name different sources of information and develop basic skills for inquiry	Differentiate between fact/opinion, reality/fiction and different viewpoints/perspectives	Investigate underlying assumptions and describe inequalities and power dynamics	Critically assess the ways in which power dynamics affect voice, influence, access to resources, decision-making and governance

continued...

Table 9.2: Citizenship Education: Topics and Elaborated Learning Objectives *(continued from previous)*

Topic 4. Different levels of identity			
Recognise how we fit into and interact with the world around us and develop intrapersonal and interpersonal skills	Examine different levels of identity and their implications for managing relationships with others	Distinguish between personal and collective identity and various social groups, and cultivate a sense of belonging to a common humanity	Critically examine ways in which different levels of identity interact and live peacefully with different social groups
Topic 5. Different communities people belong to and how these are connected			
Illustrate differences and connections between different social groups	Compare and contrast shared and different social, cultural and legal norms	Demonstrate appreciation and respect for difference and diversity, cultivate empathy and solidarity towards other individuals and social groups	Critically assess connectedness between different groups, communities and countries
Topic 6. Difference and respect for diversity			
Distinguish between sameness and difference, and recognise that everyone has rights and responsibilities	Cultivate good relationships with diverse individuals and groups	Debate on the benefits and challenges of difference and diversity	Develop and apply values, attitudes and skills to manage and engage with diverse groups and perspectives
Topic 7. Actions that can be taken individually and collectively			
Explore possible ways of taking action to improve the world we live in	Discuss the importance of individual and collective action and engage in community work	Examine how individuals and groups have taken action on issues of local, national and global importance and get engaged in responses to local, national and global issues	Develop and apply skills for effective civic engagement

continued...

CHAPTER NINE: Global Citizenship Education in Schools   253

Topic 8. Ethically responsible behaviour			
Discuss how our choices and actions affect other people and the planet and adopt responsible behaviour	Understand the concepts of social justice and ethical responsibility and learn how to apply them in everyday life	Analyse the challenges and dilemmas associated with social justice and ethical responsibility and consider the implications for individual and collective action	Critically assess issues of social justice and ethical responsibility and take action to challenge discrimination and inequality
Topic 9. Getting engaged and taking action			
Recognise the importance and benefits of civic engagement	Identify opportunities for engagement and initiate action	Develop and apply skills for active engagement and take action to promote common good	Propose action for and become agents of positive change

Source: UNESCO, 2015, p. 31

CONTRASTING PERSPECTIVES, CHALLENGES, AND CONCLUDING REFLECTIONS

Contrasting perspectives on GCE reveal an array of goals, practices, and orientations, ranging from instrumentalist to transformative. Below, we offer some contrasting perspectives, challenges, and concluding reflections based on a comparative analysis of the three vignettes in this chapter.

CONTEXT

Educational institutions are never value-neutral transmitters of knowledge, but rather value-based organizations that reflect their socio-political contexts. Teachers are political actors who—intentionally or unintentionally—convey preferred learning goals and conceptually nuanced practices. Socio-political environments and the broad intent of GCE are evident in provincial or national governments' varying policy objectives with respect to GCE and in individual teachers' orientations. Whereas UNESCO's broad intent is comprehensive and explicit in its policy guidance, both the Canadian and the Arab region approaches, not unexpectedly, are less clear in curriculum policy guidance and reveal provincial, national, and regional nuances. Predictably, concerns have been raised about what and whose knowledge counts in GCE. Some argue, as mentioned earlier, that global citizenship education may be a form of imperialism—threatening local or national ethnic, religious, or cultural allegiances. GCE may be viewed as a critique of the nation-state, suggesting its reduced importance or even demise in a globalized world. In contrast, in some armed-conflict and divided societies (for instance in Northern Ireland), GCE may be preferred as a way of avoiding the thorny issues of national identity and divided loyalties.

LEARNING GOALS

Curriculum guidance introduced across different parts of the world over the past two decades reflects the inclusion of those learning goals associated with a global dimension of citizenship. Among the three vignettes, certain common themes are apparent in stated curricular goals. All attend to questions of membership or identity, rights and responsibilities, interdependence, respect for diversity and inclusion, and cross-cultural understanding. Attention is also paid to the acquisition of knowledge and capacity-building through both formal and non-formal contexts, so as to enable young people to effectively engage in, and reflect upon, themes and social justice issues of global civic concern (in relation to such issues as human rights, the AIDS/HIV epidemic, global warming, and world poverty). Attention to particular curriculum goals, however, vary in degree. Curricula in the Arab world, for example, tend to be more transmission oriented with an emphasis on content goals, whereas a more instrumentalist orientation with an emphasis on civic literacy skills goals is evident in Canadian curricula. The rhetoric of UNESCO curricular resources highlights a transformative intent, with particular attention to the exploration of multiple values, beliefs and attitudes, and questions of injustice. Contrasting priorities and levels of clarity in curriculum guidance, however, raise questions about which learning goals ought to be emphasized, often leading to a sense of uncertainty among educators attempting to introduce global citizenship into their curriculum.

TEACHING AND LEARNING PRACTICES

There are many innovative examples of classroom, school-wide, and community-based teaching and learning practices and resources suggested across the three vignettes, yet considerable variability remains in curriculum guidance and practice. Guidance for teachers indicates

CHAPTER NINE: Global Citizenship Education in Schools   255

a need for a sophisticated repertoire of teaching and learning practices to address GCE's wide-ranging and intricate learning goals. Critical thinking activities, issue-based inquiries and analysis, cross-cultural experiences, managing instances of conflict, exploration of global issues, opportunities for authentic experiential learning, and engagement in one's communit(y/ies) are some of the practices encouraged in the UNESCO and Canadian curricular frameworks. These emphasize a transformative pedagogical orientation, in contrast to more didactic, transmission-oriented pedagogies dominant in many Arab world civic education curricula. Each initiative notes the need for suitable teacher education and other supports to address complexities inherent in GCE's successful implementation. A particular challenge is the introduction of transformative pedagogies, especially in contexts with relatively limited experience with such approaches. This will require professional learning support, both to encourage interest and knowledge of such approaches, and to develop teaching resources relevant to local needs and socio-cultural contexts. Studies suggest that learning experiences are uneven and what is intended and what is done in the name of GCE are often inconsistent (Evans, 2004; Evans et al., 2013). For example, in many contexts, teachers often avoid issues of social justice, controversy, and conflict (Bickmore, 2014; MacDonald-Vemic et al., 2015). Despite the growing interest in and availability of some global citizenship teaching resources, coherent support for GCE teacher learning or student materials can be challenging.

VARIED ORIENTATIONS AND COMPLEXITY
Each of the three cases recognizes varied orientations and complexities associated with GCE—for example, questions of overlapping identity affiliations and allegiances; diversity of perspectives; blurred boundaries between social justice and diversity; tensions among the local, national, and global; and issues of implementation in formal as well as non-formal education contexts. UNESCO in particular, and some Canadian provinces, show growing recognition of the importance of including gender and sexuality in GCE. However, there remain conceptual and practical challenges in relation to the accommodation of gender and, especially, sexual diversity concerns in different parts of the world. Promising international resources show that conceptions of globality and citizenship education always change over time in any culture and political context: for instance, historical approaches may

illustrate how women's roles in society have changed over time. In addition, local, authentic, contextualized examples can illustrate that GCE can be locally "owned" and are not being externally imposed. Similarly, while perspectives from Indigenous, non-Western, and non-majority populations are increasingly acknowledged and included in curriculum guidance, there is less evidence of promising practices.

IMPLEMENTATION

While the cases identify the use of similar curriculum delivery approaches—delivered as a discrete, stand-alone subject; integrated within existing subjects (geography, history, and social studies, and to a lesser extent, other subjects and cross-curricular documents); and/or linked with school-wide initiatives—implementation is acknowledged in each of the cases to be a major challenge, complicated by a variety of factors (e.g., political shifts, a crowded curriculum and competing priorities, lack of commitment by senior management, workload, school cultures that are not supportive of global citizenship education). These challenges are further complicated by the relatively low status accorded to explicit citizenship education—especially global citizenship education—in many schools and systems. More effective implementation processes and financial support will be required, particularly those relating to teachers' and administrators' professional learning, if school-based learning intentions are to be more fully realized.

This chapter has shown various contemporary characterizations of global citizenship education in Canada, the Arab world, and UNESCO. Despite the range of initiatives currently underway, it is clear that educating for the global dimension of citizenship is conceptually complex and hindered by uncertainty, complicating its implementation in formal schooling contexts, and for teachers intending to infuse global citizenship into their teaching repertoires. In spite of the many challenges, educators, policy-makers, and citizens worldwide are stressing the important role that education must play in facing global challenges. GCE offers many opportunities to assist youth in preparation for their membership and participation in an increasingly globalized context. Global pressures and issues are no longer abstract—they have tangible global, national, local, and individual consequences for students, teachers, schools, and communities. Infusing and rethinking global dimensions in education can enhance local curriculum, to help students understand each other's diverse backgrounds and how

CHAPTER NINE: Global Citizenship Education in Schools   257

they fit into and actively engage with questions of global consequence. By exposing young people to practices, values, and cultures different from their own, teachers can nurture a deeper appreciation for human diversity, equity, and social justice. Critical inquiry into contrasting international perspectives and practices can also enhance learning across subjects and programs, by providing stimulating contexts for reflection. Student themselves are expressing a particular interest in learning more about global themes and issues through school curriculum. Indeed, nurturing a deeper understanding and appreciation for the core goals and practices associated with GCE can help students learn to address significant challenges in informed, thoughtful, and purposeful ways. Recent developments in GCE reveal considerable interest, yet there are many unanswered questions and issues for researchers to investigate and options for educators to consider, as they both navigate its meaning and practice in classrooms, schools, and systems. The potentially transformational role of the educator and aspirational potential of GCE are emphasized here, while a level of flexibility and relevance to local contexts is also a critical feature. The work currently underway reflects steps within a longer-term process toward supporting educational institutions—both formal and non-formal—in making institutional, pedagogical, and curricular changes to make learning more relevant and meet the needs of our changing and increasingly globalized world.

QUESTIONS FOR REFLECTION AND DISCUSSION
1. What learning goals associated with global citizenship education do you find most compelling, and why? In your view, what educational elements could ensure deep engagement with themes of identity, equity, power, conflict, and difference (including their implications for relationships and action in local and global public spheres)?
2. What forms of pedagogy do you think are most suitable in achieving core learning goals associated with GCE, and why?
3. Ali Abdi (2014, p. 20) argues that some global citizenship pedagogy is insufficiently critical: "learners must be given the tools to examine the thick and connected threads of systematically oppressive processes—mainly those of

colonialism, racism and the denial of other knowledge systems—to understand why the majority of the world's populations are without basic rights and cannot meet their needs and fulfill their expectations." To what extent to you agree and/or disagree with this statement, and why?

4. Compare the three vignettes that characterize GCE curriculum directions in Canada, the Arab world, and UNESCO:
   a. What are the main attributes associated with educating for global citizenship in each context?
   b. How do you account for the apparent similarities and/or differences (e.g., historical, geo-political, philosophical)?
5. Critically examine a website that illustrates youth engagement in global citizenship. Prepare a brief profile that describes the nature of youth engagement, its purposes, its successes and challenges, and the (implied) role of the teacher (in that website material).
6. What do you see as being some of the more significant opportunities and/or challenges for teachers in infusing understandings of global citizenship into (your own or others') day-to-day teaching? What types of support do you think would be helpful?

SUGGESTED AUDIO-VISUAL RESOURCES
British Council's 5 step guide to teaching critical thinking skills and global citizenship (2013). Available at: www.youtube.com/watch?v=oMBnL5HAAJo
Schools from the United Kingdom, Kenya, and South Africa work together to create critical thinking teaching resources in this British Council–funded project. In this 20-minute video, pupils from Jo Slovo Freedom High School, Molteno, Eastern Cape discuss a *Guardian* photograph of slums next to a hotel in South America.

Teachers TV: KS2 Citizenship—Global Issues, directed by Richard Wyllie (2015). Available at: www.youtube.com/watch?v=WVgrEsHJOo4
This program looks at how resources like those supplied by NGOs, such as Comic Relief, can enhance KS2 citizenship lessons.

SUGGESTIONS FOR FURTHER READING
Amnesty International. (2013). *Education for human dignity project.* London. Available at: www.amnesty.org/en/human-rights-education/

CHAPTER NINE: Global Citizenship Education in Schools

Andreotti, Vanessa, and de Souza, Lynn M. T. (2008). *Learning to read the world through other eyes*. Derby, UK: Global Education. Available at: www.academia.edu/575387/Learning_to_Read_the_World_Through_Other_Eyes_2008_

Bryan, Audrey, and Bracken, Meliosa. (2011). *Learning to read the world? Teaching and learning about global citizenship and international development in post-primary schools*. Dublin: Irish Aid. Available at: www.ubuntu.ie/media/bryan-learning-to-read-the-world.pdf

Larsen, Marianne. (2008). *ACT! Active citizens today: Global citizenship for local schools*. London, Ontario: University of Western Ontario. Available at: www.tvdsb.on.ca/act/

Learning and Teaching Scotland. (2011). *Developing global citizens within curriculum for excellence*. Glasgow. Available at: www.educationscotland.gov.uk/Images/DevelopingGlobalCitizens_tcm4-628187.pdf

Lebanese Ministry of Education and Higher Education (n.d.). *Child safety project online*. Available at: www.crdp.org/en/desc-projects/6240-%20Child%20Safety%20Online

McGough, Hannah, and Hunt, Frances. (2012). *The global dimension: A practical handbook for teacher educators*. London: Development Education Research Center. Available at: www.ioe.ac.uk/Handbook_final%281%29.pdf

Montemurro, David, Gambhir, Mira, Evans, Mark, and Broad, Kathy (Eds.). (2014). *Inquiry into practice: Learning and teaching global matters in local classrooms*. Toronto: Ontario Institute for Studies in Education. Available at: www.oise.utoronto.ca/oise/UserFiles/File/TEACHING_GLOBAL_MATTERS_FINAL_ONLINE.pdf

OSCE Office for Democratic Institutions and Human Rights. (2009). *Human rights education in the school systems of Europe, Central Asia and North America: A compendium of good practice*. Warsaw: Author. Available at: www.osce.org/odihr/39006?download=true

Oxfam. (2008). *Getting started with global citizenship: A guide for new teachers*. Oxford: Author. Available at: www.oxfam.org.uk/~/media/Files/Education/Global%20Citizenship/ GCNewTeacherENGLAND.ashx

Oxfam. (2015). *Education for Global Citizenship: A Guide for Schools*. Oxford: Author. Available at: www.oxfam.org.uk/education/global-citizenship/global-citizenship-guides

Rodrigue, Anne, Evans, Mark, and Broad, Kathy (Eds.). (2010). *Educating for global citizenship: An ETFO curriculum development inquiry initiative*. Toronto: Elementary Teachers' Federation

of Ontario. Available at: www.etfo.ca/Resources/eResources/
GlobalCitizenship/Pages/default.aspx

Sinclair, Margaret, Davies, Lynn, Obura, Anna, & Tibbitts, Felisa. (2008). *Learning to live together: Design, monitoring and evaluation of education for life skills, citizenship, peace and human rights*. Eschborn, Germany: Deutsche Gesellschaft für Technische Zusammenarbeit GmbH. Available at: www.ineesite.org/uploads/files/resources/doc_1_Learning_to_Live_Together.pdf

UNESCO. (2013). *Education for a culture of peace, human rights, citizenship, democracy and regional integration: ECOWAS reference manual*. Dakar, Senegal: Author. Available at: unesdoc.unesco.org/images/0022/002211/221128e.pdf

UNICEF. (2011). *Educating for global citizenship: A practical guide for schools in Atlantic Canada*. Toronto: UNICEF. Available at: www.unicef.ca/sites/default/files/imce_uploads/UTILITY%20NAV/TEACHERS/DOCS/GC/Educating_for_Global_Citizenship.pdf

ONLINE RESOURCES

Asia-Pacific Centre of Education for International Understanding. www.unescoapceiu.org/en/m211.php?pn=2&sn=1&sn2=1&seq=34

British Council's Connecting Classrooms. schoolsonline.britishcouncil.org/

E-Pals. www.epals.com/#!/main

The Freire Project. www.freireproject.org

Global Dimension: The World in Your Classroom. globaldimension.org.uk/

Global Education Network Europe (GENE). www.gene.eu

Global Youth Action Network. gyan.tigweb.org/

Longview Foundation. longviewfdn.org/

New Pedagogies for Deep Learning Project. npdl.global

Taking It Global. www.tigweb.org

UNESCO Associated Schools Project Network. www.unesco.org/new/en/education/networks/global-networks/aspnet/

UNESCO Clearinghouse on Global Citizenship Education, hosted by the Asia-Pacific Centre of Education for International Understanding (APCEIU). www.gcedclearinghouse.org/

UNESCO Global Citizenship Education Database. www.unesco.org/new/en/education/resources/in-focus-articles/global-%20citizenship-education/documents-unesdoc/

UNICEF Canada's Rights Respecting Schools Project.
rightsrespectingschools.ca/
University of Alberta, Centre for Global Citizenship Education and
Research. www.cgcer.ualberta.ca/AboutCGCER.aspx
University of Ottawa, Developing a Global Perspective for Educators.
www.developingaglobalperspective.ca/welcome/

NOTES

1. Curriculum policy examples include: British Columbia, Ministry of Education, Social Justice 12, Integrated Resource Package, 2008; Halifax Regional School Board, Nova Scotia, Race Relations, Cross-Cultural Understanding, and Human Rights Policy Framework, 2007; Manitoba Education, Grade 12 Global Issues: Citizenship and Sustainability, 2011; Quebec Education Program, 2005.
2. Faculties of Education integrating aspects of global citizenship education into undergraduate and initial teacher education programs include, for example: University of Alberta, University of Ottawa, University of Prince Edward Island, University of Toronto, University of British Columbia.
3. Countries include: Britain, the United States, Russia, the Czech Republic, Spain, Poland, Brazil, France, Italy, Turkey, Lebanon, Germany, Mexico, China, Japan, Greece, Jordan, India, and Pakistan.
4. As evidenced, for example, in citizenship education approaches advocated in Lebanon (Kiwan, 2015). *Adyan International Conference on Intercultural Citizenship: Education for Peace and Co-existence, in Beirut, Lebanon, April 24–25, 2015; Summary Report on the Conference.*
5. From UNESCO Paris, June 2015.
6. See twitter.com/menitnetwork.
7. See schoolsonline.britishcouncil.org/linking-programmes-worldwide/connecting-classrooms/spotlight/Lebanon

REFERENCES

Aaberg, Rebecca (2013, March 4). Carnegie's Muhammad Faour discusses democracy education in the Arab world. Retrieved from www.ccd21.org/news/cd-ccd/faour_arab_world.html

Abdi, Ali A. (2014). Reflecting on global dimensions of contemporary education. In D. Montemurro, M. Gambhir, M. Evans, and K. Broad (Eds.), *Inquiry into practice: Learning and teaching global matters in local classrooms* (pp. 19–21). Toronto: Ontario Institute for Studies in Education.

Abdi, Ali A., and Shultz, Lynette (Eds.) (2008). *Educating for human rights and global citizenship*. New York: SUNY Press.

Abdi, Ali A., Shultz, Lynette, and Pillay, Thashika (Eds.) (2015). *Decolonizing Global Citizenship Education*. Rotterdam, the Netherlands: Sense Publishers.

Aleinikoff, Thomas Alexander, and Klusmeyer, Douglas B. (Eds.) (2001). *Citizenship today: Global perspectives and practices.* Washington, DC: Carnegie Endowment for International Peace.

Andreotti, Vanessa (2006). Soft versus critical global citizenship education in development education: Policy and practice. *Policy & Practice: A Development Education Review, 3*, 40–51. Retrieved from www.developmenteducationreview.com/issue3-focus4?page=show

Arthur, James, Davies, Ian, and Hahn, Carole (Eds.) (2008). *The Sage handbook of education for citizenship and democracy.* Los Angeles: Sage.

Banks, James A. (Ed.) (2004). *Diversity and citizenship education: Global perspectives.* San Francisco: Jossey-Bass.

Banks, James A. (2008). Diversity, group identity, and citizenship education in a global age. *Educational Researcher, 37*(3), 129–139.

Bickmore, Kathy (2006). Democratic social cohesion (assimilation)? Representations of social conflict in Canadian public school curricula. *Canadian Journal of Education, 29*(2), 359–386.

Bickmore, Kathy (2007). Linking global with local: Cross-cultural conflict education in urban Canadian schools. In F. Leach, M. Dunne, & R. Masika (Eds.), *Education, conflict and reconciliation: International perspectives.* Oxford: Peter Lang. 237–252.

Bickmore, Kathy (2009). Global education to build peace. In T. F. Kirkwood-Tucker (Ed.), *Vision in global education: The globalization of curriculum and pedagogy in teacher education and schools.* New York: Peter Lang. 270–285.

Bickmore, Kathy (2014). Citizenship education in Canada: "Democratic" engagement with differences, conflicts and equity issues? *Citizenship Teaching & Learning, 9*(3), 257–278.

Cogan, John J., and Grossman, David L. (2009). Characteristics of globally minded teachers: A twenty-first century view. In T. F. Kirkwood-Tucker (Ed.), *Visions in global education: The globalization of curriculum and pedagogy in teacher education and schools: Perspectives from Canada, Russia, and the United States* (pp. 240–255). New York: Peter Lang.

Cook, Sharon Anne (2014). Reflections of a peace educator: The power and challenges of peace education with pre-service teachers. *Curriculum Inquiry, 44*(4), 489–507.

Davies, Ian, Evans, Mark, and Reid, Alan (2005). Globalizing citizenship education? A critique of "global education" and "citizenship education." *British Journal of Educational Studies, 53*(1), 66–87.

Davies, Lynn (2006). Global citizenship: Abstraction or framework for action? *Educational Review, 58*(1), 5–25.

Dewey, John (1933). *How We Think.* Boston and Washington DC: Heath & Co.

Eidoo, Sameena, Ingram, Leigh-Anne, MacDonald, Angela, Nabavi, Maryam, Pashby, Karen, and Stille, Saskia (2011). Through the kaleidoscope:

Intersections between theoretical perspectives and classroom implications in critical global citizenship education. *Canadian Journal of Education, 34*(4), 59–85.

Evans, Mark (2004). *Citizenship education pedagogy: Teachers' characterizations (What teachers say and what teachers do)* (Unpublished dissertation). University of York, England.

Evans, Mark, Davies, Ian, Dean, Bernadette, and Waghid, Yusef (2008). Educating for global citizenship in schools: Emerging understandings. In K. Mundy, K. Bickmore, R. Hayhoe, M. Madden, and K. Majidi (Eds.), *Comparative and international education: Issues for teachers* (pp. 273–298). New York: Teachers College Press.

Evans, Mark, Ingram, Leigh-Anne, MacDonald, Angela, and Weber, Nadya (2009). Mapping the "global dimension" of citizenship education in Canada: The complex interplay of theory, practice, and context. *Citizenship Teaching and Learning, 5*(2), 16–34.

Evans, Mark, Ingram, Leigh-Anne, MacDonald, Angela, and Weber, Nadya (2013). Educating for the global dimension of citizenship in schools in Canada: A study in three metropolitan regions. SSHRC Report.

Faour, Muhammad (2012). *Religious education and pluralism in Egypt and Tunisia*. Washington, DC: Carnegie Endowment for International Peace.

Faour, Muhammad, and Muasher, Marwan (2012). *The Arab world's education report card: School climate and citizenship skills*. Washington, DC: Carnegie Endowment for International Peace.

Freire, Paulo (1970). *Pedagogy of the oppressed*. New York: Herder and Herder.

Guo, Linyuan (2013). Translating global citizenship education into pedagogic actions in classroom settings. *Education Review, 3*(2), 8–9.

Guo, Linyuan (2014). Preparing teachers to educate for 21st century global citizenship: Envisioning and enacting. *Journal of Global Citizenship and Equity Education, 4*(1), 1–21.

Hansard Society (2011). Social media and the new Arab Spring. Available online at www.hansardsociety.org.uk/blogs/edemocracy/archive/2011/04/19/social-media-and-the-new-arab-spring.aspx (accessed February 4, 2013).

Harshman, Jason, Augustine, Tami, and Merryfield, Merry M. (Eds.) (2015). *Research in global citizenship education*. Charlotte, NC: Information Age Publishing.

Heater, Derek (2002). *World citizenship: Cosmopolitan thinking and its opponents*. London: Continuum.

Hébert, Yvonne, and Sears, Alan (2002). *Citizenship education*. Toronto: Canadian Education Association. Retrieved from www.cea-ace.ca/sites/default/files/cea-2004-citizenship-education.pdf

Held, David, McGrew, Anthony, Goldblatt, David, and Perraton, Jonathan (1999). *Global transformations: Politics, economics, and culture*. Cambridge: Polity Press.

Hodgetts, A. Bernie (1968). *What culture? What heritage? A study of civic education in Canada*. Toronto: Ontario Institute for Studies in Education.

Holland, Dick (2004). *Hope for a new vision: The emergence of global citizenship in Ontario*. (unpublished master's thesis). Ontario Institute for Studies in Education/University of Toronto.

Ichilov, Orit (1998). *Citizenship and citizenship education in a changing world*. London: Woburn Press.

Isin, Engin F., and Turner, Bryan S. (Eds.) (2003). *Handbook of citizenship studies*. London: Sage.

Joshee, Reva (2004). Citizenship and multicultural education in Canada: From assimilation to social cohesion. In J. A. Banks, (Ed.), *Diversity and citizenship education: Global perspectives* (pp. 127–158). San Francisco: Jossey-Bass.

Kiwan, Dina (2008). *Education for inclusive citizenship*. London: Routledge.

Kiwan, Dina (2014). Emerging forms of citizenship in the Arab world. In E. F. Isin and P. Nyers (Eds.), *Routledge global handbook of citizenship studies* (pp. 307–316). New York: Routledge.

Kiwan, Dina (forthcoming). *The implications of global citizenship education (GCED) on learning, curriculum and competency development in the Arab States*. Beirut, Lebanon: UNESCO.

Kolb, David A. (1984). *Experiential learning: Experience as the source of learning and development*. Englewood Cliffs, NJ: Prentice Hall.

Kymlicka, Will (1998). Multicultural citizenship. In G. Shafir (Ed.), *The citizenship debates* (pp. 167–188). Minneapolis: University of Minnesota Press.

Larsen, Marianne, and Faden, Lisa (2008). Supporting the growth of global citizenship educators. Brock Education: A Journal of General Inquiry. Special issue—Citizenship Education in an Era of Globalization. *Canadian Perspectives, 17*(1), 71–86.

MacDonald-Vemic, Angela, Evans, Mark, Ingram, Leigh-Anne, and Weber, Nadya (2015). A question of how: A report on teachers' instructional practices when educating for global citizenship in Canada. In J. Harshman, T. Augustine, and M. M. Merryfield (Eds.), *Research in global citizenship education* (pp. 83–118). Charlotte, NC: Information Age Publishing.

Marshall, Thomas H. (1950). *Citizenship and social class: And other essays*. Cambridge: Cambridge University Press.

McLaughlin, Terence H. (1992). Citizenship, diversity, and education: A philosophical perspective. *Journal of Moral Education, 21*(3), 235–247.

McLean, Lorna R., Cook, Sharon A., and Crowe, Tracy (2006). Educating the next generation of global citizens through teacher education, one new teacher at a time. *Canadian Social Studies Journal, 40*(1), 1–7.

McLean, Lorna R., and Ng-A-Fook, Nicholas (2013). Developing a global perspective for educators, *Education Review, 3*(2), 1.

Merryfield, Merry M. (1998). Pedagogy for global perspectives in education: Studies of teachers' thinking and practice. *Theory & Research in Social Education, 26*(3), 342–379.

Mundy, Karen, and Manion, Caroline (2008). Global education in Canadian elementary schools: An exploratory study. *Canadian Journal of Education, 31*(4), 941–974.

Osborne, Ken (2001). Democracy, democratic citizenship, and education. In J. P. Portelli and R. P. Solomon (Eds.), *The erosion of democracy in education: Critique to possibilities* (pp. 29–61). Calgary: Detselig Enterprises Ltd.

Osler, Audrey, and Starkey, Hugh (2003). Learning for cosmopolitan citizenship: Theoretical debates and young people's experiences. *Education Review, 55*(3), 243–254.

Osler, Audrey, and Starkey, Hugh (2006). *Cosmopolitan citizenship, changing citizenship: Democracy and inclusion in education.* Maidenhead, England: Open University Press.

O'Sullivan, Brian (1999). Global change and educational reform in Ontario and Canada. *Canadian Journal of Education, 24*(3), 311–325.

O'Sullivan, Michael, and Pashby, Karen (2008). *Citizenship education in the era of globalization: Canadian perspectives.* Rotterdam, the Netherlands: Sense Publishers.

Oxley, Laura, and Morris, Paul (2013). Global citizenship: A typology for distinguishing its multiple conceptions. *British Journal of Educational Studies, 61*(3), 301–325.

Parker, Walter C. (Ed.) (1996). *Educating the democratic mind.* Albany: SUNY Press.

Peters, Michael A., Britton, Alan, and Blee, Harry (Eds.) (2008). *Global citizenship education: Philosophy, theory and pedagogy.* Rotterdam, the Netherlands: Sense Publishers.

Pew Research Center (2012). *Social networking popular across globe: Arab publics most likely to express political views online.* Washington, DC: Author. Retrieved from www.pewglobal.org/files/2012/12/Pew-Global-Attitudes-Project-Technology-Report-FINAL-December-12-2012.pdf

Pike, Graham (2000). Global education and national identity: In pursuit of meaning. *Theory into Practice, 39*(2), 64–73.

Pike, Graham (2008). Reconstructing the legend: Educating for global citizenship. In A. A. Abdi and L. Shultz (Eds.), *Educating for human rights and global citizenship* (pp. 223–237). New York: SUNY Press.

Pike, Graham, and Selby, David (1988). *Global teacher, global learner.* London: Hodder and Stoughton.

Pike, Graham, and Selby, David (2000). *In the global classroom 2.* Toronto: Pippin.

Portelli, John P., and Solomon, Patrick (Eds.) (2001). *The erosion of democracy in education.* Calgary: Detselig Enterprises Ltd.

Rapoport, Anatoli (2015). Global citizenship education: Classroom teachers' perspectives and approaches. In J. Harshman, T. Augustine, and M. M. Merryfield (Eds.), *Research in global citizenship education* (pp. 119-136). Charlotte, NC: Information Age Publishing.

Richardson, George H. (2004). Global education and the challenge of globalization. In A. Sears and I. Wright (Eds.), *Challenges and prospects in Canadian social studies* (pp. 138-149). Vancouver: Pacific Education Press.

Richardson, George H., and Abbott, Laurence (2009). Between the national and the global: Exploring tensions in Canadian citizenship education. *Studies in Ethnicity and Nationalism*, 9(3), 377-394.

Schattle, Hans (2008). *The practices of global citizenship*. Lanham, MD: Rowman & Littlefield.

Schweisfurth, Michele (2006). Education for global citizenship: Teacher agency and curricular structure in Ontario schools. *Education Review*, 58(1), 41-50.

Sears, Alan (1996). Something different to everyone: Conceptions of citizenship and citizenship education. *Canadian and International Education*, 25(2), 1-15.

Sears, Alan (2004). In search of good citizens: Citizenship education and social studies in Canada. In A. Sears and I. Wright (Eds.), *Challenges and Prospects in Canadian Social Studies* (pp. 90-106). Vancouver: Pacific Education Press.

Shultz, Lynette (2007). Educating for global citizenship: Conflicting agendas and understandings. *The Alberta Journal of Educational Research*, 53(3), 248-258.

Sipos, Yona, Battisti, Bryce, and Grimm, Kurt (2008). Achieving Transformative Sustainability Learning: Engaging Head, Hands and Heart. *International Journal of Sustainability in Higher Education*, 9(1), 68-86.

South House Exchange (2001). *Education for peace, human rights, democracy, international understanding, and tolerance*. Ottawa: Council of Ministers of Education, Canada and Canadian Commission of UNESCO. Retrieved from citeseerx.ist.psu.edu/viewdoc/download?doi=10.1.1.393.7902&rep=rep1&type=pdf

Stevick, Doyle, and Levinson, Bradley (2007). *Reimagining civic education: How diverse societies form democratic citizens*. Lanham, MD: Rowman & Littlefield.

Strong-Boag, Veronica (1996). Claiming a place in the nation: Citizenship education and the challenge of feminists, Natives, and workers in post-confederation Canada. *Canadian and International Education*, 25(2), 128-145.

UNDP (2008a). *The national human development report 2008-2009: Towards a citizen state*. Beirut, Lebanon: Author. Retrieved from www.lb.undp.org/content/dam/lebanon/docs/Governance/Publications/NHDR_Full_Report1_En.pdf

UNDP (2008b). *Education and citizenship: Concepts, attitudes, skills and actions: Analysis of survey results of 9th grade students in Lebanon*. Beirut, Lebanon: Author. Retrieved from search.shamaa.org/PDF/a13293/UNDPa13293.pdf

UNESCO (2013a). *Global citizenship education: An emerging perspective* (Outcome document of the technical consultation on global citizenship education). Paris: Author. Retrieved from unesdoc.unesco.org/images/0022/002241/224115E.pdf

UNESCO (2013b). *Intercultural competencies: Conceptual and operational framework*. Paris: Author. Retrieved from unesdoc.unesco.org/images/0021/002197/219768e.pdf

UNESCO (2014). *Global citizenship education: Preparing learners for the challenges of the 21st century*. Paris: Author. Retrieved from www.unesco.ch/fileadmin/user_upload/3_Wie/bildung/Global_Citizenship_Education.pdf

UNESCO (2015). *Global citizenship education: Topics and learning objectives*. Paris: Author. Retrieved from unesdoc.unesco.org/images/0023/002329/232993e.pdf

United Nations (n.d.). *Global education first initiative*. Retrieved from www.globaleducationfirst.org

Westheimer, Joel (2015). *What kind of citizen? Educating our children for the common good*. New York: Teachers College Press.

CHAPTER TEN

CONFLICT, PEACEBUILDING, AND EDUCATION: RETHINKING PEDAGOGIES IN DIVIDED SOCIETIES, LATIN AMERICA, AND AROUND THE WORLD

Kathy Bickmore

INTRODUCTION

Conflict—disputes, distrust, incompatible interests, not necessarily violence—is inevitable in life, but, despite what we see in news and history books, it is often addressed peacefully: "Actually, peace is not news because most people live in peace with their neighbors most of the time, and most countries live in peace with neighboring countries most of the time" (Alger, 1995, p. 128). Education alone cannot resolve (and may even legitimize) systemic issues that exacerbate destructive conflict— such as resource scarcity, concentration of power, social exclusion, or narratives of enmity and aggressive nationalism. However, education may build capacity and social relationships for democratic, inclusive, and just conflict management (transformative peacebuilding) by influencing individual and collective understandings, competencies, values, norms, opportunities, agency, and status equity.

Comparative international education as a field has always carried a concern for peace, including international understanding and amelioration of harms such as injustice and poverty (Burns, 2008). This chapter reviews international and comparative scholarship on education for democratic peacebuilding, primarily in societies suffering current or recent escalated destructive conflict (repression, gang violence, war, or division).

EDUCATION AND VIOLENT CONFLICT

Around the world, formal (school) and non-formal (outside school) education may exacerbate violence, at least as often as it teaches or practices non-violent, democratic responses to conflict. As political scientist Marc Ross (1993) found by analyzing ethnographies of high-conflict and low-conflict societies, conflicts are rooted in both tangible, socially structured interests (inequities, competing needs for resources), and intangible psycho-cultural narratives (beliefs, values, fears—what matters to people and why). This applies to education.

Social-structurally, education may reinforce destructive conflict—for instance by being unequally distributed, or through language or (de)segregation practices that disadvantage or limit the autonomy of certain groups (Davies, 2005). *Culturally,* education may legitimize beliefs and narratives of national, ethnic, or gender-based chauvinism and social inequity, or normalize (some or all) violence and militarism. How people experience and handle conflict depends on their location in the changing social, political, and cultural contexts that shape their learning and their options for responding.

Structural, cultural, and direct physical violence disproportionately harm people with the least social power, such as girls and marginalized groups (see Chapter Seven), thereby deepening social inequality (Leach & Dunne, 2007). For example, segregated residential schools, forced upon Aboriginal peoples in North America, deepened still-ongoing colonial oppression through physical, sexual, spiritual, and cultural violence (see Chapter Six).

Most major armed conflicts today are civil wars and insurgencies, not inter-state (Smith, 2012). Schools and teachers, because of their relationship to human rights and to nation-state employers, are often specifically targeted in terrorism and war (Novelli, 2010; Williams, 2004). Resources allocated to armaments are thereby denied to human needs or to education. Conversely, after Costa Rica abolished its army in 1948 and allocated the savings to public education and health, it became the most prosperous and peaceful country in Central America (Ware et al., 2005, p. 129). Clearly, escalated violence is a barrier to (any) education.

Violence takes many forms. Norwegian peace studies theorist Galtung (1975) refers to social structural inequity, discrimination, and exclusion—which themselves constitute (indirect) harm and may provoke direct physical violence—as "structural violence." "Cultural violence"

(Galtung, 1990) means collective beliefs and attitudes that legitimize enmity, direct violence, and structural violence. Alternatively, institutional factors, such as support for achievement equity within schools, may help to shape the possibilities for peace by reducing structural violence (Akiba, LeTendre, Baker, & Goesling, 2003). US cultural theorist Rob Nixon (2011) uses the term "slow violence" to describe gradual or delayed massive harm, occurring through accretion or attrition, like environmental damage. Resistance to such violence, Nixon argues, involves mobilizing dramatic images and narratives that make visible the violence of formerly anonymous disasters—a kind of informal (media) education.

DIFFERING GOALS FOR PEACE EDUCATION

Paradoxically, though education can exacerbate destructive social conflict, educational initiatives and reforms also can be essential elements of peacebuilding. Beyond facilitating development of capacities, relationships, opportunities, access, and confidence, education can increase people's understanding of the nature and extent of conflicts, their negative consequences, especially for weaker parties, and the possibilities for change—thereby motivating and equipping people to act, to shift power away from un-peaceful politics and social patterns. Direct, explicit forms of peace education may be most feasible during the calmer phases of conflict cycles—in long-range prevention, and in reconstruction after a peacemaking process has begun to work. However, this chapter documents viable examples of peace education, even in very difficult situations.

Peace, too, takes many forms. Thus, education for peace may have remarkably different goals, especially comparing higher- and lower-conflict contexts (Salomon, 2002, 2011). The *absence* of direct physical violence at a certain place and time, without resolution or transformation of the factors causing the problem, is called "negative peace" (Galtung, 1969). In contrast, "positive peace" refers to the ongoing *presence* of just, democratic mechanisms and social support for sustainable, ongoing redress of structural and cultural violence as well as individual disputes (ibid.).

Thus, education for constructive, democratic, non-violent conflict and peacebuilding (positive peace) is not a simple matter of adding new learning activities: it means transforming school structures, policies, curriculum, and pedagogical practices.

CHAPTER TEN: Conflict, Peacebuilding, and Education

There are three basic approaches to achieving (different kinds of) peace (Galtung, 1976). *Peacekeeping* security measures are designed to impede direct physical violence (to achieve negative peace) through control. *Peacemaking* (negotiation, mediation, and other dialogue to understand conflicts and identify mutually acceptable resolutions) also takes place after conflict emerges, but addresses its causes and solutions, not only its aggressive symptoms. *Peacebuilding* means complex long-term transformation of cultural and social systems, to develop sustainable positive peace by redressing the beliefs and practices that cause exploitation, marginalization, and dehumanization. Peacemaking and peacemaking education are necessary but not sufficient for peacebuilding, which also includes inclusion and equity.

> "First, the form of peace education has to be compatible with the idea of peace, that is, it has to exclude not only direct violence but also structural violence. This is important because...in the structure is the message."
> —Johan Galtung
> (1975, in Bajaj, 2008, p. 50)

There remains around the world a remarkable faith in (transformed) education's capacity to help communities to reconstruct, re-humanize, and develop, even after devastating violence (Gill & Niens, 2014b). Often among the first emergency assistance for refugees and war-affected children is to establish schooling, even where there is no functioning nation-state (Tomlinson & Benefield, 2005; Waters & LeBlanc, 2005). Education provision is a key, often gender-responsive initiative intended to facilitate psycho-social wellness, to mitigate the impact as well as the likelihood of further violence (Kirk, 2011; Skovdal & Campbell, 2015). A sub-field has sprung up around education in violent contexts that are variously called emergencies, fragile states, or conflict zones (INEE, 2010; Mundy & Dryden-Peterson, 2011; Rappleye & Paulson, 2007). Another common term, *post-conflict*, confuses (continuing, unresolved) conflict with (ceased or reduced) armed violence. Some of this work demonstrates the negative impact of armed conflict on schooling, and the value of providing or resuming regular education for children displaced or disrupted by war (Shields & Paulson, 2015). This chapter addresses primarily the other causal direction: the longer-term preventative (or escalatory, or negligible) impacts that various aspects of and approaches to education can have on future violence. Citing Ernest Gellner, International Bureau of Education scholars Tawil and Harley (2004) argue that a "monopoly of legitimate education in modern nation-states may be more important than the monopoly of legitimate violence" (p. 11). In other words, public education (expansion and reform) may be more relevant to building sustainable social cohesion and peace than military or policing.

A caution: nation-states do *not* always have a monopoly on violence, and state violence is not always "legitimate." For instance, in parts of Latin America, high levels of violence linked to drug trafficking, gangs, and corruption, as well as some insurgencies, disproportionately harm women and poor people (Pearce, 2010; Staubhaar, 2012). Both domestically and via international "aid," states increasingly confront violence (framed as criminality) with "securitization" practices that deny human rights and tend to multiply both the violence and its underlying grievances (also Ghali, 2014; Novelli, 2011).

Such securitization, in the form of punitive discipline regimes (repressive attempts at peacekeeping control), is also increasingly prevalent inside some school systems, in particular Mexico's (Zurita Rivera, 2012).

> "Rather than find solutions to [violence] problems, the state gains huge political capital from its ongoing confrontations at the same time as it allies with pathological and corrupt violent actors outside the state in order to gain temporary victories."
> —Jenny Pearce (2010, p. 299)

The work of Brazilian socialist education scholar Paulo Freire (1970) has profoundly influenced peace and conflict educators' pedagogies and efforts to address structural violence (Bartlett, 2008). Campaigns to empower poor people, inspired by Freire, have been mounted in Cuba and Nicaragua in Latin America, and Guinea-Bissau in Africa. These initiatives have engaged learners in "conscientization" dialogue, expressing the realities of their own oppression so that they could rise up and transform their situations (Arnove, 1999; Freire, 1978). These experiences show that it is challenging, but not impossible, to facilitate dialogue-based learning to build upon the local cultural knowledge of participants.

Like Freirean praxis, peace and conflict education explicitly intends to change the world, to make it more humane and less violent. This value-laden goal makes its implementation dependent on the social and political conditions, cultures, and levels of consensus in each environment (Bar-Tal, 2002). Yet many prominent international peace education initiatives, including those advocating the Culture of Peace (UNESCO, 2001), the subsequent initiative for Rapprochement of Cultures (UNESCO, 2014), and the Hague Agenda for Peace and Justice for the 21st Century (Hague-Appeal, 1999), emphasize persuading individuals to develop interpersonal communication and problem-solving skills and "universal" values such as non-violence, tolerance, justice, solidarity, human rights, and environmental sustainability (Ellison, 2014; Ross, 2010; Weinstein, Freedman, & Hughson, 2007).

An influential proponent of this "culture of peace" work, US educator Betty Reardon, argues that women's actual roles in many societies constitute evidence that peaceful, nurturing behaviour occurs as naturally among humans as does aggression, and that positive peacebuilding requires people to develop love for the Other, including the Others each of us carry inside ourselves (Reardon & Snauwaert, 2015).

There is little evidence that directly teaching values can reliably cause changes in behaviour. Based on a review of research on social and anti-bias learning, Clark McCauley (2002) argues that "feet first" education (enacting actual changes in behaviour) is more likely to change hearts and minds than "head first" education (teaching values and principles). For example, he shows that people have unlearned racism by engaging in desegregated situations offering institutional support for non-discrimination—"head" following "feet," rather than the other way around. Further, too much value consensus (indoctrination) can stifle diversity and creativity. So, "for any type of critique to be of interest, both data and values have to be

> "Critical and liberating dialogue, which presupposes action, must be carried on with the oppressed at whatever the stage of their struggle for liberation. The content of that dialogue can and should vary in accordance with historical conditions and the level at which the oppressed perceive reality."
>
> —Paulo Freire (1996, p. 26)

> "A culture of peace will be achieved when citizens of the world understand global problems, have the skills to resolve conflicts and struggle for justice non-violently, live by international standards of human rights and equity, appreciate cultural diversity, and respect the Earth and each other. Such learning can be only be achieved by systematic education for peace."
>
> —Hague Agenda for Peace and Justice for the 21st Century (1999)

present" (Galtung, 2008, p. 54). Thus peace education entwines judgment (values, feelings, and deliberation about action choices) with action, lived experience, and evidence.

Sustained peacebuilding requires broad, inclusive participation over time; thus government-funded schools are important (though challenging) contexts to transform, to improve prospects for peace. Peacebuilding requires development of concrete skills, understanding, empathetic imagination (perspective recognition), and democratic agency—achieved through frequent, varied opportunities to practise handling conflict constructively, such as facilitated discussion of conflictual issues, deliberation toward collective decisions, and resolution of disputes through mediation. Temporary *negative peace* (cessation of direct violence) can be achieved through ceasefire and peacekeeping control. However, sustainable *positive peace*—presence of capacities, norms, and institutional processes for handling conflicts fairly and non-violently—depends upon ongoing education and actual practice.

EDUCATION IN DIVERSE CONFLICT ZONES

International comparison may facilitate understanding, but application of models from one social context to another can be problematic. Peacebuilding education faces different conflict contexts in the global South and in societies facing or trying to heal from escalated armed conflict, compared to the privileged and relatively peaceful global North (Novelli & Lopes Cardozo, 2008; Salomon, 2011). Paradoxically, most peace education theory and research (including international interventions) have been imported or imposed—designed in relatively secure societies of the global North (IPEP, 2005; Sobe, 2009). When existing peace education research does study conflict zones, a preponderance examines global Northern contexts, particularly Israel, Northern Ireland, Cyprus, Bosnia, and Kosovo (Bekerman & Zembylas, 2012; McGlynn, 2009; Salomon & Cairns, 2010; Vriens, 1999). Each conflict is embedded in different cultures and histories of pain; thus peace education curricula and research may miss elements important in many conflict zones.

Non-formal peacemaking educator John Paul Lederach (1995, 2003), based on his work in armed-conflict zones, argues that top-down "prescriptive" conflict resolution training, rooted in the individualistic and rationalistic cultures of the global North, is often inappropriate in particular local conflict contexts. Alternatively, "elicitive" pedagogies are

CHAPTER TEN: Conflict, Peacebuilding, and Education 275

designed to name, investigate, and build on the implicit conflict knowledge rooted in any culture's experiences, stories, and proverbs.

Most contemporary peace education *theory* includes principles and strategies for addressing aspects of structural and cultural violence— that is, to achieve justice as well as harmonious relations (Bajaj, 2015; Curle, Freire, & Galtung, 1974; Gill & Niens, 2014a; Harris & Morrison, 2003). At the same time, much peace education *practice* (referenced above) emphasizes the interpersonal-level conflict communication skills, values, beliefs, and empathetic tolerance for the Other, sometimes accompanied by bland national citizenship narratives—avoiding the difficult political conflicts at the root of much large-scale violence.

> "'[C]ulture' should not be understood by conflict resolvers and trainers primarily in technical terms as a challenge to be mastered and overcome. Culture is rooted in social knowledge and represents a vast resource, a rich seedbed for producing a multitude of approaches and models in conflict resolution."
> —John Paul Lederach (1995, p. 40)

People growing up in different social contexts presumably glean from their environments, and consequently need from formal education, different narratives, skills, understandings, and practice opportunities. Knowledges and norms taught in school may coexist uneasily, especially in high-conflict environments, with what's learned in the family, community, religion, and popular media. Richard Merelman (1990), reviewing research in political socialization, theorizes that in highly contested regimes, children grow up embedded in visible and salient inter-group conflicts. These children may see conflict as normal and develop early understanding of how conflicts work, although they may need to learn how to re-humanize across differences and democratize social institutions. In contrast, Merelman argues, in relatively uncontested regimes (such as Canada—though groups disagree, the stability of the government is not threatened), inter-group conflicts are less visible, especially to dominant groups. In these situations, many young people would have little experience with recognizing competing worldviews, and may learn to view conflict as abnormal and dissenters or marginalized people as bad. Thus the values embedded in peace and conflict education may be more visible (contested) or more hidden (assumed), and have different ramifications for people in different social identity and risk positions. Below are some key types of peace education programming to compare.

CONFLICTING IDENTITIES, NARRATIVES, AND HISTORY IN CURRICULUM

Unfortunately, education too often recirculates hatred of the Other across generations (Jansen, 2009). Curriculum and textbooks used on different sides of many conflicts—such as Israel/Palestine, Lebanon, Bosnia and Herzegovina, Kosovo—present completely different narratives of identity, history, and causation (Frayha, 2004; Harber, 2004). For example, Greek Cypriot teachers' nationalistic discourse has presented Turks and Turkish Cypriots as barbarians, as does discourse about Greeks and Greek Cypriots in Turkish Cypriot classrooms—reinforcing a culture of violence and division (Hadjipavlou, 2002). Violence against lower-caste and Sinhalese or Tamil people has been legitimized in Indian and Sri Lankan schools (Bush & Saltarelli, 2000). Some Rwandan schools' and teachers' active or indirect support for dehumanization, and for deference to authority, helped pave the way for genocidal violence (King, 2014). However, formal and non-formal education practices *can* transform antagonistic group identities toward just, democratic, non-violent coexistence.

Cultural practices that shape people's sense of collective identity, thinking, and feeling about conflict include discourses, symbols, and narratives. History education is often hotly contested because it is where such narratives are most visible (Williams, 2014). Interviews with 250 Northern Ireland secondary students, for example, showed strong identity-group influences on students' notions of history, although students knew about competing narratives and hoped school would help them to balance multiple perspectives (Barton & McCully, 2012). Similarly, Palestinian and Orthodox and non-Orthodox Jewish Israeli youth have developed differing notions of national identity, and different narratives about each group's citizenship roles (Ichilov, 2005). Textbook history narratives of the 1967 war blamed Arabs for provocations and presented the Israeli nation-state as heroic (Firer, 2002). Subsequent history textbooks had "a more open and complex perspective," but the still-predominant Zionist narrative left negligible space for meaningful cross-cultural understanding (Al-Haj, 2005). However, alternative narratives can encourage conflict transformation (Funk & Said, 2004; Ross, 2007).

Some small projects working with educators or school children do constructively address conflicting perspectives on the painful past and present (in Israel, see Netzer, 2008). In Rwanda and other societies

CHAPTER TEN: Conflict, Peacebuilding, and Education 277

recovering from identity-based armed conflict, an initiative based on the Facing History and Ourselves program introduced new approaches to pedagogy and multi-perspective first-person testimonies and other historical resources, and facilitated difficult dialogue in teacher professional learning and collaborative curriculum development (Freedman, Weinstein, Murphy, & Longman, 2008). In Sri Lanka, pilot peace, human rights, national integration education projects have created alternative history curricula for various grade levels (Perera, Wijetunge, & Balasooriya, 2004). A joint commission of Japanese, Korean, and Chinese scholars created a new (unfortunately little-used) history text that openly addresses Japan's violent imperialist incursions in East Asia: where these 50 historians could not reach agreement, their book presents three parallel narratives representing alternative views of particular events (Hayhoe, 1998; Wang, 2009). Thus history curriculum carries politically powerful perspectives that may reinforce social conflicts, but that can be supplemented or recreated to facilitate peacebuilding.

History education conflicts are especially difficult to resolve when that history includes recent human rights violation or genocide. For instance, recent national curriculum in Guatemala recognizes multiple cultural identities and Indigenous Mayan values and languages, but is contested and unevenly implemented (Herdoízo-Estévez & Lenk, 2010; Salazar Tetzagüic & Grigsgy, 2004). Some Mexican curriculum, in contrast, presents Indigenous peoples in generic heritage terms, not as participants in contemporary interculturality (Rodríguez Ledesma, 2013). Some scholars see intercultural citizenship education as assimilation, even "cultural genocide," that substitutes surface integration for true recognition of sovereignty, culture, and harm done (Bear Nicholas, 1996). Others argue that "treaty education" and other respectful engagement with Indigenous knowledges and difficult histories can help to alleviate structural and symbolic violence (Sumida Huaman, 2011; Tupper, 2014). When historical trauma has occurred within the (conflicting) lived memories of teachers and students' families, as in Chile's course about the dictatorship, it is bound to evoke strong emotions: these can be educative, but also difficult to address in a fair and caring manner (Magendzo & Toledo, 2009). Yet, these scholars agree, leaving such important histories out of the curriculum is not a democratic option.

While formal education is heavily influenced by the nation-state, media culture can offer alternative openings for conflict transformation, such as sharing alternative information, creating space for dialogue, and acknowledging harm. For example, a mass popular education effort in Australia, Sorry Day, commemorated shameful practices toward Australian Aborigines (Bond, 2005). Public events such as Truth and Reconciliation Commission hearings also pedagogically encode particular "truths" to reshape the future (Nagy, 2014; Soudien, 2002). Thus education can address competing narratives surrounding complex conflict and violence.

DIALOGUE WITH THE OTHER: INTER-GROUP CONTACT AND PREJUDICE REDUCTION

The most widely practised and studied form of education designed to reduce inter-group enmity is "inter-group contact" dialogue. Peacebuilding dialogue for reconciliation requires participants to acknowledge harm done, and to take initiative to alleviate that harm and rebuild non-violent relationships (Assefa, 2005). Planned inter-group contact encounters are often small, voluntary, non-formal programs that bring together individuals from adversary groups, face-to-face, for facilitated sharing, cooperative activity, and dialogue about the conflict between their groups, sometimes proceeding to deliberation to plan joint problem-solving action (Kaufman, 2005). Although such initiatives usually involve far fewer people than would public schooling reforms such as desegregation or curriculum change, contact program participants often report life-changing personal impacts. International research on such initiatives sheds light on pedagogies for peacebuilding in a range of contexts.

Often there is a remarkable amount of prejudice and misinformation to unlearn. For example, American peacebuilding scholar Mohammed Abu-Nimer, working with Israeli and Arab children in one contact program, saw children looking for each other's tails (cited in Ware et al., 2005, p. 51). Gordon Allport's 1954 "contact hypothesis" articulates certain conditions under which inter-group contact would be likely to reduce prejudice and increase openness to the Other's perspectives: process and participant selection designed to equalize status between groups; close, prolonged contact; cross-group cooperation toward common goals; and institutional environments that support prejudice reduction (Tal-Or, Boninger, & Gleicher, 2002). Unfortunately these conditions are often not met (Pettigrew & Tropp, 2000). Similar inter-group dialogue programming is implemented in relatively peaceful contexts, such as North America, where racism remains a problem

(Dessel & Rogge, 2008). While many such prejudice reduction initiatives are marginal efforts of short duration, undertaken without much social-institutional support for status equalization or behaviour change, a few have developed into sustained, successful efforts.

One inter-group contact initiative is Let's Talk: students from the Republic of Ireland, Northern Ireland, England, and Australia participated in workshops discussing contentious issues and youth referenda, and developed openness, political awareness, and less adversarial hybrid identities (Davies, 2004, pp. 137–139).

A contact program in Israel included teacher professional development, internet dialogue, and some face-to-face time between Israeli Jewish and Bedouin secondary students: pre- and post-test of participants' attitudes toward their own and Others' ethnic identities demonstrated small positive effects, unevenly across groups (Katz & Yablon, 2003).

> "Education on its own will not create world peace. Nor will a school be able to heal and control children living in violent or drug-related communities...[but] I do think schools can interrupt the processes towards more violence."
> —Lynn Davies (2004, p. 223)

Speak Your Piece was a more comprehensive program in Northern Ireland, linked to an ongoing Education for Mutual Understanding curriculum requirement. It employed youth worker facilitators, television programs, conflict resolution skill teaching, and class discussion—mostly in identity (segregated homeschool) groups, but also including some inter-group contact, directly and via computer conferencing. The teacher-researchers believed their pilot year, 1996–97, had been fairly successful in facilitating open, forthright, and inclusive dialogue on controversial issues, to "generate respect for the right to express points of view and to show sensitivity to personal biographies" (McCully, O'Doherty, & Smyth, 1999, p. 126). While some inter-group contact initiatives may affect some participants' understandings and attitudes, by 2000 they had had negligible impact on tangible behaviour such as housing segregation, cross-group friendships, voting patterns, or willingness to participate in integrated education (Cairns & Hewstone, 2002).

In many protracted conflict situations, opportunities for constructive or sustained inter-group contact do not arise naturally, without preparation. Thus, although success is not assured, people continue to create contact dialogue and other bridge-building programs around the world.

PEACEBUILDING EDUCATION: ARTS, MEDIA, DISCOURSES, SHARED AND PLURAL IDENTITIES

Peace education initiatives may engage people through language, popular culture, electronic technology, and arts (Bratic, 2013; Davies, 2014; Lederach, 2005; Oxford, 2013). For instance, the Hello Peace initiative of Families Forum, an organization of Israeli Jews and Palestinians whose relatives had been killed in that conflict, encouraged people to telephone a number that connected them to a willing person on the "other side." After over 480,000 calls (2002–04), many participants reported significant impacts on themselves, their friends and relatives, and somewhat on those indirectly exposed through media or word of mouth (Barnea & Shinar, 2005). Other well-known prejudice-reduction initiatives in various conflictual societies include the many *Sesame Street*–type children's television programs (Stevenson-Krausz, 2013). One such program, for ethnic Albanian, Macedonian, Roma, and Turkish children, showed significant positive effects on children's understandings of themselves and Others (Shochat, 2003). Beyond children's education, such initiatives represent ongoing cross-party cooperation among the diverse adults who design the programs (Kay, 2013).

Integrated schooling transforms shared, daily inter-group experiences over sustained periods, thereby fulfilling tenets of contact theory (McGlynn, Zembylas, & Bekerman, 2013). In a system still segregated by religion and social class, by 2006 about 6 percent of Northern Irish pupils attended 57 voluntarily integrated schools, led by a Catholic or a Protestant principal. Integrated schooling is even rarer in Israel, whose separate Arabic and Jewish educational systems use different curricula and languages of instruction. The four integrated Jewish-Palestinian schools in 2006 had Jewish and Palestinian co-principals, offering bilingual as well as bicultural education. Many parents' motivations to place their children in these integrated environments emphasized schools' perceived academic excellence (including, for Palestinians, Hebrew language practice) more than peace (McGlynn, 2009). Interviews with government officials, and the principals of six typical Northern Irish integrated schools and the four Israeli-Palestinian schools, showed that inter-group differences were typically managed differently. The Irish integrated schools emphasized *individual* differences and *common* identity, whereas the Israeli-Palestinian schools emphasized development of mutual understanding while *maintaining* and affirming each *distinct* ethnic identity (ibid.). Based on their comparative research, the authors argued for proactively critical pluralist, anti-racist peacebuilding education in integrated social conflict environments.

Some education for peace silences rather than confronts painful conflicts. "Single identity" approaches to peace education, in contrast to inter-group contact, emphasize de-categorization (viewing people as individuals rather than as "one of them") and shared superordinate identities that cross-cut adversary polarizations (Church, Visser, & Johnson, 2004). These approaches are attractive to nation-states and common in formal "citizenship" education, since the superordinate identities are usually nation-states, such as "multicultural Canada" (Meyer, Bromley, & Ramirez, 2010). Teaching essentialized nationalist identities—as in Greece, Hong Kong, and Hungary—denies social diversity, leaving students unprepared to handle identity conflict (Mátrai, 2002). In contrast, contemporary German curriculum explicitly addresses the historical impact of identity conflict, Nazism, and intolerance, and teaches for inter-group solidarity (ibid.). A sometimes coexisting but less conflict-avoidant approach is to recognize multidimensional diverse (not bipolar) identities, and to include conflict resolution education that foregrounds equality demands by "have not" groups (Steiner-Khamsi, 2003).

Where authorities silence discussion of difficult conflicts (seeking stability to protect their positions), young people learn axes of dehumanization elsewhere. For example, in Quebec and France, official secularism in schools has functioned as conflict avoidance, limiting expression of cultural or religious diversity (Limage, 2003; Niens & Chastenay, 2008). Teaching any particular version of religion as the exclusive truth, as for instance in Palestinian and Pakistani schools, similarly would repress within-group diversity and dissent (Ahmad, 2004; Haidar, 2003). Despite inevitable risks in authoritarian or polarized societies, educative discussion of social and political identity and conflict questions is associated with higher engagement (in classroom and society) in many contexts (Baildon, 2014; Bickmore, 2014a; Schulz et al., 2010).

Formal democratic political system elements such as civic debate, constitutions and rights documents, parliaments, and courts are (imperfect) conflict management mechanisms. Thus citizen political engagement can indirectly contribute to peacemaking and/or peacebuilding. However, like many youth around the world, Mexican youth have expressed disinterest, distrust, and lack of knowledge about formal politics, and reported participating in civic organizations or political parties less frequently than, for example, Chilean and Colombian youth (Guevara & Tirado, 2006). Majorities held the cynical (but realistic) view that politicians and big business, not ordinary citizens, held power. Most of the Mexicans surveyed, however, had engaged in "private solidarity" such as contributing aid after disasters, and about a quarter had volunteered in their communities (Reimers & Cardenas, 2010). Similarly, Canadian young people often do not express much interest in formal electoral party politics, and instead favour direct engagement to address problems of personal interest (Hughes & Sears, 2008). Yet, large-scale transitional justice for peacebuilding requires broad re-engagement, rebuilding, and transformation of unjust or unworkable social institutions (Arthur, 2011; Fisher, 2013). Are formal education systems helping to equip and engage young people in such social transformation?

LIVED CITIZENSHIP IN UN-PEACEFUL COMMUNITIES: AN EXAMPLE FROM COLOMBIA

Not all societies coping with serious escalated violence suffer identity-based "ethnic" polarization. Some Latin American countries are suffering appalling levels of armed violence, mostly not political insurgency but associated with drug trafficking and corruption. Such pervasive direct violence, and the associated securitization practices that escalate both structural and direct violence, negatively impact the lived citizenship experience, trust level, and engagement of young people (also Cox et al., 2014, pp. 8–10). In Mexico and Colombia, significant school violence rates are higher in non-affluent communities (Chaux, 2011; IEP, 2015; Reimers & Cardenas, 2010, p. 154). The complex implications of education in these kinds of violent conflict zones are under-studied (Matsumoto, 2015), but I present below some context and a Colombian example.

To practise even interpersonal conflict communication and problem solving requires a certain amount of autonomy and opportunity, embodied in relatively democratic and non-violent, rather than authoritarian or exclusionary, institutional and community practices. The ways schools handle authority and governance, discipline, conflict, diversity, equity, dissent, and status competition shape participants' lived curriculum for peace/conflict citizenship (Bickmore, 2011a). Peacekeeping control and intolerance for dissent imply different citizenship roles than dialogue, joint justice work, and shared governance. In punitive, inequitable school climates, marginalized students carry different roles than high-status students (Bickmore & MacDonald, 2010). Such implicit models and practice for handling conflict may be reinforced (or not) by explicit curricula, which tend to emphasize ethics and responsibility more than creative agency or civic action (Bickmore, 2014b; Kennelly & Llewellyn, 2011; Levinson, 2007). Such implicit peace education need not be unconscious, and may be more feasible than "explicit" peace programming, in difficult conflictual contexts (Bar-Tal, Rosen, & Nets-Zehngut, 2010).

The burgeoning movement for restorative justice practices aims to transform lived citizenship education in schools, and also usually includes some explicit teaching of interpersonal conflict communication. Restorative peacemaking initiatives replace punitive, inequitable anti-violence systems with a range of activities designed to nurture caring and inclusive relationships, learning from conflicts, and joint problem-solving (Morrison & Vaandering, 2012; Schimmel, 2012). The forms of restorative peacemaking circles and conferencing processes currently influential around the world are rooted in the Aboriginal cultures of New Zealand and North America (Pranis, Stuart, & Wedge, 2003). Peacemaking circles, more than simpler facilitated dialogue processes such as peer mediation, can accommodate multiple stakeholders and address power imbalances (Bickmore, 2012). Due to their inclusive, non-hierarchical structure, peacemaking circles can be responsive to the particular social and cultural contexts of participants. Such processes hold potential for powerful affective and cognitive learning opportunities, including support, guided practice, and constructive feedback (Bickmore, 2013; McCluskey et al., 2008; Morrison, 2007). In practice, however, only some such initiatives challenge inequitable social relations in schools (Vaandering, 2010).

What is left *out* of many peace, restorative justice, and citizenship education initiatives—larger-scale social conflicts, social-structural injustice, and conflicting perspectives on sensitive narratives and political tensions specific to each context—also has implications for young people's citizenship roles. Although restorative justice and peacebuilding education *theories* (cited above) locate destructive conflict in community relationships that include inequities, some citizenship and peacemaking education *practices* at least implicitly locate the problem in (disruptive) individuals. For instance, a group of Swedish scholars apply Foucault's (2003) theory of "governmentality" to analyze two social-emotional learning programs:

> Such citizens are themselves made responsible for the setting and realisation of goals that are in line with what a "normal" and "good" citizen consists in....Problems such as disturbances and disorder, school difficulties, and unemployment are largely understood as the result of a set of "risk factors," and then particularly individual deficiencies or incompetence of various kinds, rather than as a result of societal conditions, such as family circumstances, poverty, structural inequalities and social relations. (Dahlstedt, Fejes, & Schönning, 2011, p. 410)

Thus teaching interpersonal skills and values to individuals, while ignoring fundamental systemic and cultural causes of destructive conflict and violence, could divert responsibility away from social institutions and democratic governance. Such programming could constitute a form of "gentle peacekeeping" (Bickmore, 2011b), reinforcing an antidemocratic securitization agenda (Pearce, 2010). Yet clearly, individual capacities such as recognizing the anatomy of conflicts, comprehending and persuasively expressing contrasting viewpoints, and participating in non-violent collective decision-making are necessary (though not sufficient) for democratic citizenship and peacebuilding. The following Colombian example may facilitate reflection on this dilemma.

There exist in Latin America some exemplary democratic and peacemaking education initiatives (e.g., Abrego, 2010). One of the largest-scale is Escuela Nueva (see Chapter Three), founded in rural Colombia in 1975, now with affiliate projects in Mexico and elsewhere. This multi-grade comprehensive school model emphasizes democratic culture, cooperation, and joint decision-making, and has documented positive effects on students' peaceful social interaction and democratic participation as well as academic performance (Forero-Pineda, Escobar-Rodríguez, & Molina, 2006; Pitt, 2002).

Examples of mandated interpersonal conflict resolution curriculum include two programs designed to implement the Colombian Ministry of Education's National Program of Citizenship Competencies, established in 2004. *Aulas en Paz* (Classrooms in Peace) and *Juegos de Paz* (Peace Games), first implemented in 2006, were adapted primarily from international resources and developmental psychology principles "borrowed" from the United States. The Aulas en Paz program focuses on reducing aggressive behaviour by teaching peaceful interaction, emotional awareness, anger management, active listening, assertive conflict communication, and creative conflict resolution, with minimal attention to bias awareness such as not bullying socially different peers (Chaux, 2007; Chaux et al., 2008). It includes implementation of 24 "citizenship" lessons and 16 lessons infused in language classes for all students (Grades 2–5) in their classrooms, and a series of special pull-out workshops for children considered especially aggressive (mixed in each group with students considered non-violent). Aulas en Paz does not encourage students to discuss sensitive social or political issues, nor to question the cultural narratives that legitimize enmity.

Juegos de Paz also avoids political controversies, but does attend to democratic decision-making; citizen participation, including service learning projects addressing problems in the community; and positive awareness of plural social identities (Diazgranados et al., 2014). Its main activities have been intensive teacher trainings followed by on-site coaching by visiting experts. So far, the (positive) evaluations of these programs mainly report reduced frequency of, or inclinations toward, aggressive interpersonal behaviour, rather than broader peacebuilding citizenship outcomes (Diazgranados & Noonan, 2015; Ramos, Nieto, & Chaux, 2007). The (optimistic) theory is that such negative peace (violence reduction) results in part from developing individuals' conflict management competencies and, indirectly through the student-centred pedagogies, improving their relationships with peers, teachers, and (in Juegos de Paz service learning) their local communities. Chaux explains:

> For sure, violent armed conflicts...will not be stopped by programs like *Aulas en Paz* or the National Program of Citizenship Competencies alone. However...these educational programs might be providing the competencies necessary to reduce the development of aggression caused by exposure to violence and to create peaceful relationships among children. In this way, children who could have grown up to participate in violence might contribute to the construction of a more peaceful society. (Chaux, 2009, p. 90)

Interpersonal peacemaking education, inter-group contact dialogue, and rewriting history curriculum constitute alternative approaches to making peace through education.

CONCLUSION

Education for democratic peacebuilding is conflict education (that is, it addresses conflict). There is no way to get to sustainable peace without confronting the problems underlying systemic and direct conflict and violence. To educate for sustainable peacebuilding is to facilitate broad development of processes, relationships, skills, and understandings for handling differences and problems, rather than prescribe narrowly predefined knowledge or procedures. Poor and marginalized social groups, hardest hit by direct and "slow" violence, especially need access to high-quality conflict/peace education to build (individually and collectively) such agentic democratic citizen roles, relationships, and capacities.

Every social-political-cultural system has distinct understandings, norms, and axes of inequality. Thus the cultural resources (and learning needed) to build peace, somewhat different in each context, are embedded in each community's narratives and languages, implicit feelings as well as rational thoughts, and all kinds of learning settings. While constructive conflict resolution and peacebuilding education are possible even when violence has escalated dangerously, they are generally easiest to implement and sustain in non-emergency situations (paradoxically, when conflict might seem avoidable). Yet, the political will to implement peacebuilding education may be motivated by escalated direct violence. Comparative international study of conflict and peacebuilding education, in different kinds of conflictual settings, can generate awareness of a wide variety of experiences and insights, to offer a critical perspective on the risks and opportunities in local learning contexts.

QUESTIONS FOR REFLECTION AND DISCUSSION
1. How have schools and classrooms in your experience (in various cultural and political settings) addressed peace, conflict, justice, and controversy? What are advantages and disadvantages of each climate and curriculum?
2. How could students' diversities (such as national loyalties, religious affiliations, gender, feminism) be resources for developing their class' facility and comfort with life's inevitable conflicts, uncertainties, and issues? How might a

CHAPTER TEN: Conflict, Peacebuilding, and Education 287

teacher meaningfully introduce peace and conflict topics in a homogenous classroom setting? In an escalated conflict setting?
3. Compare contrasting approaches to peace/conflict education from the chapter: What would enable or constrain the feasibility of each initiative (such as time and resource needs, institutional changes)? What might participants learn, relevant (or not) to democratic peacebuilding?

SUGGESTED AUDIO-VISUAL RESOURCES
Oasis of Peace, produced by Available Light Productions, in Inspirations, 1 (2007). Available at: search.alexanderstreet.com/preview/work/bibliographic_entity%7Cvideo_work%7C1783478
This 27-minute film shows the approaches and challenges of a bilingual-bicultural school in Israel, called *Neve Shalom-Wahat al-Salam* (Oasis of Peace), where Jewish and Palestinian children are taught together in their own languages.

Peace Process: Belfast Schools, produced by Brook Lapping Productions, in Lesson Starters (2010). Available at: search.alexanderstreet.com/preview/work/1782639
In this five-minute video, staff from two Belfast schools, one Protestant and one Catholic, explain how they get their pupils to integrate and bring about a sense of community cohesion between their schools.

SUGGESTIONS FOR FURTHER READING
Barton, Keith, & McCully, Alan. (2007). Teaching controversial issues... where controversial issues really matter. *Teaching History, 127*, 13–19.
Bickmore, Kathy (Ed.). (2014). *Peacebuilding (in) education: Democratic approaches to conflict in schools and classrooms.* Theme Issue. *Curriculum Inquiry, 44*(4), 553–582.
Bush, Kenneth, & Saltarelli, Diana. (2000). *The two faces of education in ethnic conflict: Towards a peacebuilding education for children.* Florence, Italy: UNICEF Innocenti Research Centre. [chapters 1–2].
Davies, Lynn. (2008). *Educating against extremism.* Stoke on Trent, UK: Trentham Books.
Dean, Bernadette, & Joldoshalieva, Rahat. (2007). Key strategies for teachers new to conflictual issues. In Hilary Claire & Cathie Holden (Eds.), *The challenge of teaching conflictual issues* (pp. 175–188). London: Trentham Books.

Galtung, Johan. (2008). Form and content of peace education. In Monisha Bajaj (Ed.), *Encyclopedia of peace education* (pp. 49–58). Charlotte, NC: Information Age Publishing.

King, Elisabeth. (2014). *From classrooms to conflict in Rwanda.* New York: Cambridge University Press.

Lederach, John Paul. (1995). *Preparing for peace: Conflict transformation across cultures.* Syracuse: Syracuse University Press.

Magendzo, Abraham, & Toledo, María Isabel. (2009). Moral dilemmas in teaching recent history related to the violation of human rights in Chile. *Journal of Moral Education, 38*(4), 445–465.

McGlynn, Claire, Zembylas, Michalinos, & Bekerman, Zvi (Eds.). (2013). *Integrated education in conflicted societies.* New York: Palgrave Macmillan.

Mundy, Karen, & Dryden-Peterson, Sarah (Eds.). (2011). *Educating children in conflict zones: Research, policy, and practice for systemic change—a tribute to Jackie Kirk.* New York: Teachers College Press.

Niens, Ulrike, & Cairns, Ed. (2005). Conflict, contact, and education in Northern Ireland. *Theory Into Practice, 44*(4), 337–344.

Niens, Ulrike, & Chastenay, Marie-Helene. (2008). Educating for peace? Citizenship education in Quebec and Northern Ireland. *Comparative Education Review, 52*(4), 519–540.

Ross, Marc Howard. (2010). Peace education and political science. In Gavriel Salomon & Ed Cairns (Eds.), *Handbook on peace education* (pp. 121–133). New York: Psychology Press/Taylor & Francis.

REFERENCES

Abrego, María Guadalupe. (2010). La situación de la educación para la paz en Mexico en la actualidad. *Espacios Públicos, 2010*(13), 149–164. Retrieved from redalyc.uaemex.mx/src/inicio/ArtPdfRed.jsp?iCve=6761319901

Ahmad, Iftikhar. (2004). Islam, democracy and citizenship education: An examination of the social studies curriculum in Pakistan. *Current Issues in Comparative Education, 7*(1), 39–49.

Akiba, Motoko, LeTendre, Gerald K., Baker, David P., & Goesling, Brian. (2003). Student victimization: National and school system effects on school violence in 37 nations. *American Educational Research Journal, 39*(4) (Winter), 829–853.

Al-Haj, Majid. (2005). National ethos, multicultural education, and the new history textbooks in Israel. *Curriculum Inquiry, 35*(1), 47–71.

Alger, Chadwick. (1995). Building peace: A global learning process. In Merry Merryfield & Richard Remy (Eds.), *Teaching about international conflict and peace* (pp. 127–162). Albany: SUNY Press.

Arnove, Robert. (1999). Reframing comparative education: The dialectic of the global and the local. In Robert Arnove & Carlos A. Torres (Eds.), *Comparative education: The dialectic of the global and the local* (pp. 1–23). Lanham, MD: Rowman & Littlefield.

Arthur, Paige. (2011). *Identities in transition: Challenges for transitional justice in divided societies*. Cambridge; New York: Cambridge University Press.

Assefa, Hizkias. (2005). Reconciliation: Challenges, responses, and the role of civil society. In Paul Van Tongeren, Marte Hellema, & Juliette Verhoeven (Eds.), *People building peace II: Successful stories of civil society* (pp. 637–644). London; Boulder: Lynne Rienner Publishers.

Baildon, Mark. (2014). *Controversial history education in Asian contexts*. New York: Routledge.

Bajaj, Monisha. (Ed.). (2008). *Encyclopedia of peace education*. Charlotte, NC: Information Age Publishing.

Bajaj, Monisha. (2015). "Pedagogies of resistance" and critical peace education praxis. *Journal of Peace Education, 12*(2), 154–166. doi:10.1080/17400201.2014.991914

Bar-Tal, Daniel. (2002). The elusive nature of peace education. In Gavriel Salomon & Baruch Nevo (Eds.), *Peace education: The concept, principles, and practices around the world* (pp. 27–36). Mahwah, NJ: Lawrence Erlbaum Associates.

Bar-Tal, Daniel, Rosen, Yigal, & Nets-Zehngut, Rafi. (2010). Peace education in societies involved in intractable conflict. In Gavriel Salomon & Ed Cairns (Eds.), *Handbook on peace education* (pp. 121–133). New York: Psychology Press/Taylor & Francis.

Barnea, Aaron, & Shinar, Ofer. (2005). Building trust, promoting hope: The Families Forum Hello Peace project in Israel and Palestine. In Paul van Tongeren, Malin Brenk, Marte Hellema, & Juliette Verhoeven (Eds.), *People building peace II: Successful stories of civil society* (pp. 495–500). London; Boulder: Lynne Rienner Publishers.

Bartlett, Lesley. (2008). Paulo Freire and peace education. In Monisha Bajaj (Ed.), *Encyclopedia of Peace Education* (pp. 39–45). Charlotte, NC: Information Age Publishing.

Barton, Keith, & McCully, Alan. (2012). Trying to "see things differently": Northern Ireland students' struggle to understand alternative historical perspectives. *Theory & Research in Social Education, 40*, 371–408. doi:10.1080/00933104.2012.710928

Bear Nicholas, Andrea. (1996). Citizenship education and Aboriginal people: The humanitarian art of cultural genocide. *Canadian and International Education, 25*(2), 59–107.

Bekerman, Zvi, & Zembylas, Michalinos. (2012). *Teaching contested narratives: Identity, memory, and reconciliation in peace education and beyond*. Cambridge; New York: Cambridge University Press.

Bickmore, Kathy. (2011a). Policies and programming for safer schools: Are "anti-bullying" approaches impeding education for peacebuilding? *Educational Policy, 25*(4), 648–687.

Bickmore, Kathy. (2011b). Keeping, making, and building peace in school. *Social Education ("Research and Practice" section), 75*(1), 42–46.

Bickmore, Kathy (2012). Peacebuilding dialogue as democratic education: Conflictual issues, restorative problem-solving, and student diversity in classrooms. In James Arthur & Hilary Cremin (Eds.), *Debates in Citizenship Education* (pp. 115–131). London: Routledge.

Bickmore, Kathy (2013). Circle dialogue processes in elementary classrooms: Locations for restorative and educative work. In Hilary Cremin, Edward Sellman, & Gillian McCluskey (Eds.), *Restorative approaches to conflict in schools* (pp. 175–191). London: Routledge.

Bickmore, Kathy (2014a). Peace-building dialogue pedagogies in Canadian classrooms. *Curriculum Inquiry, 44*(4), 553–582.

Bickmore, Kathy (2014b). Citizenship education in Canada: "Democratic" engagement with differences, conflicts, and equity issues? *Citizenship Teaching and Learning, 9*(3), 257–278.

Bickmore, Kathy, & MacDonald, Angela. (2010). Student leadership opportunities for making "peace" in Canada's urban schools: Contradictions in practice. *Interamerican Journal of Education for Democracy/ Revista Interamericana de Educación para la Democracia, 3*(2), 126–152.

Bond, John. (2005). From saying "sorry" to a journey of healing: National Sorry Day in Australia. In Paul Van Tongeren, Marte Hellema, & Juliette Verhoeven (Eds.), *people building peace II: Successful stories of civil society* (pp. 647–653). London; Boulder: Lynne Rienner Publishers.

Bratic, Vladimir. (2013). *Twenty years of peacebuilding media in conflict: Strategic framework*. Retrieved from Roanoke, Virginia: www.upeace.org/OKN/ working papers/UniversityForPeaceOKN-TwentyYearsOfPeacebuildingMedi aInConflictOctober2013.pdf

Burns, Robin. (2008). Comparative and international education and peace education. In Monisha Bajaj (Ed.), *Encyclopedia of peace education* (pp. 117–125). Charlotte, NC: Information Age Publishing.

Bush, Kenneth, & Saltarelli, Diana. (2000). *The two faces of education in ethnic conflict: Towards a peacebuilding education for children*. Retrieved from Florence, Italy: www.unicef-irc.org/publications/pdf/insight4.pdf

Cairns, Ed, & Hewstone, Miles. (2002). Northern Ireland: The impact of peacemaking in Northern Ireland on intergroup behavior. In Gavriel Salomon & Baruch Nevo (Eds.), *Peace education: The concept, principles, & practices around the world* (pp. 217–228). Mahwah, NJ: Lawrence Erlbaum Associates.

Chaux, Enrique. (2007). Aulas en Paz: A multicomponent program for the promotion of peaceful relationships and citizenship competencies. *Conflict Resolution Quarterly, 25*(1), 79–86. doi:10.1002/crq.193

Chaux, Enrique. (2009). Citizenship competencies in the midst of a violent political conflict: The Colombian educational response. *Harvard Educational Review, 79*(1), 84–93.

Chaux, Enrique. (2011). Múltiples Perspectivas Sobre un Problema Complejo: Comentarios Sobre Cinco Investigaciones en Violencia Escolar. *Psykhe (Santiago), 20*, 79–86. Retrieved from www.scielo.cl/scielo.php?script=sci_arttext&pid=S0718-22282011000200007&nrm=iso

Chaux, Enrique, Bustamante, Andrea, Castellanos, Melisa, Jiménez, Manuela, Nieto, Ana María, Rodríguez, Gloria Inés,...Velásquez, Ana María. (2008). Aulas en Paz: Estrategias pedagógicas. *Revista Interamericana de Educación para la Democracia/Interamerican Journal of Education for Democracy, 1*(2), 123–145.

Church, Cheyanne, Visser, Anna, & Johnson, Laurie Shepherd. (2004). A path to peace or persistence? The "single identity" approach to conflict resolution in Northern Ireland. *Conflict Resolution Quarterly, 21*(3), 273–293.

Cox, Cristián, Bascopé, Martín, Castillo, Juan Carlos, Miranda, Daniel, & Bonhomme, Macarena. (2014). *Educación ciudadana en América Latina: Prioridades de los currículos escolares*. Retrieved from Geneva: www.ibe.unesco.org/en/services/online-materials/publications/ibe-working-papers.html

Curle, Adam, Freire, Paulo, & Galtung, Johan. (1974). What can education contribute towards peace and social justice? Curle, Freire, Galtung panel. In Magnus Haavelsrud (Ed.), *Education for peace: reflection and action* (pp. 64–97). Keele, UK: University of Keele.

Dahlstedt, Magnus, Fejes, Andreas, & Schönning, Elin. (2011). The will to (de)liberate: Shaping governable citizens through cognitive behavioural programmes in school. *Journal of Education Policy, 26*(3), 399–414. Retrieved from dx.doi.org/10.1080/02680939.2010.516841

Davies, Lynn. (2004). *Education and Conflict: Complexity and Chaos*. London: Routledge-Falmer.

Davies, Lynn. (2005). Schools and war: Urgent agendas for comparative and international education. *Compare, 35*(4), 357–371.

Davies, Lynn. (2014). Interrupting extremism by creating educative turbulence. *Curriculum Inquiry, 44*(4), 450–468.

Dessel, Adrienne, & Rogge, Mary E. (2008). Evaluation of intergroup dialogue: A review of the empirical literature. *Conflict Resolution Quarterly, 26*(2), 199–238.

Diazgranados, Silvia, & Noonan, James. (2015). The relationship of safe and participatory school environments and supportive attitudes toward violence: Evidence from the Colombian Saber test of Citizenship Competencies. *Education, Citizenship and Social Justice, 10*(1), 79–94.

Diazgranados, Silvia, Noonan, James, Brion-Meisels, Steven, Saldarriagac, Lisa, Dazac, Berta C., Chávez, Minerva, & Antonellise, Irene. (2014). Transformative peace education with teachers: Lessons from Juegos de Paz in Colombia. *Journal of Peace Education, 11*, 150–161. Retrieved from dx.doi.org/10.1080/17400201.2014.898627

Ellison, Christine Smith. (2014). The role of education in peacebuilding: An analysis of five change theories in Sierra Leone. *Compare, 44*(2), 186–207. Retrieved from dx.doi.org/10.1080/03057925.2012.734138

Firer, Ruth. (2002). The Gordian Knot between peace education and war education. In Gavriel Salomon & Baruch Nevo (Eds.), *Peace education: The concept, principles, & practices around the world* (pp. 55–61). Mahwah, NJ: Lawrence Erlbaum Associates.

Fisher, Kirsten. (2013). *Transitional justice for child soldiers: Accountability and social reconstruction in post-conflict contexts.* New York: Palgrave Macmillan.

Forero-Pineda, Clemente, Escobar-Rodríguez, Daniel, & Molina, Daniel Ken. (2006). Escuela Nueva's impact on the peaceful social interaction of children in Colombia. In Angela W. Little (Ed.), *Education for All and multigrade teaching: Challenges and opportunities* (pp. 265–300). Amsterdam: Springer.

Foucault, Michel. (2003). Technologies of the self. In Paul Rabinow & Nikolas Rose (Eds.), *The essential Foucault: Selections from the essential works of Foucault 1954–1984* (pp. 145–169). New York: The New Press.

Frayha, Nemer. (2004). Developing curriculum as a means to bridging national divisions in Lebanon. In Sobhi Tawil & Alexandra Harley (Eds.), *Education, conflict & social cohesion* (pp. 159–206). Geneva: UNESCO/International Bureau of Education.

Freedman, Sarah Warshauer, Weinstein, Harvey M., Murphy, Karen, & Longman, Timothy. (2008). Teaching history after identity-based conflicts: The Rwanda experience. *Comparative Education Review, 52*(4), 663–690.

Freire, Paulo. (1970). *Pedagogy of the oppressed.* New York: Seabury Press.

Freire, Paulo. (1978). *Pedagogy in process: The letters to Guinea-Bisseau.* New York: Seabury.

Freire, Paulo. (1996). *Pedagogy of the heart.* New York: Continuum.

Funk, Nathan C., & Said, Abdul Aziz. (2004). Islam and the West: Narratives of conflict and conflict transformation. *International Journal of Peace Studies, 9*(1), 1–28.

Galtung, Johan. (1969). Violence, peace, and peace research. *Journal of Peace Research, 6*(3), 167–192.

Galtung, Johan. (1975). *Peace: Research, education, action.* Copenhagen: Ejlers.

Galtung, Johan. (1976). Three approaches to peace: Peacekeeping, peacemaking, peacebuilding. In Johan Galtung (Ed.), *Peace, war and defense: Essays in peace research* (vol. 2) (pp. 297–298). Copenhagen: Ejlers.

Galtung, Johan. (1990). Cultural violence. *Journal of Peace Research, 27*(3), 291–305. Retrieved from www.jstor.org/stable/423472

Galtung, Johan. (2008). Form and content of peace education [revised version of 1968/1975 Peace: Research, education, action]. In Monisha Bajaj (Ed.), *Encyclopedia of peace education* (pp. 49–58). Charlotte, NC: Information Age Publishing.

Ghali, Mona. (2014). *Education and (in)security: The Canadian International Development Agency's education sector aid to conflict affected states: 2000–2013* (PhD dissertation). University of Toronto.

Gill, Scherto, & Niens, Ulrike. (2014a). Education as humanisation: A theoretical review on the role of dialogic pedagogy in peacebuilding education. *Compare {Special Issue: Education as humanisation: Dialogic pedagogy in post-conflict peacebuilding, guest edited by S. Gill & U. Niens}, 44*(1), 10–31.

Gill, Scherto, & Niens, Ulrike. (2014b). Education as humanisation: Dialogic pedagogy in post-conflict peacebuilding. *Compare: A Journal of Comparative and International Education, 44*(1), 1–9. doi:10.1080/03057925.2013.864522

Guevara, Gilberto, & Tirado, Felipe. (2006). Conocimientos cívicos en Mexico: Un estudio comparativo internacional. *Revista Mexicana de Investigación Educativa (Consejo Mexicano de Investigación Educativa), 11*(30), 995–1018.

Hadjipavlou, Maria. (2002). Cyprus: A partnership between conflict resolution and peace education. In Gavriel Salomon & Baruch Nevo (Eds.), *Peace education: The concept, principles, & practices around the world* (pp. 193–208). Mahwah, NJ: Lawrence Erlbaum Associates.

Hague-Appeal. (1999). *The Hague Agenda for Peace and Justice for the 21st Century*. Retrieved from Geneva: www.haguepeace.org/resources/HagueAgendaPeace+Justice4The21stCentury.pdf

Haidar, Aziz. (2003). Minority education in the Palestinian Authority. In Yaacov Iram & Hillel Wahrman (Eds.), *Education of minorities and peace education in pluralistic societies* (pp. 149–167). Westport, CT: Praeger Publishers.

Harber, Clive. (2004). *Schooling as violence: How schools harm pupils and societies*. London: Routledge-Falmer.

Harris, Ian, & Morrison, Mary Lee. (2003). *Peace education* (2nd ed.). Jefferson, NC: McFarland.

Hayhoe, Ruth. (1998). Dilemmas in Japan's intellectual culture. *Minerva, 36*, 1–19.

Herdoízo-Estévez, Magdalena, & Lenk, Sonia. (2010). Intercultural dialogue: Discourse and realities of Indigenous and Mestizos in Ecuador and Guatemala. *Interamerican Journal of Education for Democracy/Revista Interamericana de Educación para la Democracia, 3*(2), 196–223.

Hughes, Andrew, & Sears, Alan. (2008). The struggle for citizenship education in Canada: The centre cannot hold. In James Arthur, Ian Davies, & Carole Hahn (Eds.), *Sage handbook of education for citizenship and democracy* (pp. 124–138). London: Sage Publications.

Ichilov, Orit. (2005). Pride in one's country and citizenship orientations in a divided society. *Comparative Education Review, 49*(1), 44–61.

IEP, Institute for Economics and Peace. (2015). *Mexico peace index 2015: Analyzing the changing dynamics of peace in Mexico*. Retrieved from Mexico City: economicsandpeace.org

INEE, Interagency Network for Education in Emergencies. (2010). *Minimum standards for education: Preparedness, response, recovery* (2nd ed.). Retrieved from New York: toolkit.ineesite.org/toolkit/INEEcms/uploads/1012/INEE_GuideBook_EN_2012 LoRes.pdf

IPEP, Interagency Peace Education Programme. (2005). *Analytical review of selected peace education materials.* Retrieved from Paris: www.ineesite.org/uploads/files/resources/subdoc_1_676_Analytical_Review_of_Selected_Peace_Ed_Materials.pdf

Jansen, Jonathan. (2009). *Knowledge in the blood: Confronting race and the apartheid past.* Stanford: Stanford University Press.

Katz, Yaacov, & Yablon, Yaacov. (2003). Promoting intergroup attitudes in Israel through internet technology. In Yaacov Iram & Hillel Wahrman (Eds.), *Education of minorities and peace education in pluralistic societies* (pp. 169-179). Westport, CT: Praeger Publishers.

Kaufman, Edy. (2005). Dialogue-based processes: A vehicle for peacebuilding. In Paul van Tongeren, Malin Brenk, Marte Hellema, & Juliette Verhoeven (Eds.), *People building peace II: Successful stories of civil society* (pp. 473-487). London; Boulder: Lynne Rienner Publishers.

Kay, Tamara. (2013). Educating children on the longest street in the world. *Global Dialogue, 2*(5), 2 pages.

Kennelly, Jacqueline, & Llewellyn, Kristina. (2011). Educating for active compliance: Discursive constructions in citizenship education. *Citizenship Studies, 15*(6-7), 897-914.

King, Elisabeth. (2014). *From classrooms to conflict in Rwanda.* New York: Cambridge University Press.

Kirk, Jackie. (2011). Education and fragile states [revised from 2007, Education and fragile states]. In Karen Mundy & Sarah Dryden-Peterson (Eds.), *Educating children in conflict zones: Research, policy, and practice for systemic change–a tribute to Jackie Kirk* (pp. 15-31). New York: Teachers College Press.

Leach, Fiona, & Dunne, Máiréad (Eds.). (2007). *Education, conflict and reconciliation: International perspectives.* Bern: Peter Lang.

Lederach, John Paul. (1995). *Preparing for peace: Conflict transformation across cultures.* Syracuse: Syracuse University Press.

Lederach, John Paul. (2003). *The little book of conflict transformation.* Intercourse, PA: Good Books.

Lederach, John Paul. (2005). The arts and peacebuilding: Using imagination and creativity. In Paul van Tongeren, Malin Brenk, Marte Hellema, & Juliette Verhoeven (Eds.), *People building peace II: Successful stories of civil society* (pp. 283-292). London; Boulder: Lynne Rienner Publishers.

Levinson, Bradley. (2007). Forming and implementing a new secondary civic education program in Mexico. In E. Doyle Stevick & Bradley Levinson (Eds.), *Reimagining Civic Education* (pp. 245-271). Lanham, MD: Rowman & Littlefield.

Limage, Leslie. (2003). Education and Muslim identity: The case of France. In Edward Beauchamp (Ed.), *Comparative education reader* (pp. 111–138). New York: Routledge-Falmer.

Magendzo, Abraham, & Toledo, María Isabel. (2009). Moral dilemmas in teaching recent history related to the violation of human rights in Chile. *Journal of Moral Education, 38*(4), 445–465.

Mátrai, Zsuzsa. (2002). National identity conflicts and civic education: A comparison of five countries. In Gita Steiner-Khamsi, Judith Torney-Purta, & John Schwille (Eds.), *New paradigms and recurring paradoxes in education for citizenship: An international comparison* (pp. 85–104). Amsterdam: JAI/Elsevier Science.

Matsumoto, Mitsuko. (2015). Schooling's "contribution" to contemporary violent conflict: Review of theoretical ideas and case studies in the field of education and conflict. *Research in Comparative and International Education, 10*(2), 238–256. doi:10.1177/1745499915571708

McCauley, Clark. (2002). Head first versus feet first in peace education. In Gavriel Salomon & Baruch Nevo (Eds.), *Peace education: The concept, principles, and practices around the world* (pp. 247–258). Mahwah, NJ: Lawrence Erlbaum Associates.

McCluskey, Gillean, Lloyd, Gwynedd, Kane, Jean, Riddell, Sheila, Stead, Joan, & Weedon, Elisabet. (2008). Can restorative practices in schools make a difference? *Educational Review, 60*(4), 405–417.

McCully, Alan, O'Doherty, Marian, & Smyth, Paul. (1999). The Speak Your Piece project: Exploring controversial issues in Northern Ireland. In Linda Rennie Forcey & Ian Murray Harris (Eds.), *Peacebuilding for adolescents* (pp. 119–138). New York: Peter Lang.

McGlynn, Claire. (2009). *Peace education in conflict and post-conflict societies: Comparative perspectives*. New York: Palgrave Macmillan.

McGlynn, Claire, Zembylas, Michalinos, & Bekerman, Zvi (Eds.). (2013). *Integrated education in conflicted societies* (1st ed.). New York: Palgrave Macmillan.

Merelman, Richard. (1990). The role of conflict in children's political learning. In Orit Ichilov (Ed.), *Political socialization, citizenship education, and democracy* (pp. 47–65). New York: Teachers College Press.

Meyer, John W., Bromley, Patricia, & Ramirez, Francisco. (2010). Human rights in social science textbooks: Cross-national analysis, 1970–2008. *Sociology of Education, 83*(4), 111–134.

Morrison, Brenda. (2007). *Restoring safe school communities: A whole school response to bullying, violence and alienation*. Leichhardt, New South Wales, Australia: Federation Press.

Morrison, Brenda, & Vaandering, Dorothy. (2012). Restorative justice: Pedagogy, praxis, and discipline. *Journal of School Violence, 11*(2), 138–155.

Mundy, Karen, & Dryden-Peterson, Sarah (Eds.). (2011). *Educating children in conflict zones: Research, policy, and practice for systemic change–a tribute to Jackie Kirk*. New York: Teachers College Press.

Nagy, Rosemary. (2014). The Truth and Reconciliation Commission of Canada: Genesis and design. *Canadian Journal of Law and Society, 29*(2), 199–217. Retrieved from muse.jhu.edu/

Netzer, David. (2008). Painful past in the service of Israeli Jewish-Arab dialogue: The work of the Center for Humanistic Education at the Ghetto Fighters House in Israel. *In Factis Pax, 2*(2), 282–291.

Niens, Ulrike, & Chastenay, Marie-Helene. (2008). Educating for peace? Citizenship education in Quebec and Northern Ireland. *Comparative Education Review, 52*(4), 519–540.

Nixon, Rob. (2011). Introduction. *Slow violence and the environmentalism of the poor* (pp. 1–44). Cambridge, MA: Harvard University Press.

Novelli, Mario. (2010). Education, conflict and social (in)justice: Insights from Colombia. *Educational Review, 62*(3), 271–285. doi:10.1080/00131911.2010.503598

Novelli, Mario. (2011). Are we all soldiers now? The dangers of the securitization of education and conflict. In Karen Mundy & Sarah Dryden-Peterson (Eds.), *Educating children in conflict zones: Research, policy, and practice for systemic change–a tribute to Jackie Kirk* (pp. 49–65). New York: Teachers College Press.

Novelli, Mario, & Lopes Cardozo, Mieke. (2008). Conflict, education and the global south: New critical directions. *International Journal of Educational Development, 28*, 473–488. Retrieved from www.sciencedirect.com

Oxford, Rebecca L. (2013). *The language of peace: Communicating to create harmony*. Charlotte, NC: Information Age Publishing.

Pearce, Jenny. (2010). Perverse state formation and securitized democracy in Latin America. *Democratization, 17*(2), 286–306. doi:10.1080/13510341003588716

Perera, Lal, Wijetunge, Swarna, & Balasooriya, A S. (2004). Education reform and political violence in Sri Lanka. In Sobhi Tawil & Alexandra Harley (Eds.), *Education, conflict & social cohesion* (pp. 375–433). Geneva: UNESCO/ International Bureau of Education.

Pettigrew, Thomas, & Tropp, Linda. (2000). Does intergroup contact reduce prejudice? Recent meta-analytic findings. In Stuart Oskamp (Ed.), *Reducing prejudice and discrimination* (pp. 93–114). Mahwah, NJ: Lawrence Earlbaum Associates.

Pitt, Jennifer J. (2002). *Civic education and citizenship in Escuela Nueva schools in Colombia* (MA Thesis). University of Toronto.

Pranis, Kay, Stuart, Barry, & Wedge, Mark. (2003). *Peacemaking circles: From crime to community*. St. Paul, MN: Living Justice Press.

Ramos, Cecilia, Nieto, Ana María, & Chaux, Enrique. (2007). Aulas en Paz: Resultados preliminares de un programa multi-componente. *Revista Interamericana de Educación para la Democracia/Interamerican Journal of Education for Democracy, 1*(1), 36–56.

Rappleye, Jeremy, & Paulson, Julia. (2007). Educational transfer in situations affected by conflict: Towards a common research endeavour. *Research in Comparative and International Education, 2*(3), 252–271. doi:10.2304/rcie.2007.2.3.252

Reardon, Betty A., & Snauwaert, Dale T. (2015). *Betty A. Reardon: Key texts in gender and peace* (vol. 31). *SpringerBriefs on Pioneers in Science and Practice.* Cham: Springer-Verlag International Publishers.

Reimers, Fernando, & Cardenas, Sergio. (2010). Youth civic engagement in Mexico. In Lonnie R. Sherrod, Judith Torney-Purta, & Constance A. Flanagan (Eds.), *Handbook of research on civic engagement in youth* (pp. 139–160). Hoboken, NJ: John Wiley & Sons.

Rodríguez Ledesma, Xavier. (2013). Qué historia para qué ciudadanía? La enseñanza de la historia en la educación básica en México. *Praxis Educativa (Brasil), 8*(2), 537–558. doi:10.5212/PraxEduc.v.8i2.0009

Ross, Marc Howard. (1993). *The culture of conflict.* New Haven, CT: Yale University Press.

Ross, Marc Howard. (2007). *Cultural contestation in ethnic conflict.* Cambridge: Cambridge University Press.

Ross, Marc Howard. (2010). Peace education and political science. In Gavriel Salomon & Ed Cairns (Eds.), *Handbook on peace education* (pp. 121–133). New York: Psychology Press/Taylor & Francis.

Salazar Tetzagüic, Manuel de Jesús, & Grigsgy, Katherine. (2004). Guatemala. In Sobhi Tawil & Alexandra Harley (Eds.), *Education, conflict & social cohesion* (pp. 85–158). Geneva: UNESCO/International Bureau of Education.

Salomon, Gavriel. (2002). The nature of peace education: Not all programs are created equal. In Gavriel Salomon & Baruch Nevo (Eds.), *Peace education: The concept, principles, & practices around the world* (pp. 3–25). Mahwah, NJ: Lawrence Erlbaum Associates.

Salomon, Gavriel. (2011). Four major challenges facing peace education in regions of intractable conflict. *Peace and Conflict: Journal of Peace Psychology, 17*(1), 46–59. doi:10.1080/10781919.2010.495001

Salomon, Gavriel, & Cairns, Ed (Eds.). (2010). *Handbook on peace education.* New York: Psychology Press.

Schimmel, N. (2012). The moral case for restorative justice as a corollary of the responsibility to protect: A Rwandan case study of the insufficiency of impact of retributive justice on the rights and well-being of genocide survivors. *Journal of Human Rights, 11*(2), 161–188. doi:10.1080/14754835.2012.674454

Schulz, Wolfram, Ainley, John, Fraillon, Julian, Kerr, David, & Losito, Bruno. (2010). *ICCS 2009 International Report: Civic knowledge, attitudes and engagement among lower secondary school students in thirty-eight countries.* Retrieved from Amsterdam: www.iea.nl/fileadmin/user_upload/Publications/Electronic_versions/ICCS_2009_International_Report.pdf

Shields, Robin, & Paulson, Julia. (2015). "Development in reverse"? A longitudinal analysis of armed conflict, fragility and school enrolment. *Comparative Education, 51*(2), 212–230. doi:10.1080/03050068.2014.953314

Shochat, Lisa. (2003). *Our Neighborhood*: Using entertaining children's television to promote interethnic understanding in Macedonia. *Conflict Resolution Quarterly, 21*(1), 79–93.

Skovdal, Morten, & Campbell, Catherine. (2015). Beyond education: What role can schools play in the support and protection of children in extreme settings? *International Journal of Educational Development, 41*, 175–183.

Smith, Dan. (2012). *The Penguin state of the world atlas* (9th ed.). New York: Penguin.

Sobe, Noah W. (2009). Educational reconstruction "By the dawn's early light": Violent political conflict and American overseas educational reform. *Harvard Educational Review, 79*(1), 123–131.

Soudien, Crain. (2002). Memory work and the remaking of the future: A critical look at the pedagogical value of the Truth and Reconciliation Commission for peace. In Gavriel Salomon & Baruch Nevo (Eds.), *Peace education: The concept, principles, & practices around the world* (pp. 155–161). Mahwah, NJ: Lawrence Erlbaum Associates.

Staubhaar, Rolf. (2012). A broader definition of fragile states: The communities and schools of Brazil's *Favelas*. *Current Issues in Comparative Education, 15*(1), 41–51.

Steiner-Khamsi, Gita. (2003). Cultural recognition or social redistribution: Predicaments of minority education. In Yaacov Iram & Hillel Wahrman (Eds.), *Education of minorities and peace education in pluralistic societies* (pp. 15–28). Westport, CT: Praeger Publishers.

Stevenson-Krausz, Meghan. (2013). *There's peace on the street: Using* Sesame Street *to rehumanise the Other in conflict zones* (MSc thesis). London School of Economics, online. Retrieved from https://www.academia.edu/6892192/There_s_Peace_on_the_Street_Using_Sesame_Street_to_Rehumanise_the_Other_in_Conflict_Zones

Sumida Huaman, Elizabeth. (2011). Transforming education, transforming society: The co-construction of critical peace education and Indigenous education. *Journal of Peace Education, 8*(3), 243–258. doi:10.1080/17400201.2011.621374

Tal-Or, Nurit, Boninger, David, & Gleicher, Faith. (2002). Understanding the conditions necessary for intergroup contact to reduce prejudice. In Gavriel Salomon & Baruch Nevo (Eds.), *Peace education: The concept, principles, and practices around the world* (pp. 89–107). Mahwah, NJ: Lawrence Earlbaum Associates.

Tawil, Sobhi, & Harley, Alexandra (Eds.). (2004). *Education, conflict & social cohesion*. Geneva: UNESCO/International Bureau of Education.

Tomlinson, Kathryn, & Benefield, Pauline. (2005). *Education and conflict: Research and research possiblities*. Retrieved from www.ineesite.org/default. asp

Tupper, Jennifer. (2014). The possibilities for reconciliation through difficult dialogues: Treaty education as peacebuilding. *Curriculum Inquiry, 44*(4), 469–488.

UNESCO. (2001). *International Decade for a Culture of Peace and Nonviolence for the Children of the World*. Retrieved from Paris (online): en.unesco.org/cultureofpeace

UNESCO. (2014). *Action plan for the International Decade for the Rapprochement of Cultures*. Retrieved from Paris: unesdoc.unesco.org/images/0022/002266/226664e.pdf

Vaandering, Dorothy. (2010). The significance of critical theory for restorative justice in education. *Review of Education, Pedagogy, and Cultural Studies, 32*(2), 145–176. doi:10.1080/10714411003799165

Vriens, Leonard. (1999). Children, war and peace: A review of fifty years of research from the perspective of a balanced concept of peace education. In Amiram Raviv, Louis Oppenheimer, & Daniel Bar-Tal (Eds.), *How children understand war and peace* (pp. 27–58). San Francisco: Jossey Bass.

Wang, Zheng. (2009). Old wounds, new narratives: Joint history textbook writing and peace building in East Asia. *History and Memory, 21*(1), 101–126. doi:10.2979/his.2009.21.1.101

Ware, Helen, Greener, Peter, Iribarnegaray, Deanna, Jenkins, Bert, Lautensach, Sabina, Matthews, Dylan,...Spence, Rebecca. (2005). *The no-nonsense guide to conflict and peace*. Oxford; Toronto: New Internationalist Publications/Between the Lines.

Waters, Tony, & LeBlanc, Kim. (2005). Refugees and education: Mass public schooling without a nation-state. *Comparative Education Review, 49*(2), 129–147.

Weinstein, Harvey, Freedman, Sarah Warshauer, & Hughson, Holly. (2007). School voices: Challenges facing education systems after identity-based conflicts. *Education, Citizenship and Social Justice, 2*(1), 41–71.

Williams, James H. (2004). Civil conflict, education, and the work of schools: Twelve propositions. *Conflict Resolution Quarterly, 21*(4), 471–481.

Williams, James H. (Ed.). (2014). *(Re)constructing memory: School textbooks and the imagination of the nation*. Rotterdam, the Netherlands; Boston: Sense Publishers.

Zurita Rivera, Úrsula. (2012). Las escuelas Mexicanas y la legislación sobre la convivencia, la seguridad y la violencia escolar. *Educación y Territorio, 2*(1), 19–36.

SECTION III

EDUCATION IN THE WORLD SYSTEM: GLOBALIZATION AND DEVELOPMENT

CHAPTER ELEVEN
EDUCATION FOR ALL: COMPARATIVE SOCIOLOGY OF SCHOOLING IN AFRICA AND BEYOND

Karen Mundy and Robyn Read

INTRODUCTION

Why do we have publicly provided mass education? How did going to school become a central expectation of children, parents, and communities around the world? Does going to school really provide the degree of opportunity and social equalization that we anticipate from it? And why, given the widespread endorsement of education as a fundamental right, do so many children miss out on schooling or receive an education of poor quality in many parts of the world? These are questions that have engrossed comparative educationists as well as sociologists of education since at least the end of the Second World War. They are still subject to lively debate today.

In this chapter, we review these debates with special attention to the historical experience of schooling in two countries in East Africa: Tanzania and Kenya. The first section of the chapter looks at the origins of the notion of a universal right to education, and how schooling became the international standard for childhood socialization. The second section considers various interpretations of the effort to expand mass education in the developing world after 1945. We look at whether the post-1945 expansion of formal schooling was mainly about national economic development, or whether it arose as part of a new thrust by Western countries for "cultural imperialism." In section three, we consider why in the 1980s and 1990s educational opportunity eroded in many of the poorest parts of the world, and ask what this erosion had to do with globalization. Section four reflects on the revival of "Education for All" (EFA) over the past decade, while section five looks at the EFA experiences of Tanzania and Kenya. Through this historical overview and exploration of EFA, we can better understand the ongoing debate about the purposes and effects of mass schooling today.

THE RIGHT TO EDUCATION IN WORLD HISTORICAL PERSPECTIVE

The idea that children have a right to attend school is now so widely accepted that it is hard to believe that schooling was not seen as an essential part of childhood in most parts of the world a mere one hundred years ago. Yet in the two-hundred-year period from the late 18th century to the late 20th century, "schooling"—formal, age-graded, classroom-based instruction—spread across Western societies and became the international standard for childhood socialization. Initially designed for the elite, by the early 20th century schooling (at least at the primary level) was increasingly being offered to all citizens, typically in systems run and funded by nation-states. The institution of schooling had become so widespread by the middle of the 20th century that the international community promised to uphold a "universal" right to education: first through the creation of the United Nations Educational, Scientific, and Cultural Organization (UNESCO) in 1944; and secondly through Article 26 of the 1948 Universal Declaration of Human Rights, which states:

> Everyone has the right to education. Education shall be free, at least in the elementary and fundamental stages. Elementary education shall be compulsory. Technical and professional education shall be made generally available and higher education shall be equally accessible to all on the basis of merit. (General Assembly of the United Nations, 1948)

But why did schooling spread so rapidly and become a universal, internationally recognized entitlement? In the 1960s and 1970s, sociologists and comparative education scholars argued quite heatedly about this. Their arguments are consequential because they continue to shape the way researchers and educators think about the right to education and the consequences of schooling today. Four basic explanations emerged from scholars who focused on the spread of schooling in the West:

1. Functionalist arguments portrayed schooling as a response to the needs of modernizing societies, driven by the demands of new forms of economic and political organization as societies move from pre-modern to modern stages of development. Functionalist arguments underlie much of what we hear about schooling in the popular media and political discourse, including the idea that schooling produces a more modern and more productive citizen-worker, and thus is essential for economic growth.
2. Marxist and critical sociologists of education argued against this conflict-free view of schooling. Research on the social history of schooling in Britain and the United States suggested that schooling expanded rapidly because it played a role in the development of industrial capitalism during the 19th century. Schooling created a tractable, time-conscious workforce for new industries out of agricultural peasant populations. Schooling in this view is part of a larger process of class imposition or social reproduction (Bowles & Gintis, 1977; Muller, Ringer, & Simon, 1989).
3. A third argument, drawing from the work of Max Weber, emphasized the leadership of newly forming territorial nation-states in the spread of schooling (Collins, 2000; Fuller, 1991; Fuller & Rubinson, 1992). Weberian scholars argued that new state authorities promoted compulsory schooling because it helped create a body of citizens that identified with (and were loyal to) the new territorial nation-state. Drawing primarily upon histories of schooling in Prussia and in France, they showed how schools were used to integrate different language groups and promote respect for secular authority. Weberian scholars confronted the class-imposition hypothesis with data showing that many industrialists in Britain and North America opposed the spread of mass schooling in the 19th century. They challenged the functionalist hypothesis by showing that schooling had often spread before economic modernization and industrialization took place.
4. A fourth line of scholarship asked whether schooling was indeed imposed, either by state authorities or capitalists. Here

scholars pointed out that popular movements—often including organizations of workers, parents, and social reformers—played a significant part in the spread of schooling. These actors demanded access to schooling and educational resources from national governments, and were particularly successful in the era after 1945 (Dale, 1989; Marshall, 1961). Blending Weberian and neo-Marxist arguments, these scholars argued that the extension of universal access to schooling played a strong "legitimation" role in modern capitalist states: it met popular demands with promises of equality of opportunity. In turn, the notion that schooling should be equally available to all became one of the guiding norms of the industrial welfare state in the 20th century. In this construction, the expansion of state promises for universal and equitable access to schooling is looked at as part of a "social settlement" that was worked out in specific national contexts between state, capital, and organized social forces.

In addition to these four fundamental arguments, Stanford sociologists John Meyer and Francisco Ramirez have added a fifth, overarching contention (Meyer et al., 1997; Ramirez & Boli, 1987). Meyer and Ramirez argue that as schooling became institutionalized in the Western world, it achieved widespread recognition as the standard for childhood socialization in the international community. Schooling became part of a standard world cultural model that spread through processes of diffusion and imitation. This theory, known as world institutionalism, argues that schooling is a fundamental feature of an emergent, single, world culture.

As we shall see below, each of these five arguments has been extended in research on schooling in the non-Western world. In this context, functionalist arguments tend to describe the expansion of schooling as a response to modernization: necessary for national development and the creation of the modern, productive citizen. World system and neo-Marxist scholars view the spread of schooling as part of the extension of a capitalist world order, often describing it as a form of cultural imperialism that displaces local cultures and values while legitimating unequal forms of economic integration. Weberian analysts focus more carefully on the political and bureaucratic features of developing country states and governments, arguing that Third World governments expand schooling in order to consolidate territorial sovereignty and enhance their legitimacy within the international community of states. A fourth group of scholars is interested in the role played by popular movements in the construction of local meanings and local social settlements; while a fifth, drawing on Meyer's and Ramirez's work, focuses on the way that schooling has become increasingly standardized, so that even social studies curricula look alike.

In general, comparative education scholars agree that if capitalism, the state, and/or popular demand drove the spread of mass compulsory schooling in the West, we might expect that these factors would continue to shape changes in the policies and practices of schooling in the developing world. Most also agree that schooling has become so institutionalized that arguments among these different social actors about schooling no longer focus on whether or not schooling is important, but on what kind of schooling works best. Finally, most comparative education scholars agree that national educational choices are shaped by a transnational or world system, though they disagree on what the most influential features of this system are.

Throughout this book we have invited you to examine these arguments by exploring recent policy changes in education. For example, what has driven the rise of school improvement reforms or national testing regimes, topics covered in Chapters Five and Thirteen? Have states, popular movements, economic interest groups, or the international community played a part? We will also consider how these different "forces"—the state, capital, organized social movements, and the international system—shape the educational trajectories of children in developing countries today.

EDUCATION, AID, AND DEVELOPMENT

In the 1950s and 1960s, the governments of newly independent countries around the world promised their citizens that they would expand access to schooling, replacing the highly restrictive systems inherited from colonialism with universal access. Universal primary education became a central part of the national development plans of postcolonial societies. Parents and children picked up the baton. Between 1960 and 1975, the number of children in school in developing countries increased by 122 percent (Farrell, 1999, pp. 148–149). Within years of independence, compulsory school laws were passed in virtually every country (Benavot & Resnik, 2006).

The international community supported these postcolonial efforts to expand mass systems of public education. Aid to education, provided primarily through bilateral development aid (such as that given by Global Affairs Canada—formerly the Canadian International Development Agency—and the United States Agency for International Development), was used to develop the allegiance of postcolonial states to the West during the Cold War; it also helped build economic ties to industrialized countries. But this was only part of the story. Educational aid also reflected the enormous commitment to education being made across Western welfare states after 1945, where expansion of access (at secondary and tertiary levels) and equality of opportunity had become central commitments. The idea that education could bridge social inequality was universally accepted, and countries with the most expansive domestic welfare states tended to offer international aid as an extension of their commitments to social equality at home (Mundy, 1998). Large numbers of Western volunteers travelled overseas to teach, reinforcing mounting public support for the idea that rich countries should do their share to ensure that every child would get a chance to go to school.

Substantial research literature on the role of education in the development of the newly independent countries of the South emerged in this period. Sociologists and political scientists carried out careful empirical work on the role played by education in constructing "modern" attitudes and behaviours (Inkeles & Holsinger, 1974; McClelland, 1961). Economists seeking to understand economic take-off discovered a residual role for a phenomenon that came to be labelled "human capital," and quickly embarked on rate of return studies to substantiate the claim that education enhances economic productivity (Becker, 1962; Harbison & Meyers, 1964; Schultz, 1960). Both modernization theories and human capital theory promoted a functional view of schooling as an essential ingredient for national development. Education was linked to economic growth (greater national wealth); social development (more equitable distribution of wealth or opportunity); and political development (the creation of democratic systems) (Farrell, 1999).

By the early 1970s, however, many scholars began to question the ambitions that lay behind the spread of modern schooling systems. Researchers challenged the earlier confidence in education's role in political modernization and economic growth, as well as its positive effects on social equality. Political scientist David Abernathy (1969) and sociologist Philip Foster (1965), for example, used their research in West Africa to question the wisdom of expanding education in contexts where economic growth was limited. Without the expansion of modern employment, Foster, Abernathy, and others warned that schooling might lead to widespread political dissatisfaction among the young, an unwillingness to work in agriculture, and subsequent political destabilization (Huntington, 1968). Other researchers began to show that while wealthier countries tend to have better educated populations, the expansion of schooling provides no guarantee of economic growth (Hannum & Buchmann, 2005). The effects of educational expansion are sensitive to context: for example, national political stability and position in the global trading system each structure the effects of schooling on individual, community, and national development (ibid.).

Questions about the role played by schools in the achievement of social equality were also raised. In the United States and the United Kingdom, educational sociologists such as A. H. Halsey and James Coleman collected detailed data suggesting that schooling had minimal impact in altering the socio-economic status and life chances of children (Coleman et al., 1966; Halsey, Heath, & Ridge, 1980). Family socio-economic background played a much larger role. Initial research from the developing world seemed to suggest that schooling did a better job of promoting intergenerational mobility in poor countries, but again, this outcome relied heavily upon the availability of new jobs, and in turn on high rates of economic growth (Farrell, 1999). Subsequent research showed that even in contexts of economic growth, the equity-enhancing effects of each level of schooling seemed to weaken as it became universally available, passing pressure for access upwards to the next level in the educational system (Hannum & Buchmann, 2003). In most cases, elites manage to maintain their status by getting more education than the masses. Furthermore, although schooling could be shown to have positive effects on fertility (lowering the number of children) and on maternal ability to ensure children's health, it often also reinforced ethnic and gender inequality (Hannum & Buchmann, 2003; Stromquist, 2003).

Comparative education scholars were sharply influenced by these research findings, as well as by rising criticisms of education from intellectuals in the Global South. A wave of theoretical and empirical work influenced by neo-Marxism explicated in detail the mechanisms through which schooling fed the reproduction of capitalist social relations on a global scale (Carnoy & Levin, 1985; Willis, 1981). Led by Frantz

Fanon, Ivan Illich, and Martin Carnoy, a countermovement of education and development theories emerged which blended neo-Marxist sociologies of education with dependency arguments to produce a hard-hitting critique of Western education as "cultural imperialism." Comparativists posited that the expansion of education in the South was part of a larger process of neo-colonialism, in which developing countries were integrated into a world economic system as supporting satellites of the West (Arnove, 1980).

Educational systems were thought to be playing several different roles in extending a new form of dependency. In the poorest and most marginal countries, schooling produced elite classes who identified with the values and culture of the West and were willing to exploit their own populations to emulate Western lifestyles. Schooling also acted as a legitimating mechanism that laid responsibility for failure in the world economy on the nation and the individual, rather than on the unequal and exploitative features of the world system itself (Fuller, 1991; Illich, 1971). Even in countries experiencing economic growth, schooling could still be viewed as producing a form of dependency: in this case habituating workers to competition in a global system of trade.

Alongside these criticisms from the left, the 1970s also saw the emergence of a variety of movements inside the developing world that focused on finding alternatives to dependent development. In Africa, for example, political leaders such as Kwame Nkrumah and Julius Nyerere pioneered the idea of African socialism as an alternative to neo-imperialism (Nkrumah, 1970; Nyerere, 1969). Leading African thinkers, including novelists Chinua Achebe and Ngugi wa Thiong'o, began to expose the cultural dimensions of neo-colonialism and explored African philosophy and Indigenous forms of knowledge as alternatives to Western approaches to learning (Fanon, 1968; Ngugi wa Thiong'o, 1986a, 1986b; Stromquist, 2003) (See Chapter Six by Madjidi and Restoule). The spirit of these efforts is captured in the recent work of George Dei, who argues for

> an approach to African development that is anchored in a retrieval, revitalization, and restoration of the indigenous African sense of shared, sustainable, and just social values. I contend that African peoples must re-appropriate their cultural resource knowledge if they are to benefit from the power of collective responsibility for social development. Indigenousness may be defined as knowledge

consciousness arising locally and in association with the long-term occupancy of a place. Indigenousness refers to the traditional norms, social values, and mental constructs that guide, organize, and regulate African ways of living in and making sense of the world. Indigenous knowledges differ from conventional knowledges in their absence of imperial and colonial imposition. The notion of indigenousness highlights the power of dynamics embedded in the production, interrogation, validation, and dissemination of global knowledge about "international development." It also recognizes the multiple and collective origins and collaborative dimensions of knowledge, and underscores that the interpretation or analysis of social reality is subject to different and sometimes oppositional perspectives. (Dei, 2000, p. 72)

Such criticisms naturally led to proposals for alternative forms of education. Julius Nyerere, the longtime president of Tanzania (1961–85), first captured this momentum in his well-known essay, "Education for Self-Reliance" (Nyerere, 1967). Nyerere's interest in self-reliance shares a great deal with Mahatma Gandhi's approach. He saw the inherited colonial education system in Tanzania as elitist in nature and oriented to Western interests and norms. Nyerere not only promised to make access to primary education free and to introduce universal adult literacy programs, he also envisioned schools as community institutions, supporting farms, workshops, and cultural activities that would help bridge the divide between school and rural society (Samoff, 2003). In a move that attracted international attention, Nyerere expanded opportunities for adult education and initiated a national literacy campaign (Kassam, 1995; Mundy, 1993).

The 1970s saw the South-North diffusion of strong, alternative pedagogical models, emanating from socialist educational experiments in the developing world and from the writing and field-tested curriculum of Paulo Freire (1970). Freire built his approach to education around the concept of "conscientization" (introduced in Chapter One), in which he integrated a commitment to education as the practice of freedom and the idea that a dialogue about the learner's own experience can be transformative. Freire criticized dominant elites for using a banking concept of education that encouraged the passivity of oppressed peoples. He argued instead that:

[T]he task of the humanists is to see that the oppressed become aware of the fact that as dual beings, "housing" the oppressors within themselves, they cannot be truly human. This task implies that revolutionary leaders do not go to the people in order to bring them a message of salvation, but in order to come to know through dialogue with them both their objective situation and their awareness of that situation—the various levels of perception of themselves and of the world in which and with which they exist. (ibid., p. 95)

As we saw in Chapter Three by Farrell, Manion, and Rincón-Gallardo, such efforts at transformative pedagogy were picked up in a range of efforts to establish alternative forms of primary education for the poor. The development of alternative approaches to education also led organizations as different as UNICEF, USAID, and the World Bank to more carefully target poor and marginalized populations in their development aid, and at minimum to pay greater rhetorical attention to issues of equality, empowerment, and poverty (Mundy, 1998).

GLOBALIZATION AND THE CRISIS OF EDUCATIONAL DEVELOPMENT IN AFRICA

Despite skepticism and debates about the role of education in development, the period from the 1960s to the mid-1970s was characterized by widespread expansion of public educational systems. In nearly all developing countries, where colonially inherited educational systems excluded the majority, changes were profound. Primary school enrolments, for example, increased more than sixfold over a 30-year period in sub-Saharan Africa (Samoff, 1999, p. 3). While fewer than half of all school-age children were in school in the early 1970s, by 1980, three-fourths attended schools (ibid.). In some countries, enrolment ratios, particularly of girls, remained quite low (for example, Francophone West Africa). But across the countries of East and Southern Africa, it was not uncommon to find near to universal access to schooling. In Tanzania, for example, primary school enrolments expanded from 903,000 children in 1971 to 3,500,000 in 1981: a rate of gross enrolment close to 90 percent (Vavrus, 2005, p. 181).

However, this dramatic and rapid expansion of schooling stalled after 1980. Some countries, such as Tanzania and Kenya, experienced a severe

CHAPTER ELEVEN: Education for All 313

reversal in the ratio of children enrolled in school. The central government and local communities in these countries reintroduced school fees. Educational infrastructure—school buildings, school materials, trained administrators and teachers—deteriorated dramatically, so that even when in school, children received an education of shockingly poor quality. A 1989 UNESCO report from Tanzania (where primary enrolment rates had plummeted to below 75 percent), describes the crisis:

> It is not uncommon to find a teacher standing in front of 80–100 pupils who are sitting on a dirt floor in a room without a roof, trying to convey orally the limited knowledge he has, and the pupils trying to take notes on a piece of wrinkled paper using as a writing board the back of the pupil in front of him. There is no teacher guide for the teacher and no textbooks for the children. (As cited in Samoff, 1999, p. 6)

Why did this deterioration in access to and quality of education occur? There are several answers to this question. First, African economies, already the most marginal in the global trading system, became even more peripheral during the great wave of economic globalization that began after 1975, in part because rich countries continued to raise barriers to agricultural and other primary commodities from the South. Many African governments also faced a sharp debt overhang, built up over years of borrowing from the West and its institutions for their development. As African government revenues declined, so too did available resources for schooling. Even governments that maintained a strong commitment to education saw per capita spending on education deteriorate by an average of $5 across the continent, to an average level of $85 per capita in 1995 (ibid., p. 7).

Second, many governments in Africa were poor stewards of their nations. High levels of corruption and nepotism, weak administrative capacity, a tendency toward war, and relatively undemocratic political systems characterized many of the governments of the continent. In these contexts, intermittent promises of access to schooling were often used to broker patrimonial (father-child) relations between politicians and local communities. Used in this way, schooling divided opposition and created "clients" rather than citizens with common perceptions and commitments to social and political rights. In contrast to rich country welfare states, where a strong national social settlement ensured access to education as a right of citizenship, in African countries education was often perceived as a tool of patronage. The hierarchical nature of many African school systems, as inherited from the colonial era, further entrenched inequalities. Administratively, African school systems tended to be organized in a top-down, centralized manner, with little room for participation or innovation (ibid., p. 13).

Finally, external political and institutional factors lay at the root of this crisis. From the late 1970s, African countries faced an increasingly harsh and punitive international community. The wealthier countries of the West were focused on domestic economic reforms to improve their own competitiveness in a globalized economic system, and were less willing to fund international development activities. Rich country governments refused to provide substantial debt relief or to drop trade barriers to the primary commodities produced by developing world countries. Instead they encouraged countries to adopt a set of "belt tightening" and liberalization reforms, often through their engagement with the International Monetary Fund (IMF) and the World Bank. "Structural Adjustment Programs" encouraged governments to place a cap on public spending, often with severe effects on educational provision. In cases such as Tanzania and Kenya, these caps on spending led to the reintroduction of user fees in health and education (Reimers, 1994).

From the late 1980s, externally influenced educational reforms went even further than the constraints and costs imposed by macroeconomic adjustment. Developing countries were hit by a set of educational reform proposals that had emerged across rich countries of the world, where policy-makers had begun to question the sustainability of expansionary trends in public funding for education, and were seeking reforms that might guarantee greater efficiency as well as national competitiveness. The first generation of what we might think of as "globalization-driven" reforms in education began in the mid-to-late 1970s when governments began to introduce "finance-driven" measures (cost cutting and the search for new, private sources of finance, for example). A second generation of reforms focused on "competitiveness": the efficient use of schooling to improve the productivity of the domestic labour force (Carnoy, 1999). Such reforms, reviewed by Anderson and Sivasubramaniam in Chapter Five of this volume, included standards-based reform (principally the introduction of national testing regimes) and experiments in school choice and the privatization of educational service delivery (to increase inter-school competition and parental/student motivation) (Hanushek,

1995). Finance- and competitiveness-driven reforms tended to squeeze out the expansive, equity-driven mandates of post–Second World War educational systems (Ball, 1998; Dale, 2000). In turn, they eroded education's role in extending a social compact or settlement to the citizens of the Global South.

In Africa, these reform measures were carried forward forcefully by the World Bank, which by the mid-1980s had emerged as the largest single financer of educational development as well as the largest education policy think-tank in the world (Carnoy, 1995; Colclough, 1991; Reimers, 1994). The World Bank's 1988 landmark publication, *Education in Sub-Saharan Africa: Policies for Adjustment, Revitalization and Expansion,* suggested that earlier goals of equality themselves could only be met through a substantial liberalization of educational systems. National systems of public education needed to be protected from elite capture, and returned to public accountability through the introduction of market-like mechanisms. Governments were told that they needed to encourage the private provision of education (directly funded by learners) not only because public finances could not afford universal systems, but also because private provision would enhance efficiency and quality. Governments were encouraged to step back from centralized systems of management and return schools to local control (albeit with new regulatory and accountability controls, such as national testing regimes) (Hinchcliffe, 1993).

The impact of these reforms across Africa and the developing world were mixed. Macroeconomic reforms, despite their initially steep human costs, brought about a modest renewal of economic growth in countries such as Tanzania, Kenya, and Malawi. At the same time, they have been criticized for their negative impact on social equality, since the beneficiaries of economic growth are primarily in the modern sector of the economy, while producers in traditional sectors, such as agriculture, continue to face trade barriers from the North. Further, without debt relief, governments were hard pressed to fund renewal of productive infrastructure: they simply could not compete in the global market. These economic constraints created a steep barrier for educational change. Competition-driven educational reforms—including the decentralization of education, the encouragement of private service delivery, and the devolution of financing to local communities—had negative impacts on access and equality. Many reforms floundered because they were introduced to already fragile systems with no new resources (Moulton, Mundy,

Welmond, & Williams, 2002). Most observers agree that inequality of educational opportunity increased considerably in Tanzania between 1980 and 2000, "with a growing gap between those who can afford user fees and other school related expenses, and those who cannot" (Vavrus, 2005, p. 183).

THE REVIVAL OF "EDUCATION FOR ALL" AFTER 2000

The 1990s saw a precipitous decline in overall flows of aid, and an even steeper decline in aid for education. Despite the ambitious goals for education established by the international community at the World Conference on Education for All in Jomtien, Thailand, in 1990, little progress was made in the 10 years that followed (Chabbott, 2003; Delamonica, Mehrotra, & Vandemoortele, 2001; Torres, 2000). The international community came together again in 2000, at the World Education Forum in Dakar, Senegal, to reconfirm their mutual commitment to EFA, this time setting a 15-year target with the promise that "no countries seriously committed to Education for All will be thwarted in their achievement of this goal by a lack of resources" (Article 10, Dakar Framework for Action). The international community further demonstrated their commitment to universal primary education by including this concept in two of the eight Millennium Development Goals endorsed by 189 countries in September 2000 (Glewwe & Zhao, 2005).

In the years after 2000, the international context for development in Africa and other parts of the developing world took a more positive turn. After more than a decade of declining aid and neoliberal policy reforms, rich country governments and the multilateral institutions began to develop a consensus about international poverty and inequality that links international development to democracy, good governance, and human rights in a more extensive manner than ever before, while also strongly asserting the primacy of markets and capitalism (Noel, 2005).

The 2004 Rome Declaration on Aid Harmonization, and the endorsement of the 2005 Paris Declaration on Aid Effectiveness and the 2008 Accra Agenda for Action, led to important shifts in donor behaviour. Rich nations were asked to provide a long-term, steady, and reliable source of funding for the recurrent costs of schooling in the poorest countries of the world, and major improvements were made in terms of donor coordination, concentration of aid on the poorest countries, and the untying of aid. Additionally, these declarations underlined the

CHAPTER ELEVEN: Education for All

importance of country-level ownership of the development process, noting that developing countries should have broader participation in the policy formation, stronger leadership on aid coordination, and that country-level systems should be used for aid delivery (OECD, n.d.).

Schooling re-emerged as a central part of this new international consensus, in part because it fit with both the neoliberal and pro-economic globalization approaches to development endorsed by the International Monetary Fund (IMF) and the World Bank—which began to look for the achievement of universal access to basic education in their country lending programs (Mundy, 2006, 2002), and the more equity-conscious and globalization-skeptic approaches adopted by the United Nations (Therien, 2004; Ruggie, 2003). In response, donors began to pool their funds, provide sector-wide funding (where aid is given to support a sector budget), and provide direct budget support (where aid is channelled directly into a government's budget)—a first in the history of international development cooperation, which has generally shied away from directly paying for teachers' salaries and other recurrent costs of mass education.

In the years following Dakar, better targeted aid combined with significant increases in national education budgets in the developing world resulted in significant gains in access to primary education. New forms of global coordination from both multilateral and civil society organizations emerged, and by the end of the decade the private sector had taken on new and expanding roles in EFA. Furthermore, the rise of the global middle class in the 2000s changed the economic landscape, bringing new bilateral donors onto the scene. Of these, China is probably the most significant, with rapid expansion in its foreign aid efforts, particularly in sub-Saharan Africa, which has been a major recipient of Chinese aid (World Bank, 2015a).

Additionally, under the framework of evidence-based development, the 2000s also saw an explosion of data being produced and used by a wider variety of actors. This includes increasing use of household survey data to help map inequalities in education (see UNESCO & UNICEF, 2015); greater use of national assessment data to measure student outcomes and system equity; a focus on rigorous methods for understanding the impact of education interventions, including a surge in the use of Randomized Control Trials (McEwan, 2015); and increasing participation in data collection and evaluation by non-governmental organizations in the developing world.

The above factors combined resulted in significant progress in the years following Dakar. The number of out-of-school children and adolescents decreased, falling from 204 million in 1999 to an estimated 121 million by 2012 (UNESCO, 2015, p. 3). Since 1999, the incidence of severe gender disparity (fewer than nine girls for every ten boys in primary schooling) decreased from 33 to 16 countries, and secondary level gender disparities are declining in all but a few countries (UNESCO, 2015, p. 15). This narrowing of the gender gap in primary enrolment has been heralded as one of the biggest successes of EFA.

However, by 2005, as the global financial crisis loomed, aid for education stagnated and so did global progress toward EFA. Between 2010 and 2012, total aid to the education sector fell by 10 percent (UNESCO, 2015, p. 261). In contrast, the health sector saw global funding rise continuously during the 2000s, and significant levels of new funding were allocated to global health funds (i.e., the Global Fund and GAVI, the Vaccine Alliance): for example, between 2001 and 2010 donor countries contributed US$22 billion to the Global Fund to Fight AIDS, Tuberculosis and Malaria, approximately 10 times as much as they contributed to the Global Partnership for Education (UNESCO, 2012).

Additionally, over the course of the decade it became increasingly clear that efforts to rapidly expand access to primary education had not resulted in better learning outcomes (Hanushek & Woessmann, 2007; Pritchett, 2013). As a result, the focus shifted away from access, toward a greater focus on the quality of education provided (UNESCO, 2005). Unfortunately, this shift came too late for many. By 2015 it was clear that the world would not only fail to meet the EFA targets laid out at Jomtien and Dakar, but, as demonstrated by the growing number of out-of-school children, which rose by 2.4 million between 2010 and 2013 (UNESCO Institute for Statistics & EFA GMR, 2015, p. 1), we are actually getting farther away from the target. To add to this, in 32 countries, mostly in sub-Saharan Africa, 20 percent of those that do enrol in primary schooling will drop out before completing the last grade (ibid., p. 84).

By 2013, 59 million children and almost 65 million adolescents remained out of school (ibid.), and while the global average gains made over the decade were certainly significant, wide disparities continue to exist within some countries and regions (Lewin 2011, 2009). A series of complex and intersecting disadvantages work together to ensure the most marginalized children (including children with special needs, children from lower-income families, those living in rural and remote areas, and those who come from marginalized groups within countries) do not enter or persist in school.

Despite better donor cooperation, education aid was poorly targeted to the countries and populations most in need. For example, sub-Saharan Africa, home to more than half of the world's out-of-school children, received on average 47 percent of all aid to basic education in 2004, but by 2010 this level had fallen to 31 percent (UNESCO, 2015, p. 264). Furthermore, the right to education remains especially perilous for children living in contexts of conflict and political instability, and the global community has continuously failed to introduce reliable and consistent assistance to these regions (General Assembly of the United Nations, 2010; Mundy & Dryden-Peterson, 2011; Talbot, 2013).

It is also important to note that after Dakar, efforts to advance education around the world became synonymous with the two education targets included in the widely endorsed Millennium Development Goals: universal access to primary education and gender equity in elementary education. Thus, while we have seen significant gains in these two areas, many of the broader EFA goals adopted at the World Education Forums in Dakar and Jomtien (i.e., early childhood education, youth training, and adult literacy) have been neglected.

EDUCATION FOR ALL: THE VIEW FROM TANZANIA AND KENYA

Current challenges and dilemmas of educational development can be illustrated by two East African countries, Tanzania and Kenya. Both countries share a long history of governmental efforts to use education to support economic and social development, and in the early 2000s both announced national policies supporting universal, free access to primary education. However, while Tanzania pioneered a form of African socialism, as discussed earlier in this chapter, Kenya shunned efforts at centralized socialism and instead adopted a market-oriented approach to development. As a result, early EFA experiences in Kenya and Tanzania are quite different.

At independence, Kenya began with much higher levels of participation in school than Tanzania (Cooksey, Court & Makau, 1994). Unlike Tanzania, which had severely limited access to secondary schooling in order to fund primary education, the Kenyan government did not constrain expansion at the secondary level. Instead, it encouraged communities to build their own secondary schools through a movement known as *harambee*—Swahili for "let us all pull together." As secondary schooling rapidly expanded in Kenya during the 1970s, the government did little to guide its expansion in terms of either quality or distribution.

Kenya, again in contrast to Tanzania, paid little attention to reforming its school curriculum to build a distinct national identity or alternative approach to development (Cooksey, Court & Makau, 1994; Sivasubramaniam & Mundy, 2006). Nor did it enforce its promise of free primary education. Despite announcements ending formal fees in 1974 and 1979, individual schools were quietly allowed to re-institute fees for attendance. Thus, although the central government maintained control over the educational system through a national examination system and school inspections, wealthy communities were able to build more and better schools, and large geographic disparities emerged in terms of opportunity and quality. At the same time, harambee schools offered an

Figure 11.1: Map of Tanzania and Kenya

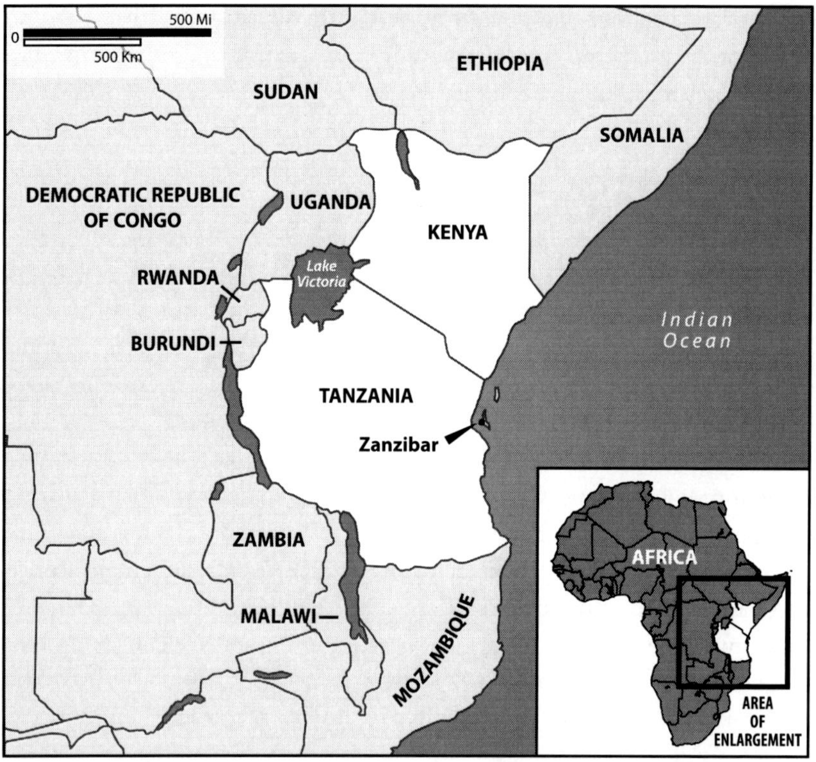

Source: Map created by Scott Wallace

outlet for popular educational aspirations, and as a result, disparities in educational opportunity were rarely blamed on the central government (Buchmann, 1999).

In the early 1980s, both Tanzania and Kenya entered a period of severe economic constraint, accompanied by neoliberal economic and educational reforms (Samoff, 1990). In both countries, primary schooling began to deteriorate, and national policies toward education began to change. In Kenya, the government introduced a new primary cycle of eight years with a new focus on pre-vocational training for self-employment, introduced secondary and tertiary quotas, and announced that educational policies would be closed to public debate. However, the Kenyan government continued to respond to popular demands for access to higher education, and in the late 1980s it expanded university enrolments, further depriving elementary education of finances. Meanwhile, in Tanzania, the government removed the cap on secondary school enrolments, encouraged communities to sponsor private secondary schools, and opened new university spaces. Tanzania's innovative literacy and adult education programs were neglected, and efforts to create a curriculum reflective of local issues and African socialism fell by the wayside. In both countries steep declines in educational quality were accompanied by the stagnation and later erosion of enrolments.

By the late 1980s, both Tanzania and Kenya began to experience external pressures to introduce cost-sharing policies into their education systems as part of structural adjustment lending. Neither country received significant increases in external aid, despite their economic crises. Indeed, charges of corruption within the Kenyan government led several donors to cease their external aid programs altogether.

In the early 2000s, political liberalization allowed for the development of an increasingly vocal network of civil society organizations across Africa, which not only advocated for equity-driven approaches to national development, but also worked with transnational advocacy groups to ensure that international organizations altered their social policy prescriptions. In the Tanzanian case, research produced by the NGO Maarifa ni Ufunguo on the negative impact of user fees in education was then used by American NGOs to lobby members of the US House and Senate. Eventually legislation was passed prohibiting the US government from funding the World Bank if it imposed any form of user fees as part of its loan conditionality. The World Bank subsequently removed user fees from its loan conditions, and the government of

Tanzania declared free primary education (FPE) and officially abolished user fees in 2003 (Maarifa ni Ufunguo, 2000; Kuder, 2004). The public response to the declaration of free education was overwhelming and immediate: overnight, approximately 1.6 million new students entered the primary system (Haggerty & Mundy, 2006).

The Tanzania experience stimulated a number of other African governments to remove user fees and declare universal FPE. In Kenya, the announcement of FPE came in late 2002, and as in Tanzania, the popular response to this announcement was overwhelming: following the implementation of FPE, 1.2 million out-of-school children were absorbed into formal primary schools and 200,000 into non-formal education centres. In both cases, there had been little planning for such a large response, and only a very limited budget for it. As a result, the first few years of FPE were somewhat chaotic.

Over the following decade, both Kenya and Tanzania made significant progress toward EFA. Yet, for both countries, FPE raised a host of questions. The question of how to finance FPE was of particular concern. In response to international pressure for developing countries to increase the share of national income devoted to education, the governments of both countries increased domestic funding for education. In Kenya this meant committing over 5 percent of its GDP (gross domestic product) to education over the decade, which by 2010 equalled 20.6 percent of the government's overall budget. In Tanzania spending on education rose from 2 percent of its GDP in 1999 to 6.2 percent by 2010, but more recent data shows this trend has started to reverse, with the government committing 19.6 percent of its total budget to education in 2010, decreasing to 15.9 percent by 2014 (World Bank, 2015b).

Despite these increases in domestic funding, in both instances FPE continues to rely on international aid. From 2005 to 2010, foreign donors financed a large share of Tanzania's education budget, rising from more than US$65 million in 2005 to over US$236 by 2010 (OECD, 2015), and by 2013 Tanzania had at least 23 active donors working in the country (Rose, Steer, Smith, & Zubairi, 2013). Over the same period Kenya was much less dependent on foreign aid, but still required external funding to meet new levels of enrolment. Such dependency puts the future of FPE in a very vulnerable position, as small changes in donor funding place the education of thousands of children at risk. These high levels of dependency also tend to lead to donor-driven policies, rather than local control and ownership (Samoff, 2004). In both Tanzania and Kenya,

CHAPTER ELEVEN: Education for All 323

the strength of external influence was amplified by a decision among donors to pool their resources and develop regular measures to jointly monitor government expenditures and implementation of policies.

At the local level, the rapid expansion of access to education in Tanzania and Kenya had sharp implications for the quality of learning, and class sizes of over 100 students were not unusual at the primary level in either country. Materials and classroom equipment were in short supply, and although many donors funded teacher training, there was no related support for teacher salaries, resulting in significant teacher shortages.

Today, both Kenya and Tanzania are among the fastest-growing economies in Africa, with Kenya's GDP per capita growing from US$977.80 in 2010 to US$1,337.90 by 2014, and with Tanzania seeing a growth from US$712.20 to US$998.10 over the same period (World Bank, 2016). However, despite this promising economic growth, both countries failed to meet their EFA targets before the 2015 deadline. Teacher shortages continue to be a major issue, even while substantive improvements have been made in lowering the student-teacher ratio. In Tanzania the average teacher-to-student ratios were lowered from 1:58 in 2003 to 1:43 by 2013 (MoE Tanzania, 2015, p. 40), but regional disparities persist within the country. AIDS continues to be a major threat, with the government estimating that the education sector could lose more than 27,000 teachers to AIDS by 2020 (ibid., p. 47).

In Kenya, children have a better chance to learn, with a net enrolment in 2013 of 95.9 percent (Republic of Kenya, 2014, p. 63), and more than three-quarters of those children making it past Grade 4. Additionally, in 2007 the government bowed to increased pressure for secondary education, announcing it would now provide free secondary education. Unfortunately, much like earlier promises for free education, schools continue to charge fees that are beyond the ability of many families to pay. Fortunately, due to the civil societies' past efforts, parents now feel empowered to act, and some parents have taken issues to the courts in order to force the government to meet its promise for free secondary education (Daniel, 2014; Kakah, 2015).

Additionally, the Kenyan case serves as a prime example of how schooling does not equal learning. The civil society group UWEZO's most recent national learning assessment found that one-third of all children in class three cannot read at the class two level. UWEZO also found teacher absenteeism to be a major obstacle, with 10 percent of all teachers absent on any given day (UWEZO, 2012, p. 1). Like Tanzania, there are large disparities across the country, and for the poorest households only 23 percent of girls and 29 percent of boys complete primary education (EFA GMR, 2014, p. 4). In turn, parents are increasingly turning to private providers with the hopes that the private sector can provide the quality education the government cannot, including poor families, which make great sacrifices in order to enrol their children in low-fee private schools. Unfortunately, the quality of these schools, which often rely on untrained teachers, is greatly mixed, and the growth of private provision has not resulted in promised learning outcomes.

The Kenyan and Tanzanian governments are under enormous pressure today—both from domestic groups and from international actors—to maintain momentum toward EFA, and the fragile democratic regimes at the centre of politics in these two countries have nonetheless staked their claims for political legitimacy on the promise of universal free education. It is not surprising, then, to see governments in both countries scrambling to find ways of harnessing private sector partnerships to expand education, and endorsing donor-advocated reforms such as the decentralization of school management and budgets. Such reforms deflect attention away from the central government and also offer mechanisms for doing more with less (Robertson, Mundy, Verger, & Menashy, 2012). They add to the heightened complexity and interdependencies that now frame achievement of the universal right to education in these and other developing countries.

CONCLUSION

The Tanzanian and Kenyan examples highlight many of the dilemmas and challenges surrounding the international call for universal primary education. Domestically, an orientation toward greater equity, self-reliance, and public accountability across primary and later levels of schooling promises enormous returns. However, these returns can only be realized if, at the level of the world system, there are guarantees of long-term funding for the poorest countries, cancellation of debt, and access to the agricultural and other product markets in rich countries. The emergence of a transnationally organized global public that is critical of globalization and global economic inequalities, and that views the right to education as an important venue for expressing a commitment to redistributive justice on a global scale, is a hopeful sign. Such transnational networks continue to help pressure rich country governments to provide reliable, long-term international funding, and also help ensure that the voices of local civil society groups, closest to indigenous knowledge and the everyday experiences of schooling, are heard by national educational policy-makers.

Despite the world's collective failure to reach the EFA targets by the 2015 deadline, the global community remains committed to this goal. In September 2015, the 2030 Agenda for Sustainable Development, commonly known as the Sustainable Development Goals (SDGs), was launched. Education is the focus of SDG4: Education 2030, which aims to "Ensure inclusive and equitable quality education and promote lifelong learning opportunities for all" (UNESCO, 2015). This not only reaffirms the vision for EFA set out in Jomtien and Dakar, but also expands upon that vision to include 10 specific targets that address universal secondary education, expanded access to early childhood education, and technical and vocational training, as well as highlight the need for quality education to improve learning outcomes, and a commitment to better address the educational needs of children living in conflict-affected areas. Additionally, 2015 saw educational stakeholders from all across the world gather for the World Education Forum, held in Incheon, Korea, in order to set new targets for education. In November 2015, the resulting *Education 2030 Incheon Declaration and Framework for Action: Towards Inclusive and equitable Quality Education and Lifelong Learning for All* (Education 2030, 2015), was formally adopted by UNESCO and its member states, reaffirming the global commitment to education for the next 15 years.

Overall, despite the optimism that a new set of global goals brings, the democratization of opportunities for learning in the developing world remains a fragile and easily reversible process. For children in many of the world's poorest countries, access to schooling has been a hollow privilege. While schooling may bring children into a global community of childhood rights and expectations, it often also sorts children into poverty and alienates them from their local cultures in ways that harm local self-reliance. The challenge of offering every child an equal opportunity to learn involves not just more schooling, but better models of schooling that will prepare them for active roles in social transformation.

QUESTIONS FOR REFLECTION AND DISCUSSION
1. What drives the demand for and expansion of schooling at basic and at higher education levels? Are the drivers in Kenya

and Tanzania similar to or different from those in your own cultural context?
2. How do you view the chances of success for recent international efforts to achieve EFA?
3. What can experiences of schooling in the South teach us about benefits and challenges within our own educational systems?
4. How does schooling in North America sort children into different kinds of life chances? How does this compare with educational life chances in countries such as Tanzania or Kenya?

SUGGESTED AUDIO-VISUAL RESOURCES
The First Grader, directed by Justin Chadwick (2010). Available at: www.thefirstgrader-themovie.com/
Set in a remote Kenyan community, this film follows an 84-year-old man fighting for his right to receive education. This true story highlights the complexity of providing free primary education for all in Kenya.

Back to School, part of the Wide Angle PBS Series of International Documentaries. Available at: www.pbs.org/wnet/wideangle/episodes/time-for-school-series/introduction/?p=4340
Back to School, the second part of the *Time for School* film series, follows the school experiences of seven children in seven different countries, trying to beat the odds and get an education. The series documented the experiences of these children to 2015, the year the international community targeted for universal access to primary education.

SUGGESTIONS FOR FURTHER READING
Abdi, Ali. (2005). African Philosophies of Education: Counter-Colonial Criticisms. In Ali Abdi and Ailie Cleghorn (Eds.), *Issues in African Education: Sociological Perspectives* (pp. 25–42). New York: Palgrave Macmillan.
Achebe, Chinua. (1958). *Things Fall Apart*. London: Heinemann.
Anderson-Levitt, Kathryn. (2005). The Schoolyard Gate: Schooling and Childhood in Global Perspective. *Journal of Social History*, *38*(4): 987–1006.
Buchmann, Claudia. (1999). The State and Schooling in Kenya: Historical Developments and Current Challenges. *Africa Today*, *46*(1): 95–115.
Cooksey, Brian, Court, David, and Makau, Ben. (1994). Education for Self- Reliance and Harambee. In Joel Barkan (Ed.), *Beyond*

Capitalism and Socialism in Kenya and Tanzania (pp. 201–234). London: Lynne Rienner.

Fanon, Frantz. (1968). *The Wretched of the Earth.* New York: Grove Press.

Freire, Paulo. (1970). *Pedagogy of the Oppressed.* New York: Continuum.

Fuller, Bruce. (1991). *Growing Up Modern: The Western States Build Third World Schools.* New York: Routledge.

Lewis, Stephen. (2005). Education: An Avalanche of Studies, Little Studying. Chap. 3 in *Race Against Time.* Toronto: Anansi Press.

Mundy, Karen. (2006). EFA and the New Development Compact. *International Review of Education, 52*(1): 23–48.

Nyerere, Julius K. (1967). Education for Self Reliance. In *Ujamaa: Essays on Socialism* (pp. 1–12). Dar es Salaam, Tanzania: Oxford University Press.

Samoff, Joel. (1990). "Modernizing" a Socialist Vision: Education in Tanzania. In Martin Carnoy and Joel Samoff (Eds.), *Education and Social Transition in the Third World* (pp. 209-273). Princeton, NJ: Princeton University Press.

Samoff, Joel. (1999). No Teacher Guide, No Textbook, No Chairs: Contending with Crisis in African Education. In Robert F. Arnove and Carlos A. Torres (Eds.), *Comparative Education: The Dialectic of the Global and the Local* (pp. 409–445). New York: Rowman and Littlefield.

Semali, Ladislaus. (1999). Community as Classroom: Dilemmas of Valuing African Indigenous Literacy in Education. *International Review of Education, 45*(3–4): 305–319.

Serpell, Robert. (1999). Local Accountability to Rural Communities: A Challenge for Education Planning in Africa. In Fiona E. Leach and Angela W. Little (Eds.), *Education, Cultures, and Economics: Dilemmas for Development* (pp. 111–142). London: Routledge.

Wa Thiong'o, Ngugi. (1986). *Decolonising the Mind: The Politics of Language in African Literature.* London: James Curry.

REFERENCES

Abernathy, David. (1969). *The Political Dilemma of Popular Education: An African Case.* Stanford, CA: Stanford University Press.

Arnove, Robert F. (1980). Comparative Education and World Systems Analysis. *Comparative Education Review, 24*(1): 48–62.

Ball, Stephen. (1998). Big Policies/Small World: An Introduction to International Perspectives in Education Policy. *Comparative Education, 34*(2): 119–130.

Becker, Gary. (1962). Investment in Human Capital: A Theoretical Analysis. *Journal of Political Economy, 70*(5): 9–49.

Benavot, Aaron, and Resnik, Julia. (2006). Towards a Comparative Socio-Historical Analysis of Universal Basic and Secondary Education. In Joel Cohen, David Bloom, and Martin Malin (Eds.), *Educating All the Children: A Global Agenda* (123-231). Cambridge, MA: American Academy of Arts and Sciences and MIT Press.

Bowles, Samuel, and Gintis, Herbert. (1981). Contradiction and Reproduction in Educational Theory. In Len Barton (Ed.), *Schooling, Ideology, and Curriculum* (pp. 51–65). Sussex: Falmer Press.

Bowles, Samuel, and Gintis, Herbert. (1977). *Schooling in Capitalist America: Educational Reform and the Contradictions of Economic Life.* London: Routledge and Kegan Paul.

Buchmann, Claudia. (1999). The State and Schooling in Kenya: Historical Developments and Current Challenges. *Africa Today, 46*(1): 95–115.

Carnoy, Martin. (1995). Structural Adjustment and the Changing Face of Education. *International Labour Review, 134*(6): 653–673.

Carnoy, Martin. (1999). *Globalization and Educational Reform: What Planners Need to Know.* Paris: UNESCO, International Institute for Educational Planning.Carnoy, Martin, and Levin, Henry. (1985). *Schooling and Work in the Democratic State.* Stanford, CA: Stanford University Press.

Chabbott, Colette. (2003). *Constructing Education for Development: International Organizations and EFA.* New York: Routledge/Falmer.

Colclough, Christopher. (1991). Who Should Learn to Pay? An Assessment of Neo-Liberal Approaches to Education Policy. In Christopher Colclough and James Manor (Eds.), *States or Markets? Neo-Liberalism and the Development Policy Debate* (pp. 197–213). Oxford: Clarendon Press.

Coleman, James, et al. (1966). *Equality of Educational Opportunity.* Washington, DC: US Department of Health, Education and Welfare.

Collins, Randall. (2000). Comparative and Historical Patterns of Education. In Maureen T. Hallinan (Ed.), *Handbook of the Sociology of Education* (pp. 213–240). New York: Kluwer Academic and Plenum.

Cooksey, Brian, Court, David, and Makau, Ben. (1994). Education for Self-Reliance and Harambee. In Joel Barkan (Ed.), *Beyond Capitalism and Socialism in Kenya and Tanzania* (pp. 201–203). London: Lynne Rienner.

Dale, Roger. (1989). *The State and Education Policy.* Milton Keynes, UK: Open University Press.

Dale, Roger. (2000). Globalization and Education: Demonstrating a "Common World Educational Culture" or Locating a "Globally Structured Educational Agenda"? *Educational Theory, 50*(4): 427–448.

Dei, George J. S. (2000). African Development: The Relevance and Implications of "Indigenousness." In George J. S. Dei, Budd L. Hall, and Dorothy G.

Rosenberg (Eds.), *Indigenous Knowledges in Global Contexts: Multiple Readings of Our World* (pp. 70–86). Toronto: University of Toronto Press.

Delamonica, Enrique, Mehrotra Santosh, Vandemoortele Jan. (2001). *Education for All Is Affordable: A Minimum Global Cost Estimate.* UNICEF Staff Working Paper. Evaluation, Policy and Planning Series, No EPP-01-001. Florence, Italy: UNICEF.

Education 2030. (2015). *Education 2030 Incheon Declaration and Framework for Action: Towards Inclusive and Equitable Quality Education and Lifelong Learning for All.* Retrieved from www.unesco.org/new/fileadmin/MULTIMEDIA/HQ/ED/ED_new/pdf/FFA-ENG-27Oct15.pdf

Education for All Global Monitoring Report. (2014). *Teaching and Learning: Achieving Quality for All: Monitoring the Education for All Goals, Sub-Saharan Africa Factsheet.* Paris: UNESCO. Retrieved from en.unesco.org/gem-report/sites/gem-report/files/SSA_Factsheet_2014.pdf

Fanon, Frantz. (1968). *The Wretched of the Earth.* New York: Grove Press.

Farrell, Joseph P. (1999). Changing Conceptions of Equality of Education: 40 Years of Comparative Evidence. In Robert F. Arnove and Carlos A. Torres (Eds.), *Comparative Education: The Dialectic of the Global and the Local* (2nd. ed.) (pp. 148–175). New York: Rowman and Littlefield.

Foster, Philip. (1965). *Education and Social Change in Ghana.* London: Routledge.

Freire, Paulo. (1970). *Pedagogy of the Oppressed.* New York: Continuum.

Fuller, Bruce. (1991). *Growing Up Modern: The Western State Builds Third World Schools.* New York: Routledge.

Fuller, Bruce, and Rubinson, Richard. (1991). *The Political Construction of Education: The State, School Expansion, and Economic Change.* New York: Praeger.

General Assembly of the United Nations. (1948). *Universal Declaration of Human Rights*, Article 26, 1948. Available at www.un.org/Overview/rights.html

General Assembly of the United Nations. (2010). *The Right to Education in Emergency Situations (A/64/L.58).* New York: UN General Assembly.

Glewwe, Paul, and Zhao, Meng. (2005). *Attaining Universal Primary Completion by 2015: How Much Will It Cost?* American Academy of Arts and Sciences Working Paper. Retrieved from faculty.apec.umn.edu/pglewwe/documents/UBASECs6_05.pdf

Haggerty, Megan, and Mundy, Karen. (2006). *Tanzania: Civil Society Participation and the Governance of Educational Systems in the Context of Sector-Wide Approaches to Basic Education* (working paper). Toronto: OISE/University of Toronto.

Halsey, Anthony, Heath, Anthony, and Ridge, John. (1980). *Origins and Destinations: Family, Class and Education in Modern Britain.* Oxford: Clarendon.

Hannum, Emily, and Buchmann, Claudia. (2003). *The Consequences of Global Educational Expansion: Social Science Perspectives.* Cambridge, MA: American Academy of Arts and Sciences.

Hannum, Emily, and Buchmann, Claudia. (2005). Global Education Expansion and Socio-Economic Development: An Assessment of Findings from the Social Sciences. *World Development, 33*(3): 333–354.

Hanushek, Eric. (1995). Interpreting Recent Research on Schooling in Developing Countries. *The World Bank Research Observer, 10*(2): 22–46.

Hanushek, Eric, and Woessmann, Ludger. (2007). *The Role of Education Quality for Economic Growth.* World Bank Policy Research Working Paper No. 4122. New York: the World Bank.

Harbison, Frederick, and Meyers, Charles. (1964). *Education, Manpower, and Economic Growth: Strategies of Human Resource Development.* New York: McGraw-Hill.

Hinchcliffe, Keith. (1993). Neo-Liberal Prescriptions for Education Finance: Unfortunately Necessary or Inherently Desirable? *International Journal of Educational Development, 13*(2): 183–187.

Howden, Daniel. (2014, January 24). Kenyan Parents Sue Ministers over Illegal School Fees. *Guardian.* Available at www.theguardian.com/global-development/2014/jan/24/kenyan-parents-sue-illegal-school-fees

Huntington, Samuel. (1968). *Political Order in Changing Societies.* New Haven, CT: Yale University Press.

Illich, Ivan. (1971). *Deschooling Society.* New York: Harper and Row.

Inkeles, Alex, and Holsinger, Donald. (1974). *Education and Individual Modernity in Developing Countries.* Leiden, the Netherlands: Brill.

Kakah, Maureen. (2015, February 8). Parent Sues Principal over Exhorbitant School Fees. *Nairobi News.* Available at nairobinews.co.ke/parent-sues-principal-over-exorbitant-secondary-school-fees/

Kassam, Yusuf. (1995). Julius Kambarage Nyerere. In Zaghloul Morsy (Ed.), *Thinkers on Education* (pp. 247–260). Paris: UNESCO Publishing. Available at unesdoc.unesco.org/images/0010/001030/103086eo.pdf

Kuder, Jeanette L. (2004). *The Formulation of Primary Education Policy in Tanzania within a Global Governance Approach to Aid and Development* (PhD dissertation). University of Bristol.

Lewin, Keith. (2009). Access to Education in Sub-Saharan Africa: Patterns, Problems and Possibilities. *Comparative Education, 45*(2): 151–174.

Lewin, Keith. (2011). *Making Rights Realities: Researching Educational Access, Transitions and Equity.* Research report of the Consortium for Research on Educational Access, Transitions and Equity. Brighton, UK: University of Sussex.

Maarifa ni Ufunguo. (2000). *Cost Sharing: A Case Study of Education in Kilimanjaro.* Arusha, Tanzania: Maarifa ni Ufunguo.

Marshall, Thomas. (1961). *Citizenship and Social Class.* Cambridge: Cambridge University Press.

McClelland, David. (1961). *The Achieving Society.* Princeton, NJ: D. Van Nostrand.

McEwan, Patrick J. (2015). Improving Learning in Primary Schools of Developing Countries: A Meta-Analysis of Randomized Experiments. *Review of Educational Research,* 85: 353–394.
Meyer, John W., Boli, John, Thomas, George M., and Ramirez, Franscisco. (1997). World Society and the Nation-State. *American Journal of Sociology, 103*(1): 144–181.
Moulton, Jeanne, Mundy, Karen, Welmond, Michel, and Williams, James. (2002). *Education Reforms in Sub-Saharan Africa: Paradigm Lost?* Westport, CT: Greenwood Press.
Muller, Detlef, Ringer, Fritz, and Simon, Brian (Eds.). (1989). *The Rise of the Modern Educational System: Structural Change and Social Reproduction 1870–1920.* Cambridge: Cambridge University Press.
Mundy, Karen. (1993). Towards a Critical Analysis of Literacy in Southern Africa. *Comparative Education Review 37*(4): 389–411.
Mundy, Karen. (1998). Educational Multilateralism and World (Dis)Order. *Comparative Education Review, 42*(4): 448–478.
Mundy, Karen. (2002). Education in a Reformed World Bank. *International Journal of Educational Development, 22*(5): 483–508.
Mundy, Karen. (2006). EFA and the New Development Compact. *International Review of Education, 52*(1): 23–48.
Mundy, Karen, and Dryden-Peterson, Sarah (Eds.). (2011). *Educating Children in Conflict Zones: Research, Policy and Practice for Systemic Change, a Tribute to Jackie Kirk.* New York: Teachers College Press.
Ngugi wa Thiong'o, (1986a). *A Grain of Wheat.* Oxford: Heinemann.
Ngugi wa Thiong'o. (1986b). *Decolonising the Mind: The Politics of Language in African Literature.* Portsmouth, NH: Heinemann.
Nkrumah, Kwame. (1970). *Consciencism: Philosophy and Ideology for De-colonization.* New York: Monthly Review Press.
Noel, Alain. (2005). *The New Politics of Global Poverty* (unpublished manuscript, Université de Montréal, December 2005).
Nyerere, Julius. (1967). Education for Self Reliance. In *Ujamaa: Essays on Socialism* (pp. 1–12). Dar es Salaam, Tanzania: Oxford University Press.
Nyerere, Julius. (1969). *Freedom and Socialism: Uhuru na Ujamaa; A Selection from Writings and Speeches, 1965–1967.* Dar es Salaam, Tanzania: Oxford University Press.
OECD. (2015). *Query Wizard for International Development Statistics. OECD.* Retrieved from stats.oecd.org/qwids/#?x=1&y=6&f=2:87,4:1,7:2,9:85,3:246, 5:4,8:85&q=2:262,87,169+4:1+7:2+9:85+3:246+5:4+8:85+1:1+6:2005,2006, 2007,2008,2009,2010,2011,2012,2013
OECD. (no date). *Paris Declaration and Accra Agenda for Action.* Available at www.oecd.org/dac/effectiveness/parisdeclarationandaccraagendaforaction.htm
Pritchett, Lant. (2013). The World Bank and Public Sector Management: What Next? *International Review of Administrative Sciences, 79*(3), 413–419.

Ramirez, Francisco, and Boli, John. (1987). Global Patterns of Educational Institutionalization. In George M. Thomas, John H. Myers, Francisco O. Ramirez, and John Boli (Eds.), *Institutional Structure: Constituting the State, Society and the Individual* (pp. 150–172). Beverly Hills: Sage.

Reimers, Fernando. (1994). Education and Structural Adjustment in Latin America and Sub-Saharan Africa. *International Journal of Educational Development, 14*(2): 119–129.

Republic of Kenya. (2014). *Education for All 2015 National Review Report: Kenya.* Republic of Kenya, Ministry of Education, Science and Technology. Retrieved from unesdoc.unesco.org/images/0023/002316/231637e.pdf

Robertson, Susan, Mundy, Karen, Verger, Antoni, and Menashy, Francine. (2012). *Public Private Partnerships in Education: New Actors and Modes of Governance in a Globalizing World.* Cheltenham, UK: Edward Elgar.

Rose, Pauline, Steer, Liesbet, Smith, Katie, and Zubairi, Asma. (2013). *Financing for Global Education: Opportunities for Multilateral Action.* Washington, DC/Paris, Center for Universal Education at Brookings/EFA Global Monitoring Report, www.brookings.edu/~/media/research/files/reports/2013/09/financing-global-education/basic-education-financing-final--webv2.pdf

Ruggie, John G. (2003). The United Nations and Globalization: Patterns and Limits of Institutional Adaptation. *Global Governance, 9*(3): 301–322.

Samoff, Joel. (1990). "Modernizing" a Socialist Vision: Education in Tanzania. In Martin Carnoy and Joel Samoff (Eds.), *Education and Social Transition in the Third World* (pp. 209–273). Princeton, NJ: Princeton University Press.

Samoff, Joel. (1999). *No Teacher Guide, No Textbooks, No Chairs: Contending with Crisis in Africa.* Paper presented at the 43rd Annual Meeting of the African Studies Association, Philadelphia, November 11–14. Available at files.eric.ed.gov/fulltext/ED443769.pdf

Samoff, Joel. (2003). No Teacher Guide, No Textbooks, No Chairs: Contending with Crisis in African Education. In Robert Arnove and Carlos A. Torres (Eds.), *The Dialect of the Global and the Local* (2nd ed.) (pp. 409–445). Oxford: Rowan and Littlefield.

Samoff, Joel. (2004). From Funding Projects to Supporting Sectors? Observations on the Aid Relationship in Burkina Faso. *International Journal of Educational Development, 24*(4): 397–427.

Schultz, Theodore. (1960). Capital Formulation by Education. *Journal of Political Economy, 8*(6): 571–583.

Sivasubramaniam, Malini, and Mundy, Karen. (2006). *Kenya: Civil Society Participation and the Governance of Educational Systems in the Context of Sector-Wide Approaches to Basic Education.* Mimeo, Toronto: OISE/University of Toronto.

Stromquist, Nelly. (2003). Women's Education in the Twenty-First Century: Balance and Prospects. In Robert Arnove and Carlos A. Torres (Eds.),

CHAPTER ELEVEN: Education for All

Comparative Education: The Dialect of the Global and the Local (2nd ed.) (pp. 176–203). Oxford: Rowan and Littlefield.

Talbot, Christopher. (2013). *Education in Conflict and Emergencies in Light of the Post-2015 MDGs and EFA Agendas.* Working Paper 3 (January), Geneva, Switzerland: NORRAG.

Therien, Jean Phillip. (2004). The Politics of International Development: Towards a New Grand Compromise? *Economic Policy and Law: Journal of Trade and Environmental Studies* (special issue, September 2004). Available at http://www.ecolomics-international.org/epal_2004_5_therien_towards_new_grand_compromise....pdf

Torres, Rose-Marie. (2000). *One Decade of EFA: The Challenge Ahead.* Buenos Aires: International Institute of Educational Planning.

UNESCO. (2005). *EFA Global Monitoring Report 2005: The Quality Imperative.* Paris: UNESCO.

UNESCO. (2012). *EFA Global Monitoring Report 2012: Youth and Skills: Putting Education to Work.* Paris: UNESCO.

UNESCO. (2015). *EFA Global Monitoring Report 2015: Education for All 2000–2015: Achievements and Challenges.* Paris: UNESCO.

UNESCO Institute for Statistics and the Education for All Global Monitoring Report. (2015, July). *A Growing Number of Children and Adolescents Are out of School as Aid Fails to Meet the Mark.* Policy Paper 22 / Fact Sheet 31. UNESCO. Available at unesdoc.unesco.org/images/0023/002336/233610e.pdf

United Republic of Tanzania, Ministry of Education and Vocational Training. (2015). *Education for All 2015 National Review Report: United Republic of Tanzania: Mainland.* Available at unesdoc.unesco.org/images/0023/002314/231484e.pdf

UNESCO and UNICEF. (2015). *Fixing the Broken Promise of Education for All: Findings from the Global Initiative on Out of School Children.* Montreal: UNESCO Institute of Statistics.

UWEZO. (2012). *Are Our Children Learning: Annual Learning Assessment Report.* UWEZO, www.uwezo.net/wp-content/uploads/2014/05/Kenya-Report-2012-WebFinalUpdate.pdf

Vavrus, Frances. (2005). Adjusting Inequality: Education and Structural Adjustment Policies in Tanzania. *Harvard Educational Review, 75*(2): 174–201.

Willis, Paul. (1981). *Learning to Labor: How Working Class Kids Get Working Class Jobs.* New York: Columbia University Press.

World Bank. (2015a). Linkages between China and Sub-Saharan Africa. *Global Economic Prospects.* Available at www.worldbank.org/content/dam/Worldbank/GEP/GEP2015b/Global-Economic-Prospects-June-2015-China-and-Sub-Saharan-Africa.pdf

World Bank. (2015b). *Government expenditure on education, total (% of government expenditure).* Retrieved from data.worldbank.org/indicator/SE.XPD.TOTL.GB.ZS

World Bank. (2016). *GDP Per Capita (current US $)*. Retrieved from data.worldbank.org/indicator/NY.GDP.PCAP.CD

World Conference on Education for All: Meeting Basic Learning Needs. (1990). *World Declaration on Education for All and Framework for Action to Meet Basic Learning Needs Adopted by the World Conference on Education for All: Meeting Basic Learning Needs, Jomtien, Thailand, 5–9 March 1990*. New York: Inter-Agency Commission (UNDP, UNESCO, UNICEF, World Bank) for the World Conference on Education for All.

CHAPTER TWELVE
THE INTERNATIONALIZATION OF SCHOOLING: IMPLICATIONS FOR TEACHERS

Julia Resnik

INTRODUCTION

International education provided in international schools is not a new phenomenon in the world of education. However, the internationalization of schooling that refers to both the multiplication of international schools around the world, and the tendency in an increasing number of countries to incorporate international education into local schools, is a global process that started in the 1980s and has intensified in the last two decades. As such, it attracts the attention of education comparativists and it becomes a crucial element of teachers' training. Once, international schools catered mainly to mobile students (typically the children of diplomats, INGOs, and employees of transnational corporations), but at the present time they also serve local elites and middle-class groups. In the past, international education through international curriculum was the exclusivity of international schools; nowadays, more and more national or state schools, either public or private, are interested in the international dimension of education (multiculturalism, global citizenship, proficiency in English) and many adopt international curricula. This double process, the growing local demand for international schools and the addition of international education in national schools, is referred to as the internationalization of schooling, and it undermines the narrow connection that existed in the past between international schools and international education. The International Baccalaureate (IB) program exemplifies this transformation very clearly. Initially, the

IB curriculum was conceived for international private schools as a pragmatic solution for mobile families that move from country to country. In addition, the IB curriculum had the ideological objective of diffusing international understanding in the post–Second World War years. However, at present, the majority of IB schools providing the different IB programs are public schools.

This chapter deals with the internationalization of schooling, with sections focusing on the following aspects:

1. *The Transformation of International Schools and International Education*: the evolution of the internationalization of schooling.
2. *Globalization and the Internationalization of Schooling*: different sociological explanations for the internationalization of schooling.
3. *The English-Speaking Teacher Job Market—A Global and Segmented Market*: analysis of the consequences of schooling transformation on teacher labour.
4. *Who Are the Mobile Teachers?*: the incentives and factors that attract teachers to an international career.
5. *Mobile Teachers' Challenges: Cultural Challenges and Pedagogical Challenges*: the major challenges a teacher has to overcome when working abroad.
6. *Conclusions: Lack of Mobile Teacher Training*: this short concluding section focuses on the exiguous courses and programs available worldwide to serve teachers interested in initiating an international trajectory.

THE TRANSFORMATION OF INTERNATIONAL SCHOOLS AND INTERNATIONAL EDUCATION

The internationalization of schooling has been the result of parallel processes. One is the growing number of international schools, due not only to a rise in the quantity of mobile families but also, especially, to the increasing proportion of local elites demanding international education. The other is the incorporation of international education through international curricula and/or English courses in national public and private schools.

EVOLUTION OF INTERNATIONAL SCHOOLS

International schools, mainly American, British, German, Italian, French, Dutch, Russian, and lately Japanese, were first established to offer educational services to the children of expatriate workers in locations around the world. These schools provide national programs and socialize children in the language and culture of origin. The global economy and the increasing number of transnational corporations with branches all over the world undoubtedly entailed an increase in the number of globally mobile professional people whose children accompany them to a variety of postings worldwide. These mobile families, who search to educate their children according to the national programs of their country of origin, raise the demand for international schools worldwide. As an example, the network of French schools abroad comprises 480 schools in 130 countries that enrol 300,000 students and is in constant expansion.[1] One of the recently founded schools under the control of the *Agence pour l'enseignement français à l'étranger* (AEFE) is the French-Israeli junior and high school near Tel Aviv (Resnik, forthcoming). International schools that cater to mobile families offer the national education system away from the home country, or an international curricula such as the International Baccalaureate (IB).

Another type of international school corresponds to Hayden and Thompson's (2013) "Type B." Type B are "ideological" international schools established principally on an ideological basis, bringing together young people from different parts of the world to be educated together with the purpose of promoting global peace and international understanding. In this category we can cite the United World Colleges (UWC), a worldwide movement with 10 senior-secondary colleges that provide an internationally minded curriculum; UNESCO Associated Schools that emphasize world community, human rights, and international understanding; and Schola Europaea, administered by the European Union, with 14 European schools and 22,500 pupils, aiming to develop a European identity based on multilingual curriculum.[2]

The growth in the number of international schools is almost unparalleled by any other service industry. In 2000, there were 2,584 international schools worldwide teaching almost one million students. The countries dominating the market at that time were Spain, the United Arab Emirates, Hong Kong, and Thailand (99, 97, 70, and 55 international schools respectively). In 2013, the number of total international schools climbed to 6,400, teaching 3.2 million students. Asia dominates the international school market, led by the United Arab Emirates and followed by Pakistan, China, India, and Japan (Brummit & Keeling, 2013, p. 21).

The impressive increase in the number of international schools corresponds to the growing interest of local elites in international education. The traditional global consumers of international education, highly mobile expatriate professional parents, have increasingly been joined by local elite and middle-class families. The French-Israeli school established recently in Israel is a good example of this tendency: 66 percent of the students are French-born or from mobile families of different countries, and the rest of the students, 34 percent, are Israeli-born (Resnik, forthcoming). Similarly, a large part of the new segment of international education consumers comes from local communities in Asia (Lee, Hallinger, & Walker, 2012).

Another significant transformation of international schools concerns their ownership. In the past, international schools were largely a non-profit phenomenon, and today, most international schools are for profit. Since international education represents big business, the future will continue to be dominated by profit-making schools and, increasingly, by multinational school groups (Brummit & Keeling, 2013).

EVOLUTION OF INTERNATIONAL EDUCATION

International education, embodied in international curriculum, was equated in the past to international schools. Today, international education has acquired a more extensive meaning, and in addition to an international curriculum, it refers to different courses and educational objectives that aim at preparing the young generation for a global world: English proficiency, intercultural studies, international understanding, global citizenship, and so on.

Not only international schools but also many private schools that cater to local elites offered international curricula, such as the International Baccalaureate (IB), the International General Certificate of Secondary Education (GCSE) offered by Cambridge International Examinations, the International Primary Curriculum (IPC), or a curriculum imported from a national context, such as the English A level. Today, as we have seen, the number of international schools keeps growing and the number of national elite schools adopting international curricula is on the rise. Moreover, as part of the globalization process and the growing international focus in many national systems, many public schools worldwide offer international curricula (Resnik, 2012).

Among the various international curricula, the International Baccalaureate is the largest and most rapidly expanding global curriculum.

CHAPTER TWELVE: The Internationalization of Schooling 339

Many schools formerly identified as British or American shifted to the IB Diploma program providing international curricula and standards (Tarc & Mishra Tarc, 2015). Founded in Geneva in 1968 by a non-profit educational foundation, the International Baccalaureate Organization (IBO) offers four programs for students ages 3-19: the Primary Years Programme (PYP) for pupils ages 3-12, the Middle Years Programme (MYP) for students ages 11-16, and the Diploma Programme (DP) and Career-Related Programme for students ages 16-19. The number of IB schools has been growing steadily since the creation of the IBO in 1968, but since the mid-1980s the interest in these schools seems to have increased significantly: in 1978 the number of IB schools was 47; in 1985, 164; in 1995, 540; in 2000, 1,052; in 2005, 1,934; and in 2015, 4,267 (IBO, 2016a). The Asia Pacific region has experienced the most rapid gains in the number of IB schools since 2000. As of 2010, 407 schools had adopted IB programs, and by 2015, 681 more schools were added just in the Asia Pacific Region (IBO, 2016a). A social culture that places a strong value on education and high parental expectations for educational success, or "education fever," prevalent in many countries in East Asia (Seth, 2002, in Lee et al., 2012) make IB programs particularly attractive to East Asian parents.

In the past, IB programs were delivered mostly in private institutions. However, over the last 20 years we have seen a transformation of this tendency, with IB programs being offered mostly in public schools as an additional option to the official programs. This is the case of public schools in Australia, where the DP is provided in 51 independent schools and also in 11 state-funded schools (Doherty & Shield, 2012). In North America, IB programs are found predominantly in public (i.e., government-funded) schools (Lee et al., 2012). In particular, the DP has attracted many market-driven schools, such as magnet schools (Bunnell, 2008). In 2008, 920 schools offered the IB, and in 2015 the number reached 1,615, with a large majority of public schools—1,456, including 746 offering the DP. Currently more than 61 percent of IB schools in the world are American (2,633 out of 4,267) (IBO, 2016a).

The massive introduction of the DP in Ecuador, one of the world's poorest countries and one with the lowest educational level, is a case of special interest. In the past, the IB curriculum in Ecuador was provided exclusively in a small number of private schools (16 in total). Driven by a post-neoliberal equalitarian ideology and seeking to improve the national education level, the government decided to create IB classes in state schools all over the country. This decision entailed a transformation of the whole national education market, forcing many private schools to also adopt the IB in order to avoid "lagging behind" (Resnik, 2014). Today there are 236 schools offering the DP in this country (IBO, 2016b).

In addition to the adoption of well-known international curricula in state-funded schools, the internationalization of schools was encouraged by the incorporation of English-medium international tracks into public secondary schools. For instance, international sections in secondary public schools teaching in English and the native language have been on the rise in the last 30 years in several non-English-speaking European countries, like Austria, Denmark, France, Germany, and Sweden, and very particularly in the Netherlands (Weenink, 2009). Though it is a new phenomenon in China, since 2008 an increasing number of domestic schools have offered English-medium sections based on Sino-foreign joint venture programs (Brummit & Keeling, 2013).

Finally, internationalization of schooling also includes the intensification of English learning as well as the integration of an international, intercultural, or global dimension into the purpose, functions, or delivery of education (Knight, 2004, in Yemini & Fulop, 2014). Many educational systems worldwide are making substantial efforts to integrate an international dimension into local schools, fostering significant changes in the processes of instruction and learning as well as transformations at pedagogical and organizational levels (Yemini & Fulop, 2014). In China, the rapid economic, social, and cultural development has brought an escalating demand for English proficiency, and paramount efforts are made to incorporate the study of English in primary and secondary schools (Hu, 2003). In Thailand, the proliferation of international schools centred on the study of English as part of the global neoliberal policy agenda. Since the early 1980s, English language centres, international and bilingual schools, and university programs have been rapidly spreading across the face of the educational landscape in Thailand. From just 5 international schools in 1992, the number had grown to 75 by 2004, with another 170 schools and 44 universities offering bilingual programs and hundreds of training centres offering English language courses (Persaud, 2014). Schools for the elites in Brazil seem to restructure themselves according to an investment logic, offering educational products oriented to the families' new demands for internationalized education, such as special programs of foreign language learning, bilingual pedagogical projects, and trips abroad. Special programs of foreign language learning (mostly English) could start at a precocious age (since kindergarten) (Aguiar & Nogueira, 2012).

Although English proficiency is an important aspect of the internationalization of schooling, educational systems have also made an effort to introduce intercultural and global dimensions as part of their internationalization efforts. Citizenship education agendas in European countries emphasize the need to provide young people with the skills, tools, knowledge, and understanding to deal with differences, and are concerned with developing an identity (or set of identities) beyond the local and national ones (Marshall, 2009). Global citizenship education, as it has developed in the United Kingdom, for example, involves developing an understanding of the background of global problems, skills to engage in action for change, and relevant values and attitudes (Tasneem, 2005). Even in Israel, where there is no internationalization as a central policy, school administrators turn to internationally oriented external stakeholders in their efforts to introduce internationalization as added value within their schools. They integrate international dimensions mostly within extracurricular activities, such as student exchange programs, delegations abroad, and intercultural dimensions through projects focused on recognition of the "other" to deal with the diverse school population (Yemini & Fulop, 2014).

Out of respect for their multicultural student populations and the inherent international focus, many international schools traditionally offered intercultural or international understanding in their curricula. Today, with the growing international focus in many national schools worldwide and the increasingly multicultural nature of the student population, the differences between curriculum in international schools and national schools are being eroded (Hayden & Thompson, 2013).

GLOBALIZATION AND THE INTERNATIONALIZATION OF SCHOOLING

How can we explain the meteoric expansion of schooling internationalization in the last decades? Globalization processes beginning in the mid-1980s are unquestionably at the source of the growing demand for international education worldwide. We will analyze this phenomenon focusing on three aspects. First, international education as a response to the global economy and global job market; second, international education as a response to neoliberal national education policies; and third, international education as social reproduction and/or social mobility.

INTERNATIONAL EDUCATION AS A RESPONSE TO THE GLOBAL ECONOMY AND GLOBAL JOB MARKET

Leaders worldwide are aware of the need to prepare the next generations to function in a global, interconnected, and competing world. The Organization for Economic Cooperation and Development (OECD) states that the interconnectedness of the global economy, ecosystem, and political networks requires that students learn to communicate, collaborate, and problem solve with people worldwide (Saavedra & Opfer, 2012). Policy-makers speak about the need to instill a global or international view into the young generation. In the United States, concerns such as economic competitiveness, national security, and domestic diversity are driving a new push for integration of international education in K–12 schools in many states (Frey & Whitehead, 2009). As part of the No Child Left Behind policy, aiming to improve academic standards, schools serving high numbers of low-income students have been encouraged by the federal government to implement the IB (Siskin & Weinstein, 2008). Policies and practices in the United States emphasize economic development and concentrate on the benefits of "international" education for the economic competitiveness of the country (Frey & Whitehead, 2009; Ortloff, Shah, Lou, & Hamilton, 2012).

On the other side of the ocean, the primary response to the impact of globalization on education policies in the United Kingdom has been the development of relevant skills and competencies for a global economy. "Learning in a global context" is understood by the government as being about equipping "employers and their employees with the skills needed for a global economy," involving the learning of economically useful languages and the move toward "mutual recognition and improved transparency of qualifications" (DFES, 2004, p. 6, in Marshall, 2009). Also in Singapore, as part of a larger economic development policy, a renowned state elite school adopted an international curriculum to instill a global habitus into the future elite of the nation (Koh & Kenway, 2012).

In spite of the largely instrumental international agendas adopted by education systems, scholars maintain that in order to prepare well-rounded citizens for the 21st century, the economic targets should be integrated in a broader international and global education agenda. However, while workforce development and skill improvement are a part of what schools should do, they should not dominate the goals or expected outcomes of international education (Frey & Whitehead, 2009). Moreover, by providing concrete skills as well as historically and culturally informed perspectives on the global society, schools will enable students not only to be better equipped to respond to global economic forces and succeed within the 21st century, but also to contribute to the evolution of a more informed and just society (Ortloff et al., 2012).

In an era of economic and cultural globalization, parents seek to prepare their children for a global job market, and many see international education as the best choice for success. Wealthy parents are seeking alternative paths for their children to obtain the kind of education and credentials that will provide smooth passage into the global marketplace (Phillips, 2002). The attraction of an international curriculum such as the IB lies in obtaining an international rather than a state-certified form of credentials (Brown & Lauder, 2009). There are increasing demands for educational qualifications that are portable between schools and transferable between education systems, with global quality standards secured through quality assurance processes such as schools' accreditation (Cambridge & Thompson, 2004, p. 164). More specifically, analysis of the IB curriculum shows that it aims at inculcating in students the skills seen as necessary to compete in the global job market (Resnik, 2008, 2009). Surprisingly, the abilities required for productive work in the global economy resemble those required for personal fulfillment in the humanist approach to education fostered traditionally by the IB (Phillips, 2002).

INTERNATIONAL EDUCATION AS A RESPONSE TO NEOLIBERAL EDUCATION POLICIES AND MARKETIZATION OF SCHOOLING

Neoliberal educational policies adopted in many countries have been promoted worldwide by international organizations such as the OECD and the World Bank. Policies that include parents' choice, school-based management, and decentralization of education systems have been implemented to different degrees in most of the countries that are adopting international programs. Moreover, budget cuts to, and the deterioration of, public schools have directly contributed to increased participation in international alternatives.

Australia, like other OECD countries, has pursued neoliberal policies promoting market choice in education. This ambit has recently expanded to offering a branded alternative in private and government schools with local catchments, enabled by regulatory regimes encouraging competition with state schooling and its official curriculum. Australian states attempted to attract middle-class children to state schools, which had experienced a retreat of the middle class in the 1990s in response to neoliberal marketing policies. The growing interest in the IB in both state and private schools in Australia corresponded to a quest by middle-class parents for a "rare" educational product, which represents a "sign of distinction" (Doherty, 2009). Similarly, in the United States and in Western Canada, state/provincial schools have adopted the IB to create a "private school" aura to attract students from middle- and upper-class families and accommodate neoliberal parents' desire "for high academic standards" (Tarc, 2009, p. 68). The adoption of the DP by public schools in Canada has to be understood within a larger context of neoliberal educational reform, which sees schools pressed to distinguish themselves from other schools in order to attract academically able students and maintain enrolment (Tarc & Beatty, 2012). More specifically, a study that focused on Ontario confirmed the DP operates as a product of distinction in the education market, predominantly serving middle-class students (Baker, 2014). The European track in public *lycées* in France has provided a means by which middle-class families could avoid the school zoning map (*carte scolaire*) and the social integration it implied (Van Zanten, 2009). Competitive pressures are fierce in the Dutch education arena, and school managers' mode of engagement is market oriented, giving priority to the position of the school. The marketization of education gives room to middle-class parents' desires to create separate educational settings. More generally speaking, the presence of international schools in national education systems might push both state-funded and independent schools to introduce international elements in order to remain attractive for social elites (Weenink, 2009).

INTERNATIONAL EDUCATION AND SOCIAL STRUCTURE: SOCIAL REPRODUCTION OR SOCIAL MOBILITY?

Globalization entails the formation of a new class structure that includes a growing world class demanding world-class education for its children (Ilon, 1997, p. 620). The demand for international education is

CHAPTER TWELVE: The Internationalization of Schooling 345

a strategy of the upper class to keep its advantages since international managers' children reproduce their parents' international cultural capital by attending international schools (Wagner, 2007). A global educational path from international schools through elite universities into the high-end segments of the global market might denote the emergence of a global ruling class that includes global and indigenous elites (Brown & Lauder, 2009). The DP provided as an additional option to the official program in schools in Australia creates a curricular market that permits a curricular choice and contributes to the reproduction of advantage that is accomplished through choice behaviours in stratified educational markets (Doherty, Luke, Shield, & Hincksman, 2012). In the southern part of the globe, elitist IB schools are chosen for their status, for the "distinction" they represent and the cultural capital they confer. For the parent, this translates into an expectation that an international education will promote better marketplace value for their children (Gardner-McTaggart, 2014). The creation of separate international education settings in state-funded schools in the Netherlands on the basis of class-related abilities of pupils is part of the reproduction strategies of the privileged social layers. The celebration of excellence in education legitimizes, and in fact glorifies, the social hierarchy (Weenink, 2009). More generally, national education systems legitimate cosmopolitanism as a desirable disposition at the global level, while simultaneously distributing it unequally among different groups of actors according to their geographical locations and the volume of economic, cultural, and social capital their families possess (Igarashi & Saito, 2014).

Some authors contend that international education not only contributes to social reproduction but also serves as a way to climb the social ladder. In the Netherlands, parents believe that registering their children in international tracks in public schools will facilitate social mobility (Weenink, 2009). Traditional elites and rising middle classes in Brazil are investing more and more in internationalized resources (international and bilingual schools, trips abroad, etc.), the former in an attempt to reproduce their advantages, the latter as a strategy of social mobility (Nogueira & Aguiar, 2008). Similarly, attending the Franco-Israeli school in Tel Aviv is perceived as contributing to social reproduction of local elites and mobile families, but also as a tool of social mobility for middle-class Israeli parents and to avoid downward mobility among French immigrants (Resnik, forthcoming).

THE ENGLISH-SPEAKING TEACHER JOB MARKET—A GLOBAL AND SEGMENTED MARKET

The development of international education in developed and developing countries in recent decades has opened a global teacher labour market in which highly qualified English-speaking teachers have become an increasingly valuable workforce (Resnik, 2014). International schools are competing not only among themselves to hire teachers, but also with state schools adopting international programs or offering English courses. The global movement of teachers includes mainly English-speaking teachers from a variety of countries such as the United States, Canada, New Zealand, the United Kingdom, Australia, and South Africa. "Global teachers" can refer to teachers hired to teach in Western countries that suffer from shortages of teachers in certain disciplines (sciences, mathematics, etc.) or geographical locations. In this chapter, however, we address a different group of mobile teachers: emigrant teachers (Reid, Collins, & Singh, 2014), those who travel to teach abroad in international schools or schools providing international curricula.

In 2000 there were a total of 90,000 full-time staff members employed in international schools.[3] Today that number has more than tripled to 300,000. Research predicts that demand for qualified English-speaking teachers will reach 529,000 in 2020 (Brummit & Keeling, 2013, p. 27). Since these numbers relate only to a narrow definition of international schools and do not include schools adopting an international curriculum or offering English courses, the global market for English-speaking teachers is considerably larger. The result is a growing international competition for English-speaking teachers and increasing difficulty to recruit expatriate teachers to fill all the posts available in international schools (Wigford, 2007, in Hayden & Thompson, 2011, p. 90). International schools that are developing fast in Asian and other non-English-speaking countries contribute to the international competition for teachers whose first language is English (Reid et al., 2014). Moreover, China, in which English is compulsory throughout much of schooling and universities and optional, but in high demand, in private institutions, is the largest English-language teaching market in the world (Stanley, 2012, in Reid et al., 2014). Many Chinese institutions, mainly private ones, attempt to recruit native English-speaking teachers, thus increasing even more the global competition for overseas English-speaking teachers.

What is clear is that the high demand for English-speaking teachers globally is changing the dimensions of the teaching profession and the English-speaking teacher job market. The fierce competition for highly qualified English-speaking teachers produces a segmented global market that differentiates between English-speaking teachers of different nationalities as well as an inner school segmented market that differentiates between different categories of teachers in the same school.

GLOBAL SEGMENTED MARKET
In the past, the teaching staff in international schools used to be British and American, but today, an increasing number of English-speaking teachers from New Zealand, Australia, Ireland, Canada, and South Africa are joining the staff of these schools (Hayden & Thompson, 2011). For instance, the demand for English-language teachers in non-English-speaking countries is a key driver for Australian-educated teachers to seek employment overseas. However, this mobile teacher market is far from being uniform and is segmented according to nationalities. In the southern part of the globe, international educators are often desired and hired by schools for their normative Western (out) look and "native-language" proficiency in English (Tarc & Mishra Tarc, 2015). American and British teachers are the most valued: they represent the "authentic" English speakers. In contrast, Australian teachers are less valued since the English-Australian accent is not always seen as "real" English. On the other hand, Australian emigrant teachers are highly qualified: these qualifications are sought after and assist mobility. The great majority of Australian teachers who work overseas have either one or two higher education qualifications, most commonly at either undergraduate or postgraduate level (Reid et al., 2014).

Another aspect of the global segmented market is the competition at a national level between mobile teachers and local teachers trained abroad, mostly in the United States. Because of the high costs of recruiting overseas teachers, particularly for low-income countries, international schools and schools providing international education employ largely local English-speaking teachers. These local teachers trained in foreign universities compete with mobile teachers for the same jobs. Due to the growth of English-medium schools and schools offering English courses in South America, mobile teachers or local teachers trained abroad are becoming a rare and expensive manpower. International schools in Argentina, Chile, and Ecuador can be categorized according to their international level: English-medium schools, such as the International American schools; bilingual schools providing around half of the subjects in English; and international schools with intensive English-language learning, which is usually a translation of the level of fees they charge.

The national segmentation of the English-speaking teacher market is concomitant to students' fees: only international English-medium schools recruit some overseas teachers; bilingual schools recruit mostly local teachers trained abroad, and low-fee schools recruit local teachers. In Ecuador, when the government launched a massive national campaign for the incorporation of the IB into public schools, inciting many private schools to adopt the international program, the scarcity of English-speaking teachers became critical. Teacher scarcity fostered teacher mobility and turned the labour markets "fishy": school administrators stole qualified teachers from each other, with some teachers even leaving schools in the middle of the academic year, tempted away by higher salaries (Resnik, 2014). As we can see, a change of educational policy can entail a transformation of the whole national education market, sharpening the differentiation between the various teacher segments.

INNER SCHOOL SEGMENTED MARKET
The majority of international schools, whenever possible and finances allowing, look to employ Western-trained, English-speaking teachers who preferably have previous experience in the curriculum being offered. Parents prefer to see their children served by expatriate teachers rather than by host country teachers (local-hire teachers). Nevertheless, most international schools will have on their staff at least a small number of host country teachers, often employed to teach the local language and culture (Hayden & Thompson, 2011). Therefore, international schools usually hire a mix of mobile and local teachers, paying attention to the right balance between hiring good teachers and incurring substantial costs (Canterford, 2003, p. 58).

Teaching staff in international schools can be grouped in three distinct categories:

- host country nationals
- local-hire expatriates
- overseas-hire expatriates (Garton, 2000, in Canterford, 2003)

The segmented inner school market is based on differential pay scales and special benefit pay to teachers. Teachers appointed on an "overseas hire" contract will generally have the most advantageous pay and conditions compared to those of the host country nationals. Overseas-hire expatriates are considered to be more costly and time-consuming recruits than their peers. This is because educators in this category typically require additional paperwork to be processed, housing to be secured, and a salary that is competitive enough to entice candidates to opt for one location over another (Savva, 2015). Despite being a more costly and time-consuming recruit, the demand for the overseas-hire teacher remains strong because of the prestige associated with educators coming directly from Anglophone countries (Hayden & Thompson, 2013). On the other hand, teachers hired on a local contract are often paid a fraction of what teachers hired on an overseas contract are paid, often for filling the same positions. This inner segmented market produces a contractual dissatisfaction among teachers and results in a constant source of friction among staff and between staff and administrators (Odland & Ruzicka, 2009). "Hidden resentment towards overseas teachers by local members of the staff, most commonly [the result of] differential pay scales and special benefit pay to teachers [who are doing the same job as local teachers]...result[s] in friction and sometimes overt conflict, creating a negative impact in the working environment" (Hardman, 2001, p. 128, in Canterford, 2003, p. 59).

In sum, new global teacher markets make mobility on a global scale increasingly part of the imagination of teachers and future teachers (Widegren & Doherty, 2010). Aware of the global job market and the possibilities it offers, mobile teachers position themselves where they predict the labour market will be most open to their skills, competencies, and qualifications (Adkins, 2011, in Reid et al., 2014, pp. 354–355). As the study on Australian emigrant teachers shows, global teachers overseas are exploiting the opportunities of globalization—the strong growth in Asia, powered by lowering trade and capital barriers worldwide, and the strong demand for English-language education in Asia—to further take advantage of global economic opportunities in the future (Reid et al., 2014).

WHO ARE THE MOBILE TEACHERS?

Mobile emigrant teachers may choose to work temporarily overseas and return later to their country of origin, or to move permanently. They may plan on "touring the world" by changing schools and countries continually. They may accompany a partner that has been transferred for a number of years with international companies and see teaching in an international school as a way to earn additional income. They may be thinking of immigrating to another country permanently. In the case of Australian teachers, many are attracted to Asian countries where the demand for teachers who are native English speakers is growing. Others look toward work and travel opportunities in Europe and North America. Teacher mobility often involves multi-country movements, and sometimes eventually a return to the home country, a form of circular migration (Reid et al., 2014).

Teachers applying for posts in international schools can be considered to fall into one of the following groups:

- childless career professionals
- mavericks (free and independent spirits)
- career professionals with families (Hardman, 2001, in Hayden & Thompson, 2011)

Women now constitute the largest proportion of Australian globally mobile teachers (Reid et al., 2014). Since the feminization of the teaching profession occurred in most Western countries, this process will most likely impact the mobile teacher population as well. Some female teachers travel with their families and/or partners, but increasingly, women are globally mobile on their own (Reid et al., 2014).

Motives for seeking overseas employment and a teaching post in an international school or a school providing international education vary largely. One of the main reasons motivating teachers to work abroad is the possibility of combining their career with a desire to travel the world (Hayden & Thompson, 2011). Therefore, for many mobile teachers, lifestyle and quality of life are primary considerations for their location selection. Then, by selecting their professional trajectory, teachers choose (or reject) not just a school but a country. Just as important as the location and the financial considerations are generous holidays, the ability to travel, and the excitement of living in a foreign country (Walsh, 1999, in Canterford, 2003, p. 59). This desire to see the world may explain why international schools have a highly mobile faculty and a recurring need to replenish it (Savva, 2015). And indeed, a large study by Chandler (2010) on international schools confirms the importance of location to teachers' recruitment. However, there is no apparent link between location satisfaction and teachers' retention. Therefore international schools cannot be certain of keeping teachers who like living in their location longer than those who do not. It may be that job satisfaction has a greater bearing on international school teacher retention than does location satisfaction.

Indeed, besides travelling and enjoying new cultural experiences, lucrative compensation, career advancement, and professional development opportunities are also important motives behind the decision to teach abroad (Savva, 2015). Thus, according to Hardman's study (2001, in Odland & Ruzicka, 2009), the main reason identified by a large majority of teachers for joining and remaining in an international school was professional advancement. Other important factors were a happy working climate in the school, financial incentives, and a strong sense of job challenge. A happy working climate was further defined as feeling appreciated and respected by colleagues and administration, a sense of security, and strong relationships with colleagues and students.

The increasing global competition for English-speaking teachers only exacerbates the high teacher turnover that characterizes schools that recruit a mobile staff. High turnover is critical, in particular for international schools that incur heavy costs recruiting teachers. In addition to financial costs, there are high institutional costs associated with teacher turnover in international schools (Hayden & Thompson, 1998). International schools and schools recruiting overseas teachers operate in a globalized context. To compete for quality applicants it would seem that they must compete for the job satisfaction of the teachers (Slethaug, 2010).

MOBILE TEACHERS' CHALLENGES

Teaching abroad raises cultural as well as pedagogical challenges, particularly for teachers who move for the first time from schools in their home context but also for teachers who move to a new location.

CULTURAL CHALLENGE
Starting any new job is an anxious experience, creating feelings of uncertainty and self-doubt. Starting a new job in a foreign country where most of the "customers" (parents and pupils) are from a different cultural norm is likely to be particularly stressful, as it creates the necessity of

simultaneously adapting to new cultures both in and out of the workplace (Stirzaker, 2004). Remington (2002), who studied North American educators working in international schools in Latin America, contends that each year international educators move to new countries and inevitably experience a certain degree of culture shock. Remington adds that age, gender, and previous overseas experience influence the degree of culture shock.

When moving to a new location, teachers have to overcome "transitional challenges," since living and working in another culture requires adjustments to a wide range of cultural dimensions and to new meaning systems. Transitional challenges depend on school characteristics, but in particular, on host country conditions and cultural expectations that can affect the success of a teacher moving to an international school (Joslin, 2002).

Joslin (2002) summarizes the multiple cultural dimensions that impact a teacher's work and non-work environments:

- the teacher's own cultural heritage
- the teacher's previous work culture/home country professional culture
- the school's organizational culture
- the international school's mission
- the local community culture (e.g., expatriate community)
- the regional and the host nation's culture/subcultures

The cultural expectations can be extremely challenging in some host countries and particularly for female teachers. For example, this was the case of a North American teacher who had been recruited in a conservative Muslim country. Despite her awareness of different social norms prior to taking this post, the teacher nevertheless struggled to follow rules which contrasted sharply with Western thought and philosophy. As a woman, she had to follow specific rules and accept explicit limitations in this new country. Her Western social constructs were challenged, and she had to make the necessary adjustments (Savva, 2013).

Social expectations can also be challenging, particularly in high-tuition international schools in South America. This is the case of Canadian teachers who are aware of their uncomfortable position as "in-between" the elite users (families) of international education and members of local populations working in and servicing the school. They often find themselves, literally, "in the middle" of an array of historical and political forces and unfamiliar social formation (Tarc & Mishra Tarc, 2015).

Another cultural challenge of moving abroad is connected with being the "other" in a foreign country. Commonly, the majority group in Western societies is thought not to possess ethnicity, which is usually a consequence of being a minority or "other"; whiteness is often conceived as being non-ethnic. The experience of Australian emigrant teachers in Asia, most of whom are white Anglo-Australians, demonstrates how they become an ethnic minority in countries where they teach. Nevertheless, teachers' ethnicity and intensities of "othering" experiences are often mitigated due to their English capital, deriving from their English-speaking background (Reid et al., 2014). On the other hand, the experience of difference or being "othered" contributes to instilling intercultural understanding into white and monolingual mobile teachers, often unaware of their "Whiteness" privilege (Reid et al., 2014). A superficial intercultural awareness of being "other" can be transformed into a deeper intercultural understanding among teachers. But as a study that examined the experiences of teachers from the United States and Canada in international schools abroad revealed, despite this broader understanding, not all teachers made explicit connections to their professional practice (Savva, 2013).

Feelings of "otherness" encouraged mobile teachers to form friendships almost exclusively with the school community in which they worked. As a result, teachers were sometimes seen by locals as "long-term tourists" who never quite immersed themselves in the native culture (Savva, 2013). The support of constituents of the school community is highly important for mobile teachers. Faced with the challenges of culture shock, language barriers, potentially adverse living conditions, and a host of other possible challenges, international school communities come to rely heavily on support from within their own community. Not surprisingly, teachers reported that relationships with colleagues and particularly the relationships between senior administrators and members of their staff were important factors of job satisfaction (Odland & Ruzicka, 2009).

PEDAGOGICAL CHALLENGE

Mobile teachers face two main pedagogical challenges: one, the tension between child-centred and teacher-centred learning/teaching models; the other, the increasing multicultural nature of classrooms.

The Tension between Child-Centred and Teacher-Centred Learning/Teaching Models

Western nations are more likely to have child-centred pedagogical models, while many other societies and cultures have teacher-centred models. The pedagogical style preferred in international schools is that of Western countries. And indeed, Australian teachers felt that besides English language capabilities, their curriculum knowledge and pedagogical skills were most significant to the host country (Reid et al., 2014). The student-centred, constructivist approach prevailing in international schools will pose challenges also to teachers from Western countries trained in more teacher-centred approaches (Hayden & Thompson, 2013). For instance, the teacher who has only experienced a national system such as the rather prescriptive national curriculum of England and Wales may view a creative curriculum as daunting—or as a reason for celebration (Joslin, 2002). Differences in pedagogical approaches might be a source of conflict within a school between overseas and host country teachers where adaptation to new ways of teaching is either resisted or ineffective.

Besides student-centred versus teacher-centred pedagogies, there are other learning/teaching style differences between countries, as well as different constructions of the "good teacher." For instance, performing appropriately in China means being fun, and teachers are assessed on their performance constantly. Adapting to the Chinese way necessitates "learning from local teachers as much as learning with them" as a means to approach Chinese students (Reid et al., 2014).

The Increasingly Multicultural Nature of Classrooms

Globalization has accelerated student mobility, turning classrooms more cosmopolitan, particularly in international schools or schools offering international education. This means students are more globally connected and more diverse in terms of ethnicity, with gendered subjectivities, and multilinguistic and multicultural backgrounds. The mobile teacher has to address a heterogeneous student population and to adapt her teaching to different religious and cultural backgrounds. Moreover, the diversity of the student population means that in each class the teacher faces an array of different identities as well as different expectations of the role of "student," according to the student's national or international previous schooling experience (Pearce, 2013).

In addition, the mobile teacher from the West carries with her certain understandings and expectations that can differ, to an extent, from the host country's cultural understandings. For a woman teacher, expectations about gender and gender relations can sharpen a sense of cultural difference. Moreover, a Western woman can also be seen as threatening the traditional local gender view, leading to a lack of respect in teaching relationships. How do teachers deal with gender differences? According to Reid et al.'s study (2014), some teachers negotiate gender contexts by assuming the gendered and racialized Western stereotype with humour.

An additional dilemma arises when teachers' professional and cultural identities conflict with students' backgrounds: are teachers imposing their values as educators on their students? Teachers are culturally bound to the extent that the way they think and teach, and their expectations of their students, are in fact a product of their training and learned beliefs about teaching and how students learn. Do they want these values to match their students' home culture, or for them to become free-thinking individuals who are anxious to do well and pursue their own goals? (Fail, 2011, p. 106).

Negotiating cultural and linguistic differences, as well as professional identities, will become paramount for mobile teachers in the accelerated process of schooling internationalization that increasingly includes non-Western cultures. Not surprisingly, Gillies (2001, in Odland & Ruzicka, 2009) found in his study that adaptability, flexibility, and competence are teachers' characteristics leading to success in overseas schools.

CONCLUSIONS: LACK OF MOBILE TEACHER TRAINING

The internationalization of schooling—international schools and schools adopting international education—is on the rise and so is the global demand for mobile teachers. Although the English-speaking teacher market is continuously expanding, there are very few training courses that actually focus on international education. The International Baccalaureate attempts to fill this void by offering IB courses in a few universities in the world. Two types of certificates are offered: the IB certificate in Leadership Practice[4] and the IB advanced certificate in Leadership Research.[5] These teacher training courses on international education are specific to IB programs and schools. The rest of teacher training courses are national or provincial. This lack of models for international education allows provincial or national ideologies to dominate in international schools (Slethaug, 2010, p. 35).

Because of the meagre offering of training programs in international education, teachers new to the international school sector often learn the skills required "on the job" (Hayden & Thompson, 2011). Moreover, most Australian mobile teachers do not have access to induction programs and have to deal with new institutional agendas in an ad-hoc manner (Reid et al., 2014).

What are the courses and qualifications that can prepare teachers embarking on an international teaching career? They should include programs such as ESL to deal with the growing number of non-English-speaking students attending international schools, and intercultural awareness and sensitivity to assist teachers in dealing with the large heterogeneity of students (Hayden & Thompson, 2011, p. 91). Global citizenship education (Marshall, 2009; Bates, 2012) or "education for a better world" that may replace the commonly accepted "international mindedness" notion (Roberts, 2013) should be included in mobile teacher training as it is an integral part of international curricula.

Interestingly, Savva (2013) considers that a global/international teacher experience can be beneficial for the formation of interculturally aware local teachers. International schools, the author suggests, can serve as cost-effective tools for the professional development of qualified North American teachers already working in schools, since the international school setting offers unique opportunities for meaningful intercultural experiences.

The increasing teacher mobility and the growing number of schools offering international curricula and English-speaking tracks or courses merit the inclusion of an international education option as part of teacher certification programs in departments of education worldwide.

QUESTIONS FOR REFLECTION AND DISCUSSION
1. What are the key personal characteristics a mobile teacher should possess to be more apt to succeed in an international setting? Which are innate and which could be developed?
2. What additional resources and support could be provided to address the challenges faced by mobile teachers?
3. In what ways do you think new technological developments and tools could impact the mobile teacher job market?

CHAPTER TWELVE: The Internationalization of Schooling

SUGGESTED AUDIO-VISUAL RESOURCES
South Korea—Robotic Avatars to Teach English, euronews (2014).
Available at: youtu.be/KWR7x48AwZk
In order to overcome a shortage of English teachers, South Korea piloted a program in which robotic avatars, "manned" virtually by Philippine teachers, were introduced in elementary schools to assist teachers in the classroom. It has proven to be very popular with South Korean students, and therefore the government will extend its use throughout the country.

SUGGESTIONS FOR FURTHER READING
Bailey, Lucy. (2015). Reskilled and "running ahead": Teachers in an international school talk about their work. *Journal of Research in International Education, 14*(1), 3–15.
Bunnell, Tristan. (2005). Perspectives on international schools and the nature and extent of local community contact. *Journal of Research in International Education, 4*(1), 43–63.
Bunnell, Tristan. (2006). Managing the role stress of public relations practitioners in international schools. *Educational Management Administration & Leadership, 34*(3), 385–409.
Mancuso, Steven V., Roberts, Laura, & White, George P. (2010). Teacher retention in international schools: The key role of school leadership. *Journal of Research in International Education, 9*(3), 306–323.
Murphy, Edna. (1991). *ESL: A handbook for teachers and administrators in international schools.* Bristol, PA: Multilingual Matters.
Palk, S. (2010, October 22). Robot teachers invade South Korean classrooms. *CNN.* Available at: edition.cnn.com/2010/TECH/innovation/10/22/south.korea.robot.teachers
Roskell, D. (2013). Cross-cultural transition: International teachers' experience of "culture shock." *Journal of Research in International Education, 12*(2), 155–172.
Sears, C. (1998). *Second language students in mainstream classrooms: A handbook for teachers in international schools* (Vol. 2). Toronto: Multilingual Matters.

NOTES
1. www.aefe.fr
2. www.eursc.eu
3. International schools in this case refer only to any school delivering a curriculum to any combination of infant, primary, or secondary students,

wholly or partly in English, outside an English-speaking country (Brummit and Keeling, 2013, p. 26).
4. This course is proposed in the following universities: Bath University (UK), Hong Kong University, and Flinders University Adelaide (Australia). See www.ibo.org/globalassets/digital-tookit/pd/ib-leadership-certificates-uni-en.pdf and www.bath.ac.uk/education/postgraduate/international-baccalaureate/
5. This course is proposed in the following universities: Hong Kong University, University of Victoria (Canada), University of Alberta Edmonton (Canada), Flinders University Adelaide (Australia), Bath University (UK) Institute of Education, and the University of London (UK). See www.ibo.org/globalassets/digital-tookit/pd/ib-leadership-certificates-uni-en.pdf and www.bath.ac.uk/education/postgraduate/international-baccalaureate/

REFERENCES

Aguiar, Andrea, & Nogueira, Maria Alice. (2012). Internationalisation strategies of Brazilian private schools. Special issue: International education. Resnik, Julia (Ed.), *International Studies in Sociology of Education*, 22(4), 353–368.

Baker, Wendy J. (2014). *"Curricular choice" in Ontario public secondary schools: Exploring the policy and practice of the International Baccalaureate Diploma Programme* (Doctoral dissertation). University of Western Ontario, London, Ontario. Available from: Electronic Thesis and Dissertation Repository. Paper 1969.

Bates, Richard. (2012). Is global citizenship possible, and can international schools provide it? *Journal of Research in International Education*, 11(3), 262–274.

Brown, Phillip, & Lauder, Hugh. (2009). Globalization, international education, and the formation of a transnational class? In Popkewitz, Thomas, & Rizvi, Fazal (Eds.), *Globalization and the Study of Education*. The Yearbook of the National Society for the Study of Education (pp.130–148). Oxford, UK: Blackwell.

Brummitt, Nicholas, & Keeling, Anne. (2013). Charting the growth of international schools. In Pearce, Richard (Ed.), *International education and schools: Moving beyond the first 40 years* (pp. 25–36). London: Bloomsbury.

Bunnell, Tristan. (2008). The global growth of the International Baccalaureate Diploma Programme over the first 40 years: A critical assessment. *Comparative Education*, 44(4), 409–424.

Cambridge, James, & Thompson, Jeff. (2004). Internationalism and globalization as contexts for international education. *Compare*, 34(2), 161–175.

Canterford, Glenn. (2003). Segmented labour markets in international schools. *Journal of Research in International Education*, 2(1), 47–65.

Chandler, James. (2010). The role of location in the recruitment and retention of teachers in international schools. *Journal of Research in International Education*, *9*(3), 214–226.

Doherty, Catherine. (2009). The appeal of the International Baccalaureate in Australia's educational market: A curriculum of choice for mobile futures. *Discourse: Studies in the Cultural Politics of Education*, *30*(1), 73–89.

Doherty, Catherine, Luke, Allan, Shield, Paul, & Hincksman, Candice. (2012). Choosing your niche: The social ecology of the International Baccalaureate Diploma in Australia. Special issue: International education. Resnik, Julia (Ed.), *International Studies in Sociology of Education*, *22*(4), 311–332.

Doherty, Catherine, & Shield, Paul. (2012). Teachers' work in curricular markets: Conditions of design and relations between the International Baccalaureate Diploma and the local curriculum. *Curriculum Inquiry*, *42*(3), 414–441.

Fail, Helen. (2011). Teaching and learning in international schools: A consideration of the stakeholders and their expectations. In Pearce, Richard (Ed.), *Schooling internationally: Globalisation, internationalisation and the future for international schools* (pp. 101–120). London: Routledge.

Frey, Christopher J., & Whitehead, Dawn M. (2009). International education policies and the boundaries of global citizenship in the US. *Journal of Curriculum Studies*, *41*(2), 269–290.

Gardner-McTaggart, Alexander. (2014). International elite, or global citizens? Equity, distinction and power: The International Baccalaureate and the rise of the South. *Globalisation, Societies and Education*, (ahead-of-print), 1–29.

Hayden, Mary, & Thompson, Jeff. (2013). International schools: Antecedents, current issues and metaphors for the future. In Pearce, Richard (Ed.), *International education and schools: Moving beyond the first 40 years* (pp. 3–23). London: Bloomsbury.

Hayden, Mary, & Thompson, Jeff. (2011). Teachers for the international school of the future. In Bates, Richard (Ed.), *Schooling internationally: Globalisation, internationalisation and the future for international schools* (pp. 83–100). London: Routledge.

Hayden, Mary, & Thompson, Jeff. (1998). International education: Perceptions of teachers in international schools. *International Review of Education*, *44*(5–6), 549–568.

Hu, Guangwei. (2003). English language teaching in China: Regional differences and contributing factors. *Journal of Multilingual and Multicultural Development*, *24*(4), 290–318.

Igarashi, Hiroki, & Saito, Hiro. (2014). Cosmopolitanism as cultural capital: Exploring the intersection of globalization, education and stratification. *Cultural Sociology*, *8*(3), 222–239.

Ilon, Lynn. (1997). Educational repercussions of a global system of production. In Cummings, William K., & McGinn, Noel F. (Eds.), *International handbook of education and development: Preparing schools, students and nations for the twenty-first century* (pp. 609–630). New York: Pergamon.

International Baccalaureate Organization. (2016a). *Facts and figures.* Available at: www.ibo.org/en/about-the-ib/facts-and-figures

International Baccalaureate Organization. (2016b). *Ecuador.* Available at: www.ibo.org/en/country/EC/

Joslin, Pamela. (2002). Teacher relocation reflections in the context of international schools. *Journal of Research in International Education, 1*(1), 33–62.

Koh, Aaron, & Kenway, Jane. (2012). Cultivating national leaders in an elite school: Deploying the transnational in the national interest. Special issue: International education. Resnik, Julia (Ed.), *International Studies in Sociology of Education, 22*(4), 333–351.

Lee, Moosung, Hallinger, Phillip, & Walker, Alan. (2012). Leadership challenges in international schools in the Asia Pacific region: Evidence from programme implementation of the International Baccalaureate. *International Journal of Leadership in Education, 15*(3), 289–310.

Marshall, Harriet. (2009). Educating the European citizen in the global age: Engaging with the post-national and identifying a research agenda. *Journal of Curriculum Studies, 41*(2), 247–267.

Nogueira, Maria Alice, & Aguiar, Andrea. (2008). La formation des élites et l'internationalisation des études: Peut-on parler d'une "bonne volonté internationale"? *Education et sociétés, 21*(1), 105–119.

Odland, Glenn, & Ruzicka, Mary. (2009). An investigation into teacher turnover in international schools. *Journal of Research in International Education, 8*(1), 5–29.

Ortloff, Debora Hinderliter, Shah, Payal P., Lou, Jingjing, & Hamilton, Evelyn. (2012). International education in secondary schools explored: A mixed-method examination of one Midwestern state in the USA. *Intercultural Education, 23*(2), 161–180.

Pearce, Richard. (2013). Student diversity: The core challenge to international schools. In Pearce, Richard (Ed.), *International education and schools: Moving beyond the first 40 years* (pp. 61–83). London: Bloomsbury.

Persaud, Walter H. (2014). Thai globalization through postcolonial pens. *Journal of Education and Practice, 5*(16), 167–173.

Phillips, John. (2002). The third way: Lessons from international education. *Journal of Research in International Education, 1*(2), 159–181.

Reid, Carol, Collins, Jock, & Singh, Michael. (2014). *Global teachers, Australian perspectives.* Singapore: Springer.

Remington, Michelle Annette Ganiere. (2002). *Cultural shock of North American educators living and working in international schools in Latin America* (Doctoral dissertation). University of Southern Mississippi.

Resnik, Julia. (forthcoming). *International capital consumption: Enrolling mobile, migrant, and local students in a French-Israeli school.*

Resnik, Julia. (2014). Who gets the best teachers? The incorporation of the IB program into public high schools and its impact on teacher labor market in Ecuador. In Arber, Ruth, Blackmore, Jill, & Vongalis-Macrow, Athena (Eds.), *Mobile teachers and curriculum in international schooling* (pp. 95–120). Amsterdam: Sense Publishers.

Resnik, Julia. (2012). Sociology of international education—an emerging field of research. Special issue: International education. Resnik, Julia (Ed.), *International Studies in Sociology of Education, 22*(4), 291–310.

Resnik, Julia. (2009). Multicultural education: Good for business but not for the state? IB curriculum and the global capitalism. *British Journal of Educational Studies, 57*(3), 217–244.

Resnik, Julia. (2008). The construction of the global worker through international education. In Resnik, Julia (Ed.), *The production of educational knowledge in the global era* (pp. 147–157). Rotterdam, the Netherlands: Sense Publishers.

Roberts, Boyd. (2013). International education and global engagement: Education for a better world? In Pearce, Richard (Ed.), *International education and schools: Moving beyond the first 40 years* (pp. 119–145). London: Bloomsbury.

Saavedra, Anna Rosefsky, & Opfer, V. Darleen. (2012). Learning 21st-century skills requires 21st-century teaching. *Phi Delta Kappan, 94*(2), 8–13.

Savva, Maria. (2015). Characteristics of the international educator and the strategic role of critical incidents. *Journal of Research in International Education, 14*(1), 16–28.

Savva, Maria. (2013). International schools as gateways to the intercultural development of North-American teachers. *Journal of Research in International Education, 12*(3), 214–227.

Siskin, Leslie Santee, & Weinstein, Meryle. (2008). *Supplemental survey to creating support structures and services for Title I high schools implementing the International Baccalaureate Programs supported by the U.S. Department of Education, API Initiative.* New York: Institute for Education and Social Policy, NYU.

Slethaug, Gordon. (2010). Something happened while nobody was looking: The growth of international education and the Chinese learner. In Ryan, Janette, & Slethaug, Gordon (Eds.), *International Education and the Chinese Learner* (pp. 15–36). Hong Kong: Hong Kong University Press.

Stirzaker, Rosalind. (2004). Staff induction issues surrounding induction into international schools. *Journal of Research in International Education, 3*(1), 31–49.

Tarc, Paul. (2009). *Global dreams, enduring tensions.* New York: Peter Lang.

Tarc, Paul, & Beatty, Luke. (2012). The emergence of the International Baccalaureate diploma in Ontario: Diffusion, pilot study and prospective research. *Canadian Journal of Education/Revue canadienne de l'éducation*, 35(4), 341–375.

Tarc, Paul, & Mishra Tarc, Aparna. (2015). Elite international schools in the Global South: Transnational space, class relationalities and the "middling" international schoolteacher. *British Journal of Sociology of Education*, 36(1), 34–52.

Tasneem, Ibrahim. (2005). Global citizenship education: Mainstreaming the curriculum? *Cambridge Journal of Education*, 35(2), 177–194.

Van Zanten, Agnes. (2009). Choisir son école. *Stratégies familiales et médiations locales*. Paris: PUF, coll. Lien social.

Wagner, Anne-Catherine. (2007). Les classes sociales dans la mondialisation. Paris: La Découverte.

Weenink, Don. (2009). Creating a niche in the education market: The rise of internationalised secondary education in the Netherlands. *Journal of Education Policy*, 24(4), 495–511.

Widegren, Pemilla, & Doherty, Catherine. (2010). Is the world their oyster? The global imagination of pre-service teachers. *Asia-Pacific Journal of Teacher Education*, 38(1), 5–22.

Yemini, Miri, & Fulop, Alexandra. (2014). The international, global and intercultural dimensions in schools: An analysis of four internationalised Israeli schools. *Globalisation, Societies and Education*, (ahead-of-print), 1–25.

CHAPTER THIRTEEN
INTERNATIONAL EDUCATION INDICATORS AND ASSESSMENTS: ISSUES FOR TEACHERS

Anna K. Chmielewski, Karen Mundy, and Joseph P. Farrell

INTRODUCTION

Statistics about educational achievement and other social issues increasingly influence and drive debates over public policy. Both political actors and media commentators make claims based on such statistics: we have all read headlines about the growth of income disparities and other forms of economic inequality, the growth of secondary dropout rates, or the poor literacy skills of youth. Educational statistics are also regularly used in comparing nations (and in federal nations such as Canada and the United States, to compare provinces/states). You may have noticed media reports on how a country ranks internationally, describing, for example, Canadian or American student achievement in math, science, or literacy in relation to students in other countries around the world. The tests on which these rankings are based are different from those used at the district and school levels to assess educational performance. Yet both types of tests may be thought of as part of the same global movement to gather more educational data for comparison.

Why are statistics increasingly perceived as useful? At least part of the reason stems from their ability to place disparate students, schools, provinces/states, or countries onto a single external scale for comparison. Statistics can alert teachers and local administrators to blind spots, such as areas of learning that may be neglected or groups who may be disadvantaged. But placing all students on a common scale inherently means simplifying and reducing complex information. Statistics cannot (and are not intended to) capture the nuanced, subjective knowledge of practitioners. Furthermore, it is important to remember that while statistics strive for objectivity, they are ultimately collected and interpreted by humans. Although there have been enormous advances in survey technology in recent decades, flaws in methods of data collection and survey design can still limit accuracy and representativeness. More importantly, misconceptions or even political agendas can bias interpretation, reporting, and decision-making based on educational statistics. Thus, it is crucial to read statistics with a critical eye toward "fine print" describing how the data were collected and exactly what they measure.

As citizens, students, and professional educators, there is a pressing need for us to better understand these numbers. This chapter aims to demystify some widely used international educational data, which can and do have an important influence on the careers and day-to-day practices of educators. We begin with a history of various efforts to develop statistical indicators for educational systems. We look first at international indicators that provide cross-national (or cross-provincial/state) comparisons of various core aspects of an educational system. Then we turn to international large-scale assessments (ILSAs), that is, cross-national achievement tests. ILSAs are sometimes classified as part of the set of international indicators, but the issues involved in their creation and use are sufficiently different from other indicators that they need separate treatment. We also look at how indicators and ILSAs can be combined to provide a glance or snapshot of different aspects of a nation's educational system, highlighting in particular what a comparative snapshot can tell us about Canada. Throughout this chapter, we emphasize the importance of looking critically at cross-national data on education. As a source of externally standardized information, statistics are an invaluable resource that should not be ignored by educational policy-makers and practitioners. But neither should statistics be our only source of evidence for policy-making.

INTERNATIONAL INDICATORS

Indicators are statistics used to measure and monitor systems over time and to compare across jurisdictions, such as provinces, states, or countries. International educational indicators have been with us for quite a long time. The first formal intergovernmental effort to assemble systematic international comparisons of educational systems was undertaken by the International Bureau of Education (IBE) in the early 1930s. Beginning in 1933, the IBE collected basic data about the structure of its members' educational systems, as well as information about specific policies or issues, which was published in an annual *Education Yearbook*.[1] After the Second World War and the formation of the United Nations, UNESCO (the United Nations Educational, Scientific, and Cultural Organization) assumed responsibility for such cross-national data collection and reporting. UNESCO's first questionnaire-based survey of education received responses from 57 member states in 1950. This seems a small number now, but at the time covered almost all of the independent nation-states in the world. The UNESCO survey collected data on school enrolments by level, public expenditure in education, literacy, and a variety of other features of the educational system. The resulting information was published in a *Statistical Yearbook* (which continues to be published under the title *Global Education Digest*; see UNESCO Institute of Statistics, 2012).

To comparative educators in the 1960s, it quickly became apparent that the indicators being reported by UNESCO were, for purposes of comparison, often quite misleading. Beyond questions of accuracy, it was not clear what was actually being counted in any given nation compared to the same statistical indicator in some other nation, since the educational systems of various nations were actually quite different. For example, how would one compare data on various aspects of primary schooling, when some systems end primary schooling after five years and other systems go up through Grade 8? This concern eventually led to the development in the early 1970s of the International Standard Classification of Education (ISCED), illustrated in Table 13.1, which provided standards for all nations as to what should be counted under which indicator. This classification was updated in 1997 and again in 2011 to incorporate early childhood education for children under three years old as well as more fine-grained categories of higher education ("short-cycle" or community college, bachelor's, master's, and doctoral degrees).

UNESCO was intended to be the main gatherer of international educational statistics, and in many respects still is so. However, as budgetary crises and leadership problems developed within the United Nations in the 1980s, the agency's ability to develop and improve such indices declined (Puryear, 1995). Other international agencies began developing their own indicators, often using UNESCO indicators, but adding other sources. For example, UNICEF (United Nations Children's Fund) began publishing an annual report titled *The State of the World's Children*, which includes a wide variety of indicators regarding children, including educational data. The World Bank also publishes an annual *World Development Report*, which includes tables listing a wide variety of economic, social, and educational data from most nations in the world. UNESCO began to regain some of its prominence in this area with the establishment in 1999 of the UNESCO Institute for Statistics (UIS), located at the University of Montreal, whose task is to gather quality statistical information from and for member states, and to report on the global situation of education.

Table 13.1: Original International Standard Classification of Education (ISCED)

Level	Age Range	Stage	Examples
4	22–25	6	• Postgraduate study
3	21–22	5	• Professional schools • Higher stage of university study • Teacher training
	18–19	4	• Advanced technical schools • Lower stage of university study • Teacher training
2	14–15	3	• Full- and part-time vocational schools • Upper section of high schools • Grammar schools • Gymnasiums • Teacher training
	10–11	2	• Upper section of elementary schools • Lower section of high schools • Grammar schools • Gymnasiums
1	5–7	1	• First six years of primary school
	Compulsory School Begins	0	• Nursery and kindergarten

Note: The stages are illustrated by typical examples; ages stated are also illustrative. *Source:* Adapted from Holmes and Robinsohn (1963, p. 57); see also UNESCO, 1997a, 2011

CHAPTER THIRTEEN: International Education Indicators and Assessments 367

Most education-related indicators are essentially head counts. These include total enrolment by level of schooling (or in some cases grade level), retention or dropout rates by level, enrolment ratios by level (the number of students enrolled compared to the number in the population who are age-eligible for that level), number of teachers and teacher/student ratios, government expenditures on education, teacher/faculty average salaries, adult literacy rates, and so forth. They are primarily derived from the administrative information that Ministries or Departments of Education routinely have to collect and assemble for their own administrative and management activities and obligations, or from censuses that usually occur once every decade.

Several examples of the use of such statistical indicators for comparative purposes can be found in this book. In Chapter Three, for example, they are used to describe the general status and condition of the three nations, Bangladesh, Colombia, and Mexico, and to compare them to Canada. There, in Table 3.2, we find Gross National Income (GNI) per capita, which is a rough measure of the amount of wealth available per person in the nation; a measure of income distribution, which roughly measures the percentage of that wealth available to the poorest 20 percent of that population; and the adult literacy rate. In the accompanying text there is an indication of how those wealth and distribution indicators translate into the actual value, in current international dollars, of the annual income available to the poorest 20 percent of each country's population, per capita. These are approximate figures, with no claim to precise accuracy, but they do provide a general snapshot that can help the readers locate these nations quickly in their own mental maps. Similarly, statistics are used in Chapter Eleven to compare basic education enrolment rates in Tanzania and Kenya and in Chapter Seven to demonstrate gender disparities in education.

Until the 1990s, international indicators rarely incorporated detailed layers of research (such as on students' family backgrounds, socioeconomic status, racial/ethnic identity, family private expenditures on schooling, or the quality of teaching and learning), which would provide context for the indicators surveyed. They have also been limited by the data that governments report. Because governments self-report, some of the international statistical series are of questionable or suspicious reliability and accuracy. One part of the problem is that the quality of the information provided to international agencies depends on the resources available to governments to collect such information.

Richer nations have the resources available to collect and analyze reasonably accurate information on all sorts of government concerns—but collecting such information is expensive. Thus statistics from poorer nations are often simply the best guess of government officials. It is not uncommon, for example, to find that Ministry of Education officials in poorer nations have only the vaguest idea of how many students and teachers are in their formal education system. Elaborate procedures and requirements for data collection are in place on paper but the resources to accurately gather this data are not available. Moreover, governments often deliberately misreport, for domestic and/or international political reasons, such as to exaggerate their own accomplishments or minimize the accomplishments of a previous regime.

Beyond these problems, it is difficult to know what some often-cited international indicators actually refer to, and how they are measured. Adult literacy rates are a good example of this. At one level it seems clear what literacy refers to: the ability to read text, and in some cases to write as well. Literacy statistics, however, are much more complicated than that. Scholars of literacy often distinguish among levels or types of literacy, ranging from basic or functional literacy (usually thought of as the ability to read with understanding fairly simple texts, such as local newspapers, or instructions for medicines or farming/gardening chemicals), to much more complex forms, such as the ability to read complicated texts—for example, the plays of Shakespeare. We also now speak about new kinds of literacy, such as computer or mathematical literacy. So it is important to understand what level and type of literacy is being referred to.

Furthermore, it is generally difficult and expensive to actually test people's level of literacy, especially for large population groups. So proxies are used. For example, in many international statistical series, literacy is taken as the proportion of the adult population who have completed primary school, on the assumption that it normally takes at least five or six years of primary schooling to become literate. In other cases, literacy rates are based on self-reporting from censuses, in which people often exaggerate their level of schooling and/or literacy (Farrell, 2007). For instance, Latin America is generally considered to be one of the most-schooled and literate regions of the developing world, with primary enrolment ratios for the most part well over 90 percent. However, a study done early in the current millennium, covering a large sample of adults from the region, found that of the 63 percent who reported

CHAPTER THIRTEEN: International Education Indicators and Assessments   369

completing primary schooling and being literate, only about 50 percent could actually read with understanding a short paragraph taken from the front page of a local popular newspaper (Schiefelbein, 2006).

In recent years, advances in information technology and the growth in funding for the collection of international data has led to an ever-wider range of statistical information, and to the development of more robust efforts to clarify relationships among statistical indicators. Detailed information on attitudes and lived experiences is often collected alongside administrative data through methods such as household surveys and surveys of students and teachers. As we shall see in the next section, in education such efforts have led to a sometimes bewildering proliferation of cross-national comparative data, in forms that critics argue contribute to both greater homogenization of educational systems, and greater surveillance and control. On the other hand, such data is increasingly sensitive to questions of inequality and may allow us to see whether formally agreed universal entitlements, such as the right to education, are in fact realized in the distribution of educational opportunities around the world. UNICEF's annual *Report Card* on child poverty and well-being in rich countries (UNICEF, 2013), and UNESCO's *Global Education Monitoring Report* (previously the *Education for All Global Monitoring Report*) (UNESCO, 2015) exemplify this trend.

THE BIRTH OF INTERNATIONAL LARGE-SCALE ASSESSMENTS

The term *international large-scale assessments* (ILSAs) is commonly used to refer to tests of educational achievement carried out in more than one nation using the same tests and testing methodology. The first ILSA was the First International Mathematics Study (FIMS), which was conducted in 1964, under the auspices of the International Association for the Evaluation of Educational Achievement (IEA). The IEA had been founded in 1958, growing out of a meeting at the UNESCO Institute for Education of an international group of educational psychologists, and curricular and measurement specialists from a variety of Western countries. The founding chair of the IEA and the head of the FIMS study was eminent Swedish professor of educational psychology Torsten Husén. Husén and the other founders of the IEA viewed the world as a "natural educational laboratory," encompassing far more variation than could be observed in a single national setting, and thus prime for educational research (IEA, n.d.). FIMS consisted of multiple-choice and fill-in-the-blank math problems translated into eight different languages and administered in 12 different countries. The countries were all relatively high income and located primarily in Europe, plus Australia, Israel, Japan, and the United States. (Canada did not participate in FIMS.)

In each country, tests were administered to randomly chosen, anonymized samples of about four thousand Grade 8 students and four thousand students in the pre-university stream of the final year of high school. In addition, students, teachers, and principals completed questionnaires to provide context on family and educational background, attitudes toward learning, resources, and teaching practices. The scope and ambition of FIMS were groundbreaking for its time. After the success of FIMS, the IEA went on to undertake studies in six more academic subjects in the 1970s (science, reading comprehension, literature, English and French as foreign languages, and civic education). In the 1980s and 1990s, the IEA conducted follow-up studies in many of these same subjects in order to expand on earlier findings and to study changes in education over time. With each successive study, new countries joined, including some Canadian provinces in 1980, dozens of other industrialized countries, and a small number of middle-income and developing countries, including Chile, Iran, Nigeria, Swaziland, Thailand, and Zimbabwe.

Aside from refining techniques for educational measurement, early ILSAs produced a number of interesting findings. One important issue was how to compare achievement in the final year of secondary school across countries with very different "retentivity" rates, meaning the share of students who had not left school or entered vocational training by this grade. While in comprehensive systems like Sweden's, nearly all youth were still in school and following a general stream by the end of secondary school, in selective systems like Germany's, vocational stream students graduated after Grade 9 or 10, meaning that only an elite few remained until the end of secondary school. Thus, a more appropriate comparison was at Grade 8, when virtually all students were still enrolled in school, at least in the wealthy participating countries (Husén, 1967b).

A second finding from the early ILSAs is perhaps the most important and well known: the concept of "opportunity to learn" (OTL). OTL originated as a way to explain and validate cross-national differences in achievement based on the fact that students' content exposure was not

CHAPTER THIRTEEN: International Education Indicators and Assessments 371

equally well aligned to the test in every country. Even though the tests were designed to represent an "international consensus" curriculum of agreed-upon topics, it appeared that teachers implemented curriculum differently across countries. OTL was conceptualized as the second of three levels at which the curriculum operates: (1) the "intended curriculum," which was the official curriculum of the country (or province/state), (2) the "implemented curriculum," or OTL, meaning the content that teachers actually taught in their classrooms, and (3) the "attained curriculum," or the content that students learned, as evidenced by their performance on the test. By collecting extensive curricular information from government officials and from teachers, the scholars of the early ILSAs found large discrepancies between the intended and the implemented curriculum in some countries. Further, they found that the implemented curriculum, or OTL, went a long way toward explaining cross-national differences in achievement. Finally, ILSA results drew attention to the unequal distribution of OTL within some countries, particularly those practising curricular tracking and streaming between or within schools (McDonnell, 1995).

Throughout the 1980s and 1990s, the IEA implemented many other innovative research ideas. For example, the Second International Mathematics Study (SIMS, 1980) included longitudinal (pre/post-test) designs in some countries, in order to observe how much students learn in one year. Other IEA studies went beyond collecting data only from tests and surveys. The Civic Education Study (CIVED, 1999) included impressive in-depth qualitative case studies of civic education in 24 countries (Torney-Purta, Schwille, & Amadeo, 1999). The Third International Mathematics and Science Study (TIMSS, 1995 and 1999) collected classroom video data in eight countries to allow for even greater analysis of instructional practices. These videos are now freely available online, meaning teachers themselves can access and review them. (A link is provided in the audio-visual resources at the end of this chapter.) Reflecting the attitude of seeing the world as an educational laboratory, an article based on the TIMSS video study concluded, "The opportunities to see the familiar in new light might offer many opportunities for teachers to rethink the taken-for-granted practices and see them as choices rather than inevitabilities" (Givven et al., 2005).

The founders of the IEA were academic researchers, primarily curricular and measurement specialists. They intended for ILSAs to contribute to a global body of knowledge on teaching and learning, but they did not promote educational policy changes on the basis of their findings (Pizmony-Levy, 2014). Most particularly—and perhaps most naively—they were opposed to using the test results to rank countries by performance. As Torsten Husén argued in the FIMS (1964) report, "The IEA study was not designed to compare countries; needless to say, it is not to be considered as an 'international contest'" (Husén, 1967b, p. 288). Relatedly, Husén emphasized that ILSAs could not be used to make causal arguments and claims about why certain countries achieved the results they did, or which policy changes might improve a country's results (Husén, 1967a, p. 31). ILSAs merely provided a snapshot of a country's achievement and instructional practices at a single point in time; as the popular mantra goes, "correlation does not imply causation."

However, the basic design and intention of international assessment studies did not stop their results from being used both as direct evidence for educational policy decisions and as fodder for competition among nations. The early ILSA reports listed countries' average scores in alphabetical order rather than ranked from highest to lowest, in a table buried in the middle of the reports after chapters of background material—or avoided publishing country averages altogether. Yet it was easy for politicians and journalists to reconstruct the rankings themselves based on the information in the reports. What were those rankings? In the early math and science assessments, the consistent top performer was Japan. The lowest performers tended to be the developing countries. Among the higher-income countries, the lowest performers were often the United States, Sweden, and Finland. Canada's performance was generally above average. For national policy-makers, it did not go unnoticed that top-scoring Japan was also experiencing rapid economic growth in the 1980s, and this success was assumed to be the product of a superior school system. The simplistic use of rankings linked to economic competitiveness is best illustrated by the 1983 US Department of Education report *A Nation at Risk*, which stated that across all ILSAs conducted to date, "American students were never first or second and, in comparison with other industrialized nations, were last seven times" (National Commission on Excellence in Education, 1983, p. 8), and equated this low performance to "unilateral educational disarmament" (ibid., p. 5).

The IEA's explanations for Japan's high scores were generally curriculum-focused. They noted that Japanese students experienced a high level of OTL in math. The TIMSS video study revealed that Japanese math teachers devoted more time to introducing new content and less time to reviewing old lessons than teachers in other countries (Givven et al., 2005). Yet the US standards-based reform movement that grew out of *A Nation at Risk* did not directly target improvements to OTL and instruction but instead aimed to increase standards indirectly through accountability, high-stakes testing, and decentralization of management. In this early example of educational reform justified though ILSA results, the wealth of information from the world's "educational laboratory" was reduced to simple rankings and used to support a pre-existing reform agenda. Unfortunately, the policy effects of ILSAs in later decades and in other countries have sometimes followed a similar pattern.

GLOBALIZATION, LARGE-SCALE ASSESSMENT, AND THE POLITICS OF LEAGUE TABLES

In the 1990s, as the Cold War faded from view, governments around the world focused their policies even more intensely on the challenges of globalization and international economic competition. Human capital—particularly in terms of skills in science, math, and literacy—was increasingly seen as central to national efforts to maintain economic advantage within the world economy (see Chapters One and Eleven for further discussions on human capital). The information available to measure those skills has dramatically proliferated. After 1999, the IEA changed the name of TIMSS from "Third" to "Trends" in International Mathematics and Science Study, and began conducting the study every four years at Grades 4 and 8. The IEA also runs assessments of reading skills every five years, civic education every seven years, and computer literacy every five years, and is developing a test of kindergarten early literacy (see Table 13.2 for a full listing of current ILSAs). These other subject tests have lower participation rates and receive less media attention than TIMSS, most likely because in the policy discourse, they are less linked to economic growth than are math and science.

Around 50 countries now participate in each cycle of TIMSS—yet the composition of this set of countries has changed over time. The number of Western countries participating in TIMSS has declined markedly since 1995, while the number of Middle Eastern and African countries has increased (and the number of East and Southeast Asian countries has remained high). Germany, France, most Canadian provinces, and many other countries have left TIMSS. This may seem surprising given the growing worldwide policy focus on human capital and economic growth, but the likely explanation is the advent of a new ILSA: the Programme for International Student Assessment (PISA).

PISA is run by the Organization for Economic Co-operation and Development (OECD), an intergovernmental economic and policy organization founded in 1961 that includes most of the world's wealthiest countries. The OECD is based in Paris, France, and describes itself as committed to the market economy and democracy and working to promote economic progress, world trade, and policy best practices (OECD, n.d.). One of the main functions of the OECD has been collecting and publishing its member countries' economic indicators, such as gross domestic product. The OECD also collected educational indicators, such as numbers of students enrolled in primary, secondary, and post-secondary education and government expenditures on education, releasing these in an annual publication called *Education at a Glance*. But starting in the mid-1990s, the OECD expanded its mission to measuring the skills necessary for a productive national workforce. The OECD hired a German statistician from the IEA named Andreas Schleicher to help develop a new assessment in which all OECD countries would regularly participate. PISA was conducted for the first time in 2000 and is repeated every three years. In addition to all 34 OECD member countries, the number of non-member "partner" (mostly middle-income) countries participating in PISA has quickly grown and surpassed OECD countries, making PISA the largest ILSA ever conducted. The ability to compare academic performance to all of one's major economic competitors (with the notable exceptions of China and India) is likely one reason that many wealthy countries choose to participate in PISA rather than TIMSS. Another reason is that PISA directly caters to the desire of policy-makers to draw policy lessons from ILSAs. Unlike the IEA, which historically was an organization of academics pursuing research questions that interested them, the OECD has always been an organization of governments seeking policy solutions. In recent years, the IEA has also begun to see heavier government involvement and more policy focus (Pizmony-Levy, 2014).

PISA shares many similar technical aspects with the IEA assessments, including randomly, anonymously sampling 4,000 to 4,500 students in 150 schools per country, administering student and principal contextual questionnaires, and using similar statistical methods for calculating test scores. Both PISA and the IEA assessments are nationally representative samples that include both public and private school students

CHAPTER THIRTEEN: International Education Indicators and Assessments 375

(Martin & Mullis, 2013; OECD, 2014a). But the differences between PISA and TIMSS illustrate the OECD's focus on future workforce skills. First, while TIMSS is a curriculum-based test, PISA tests mathematical, scientific, and reading "literacy," with a focus on problem solving and real-world application. While TIMSS test questions are mostly multiple-choice and fill-in-the-blank, PISA has fewer multiple-choice and more open-ended questions (ibid.). (The types of questions used in PISA and TIMSS can be compared by accessing the publicly released items for each test, which are listed among the resources at the end of this chapter.) Second, PISA's contextual surveys are less focused on curriculum. Its school principal surveys ask more questions about management practices (such as decentralization of decision-making, accountability, and school choice), and PISA does not collect teacher surveys at all. Third, rather than sampling Grade 8 or Grade 4 students, PISA samples 15-year-old students, regardless of which grade they are in (OECD, 2014a). Age 15 was chosen to correspond to the end of compulsory schooling in many member countries (at least in the late 1990s when the test was being developed; compulsory schooling has been lengthened in many countries since then) (Baird et al., 2011). Thus, PISA was intended to measure the "yield" of national educational systems for the broadest cross-section of students possible—in effect it purports to measure the economic competitiveness and skills of a nation's future labour force.

Despite its shorter history, PISA appears to have gained more international recognition than the IEA studies among policy-makers, the media, and the public. This may be due to the appeal of the OECD's explicit focus on policy relevance as well as a more intensive dissemination strategy that does not shy away from rankings. PISA releases its official reports every three years in December in a major media event, and those reports display country rankings in their first few pages. (In the 1990s, IEA studies also began publishing country rankings.) Many observers refer to these rankings by a new name: "league tables"—a term meant to invoke the relative standing of teams as reported in the sports pages of newspapers. In some countries, the release of PISA results triggers over 100 articles in the main national newspaper alone (Martens & Niemann, 2013). PISA is perceived as having a reputable "brand" among policy-makers and the press (Grek, 2009). Andreas Schleicher, the director of PISA, has become a well-known public figure, invited to give lectures to education ministries around the world and a TED Talk on the results of PISA. At least 18 national Ministries of Education have begun to set performance targets specifically benchmarked to PISA scores or rankings (Breakspear, 2012).

Unlike the IEA, the OECD attempts to identify policies and characteristics of successful systems, although it claims not to make explicit policy recommendations based on PISA. Further, the content of all OECD publications and recommendations must be approved by all OECD member states (though not the non-members), and these recommendations are not binding; countries may choose to implement them voluntarily (Bieber & Martens, 2011). Descriptions of policy best practices appear in the main PISA reports, in country-specific policy advice that the OECD produces on request, and in the video series co-produced with educational company Pearson called "Strong Performers and Successful Reformers" that profiles top-scoring systems.

One of the most consistent messages of PISA concerns educational equity. Even in its design, PISA has always had a greater emphasis on equity than do the IEA studies. PISA's practice of sampling students by age rather than by grade means that countries' results suffer if they have high rates of grade retention. PISA's student surveys also collect more information on family socio-economic context than do the IEA studies, which allows the OECD to conduct many within-country analyses of inequality between students of different socio-economic statuses, including the correlation between socio-economic status and achievement as well as the level of socio-economic segregation between schools (OECD, 2013a). But it is in the publicity surrounding some of the top-performing countries in PISA where the equity focus is most striking. Two of the surprise top-scoring countries in the first round of PISA in 2000 were Finland and Canada, both known for relatively equitable educational and social policies. Along with South Korea, the other top performer, all three countries had among the lowest levels of socio-economic segregation between schools and smallest impact of socio-economic status on achievement. In addition, Finland had among the smallest gender differences in achievement, and Canada had some of the smallest achievement gaps between immigrant and native-born students (OECD, 2004). These findings led to a major conclusion of PISA: that educational equity was compatible with educational excellence—and perhaps even led to excellence. Although both Finland's and Canada's scores declined somewhat in later years, equity remains a strong message of PISA. OECD publications urge extra support for low-achieving, socio-economically disadvantaged, immigrant and language learner students, and are critical

CHAPTER THIRTEEN: International Education Indicators and Assessments   377

of policies that tend to increase social segregation between schools, such as selective school admissions and between-school academic and vocational tracking (OECD, 2013a).

Other policies that the OECD has identified in top-scoring countries include high teacher quality, positive school climate, greater autonomy for local schools, rigorous academic standards, and accountability (OECD, 2004, 2013b). Here, the emphasis on standards, accountability, and particularly the role of assessments merits further discussion, as this has been one of the most controversial impacts of PISA and is also an area where the evidence gathered by the OECD remains inconclusive. While some of the OECD's early case studies profiled in a positive light the development of different test-based accountability systems, such as those of Ontario, Brazil, and Germany (OECD, 2004, 2010), there were also many prominent examples of successful systems operating under different models, such as Finland, which has very little standardized testing, and Korea and Japan, which have high-stakes university entrance exams but limited use of standardized testing in early grades. More recently, in the PISA 2012 results, the OECD reported that countries where more schools' achievement data were tracked by administrative authorities in fact had *lower* average PISA scores (OECD, 2013b, p. 59). Despite this somewhat inconsistent picture, what is clear from the PISA principal surveys is that the amount of test-based accountability has increased quite dramatically in many countries since the start of PISA in 2000 (ibid.).

What has been the impact of PISA on educational policy? Among OECD member countries, the response has varied greatly, from large reforms in many European and East Asian countries to little recognition of PISA in many English-speaking countries. The amount of national media coverage of PISA follows a similar pattern, with high coverage in Spain, Germany, Mexico, and Finland, and low coverage in the United States, the United Kingdom, Canada, and New Zealand. Media coverage appears unrelated to how well or poorly countries perform in PISA (Martens & Niemann, 2013). A number of countries experienced "PISA Shock" following lower-than-expected results, prompting large reforms. Germany, after disappointing results in 2000, enacted national standards, assessments in each federal state, and greater support for disadvantaged students, particularly immigrants, among other reforms (Breakspear, 2012). Perhaps the most unexpected outcome of PISA has been the "Finnish Miracle." Finnish educators themselves were quite surprised at their system's top performance in PISA 2000 and at the massive international attention it drew to the small country (Grek, 2009). Ministry officials, researchers, and journalists travelled to Finland to discover the secrets to its success, and Finnish ministry official Pasi Sahlberg's book *Finnish Lessons* became a best-seller. The Finnish craze even reached Japan, the country that had received the most international attention in the previous decade for its TIMSS results, but that had experienced a "PISA Shock" of its own when scores fell in 2003 and 2006 (although they were still far above the OECD average) (Takayama, 2009). Across Japan and other countries, scholars have observed that education reformers from both the right and the left used the external Finnish example to lend greater legitimacy to their preferred agendas (Dobbins & Martens, 2012). On the other hand, the English-speaking world has only recently begun to take notice of PISA. In the United Kingdom, PISA received little attention until after 2006 when performance appeared to fall (possibly due to correction of sampling problems in earlier waves) and a new government was interested in criticizing old policy (Baird et al., 2011). In the United States, PISA went relatively unnoticed until 2009, when the Chinese city of Shanghai participated for the first time and topped the rankings, prompting a massive response in the national media and government, which often interpreted the results for the single city of Shanghai as representing the entire country of China (Baird et al., 2011; Martens & Niemann, 2013). Overall, it appears that the policy effects of PISA are increasing over time, and that some of the most common policy responses are implementing national standards and assessments, as well as aligning these standards and assessments with PISA (Breakspear, 2012).

PISA and other ILSAs are not themselves used for accountability purposes. As ILSAs are administered only to small, randomly selected, anonymized samples of students in each country, they cannot have high stakes for individual participating students, teachers, or schools, as domestic assessments can. However, ILSAs and domestic assessments do share some similarities: Both measure achievement on a standardized scale for purposes of comparison, whether comparison of countries or of schools. Both often result in visible public rankings that may end up "naming and shaming" low-performing systems. Thus, it could be argued that, although ILSAs are not high stakes for students, they can have stakes for national actors, such as ministers of education. Finally, as described above, many countries have begun aligning their national assessments with PISA's concepts of literacy and problem solving, creating some convergence in the content of the tests themselves. (See Chapter Five by Anderson and Sivasubramaniam for more discussion of testing and assessment programs.)

PISA (as well as other ILSAs and indicator projects) also have far-reaching policy impact within the developing world. As early as 1990, the international community linked better assessment to the achievement of education as a universal right (as described by Mundy and Read in Chapter Eleven). Article 4 of the *World Declaration on Education for All* (adopted in Jomtien, Thailand, in 1990 and ratified in Dakar, Senegal, in 2000) states, "It is necessary to define acceptable levels of learning acquisition for educational programmes and to improve and apply systems of assessing learning achievement" (World Conference on Education for All, 1990, p. 36). Many developing countries produce shockingly low levels of learning acquisition: basic levels of literacy and numeracy are often not acquired during the full primary cycle, causing mounting international concern with educational quality (an issue that is sometimes neglected in the push for greater access). Beginning in the 1990s, many governments introduced national assessment programs; in several countries whose governments did not initiate assessments, citizen-led assessments emerged (e.g., in India, Pakistan, Kenya, and others) (Results for Development, 2015). According to a recent count, 65 percent of developing countries now have national assessments (Benavot & Köseleci, 2015). Regional indicator and assessment programs were undertaken in Southern Africa and Latin America—most notably the Southern and Eastern African Consortium for Monitoring Educational Quality (SACMEQ) and the Latin American Laboratory for Evaluating the Quality of Education (LLECE).[2] Many other countries simply joined in the IEA's TIMSS or the OECD's PISA program: non-OECD countries represent more than half the current participants of both assessments. The relatively demanding TIMSS and PISA tests generally draw middle-income countries, and some developing countries have stopped participating in ILSAs after disappointing results (Wiseman, 2013). Thus far, developing countries appear to favour using their own national assessments over participation in regional or international assessments (Kamens & Benavot, 2011). Participation in all of these types of assessments is heavily supported by the World Bank, which increasingly sees assessments as essential to both the efficient allocation of scarce educational resources, and providing a key way of mobilizing policy-makers around educational reform programs. There is some evidence that developing countries that participate in ILSAs also subsequently receive more foreign aid to education (Kijima, 2010). The new version of Article 4 in the UN's post-2015 Sustainable Development Goals for the first time explicitly mentions using international, regional, and national assessments to monitor educational quality. In response, both the OECD and the IEA are implementing new assessments aimed at monitoring more basic skills in developing countries (PISA for Development, TIMSS Numeracy, and PIRLS Literacy). Such efforts have raised criticisms of increasing pressure to participate in ILSAs and the creation of a de facto global curriculum. However, UNESCO officials argue that universal participation in ILSAs is unnecessary; instead, common scales can be developed for comparing disparate national assessments (Benavot & Köseleci, 2015; Rose, 2015).

CANADA AND THE INTERNATIONAL INDICATORS

What implications and issues are raised by the rapid growth of international indicator programs for educators? In this section, we answer this question by first describing Canadian involvement in international assessments, and then looking at some of the findings from these assessments and the policy debates they have stimulated. Our goal here is to provide educators with a practical guide to international indicators, and to encourage greater critical engagement with them, using the Canadian experience as an illustration.

Canada (through the national Council of Ministers of Education Canada [CMEC], Human Resources and Skills Development Canada [HRSDC], Statistics Canada [StatsCan], and the provincial Ministries of Education) has been quite an active participant in many of the major international assessment exercises since relatively early. Canada's first participation in an ILSA came in 1980 when British Columbia and Ontario took part in the Second International Mathematics Study (SIMS). As education in Canada is a provincially mandated responsibility, in most of the early ILSAs, only some provincial Ministries of Education made the decision to participate. In TIMSS 1995 and 1999, for the first time all 10 provinces participated and were reported as a single country. Throughout the IEA assessments of the 1980s and 1990s, Canada generally achieved above-average results compared to other countries. Canada has also played a leadership role in ILSA design and analysis. SIMS was headed by David Robitaille, professor of mathematics education at the University of British Columbia. Robitaille was also involved in the initial planning for TIMSS 1995. Statistics Canada led the administration of the first two surveys of literacy skills for adults ages 16–65, IALS 1994 and ALL 2003.

Table 13.2 lists the various international assessments in which Canada currently participates. Since 2003, only Ontario and Quebec have consistently participated in every year of TIMSS. Both provinces generally score above the international average, with Quebec outperforming Ontario in math and both provinces performing similarly in science (Mullis et al., 2012). Different provinces have participated in each year of the IEA's Grade 4 reading test (PIRLS) and Grade 8 computer skills test (ICILS). No Canadian provinces currently participate in the IEA's Grade 8 civics test (ICCS). PISA constitutes a marked change for Canadian participation in ILSAs because all 10 provinces (though no territories) have participated in every wave of the study. Unlike in the IEA studies, which are generally funded by the participating provincial Ministries of Education, direct costs for PISA are paid for by the federal ministry and HRSDC, with provinces, CMEC, and StatsCan as collaborating partners. Moreover, Canada is one of a handful of federal countries that chooses to select an especially large PISA sample in order to obtain reliable results for individual provinces or states. Rather than the typical PISA sample of 4,500 students, Canada selects over 20,000 students from across the 10 provinces in each wave of PISA. This enables comparison of results for all provinces, as well as for English and French systems where applicable.

As described in the previous section, Canada has received a great deal of international attention for its high and equitable performance in PISA. In particular, recent educational reforms in Ontario have been profiled in the OECD's reports on "Strong Performers and Successful Reformers" and the OECD/Pearson video series of the same name, as well as reports by McKinsey & Company and the National Centre on Education and the Economy (Tucker, 2011; OECD, 2010; Mourshed, Chijioke, & Barber, 2010). Alberta also was covered in the *Economist* (2006) for its top performance and its education policies emphasizing school choice, competition, and accountability. Inside Canada, the picture is different. As in the United Kingdom and United States, initial media attention to PISA was rather low (Grek, 2009; Martens & Niemann, 2013).

Table 13.2: A Guide to Current International Assessments in Canada

	Goals/Method	Years	Canadian Participation
Title (Organization)	**PISA**: Programme for International Student Assessment (OECD)		
	• Reading, math, and science • 15-year-olds (regardless of grade) • Tests literacy, with emphasis on problem solving and application of knowledge (does not test mastery of a curriculum) • Student and school contextual questionnaires	Every 3 years starting in 2000	All years, all provinces
	TIMSS: Trends in International Mathematics and Science Study (IEA)		
	• Science and math • Grades 4 and 8 • Curriculum-based tests (based on international consensus curriculum) • Student, teacher, and school contextual questionnaires; national context survey	Every 4 years starting in 1995	1995 & 1999: all provinces; since 2003: ON & QC in all years, BC & AB in some years
	PIRLS: Progress in Reading Literacy Study (IEA)		
	• Reading • Grade 4 • Tests literacy in both literary texts and informational documents • Student, teacher, school, and parent contextual questionnaires; national context survey	Every 5 years starting in 2001	2001: QC & ON; 2006: AB, BC, NS, QC, ON; 2011: all provinces
	Civics Education Studies: **CIVED** (1999): Civic Education Study **ICCS** (from 2009): International Civics and Citizenship Study (IEA)		
	• Civic and citizenship knowledge and attitudes • Grade 8 • Achievement test assesses civic knowledge and interpretation of democracy/citizenship, identity/intl. relations, social cohesion/diversity • Student, teacher, and school contextual questionnaires • CIVED included qualitative country case studies	CIVED 1999; ICCS every 7 years starting in 2009	Canada participated in CIVED qualitative case study only, not assessment; did not participate in ICCS

continued...

CHAPTER THIRTEEN: International Education Indicators and Assessments   383

Title (Organization)			
Surveys of Adult Skills: **IALS** (1994): International Adult Literacy Survey (StatsCan) **ALL** (2003): Adult Literacy and Lifeskills Survey (StatsCan) **PIAAC** (from 2011): Programme for the International Assessment of Adult Competencies (OECD)			
	• Literacy and numeracy skills • Adults ages 16–65 • Tests literacy in both prose and informational documents; numeracy applied to real-life situations (not curriculum-based) • Test was computer-based starting in 2011 • Participant contextual questionnaires	IALS 1994; ALL 2003; PIAAC every 10 years starting in 2011	All years, all provinces
Computer Studies: **COMPED** (1992): Computers in Education Study **SITES** (2006): Second Information Technology in Education Study **ICILS** (2013): International Computer and Information Literacy Study (IEA)			
	• Computer and information literacy • Grade 8 • Computer-based test with questions testing knowledge and tasks using simulated software applications • Student, teacher, and school contextual questionnaires; national context survey • SITES included qualitative country case studies	COMPED 1992; SITES 2006; ICILS every 5 years starting in 2013	COMPED: BC only; SITES: all provinces participated in qualitative case study; only AB & ON participated in assessment; ICILS: NL & ON only

As coverage began to grow, it was primarily focused on ranking the provinces rather than international comparisons (Stack, 2006). Generally, British Columbia and Alberta are the highest-scoring provinces, although Quebec performs well in math and Ontario in reading; the Atlantic provinces tend to have the lowest average scores (Brochu et al., 2013). Provincial league tables may have been fascinating to many Canadians because they were relatively new. When the first results of PISA 2000 were released, CMEC's federal testing program, then known as the School Achievement Indicators Program (SAIP), was less than 10 years old (CMEC, n.d.). As with international results, it is difficult to prove whether particular policies in each province are the cause for these results. Ontario's curricular reforms profiled in the OECD reports above began in 2003, after the province had already achieved relatively high scores in the first wave of PISA (Stack, 2006).

In comparison to other countries, the policy impact of PISA within Canada has been medium (Breakspear, 2012). The largest impact at the federal level has been on the federal testing program, which in 2007 was revised to be more aligned with PISA (at that time, it was also renamed from SAIP to the Pan-Canadian Assessment Program [PCAP] (CMEC, n.d.). Similarly to PISA and other ILSAs, PCAP also tests a randomly selected sample of students from within each province, and each of the English and French systems, in order to perform comparisons. Some have commented that PISA may provide external legitimacy to unified federal indicators that otherwise would have been difficult for provinces to agree on (Smith & Baker, 2001). Others have criticized PISA for increasing pressure toward standardization and uniformity across the provinces, and HRSDC's involvement in PISA as marking a new trend in federal intervention in education. PISA has also had policy effects for individual provinces. For example, Ontario has used PISA results to monitor and validate the effectiveness of its recent reforms, Prince Edward Island has implemented provincial assessments partly in response to its low initial PISA performance, and New Brunswick has set targets to improve its ranking within Canada (Baird et al., 2011). Again, these policy effects are primarily focused on domestic rather than international comparisons.

More recently, Canada's relatively small but statistically significant declines in scores in PISA 2009 and 2012 have caused alarm among policymakers and researchers and prompted calls for curricular reforms (Alphonso, 2013; the Canadian Press, 2013). Falling scores call into question the success of educational reforms implemented in many provinces over the past decade. However, it is important to recognize that these declines are relatively small—in fact, Finland's performance has fallen much more precipitously during the same period. Additionally, Canada's achievement remains among the most equitably distributed in the world, particularly for immigrant students. Yet both ILSA results and the experiences of Canadian educators remind us that socioeconomic segregation and achievement disparities are far from zero. This serves to highlight the persistent severity of educational inequality throughout the developed and developing world.

CONCLUSION: INTERNATIONAL INDICATORS—WHAT TEACHERS NEED TO KNOW

In May 2014, a group of nearly 100 professors and educators wrote an open letter to Andreas Schleicher that was published in the *Guardian*. They called for a moratorium on PISA testing until the OECD addresses a number of criticisms, including an overreliance on league tables; an overly narrow focus on economically relevant skills and neglect of students' civic, moral, and artistic development and well-being, leading to a narrowing of school curricula; partnerships with for-profit educational companies (Pearson co-produced the "Strong Performers and Successful Reformers" video series and had recently won the contract to develop the next round of PISA); and inadequate involvement of a wide range of stakeholders, such as teachers, parents, school administrators, and other international organizations such as the United Nations (Meyer et al., 2014). The OECD responded with a public statement saying that "less than 1% of the PISA reporting is devoted to league tables"; that PISA contextual surveys collect a wide range of information including student attitudes, motivation, and socio-economic factors; that PISA contractors, whether for- or not-for-profit, win contracts through open competition; and that all OECD member countries (though not non-members) have equal representation in PISA governance (OECD, 2014b). Later, Pasi Sahlberg and Boston College education professor Andy Hargreaves wrote a blog post in the *Washington Post* arguing that PISA is flawed but should be saved. While they also had misgivings about for-profit contractors, they pointed out that PISA's equity emphasis had had a positive impact on education policy, drawing global attention toward the success of relatively equitable countries such as Finland and Canada and away from market-based reform trends in the United States and United Kingdom (Sahlberg & Hargreaves, 2015).

ILSAs are clearly highly controversial. On the one hand, they have highlighted countries where all students have high OTL and equitable access to education; and they have exposed other countries' low and unequal distribution of opportunity, shaking them out of their parochialism and false assumptions that their schools are the best in the world. On the other hand, ILSAs are widely used for simplistic league table comparisons and mischaracterizations of successful systems like Finland's and Japan's, as well as for justification of test-based accountability and other reforms with limited evidence of effectiveness. Some of the responsibility for these effects is borne not by the OECD and IEA themselves but by policy-makers and journalists. Both the IEA and the OECD publish each ILSA along with thousands of pages of documentation and analyses of national contexts, much of which gets ignored. When one encounters rhetoric about ILSAs, it is important to keep in mind:

- Rankings can be misleading. They can exaggerate small differences: the country in first place and the country in fifth place may have average scores that differ by only 10 points on a 1,000-point scale. When examining changes in performance over time, it is preferable to look at changes in scores rather than changes in rankings, as rankings can be affected by new countries joining. Some news and political outlets publish truncated league tables showing only those countries that score higher than the country in question, giving the false impression that that country ranks in last place.
- It is important to look beyond country averages to the distribution of scores within countries. Every ILSA to date has found more variation within countries than between them (i.e., not every student in Korea outscores every student in Spain). Variation within countries can draw attention to unequal opportunities to learn.
- Correlation is not causation. ILSAs give us a snapshot of how countries perform at a single moment in time, but cannot tell us which policies caused these results. It is particularly faulty logic to attribute a country's performance to educational reforms that are currently underway, rather than recognizing that 15-year-old students are the products of 15 years of experiences both in and out of school—and that countries are the products of hundreds or thousands of years of historical development.

QUESTIONS FOR REFLECTION AND DISCUSSION
1. Why have governments become so interested in participating in efforts to compare their educational performance?
2. What kinds of limits should we be aware of when assessing information from international assessments and indicators?

CHAPTER THIRTEEN: International Education Indicators and Assessments   387

3. How does the collection of international assessments and indicators differ in developed and developing countries? What practical, political, and/or ethical issues does this pose?
4. In your view, do international assessments and indicators offer valuable information for educators? Explain.

SUGGESTED AUDIO-VISUAL RESOURCES
Instead of selecting a film for this chapter, we suggest that instructors explore with students the activities and audio-visual resources provided on international assessment websites. Holding this class in a computer lab would be ideal.

   a. Explore TIMSS questions: timssandpirls.bc.edu/timss2011/international-released-items.html
   b. Explore PISA questions: www.oecd.org/pisa/test
   c. Watch footage of math and science classrooms around the world from the TIMSS 1999 Video Study: www.timssvideo.com
   d. Compare and contrast the videos above with the OECD/Pearson video series "Strong Performers and Successful Reformers": www.oecd.org/pisa/pisaproducts

SUGGESTIONS FOR FURTHER READING
Council of Ministers of Education Canada. (2013). *Measuring Up: Canadian Results of the OECD PISA Study: 2012 First Results for Canadians Aged 15*. Toronto: Council of Ministers of Education Canada.
Meyer, Heinz-Dieter, and Benavot, Aaron. (2013). *PISA, Power, and Policy: The Emergence of Global Educational Governance*. Southampton: Symposium Books.
OECD. (2014). *Education at a Glance 2014: OECD Indicators*. Paris: OECD.
Pizmony-Levy, Oren, et al. (2014). On the merits of, and myths about, international assessments. [Moderated discussion]. *Quality Assurance in Education*, 22(4): 319–338.
Smith, Thomas A., and Baker, David P. (2001). Worldwide Growth and Institutionalization of Statistical Indicators for Educational Policy Making. *Peabody Journal of Education*, 76(3–4): 141–152.
UNESCO. (2015). *Education for All 2000–2015: Achievements and Challenges*. Paris: UNESCO.
UNICEF. (2007). Child Poverty in Perspective: An Overview of Child Well-Being in Rich Countries. *Innocenti Report Card 7*. Florence,

Italy: UNICEF Innocenti Research Centre. Available at: www.unicef-irc.org/ publications/pdf/rc7_eng.pdf

NOTES

1. For an overview of the IBE's *International Education Yearbook*, see UNESCO, "Unesco 50 Years for Education." (UNESCO, 1997b).
2. Information about the SACMEQ and the LLECE programs can be found online at: www.sacmeq.org and www.llece.org

REFERENCES

Alphonso, Caroline. (2013, December 3). Canada's Fall in Math-Education Ranking Sets Off Alarm Bells. *Globe and Mail*. Retrieved from www.theglobeandmail.com/news/national/education/canadas-fall-in-math-education-ranking-sets-off-red-flags/article15730663/

Baird, Jo-Anne, Isaccs, Talia, Johnson, Sandra, Stobart, Gordon, Yu, Guoxing, Sprague, Terra, and Daugherty, Richard. (2011). *Policy Effects of PISA*. Oxford: Oxford University Centre for Educational Assessment.

Benavot, Aaron, and Köseleci, Nihan. (2015). Seeking Quality in Education: The Growth of National Learning Assessments, 1990–2013. Background paper prepared for the Education for All Global Monitoring Report 2015. *Education for All 2000–2015: Achievements and Challenges*. ED/EFA/MRT/2015/PI/53.

Bieber, Tonia, and Martens, Kerstin. (2011). The OECD PISA Study as a Soft Power in Education? Lessons from Switzerland and the US. *European Journal of Education, 46*(1): 101–116.

Breakspear, Simon. (2012). *The Policy Impact of PISA: An Exploration of the Normative Effects of International Benchmarking in School System Performance*. OECD Education Working Papers, No. 71, Paris: OECD.

Brochu, Pierre, Deussing, Marie-Anne, Houme, Koffi, and Chuy, Maria. (2013). *Measuring Up: Canadian Results of the OECD PISA Study*. Toronto: Council of Ministers of Education.

CMEC. (no date). *Overview: Pan-Canadian Assessment Program (PCAP)*. Retrieved from www.cmec.ca/240/Programs-and-Initiatives/Assessment/Pan-Canadian-Assessment-Program-(PCAP)/Overview/index.html

Dobbins, Michael, and Martens, Kerstin. (2012). Towards an Education Approach À La Finlandaise? French Education Policy after PISA. *Journal of Education Policy, 27*(1): 23–43.

Farrell, Joseph P. (2007). Literacy and International Development: Education and Literacy as Basic Human Rights. In David R. Olsen and Nancy Torrance (Eds.), *Handbook of Literacy*. Cambridge: Cambridge University Press, pp. 518–534.

Givven, Karen Bogard, Hiebert, James, Jacobs, Jennifer K., Hollingsworth, Hilary, and Gallimore, Ronald. (2005). Are There National Patterns of Teaching? Evidence from the TIMSS 1999 Video Study. *Comparative Education Review, 49*(3): 311–343.

Grek, Sotiria. (2009). Governing by Numbers: The PISA "Effect" in Europe. *Journal of Education Policy, 24*(1): 23–37.

Holmes, Brian, and Robinsohn, Saul. (1963). *Relevant Data in Comparative Education.* Hamburg: UNESCO Institute for Education.

Husén, Torsten (Ed.). (1967a). *International Study of Achievement in Mathematics* (Vol. I.). Hamburg: Evaluation of Educational Achievement.

Husén, Torsten (Ed.). (1967b). *International Study of Achievement in Mathematics* (Vol. II.). Hamburg: Evaluation of Educational Achievement.

IEA. (no date). *Brief History of IEA: 55 Years of Educational Research.* Retrieved from www.iea.nl/brief_history.html

Kamens, David H., and Benavot, Aaron. (2011). National, Regional and International Learning Assessments: Trends among Developing Countries, 1960–2009. *Globalisation, Societies and Education, 9*(2): 285–300.

Kijima, Rie. (2010). Why Participate? Cross-National Assessments and Foreign Aid to Education. In Alexander W. Wiseman (Ed.), *The Impact of International Achievement Studies on National Education Policymaking.* Bradford, UK: Emerald Group Publishing, 35–61.

Martens, Kerstin, and Niemann, Dennis. (2013). When Do Numbers Count? The Differential Impact of the PISA Rating and Ranking on Education Policy in Germany and the US. *German Politics, 22*(3): 314–332.

Martin, Michael O., and Mullis, Ina V. S. (2013). Methods and Procedures in TIMSS and PIRLS 2011. Boston: TIMSS & PIRLS International Study Center, Lynch School of Education, Boston College and IEA.

McDonnell, Lorraine M. (1995). Opportunity to Learn as a Research Concept and a Policy Instrument. *Educational Evaluation and Policy Analysis, 17*(3): 305–322.

Meyer, Heinz-Dieter, et al. (2014, May 6). OECD and PISA Tests Are Damaging Education Worldwide: Academics. *Guardian.* Retrieved from www.theguardian.com/education/2014/may/06/oecd-PISA-tests-damaging-education-academics

Mourshed, Mona, Chijioke, Chinezi, and Barber, Michael. (2010). *How the World's Most Improved School Systems Keep Getting Better.* London: McKinsey & Company.

Mullis, Ina V. S., Martin, Michael O., Foy, Pierre, and Arora, Alka. (2012). *TIMSS 2011 International Results in Mathematics.* Boston: TIMSS & PIRLS International Study Center, Lynch School of Education, Boston College and IEA.

National Commission on Excellence in Education. (1983). A Nation at Risk: The Imperative for Educational Reform. In *A Report to the Nation and the Secretary of Education by the National Commission on Excellence in Education*: US Department of Education.

OECD. (2004). *What Makes School Systems Perform? Seeing School Systems through the Prism of PISA*. Paris: OECD.
OECD. (2010). *Strong Performers and Successful Reformers in Education: Lessons from PISA for the United States*. Paris: OECD.
OECD. (2013a). *PISA 2012 Results: Excellence through Equity: Giving Every Student the Chance to Succeed* (Vol. II). Paris: OECD Publishing.
OECD. (2013b). *PISA 2012 Results: What Makes Schools Successful?* (Vol. IV). Paris: OECD.
OECD. (2014a). *PISA 2012 Technical Report*. Paris: OECD.
OECD. (2014b). *Response to Points Raised in Heinz-Dieter Meyer "Open Letter."* Paris: OECD. Retrieved from www.oecd.org/PISA/aboutPISA/OECD-response-to-Heinz-Dieter-Meyer-Open-Letter.pdf
OECD. (no date). *About the OECD*. Retrieved from www.oecd.org/about/
Pizmony-Levy, Oren. (2014). Back to the Future in International Assessments. In Madhabi Chatterji and James Harvey (Eds.), *EdWeek Blog: Assessing the Assessments: K–12 Measurement and Accountability in the 21st Century*, Bethesda, MD: Education Week. Retrieved from blogs.edweek.org/edweek/assessing_the_assessments/2014/04/back_to_the_future_how_international_large-scale_assessments_came_about.html
Puryear, Jeffrey. (1995). International Education Statistics and Research: Status and Problems. *International Journal of Educational Development, 15*(1): 79–91.
Results for Development. (2015, June). *Bringing Learning to Light: The Role of Citizen-Led Assessments in Shifting the Education Agenda*. Washington, DC: R4D and the Hewlett Foundation. Retrieved from www.hewlett.org/sites/default/files/R4D%20-%20Bringing%20Learning%20to%20Light%20-%20June%202015.pdf
Rose, Pauline. (2015). Is a Global System of International Large-Scale Assessments Necessary for Tracking Progress of a Post-2015 Learning Target? *Compare, 45*(3): 486–490.
Sahlberg, Pasi, and Hargreaves, Andy. (2015, March 24). The Tower of PISA Is Badly Leaning. An Argument for Why It Should Be Saved. *Washington Post*. Retrieved from www.washingtonpost.com/news/answer-sheet/wp/2015/03/24/the-tower-of-PISA-is-badly-leaning-an-argument-for-why-it-should-be-saved/
Schiefelbein, Ernesto. (2006). *School Performance Problems in Latin America: The Potential Role of the Escuela Nueva System*. Paper presented at the Second International New Schools Congress, Medellin, Colombia.
Smith, Thomas M., and Baker, David P. (2001). Worldwide Growth and Institutionalization of Statistical Indicators for Education Policy-Making. *Peabody Journal of Education, 76*(3–4): 141–152.
Stack, Michelle. (2006). Testing, Testing, Read All about It: Canadian Press Coverage of the PISA Results. *Canadian Journal of Education, 29*(1): 49–69.

Takayama, Keita. (2009). Politics of Externalization in Reflexive Times: Reinventing Japanese Education Reform Discourses through "Finnish PISA Success." *Comparative Education Review, 54*(1): 51–75.

The Canadian Press. "Canada's Students Slipping in Math and Science, OECD Finds." *CBC News*, December 3, 2013.

The Economist. (2006, September 21). *Clever Red-Necks: It's Not Just the Economy That Is Booming; Schools Are Too*. Retrieved from www.economist.com/node/7945805

Torney-Purta, Judith, Schwille, John, and Amadeo, Jo-Ann. (1999). *Civic Education across Countries: Twenty-Four National Case Studies from the IEA Civic Education Project*. Amsterdam: International Association for the Evaluation of Educational Achievement.

Tucker, Marc S. (2011). *Standing on the Shoulders of Giants: An American Agenda for Education Reform*. Washington, DC: National Center on Education and the Economy.

UNESCO. (1997a). *International Standard Classification of Education ISCED97*. Paris: UNESCO. Retrieved from www.unesco.org/education/information/nfsunesco/doc/isced_1997.htm

UNESCO (1997b). *UNESCO 50 Years for Education*. Paris: UNESCO. Retrieved from unesdoc.unesco.org/images/0011/001102/110264eb.pdf

UNESCO. (2011). *International Standard Classification of Education ISCED 2011*. Paris: UNESCO.

UNESCO. (2015). Education for All 2000–2015: Achievements and Challenges. *Education for All Global Monitoring Report,* Paris: UNESCO.

UNESCO Institute of Statistics. (2012). *Global Education Digest: Opportunities Lost: The Impact of Grade Repetition and Early School Leaving*. Montreal: UNESCO Institute of Statistics.

UNICEF. (2013). Child Well-Being in Rich Countries: A Comparative Overview. *Innocenti Report Card 11*. Florence, Italy: UNICEF Innocenti Research Centre.

Wiseman, Alexander W. (2013). Policy Responses to PISA in Comparative Perspective. In Heinz-Dieter Meyer and Aaron Benavot (Eds.), *PISA, Power, and Policy: The Emergence of Global Educational Governance*. Southampton: Symposium Books. 303–322.

World Conference on Education for All. (1990). *Meeting Basic Learning Needs: A Vision for the 1990s*. New York: Inter-Agency Commission for World Conference on Education for All.

ABOUT THE CONTRIBUTORS

Stephen Anderson is a professor at the Ontario Institute for Studies in Education (OISE), University of Toronto, and director of OISE's Comparative, International, and Development Education Program and Centre. His professional work focuses on school improvement, teacher development, and education leadership in Canada, the United States, East Africa, Pakistan, and Latin America. His scholarly publications appear in such journals as *School Effectiveness and School Improvement*, the *International Journal of Educational Development*, *Curriculum Inquiry*, the *Canadian Journal of Education*, the *Journal of School Leadership*, *Leadership and Policy in Schools*, the *Journal of Staff Development*, and the *Journal of Educational Change*.

Monisha Bajaj is an associate professor of International and Multicultural Education at the University of San Francisco, where she directs the MA program in Human Rights Education. She is also a visiting professor and research fellow at the Institute for Reconciliation and Social Justice, University of the Free State, South Africa. Dr. Bajaj is the editor/author of six books, including *Schooling for Social Change: The Rise of Human Rights Education in India* (winner of the 2012 Jackie Kirk Outstanding Book Award of the Comparative & International Education Society). She has also developed curricula and reports for international organizations, including UNESCO and UNICEF.

Kathy Bickmore (PhD Stanford University) is a professor in Curriculum Studies and Comparative, International, and Development Education at OISE, University of Toronto. She is the guest editor of the special issue *Peace-building (in) Education: Democratic Approaches to Conflict in Schools and Classrooms* (*Curriculum Inquiry* 44:4, September 2014). Current research examines gaps (and links) between young people's lived citizenship experiences in violent neighbourhoods and their public school education in Canada and Mexico. Earlier projects include the UN University for Peace in Costa Rica, an anti-bullying initiative in Japan, and civic education in Tula, Russia. Her most recent chapters appear in *Building Democracy in Education on Diversity* and *Social Studies Today: Research and Practice, 2nd Edition*.

Anna K. Chmielewski is an assistant professor in the Department of Leadership, Higher and Adult Education at OISE, University of Toronto. Her areas of specialization include international comparisons of educational and social inequality and international large-scale assessments. Recent publications include international comparisons of curricular streaming and ability grouping, socio-economic achievement gaps, school segregation, and university access, and have appeared in the *American Educational Research Journal*, the *American Journal of Education*, and *Research in Social Stratification and Mobility*.

Mark Evans is an associate professor, teaching stream, in the Department of Curriculum, Teaching, and Learning and former associate dean of teacher education at OISE, University of Toronto. His current teaching and research focuses on youth civic engagement and activism, educating for the global dimension of citizenship, and comparative perspectives and practices in teacher education programs and accreditation processes. He is involved in a variety of education reform initiatives and research projects, locally and internationally. Additional information may be found at: http://www.oise.utoronto.ca/ctl/Faculty_Staff/Faculty_Profiles/1577/Mark_Evans.html.

Joseph P. Farrell was a professor in the Department of Curriculum, Teaching, and Learning at OISE, University of Toronto, for over 30 years. Dr. Farrell's areas of specialization included comparative and international education; planning education for social development, especially in developing countries; comparative teacher development; education policy studies; and evaluation of reform projects. He was a co-founder and dedicated contributor to the Comparative, International, and Development Education program at OISE and an Honorary Fellow of the Comparative and International Education Society (CIES) in the United States. Dr. Farrell passed away on December 8, 2012, at the age of 73. He is greatly missed.

Ruth Hayhoe is a professor at OISE, University of Toronto. Her professional engagements in Asia included foreign expert at Fudan University (1980–82), head of the cultural section of the Canadian Embassy in Beijing (1989–91), and director of the Hong Kong Institute of Education (1997–2002). Recent books include *Canadian Universities in China's Transformation: An Untold Story* (2016) and *China Through the Lens of Comparative Education* (2015). She has received many honours, including the Silver Bauhinia Star of the Hong Kong SAR Government (2002) and Commandeur dans l'ordre des Palmes académiques of the Government of France (2002).

About the Contributors

Kara Janigan has specialized in issues of gender as a teacher, teacher educator, curriculum developer, and researcher for over two decades. She has worked as a gender specialist for education projects in Central Asia (Tajikistan), Southeast Asia (Bangladesh and India), and sub-Saharan Africa (Eritrea, Ethiopia, Malawi, and Zimbabwe) for organizations such as CARE, UNICEF, and USAID. Holding a PhD in Comparative, International, and Development Education from OISE, University of Toronto, she is an adjunct professor at the Middlebury Institute of International Studies at Monterey (MIIS) and a visiting scholar at OISE.

Dina Kiwan is an associate professor at the American University of Beirut. Educated at the Universities of Oxford, Harvard, and London, she was previously a senior lecturer in Citizenship Studies at Birkbeck College, University of London, and co-director of the International Centre for Education for Democratic Citizenship (ICEDC). Her research program focuses on citizenship and civil society, extending across the domains of education, gender, human rights, immigration, and naturalization. She co-authored a curriculum guiding framework on Global Citizenship Education for UNESCO (2014) with Mark Evans, University of Toronto. She has recently completed conducting research for an Oxfam-funded project on women's participation and leadership in Lebanon, Jordan, and northern Iraq.

Jun Li is deputy director of the Education Policy Unit at the University of Hong Kong, and currently serves as chairman of the Hong Kong Educational Research Association. He is a past president of the Comparative Education Society of Hong Kong. He leads an ear-marked UGC/GRF research project on China-Africa University Partnerships in Education and Training and other projects, such as the Global Ranking Regime and the Mission of Higher Education: Comparative Case Studies of Research Assessment Exercises in Four Systems. His publications include *Quest for World-Class Teacher Education? A Multiperspectival Study on the Chinese Model of Policy Implementation* (2016) and *Portraits of 21st Century Chinese Universities* (2011).

Katia Sol Madjidi (PhD, OISE–University of Toronto) is the co-director of the Ecology of Leadership program at the Regenerative Design Institute in Bolinas, California, and an adjunct professor of International Education Management at the Middlebury Institute for International Studies at Monterey. Her areas of specialization include transformative education, Indigenous ways of knowing, and the dynamics of global change. She has more than 20 years' experience working and conducting research around the world, including in numerous Indigenous communities. For more information and to contact her, please visit www.katiasol.com.

Caroline Manion is an Assistant Professor, Teaching Stream, Comparative, International, and Development Education at the Ontario Institute for Studies in Education, University of Toronto. Her research interests include equity and social justice, teach development, school improvement, gender and education, the politics of education, and educational multilateralism and governance. Dr. Manion's research has been supported by a variety of agencies and organizations, including the Social Sciences and Humanities Research Council of Canada, the International Development Research Centre of Canada, and the Canadian International Development Agency (now Global Affairs Canada), and she has provided contract services, including educational program development and evaluation, for such groups as the Aga Khan Foundation, the United Nations Girls' Education Initiative, the Hewlett Foundation, UNESCO, and Open Society Foundation.

Vandra Lea Masemann is an anthropologist who has worked in the fields of comparative education, multicultural and anti-racist education, and international and global education. Her PhD thesis was an ethnography of a girls' boarding school in West Africa, and she has devoted a considerable portion of her career to advocating the uses of ethnographic and other qualitative methods in research in comparative education. She established the Gender and Education Committee while president of the Comparative and International Education Society (1989). She is presently adjunct associate professor at OISE, University of Toronto.

Karen Mundy is a professor of International and Comparative Education at the University of Toronto (on leave) and the chief technical officer and director of strategy, policy, and performance for the Global Partnership for Education (2014–17), a multi-stakeholder partnership whose mission is to ensure good quality education to children in the developing world. Her published research has focused on the global politics of "education for all" programs and policies; educational policy and reform in sub-Saharan Africa; and the role of civil society organizations in educational change. She has published five books and more than 50 articles and chapters.

Sarfaroz Niyozov is currently the director of the Institute for Educational Development (IED) at the Aga Khan University, and is a professor with the Department of Curriculum, Teaching, and Learning at OISE, University of

Toronto (on leave). His research interests focus on teaching, researching, teacher development, and education reform in developing, Muslim, and post-Communist contexts; and global education, international, and comparative curriculum studies/education. Dr. Niyozov has written extensively about education in post-Soviet countries and the experiences of teachers working with Muslim students in multicultural classrooms.

Robyn Read is a PhD candidate and Canada Graduate Scholar studying comparative, international, and development education at OISE, University of Toronto. Her research interests centre on the global governance of education, and her work focuses on knowledge mobilization and education policy in the developing world, with a specific interest in how research influences policy in educational development.

Julia Resnik (PhD, Tel Aviv University) is a senior lecturer at the School of Education in the Hebrew University of Jerusalem. Her main research areas are globalization of education policies, comparative education, multiculturalism, migrant children, and international education. She and other Israeli scholars have started a study on global citizenship education as part of a large international project. She has recently edited a special issue on "The Power of Numbers and Networks: Understanding the Mechanisms of Diffusion of Educational Models" in *Globalisation, Society and Education*. Dr. Resnik has published many articles in English-speaking but also in francophone peer-reviewed journals.

Jean-Paul Restoule (Ansishinaabe, Dokis First Nation) is an associate professor of Aboriginal Education at OISE, University of Toronto. He co-founded SAGE Ontario, a peer support group for graduate students whose research involves Aboriginal communities, and is an original member of the OISE working group to infuse teacher education with Aboriginal perspectives called *Deepening Knowledge, Enhancing Instruction*. His current research involves studying the adoption of Indigenous education by new and continuing teachers and looking at the ways Indigenous knowledge and education are carried out in online environments.

Santiago Rincón-Gallardo is the chief research officer at Michael Fullan's international consulting team and a visiting scholar at OISE, University of Toronto. His academic work explores how effective pedagogies for deep learning can spread at scale. He advises system leaders and educators around whole system reform. As an educator and organizer, he worked for over a decade to promote grassroots educational change initiatives in Mexican public schools serving historically marginalized communities. He holds an EdM in International Education Policy and an EdD in Education Policy, Leadership, and Instructional Practice from Harvard.

Malini Sivasubramaniam completed her PhD at the University of Toronto with a specialization in Comparative, International, and Development Education. Her dissertation examines household decision-making in low-fee private schools in Kenya. She is currently a visiting scholar with the Comparative, International, and Development Education Centre at OISE, University of Toronto. Her research interests include the privatization of education, school choice and equity for marginalized communities, and faith-based non-state actors in education.

INDEX

A
Abed, Fazle Hasan, 218, 224
Abernathy, David, 308, 309
Aboriginal people
　See also Indigenous knowledge;
　　Indigenous ways of knowing
　　and learning
　Aboriginal, as term, 156
　gender inequality and education,
　　202, 203, 206
　matriarchal societies, 202, 203
　medicine wheel, 161, 162*f*, 164,
　　166, 175, 176,
　residential school(s), 157, 202,
　　269
　restorative justice, 173, 283
Abu-Nimer, Mohammed, 278
Accelerated Schools, 129
accountability policies, 133, 136–141
Achebe, Chinua, 310
achievement gaps, 376, 394
active pedagogy, 66, 80, 102
Adivasi communities, 220*t*
Adult Literacy and Lifeskills (ALL)
　Survey, 383*t*
adult literacy rate(s), 68t, 91t, 192,
　367,368
Afghanistan, 72, 92*f*, 107, 108, 130,
　208, 212, 213, 224
Africa
　crisis of educational
　　development, 312–316
　debt, 313
　Education for All, 316–319

educational infrastructure,
　313–314
educational reforms, 315–321
Eritrea, 193–196, 194*f*, 198–199, 395
free primary education promises,
　319–324
gender disparities, 191–192, 318
out-of-school children, 190,
　318–319, 322
primary school enrolments, 312
Structural Adjustment Programs,
　314
sub-Saharan Africa, 190, 191, 192,
　312, 317, 318, 319, 395, 396
West Africa, 16, 309, 312, 396
African socialism, 310, 319,321
Aga Khan, 102, 107, 111
Aga Khan Foundation, 130, 396
Aga Khan University Institute for
　Educational Development, 130,
*Agence pour l'enseignement français à
　l'étranger (AEFE),* 337
aid (to education), 308, 316–319, 380
AIDS/HIV, 254, 318, 323
Albania, 280
Alberta, 381, 383
Alexander, Czar of Russia, 4
Allport, Gordon, 278
Altbach, Philip, 16
alternative approaches to education,
　312
　BRAC Non-Formal Primary
　　Education Program
　　(Bangladesh), 67, 72, 75*f*

community education and
community schools, 60, 66
Escuela Nueva, Colombia, 67,
70–71, 73, 75f, 77, 79, 82
Learning Community Project, 67,
71, 73, 75f,
alternative school movement, 65
American Indian, as term, 156
Anderson, Stephen, 13,18, 62,
119–151, 314, 393
Anderson-Levitt, Kathryn, 19
Anglicized Indians, 216, 217
Anglophone countries, 349
anthropological research methods
(ethnography), 188
anti-bias, anti-discriminatory
education, 273
anti-racist (and) multicultural
education, 20, 281,396
anti-sexist philosophies and
initiatives, 206
Anti-colonial (movements),213
Antonopoulos, Antonia, 81
Arab States, 191–192, 246
Argentina, 347
Aristotle, 33
armed conflict. *See* violence
Arnove, Robert, 16, 19
Asia, 3,10,17,43, 337, 338, 349,
353, 394
West Asia, 190, 192
Asia Pacific region, 339
assessments
domestic assessment programs,
378
international assessments. *See*
international assessments
Association of Southeast Asian
Nations (ASEAN), 18,249
audio-visual resources, 21, 52, 81,
114, 145, 177, 207, 229, 258, 287,
326, 357, 371, 387

Australia, 133,134, 156, 179, 212, 278,
279, 339, 344, 345–347, 358, 370
Australian Aborigines, 157, 278
Austria, 340

B
Back to School (PBS), 326
Badakhshan Autonomous Province
of Tajikistan. *See* Tajikistan
Bangladesh, 67–70, 72, 76, 79–82,
129, 134, 135, 191, 212, 214,
217–219, 224–228, 367, 395
Dhaka, Bangladesh, 218
See also alternative models; BRAC
Non-Formal Primary Education
Program (Bangladesh)
banking education (Freire), 216, 311
barefoot lawyers, 219, 224, 226–227
Basmachis, 110
Battiste, Marie, 159–160
Beijing, China, 14, 48, 50, 394
Bereday, George, 10, 13
Bickmore, Kathy, 17, 20, 268–299, 393
bilateral developmental aid, 308
bilingual schools, 287, 340, 345, 348
Bosnia and Herzegovina 274,276
BRAC Non-Formal Primary
Education Program (Bangladesh),
67, 72, 73, 75f, 77, 79, 81, 82, 129,
130, 212, 214, 217–219, 224–229,
226t
Brazil, 240, 340, 345, 377
Britain, British
British Council, 246, 258
Department for International
Development, 131
effective schools movement, 122
National Curriculum, 354
social history of schooling, 305
socio-economic status, 309
standards and accountability
approach, 136

Index 401

British colonies, colonial, 43, 216
British Columbia, 176, 380, 381, 383
Buddhism, 3, 31, 33, 37, 46
bullying. *See* violence
Burundi, 320*f*
Bhutan, 212

C

Cajete, Gregory, 162, 165
Cambridge International
  Examinations, 338
Canada
  alternative school movement, 65
  gender inequality in education,
    202–206
  global citizenship education,
    242–245, 256
  home-schooling movement, 65
  Indigenous models, 156–158, 163
  international
    assessments, 381–382, 382t
  international indicators, 380–384,
    385
  PISA results, 376–377, 381, 384
  sex-role stereotyping, 205
  standards and accountability
    approach, 136,
  teacher training institutions, 204
  testing, 136, 138
  wage gap, 206
Canadian International Development
  Agency (CIDA), 9, 243, 308, 396
Canadian Royal Commission on
  Aboriginal Peoples, 163
CARE, 395
Caribbean, 192
Carnoy, Martin, 15, 310
Career-related (education, programs,
  Programme), 339
caste discrimination, 220, 220t, 222
Castellano, Marlene Brant, 161
Central Asia

  See also Tajikistan
  culture, 88, 90, 94, 107, 111
  Muslim traditions, 102
  Pedagogy and teaching, 95–103,
    104–105
  Soviet educational culture,
    influence 102
  subject matter, 103–104
  teachers as reformers, 94, 110
Chicago, United States, 48, 50, 127
child-centred, learner-centred
  pedagogy, 89, 171, 277
child labour, 220*t*, 213, 228
child marriage, 211, 212, 226
child socialization
  and gender, 184
  in East Asia, 49
  political socialization, 275
  schooling and, 306
children's rights, 220*t*, 221, 239
Chile, 133, 217, 277, 347, 370
China
  See also East Asia; Taiwan
  American-style schooling
    structure, 40–41
  Chinese classical thought, 31
  civil service examination system,
    33, 47
  Communist revolution, 14, 41, 45
  Confucian heritage, 39, 40, 52
  Cultural Revolution, 14, 41, 44
  decentralization, adoption of,
    40–42
  early history of education, 3–4
  educational reforms, 40–42
  educational ideas, educators'
    search for alternatives 5, 6
  European models and values,
    influence 30–36, 39
  human capital theory,
    introduction of, 15
  May 4th Movement of 1919, 39

modern educational system,
  development of, 36, 39–42
  Nationalist Revolution, 39
  social order, 31, 35
  teachers in, 42
Cicero, 3
CIDA. *See* Canadian International
  Development Agency (CIDA)
citizenship education
  citizenship theory, 276
  core themes, 237t
  global citizenship. *See* global
    citizenship education
  teachers, 239, 240
  views of, 234, 235
Cold War, 30, 41, 42, 45–46, 215, 308,
  373
Coleman, James. 309
Colombia, 10, 67– 71, 79–80, 82, 129,
  282, 284, 367
  See also alternative models;
    Escuela Nueva, Colombia
colonial education, 202, 311
colonialism, colonization, 29, 30,
  91,174,179, 202, 307
Communist party, 34, 42, 103
Communist revolution, 14, 41, 45
community-based (organizations
  and educators), 212, 214
Community Rights Implementation
  Committee, 211
community schools, 60, 66
Comparative and International
  Education Society (CIES), 9,170
Comparative Education Society, 9
Comparative Education Society of
  Asia, 9
Comparative Method in Education
  (Bereday), 10
comparative research
  anthropological research
    methods, ethnography, 188

comprehensive school reform
  movement (CSR), 129–130
decentralization, 127–128
national governments,
  importance of, 19
private schools, 133–136,141
qualitative research, 188, 193
school-based management,
  127–128
school choice policies, 133–134
school improvement, 120–122
schooling in non-Western world,
  304–307
standards and accountability
  approach, 139–141
competition-driven educational
  reforms, 315–316
comprehensive school reform
  movement (CSR), 128–130, 144
compulsory schooling, 305, 307, 315
Comte, Auguste, 6
Conceptions of Citizenship
  Education model, 243
conflict
  See also violence
  armed conflict, 254, 269, 271, 274,
    285
  civil war(s), 40, 109, 269
  conflict cycle, 270
  identity-based conflicts, 277
  inter-group (ethnic) conflict, 275
  learning, effect on, 270
  meaning of, 268
  prejudice, anti-bias education,
    278–279
conflict resolution
  See also peace
  dialogue, 278–279
  inter-group contact, 278–279, 281,
    285
  narratives and history education,
    276–278

Index

peace and conflict education, 272–275
pedagogical practices, 270–274
conflict theory, 188
Confucian heritage societies, 36, 46, 51, 52
Confucianism, 37, 46
Confucius, 3, 31–32
conscientization (Freire), 16, 227, 272, 311
constructivist teaching and learning, 80, 354
contact hypothesis, contact theory, 278, 280
Convention on the Elimination of All Forms of Discrimination against Women (CEDAW), 185–186, 226t
corporal punishment, 191, 221,222
cosmopolitan citizenship, cosmopolitanism, 236, 241, 345, 354
cost-sharing policies, 321–322
Costa Rica, 269
Council of Ministers of Education Canada (CMEC), 380–381, 383
Council of Public Instruction regulation, 204
Cousin, Victor, 5
Couture, Joseph, 160, 172
critical consciousness, 214, 217, 228, 240
critical sociology, 305
Cuba, 272
cultural imperialism, 15–17, 303,306,310
Cultural Revolution, 14, 41,44
culture, 88, 90, 107,111, 236, 255, 275, 337, 348, 352
culture of peace. *See* peace
Cummings, William, 39
Cyprus, 274

D

Daoism, 31, 37
Das Kapital (Marx), 14
data collection. *See* educational statistics; international indicators
Davies, Lynn, 236, 279
decentralization, 38, 70, 91, 125, 126–128, 144, 343, 373, 375
Declaration on Human Rights Education and Training, 215
dehumanization, 271,276,281
Dei, George J.S., 17, 162,310
Delpit, Lisa, 222
Denmark, 12, 340
Deng Xiaoping, 14, 42, 44
dependency theory, 10, 15–16, 46, 189
developing countries,
development
  aid to education, 308–309, 380
  critical approach to education, 17
  cyclical school improvement planning,125
  educational innovation, history of, 120–122
  international assessment and indicator projects, 379–380
  national curricula, 72–73
  neo-colonialism, 310
  pedagogical models, 354
  relevance of comparative education findings, 9–10
  school-based management, 127–128
  schooling and national development, 308
  schools and social equality, 309
developmental aid, 15, 307–308, 322
Dewey, Alice, 40
Dewey, John, 7, 8, 31, 34, 40, 79, 240
dialogue, 278–279
dialogue among civilizations, 30, 46, 51

Diploma Programme (DP), 339, 3340, 344, 345
discrimination, 273
division of labour, 183–184

E
early marriage, 196–197, 199
East Asia
 See also specific East Asian countries
 capitalism, model of, 30
 comparative studies, 44–45, 47–51
 Confucian heritage societies, 36, 46, 51, 52
 dependency theory, challenges to, 46
 effort vs. ability, 49–50
 human capital, 44–45
 learning experiences of children, 48–50
 modern educational development, 36–51
 paradoxes in East Asian learning, 51–52
 socialization, 49–50
 teachers in, 50
 vs. Western educational values, 30–36
 world system perspective, 45–46
Eckstein, Max, 10, 13
economic development, 1, 6, 11, 15, 46, 224, 303, 342
economic growth, 44, 305, 308–310, 315, 323, 372, 373
Ecuador, 339, 347, 348
Educating for Global Citizenship, 245–247
education
 See also comparative and international education
 Cold War, 30, 41, 42, 45–46, 308, 373
 and economic development, 11
 and economic growth, 308
 international consensus, 317, 371
 right to education, in world historical perspective, 304–307
 and violence, 269–270
education fever, 339
Education and the Colonial Experience (Kelly and Altbach), 16
Education as Cultural Imperialism (Carnoy), 15
Education at a Glance (OECD), 374
Education for All (EFA)
 girls, enrolment of, 189
 global initiatives, 190
 Global Monitoring Report, 192, 369
 In Kenya, 319–324
 revival in Africa, 316–319
 in Tanzania, 319–324
 World Conference on Education for All, 316
"Education for Self-Reliance" (Nyerere), 311
Education in Sub-Saharan Africa (World Bank), 315
Education Through Imagination (Antonopoulos), 81
Education Yearbook, 365
educational achievement, 11, 46, 52, 363, 369
educational aid, 307–308
educational borrowing, 5, 59
educational policy
 cost-sharing policies, 321
 equal opportunity, 185, 325
educational convergence, 214
educational reforms
 Africa, 315
 Canada, 243–245, 381
 China, 41–42
 competition-driven, 315–316
 developing countries, 314

Index

failed attempts, in United States, 62
global reform agendas, 18–19
globalization, 314
Indigenous ways of knowing and learning, incorporation of, 170–171
Japan, post-war reforms in, 38
Kenya, 321
macroeconomic reforms, 315
as nation-building, 93
Tanzania, 321
"teacher-proof," 78
educational statistics
current statistics for girls and boys, 189–193
and educational policy, 363
in Eritrea, 193–196
gender parity, 184, 190–192
international indicators. See international indicators
misuse of statistics, 363–364, 368
usefulness of, 363
EFA. *See* Education for All (EFA)
effective schools movement, 122–125
Elementary Teachers' Federation of Ontario, 205
Emerging alternative model *vs* formal schooling, 61–67, 63–64*t*
England. *See* Britain
Ensor, Beatrice, 7
Environment, environmental rights, 220*t*
epistemology
See Indigenous ways of knowing and learning
Western vs. Indigenous frameworks, 158–159
equalitarianism, 186–188
Eritrea, 184, 193–201, 206, 395
Ermine, Willie, 160
Escuela Nueva, Colombia, 67, 70–71, 72–73, 75*f*, 76, 77, 79, 82, 129, 284

Ethiopia, 72, 193, 194*f*, 208, 320*f*, 395
ethnic identity, 281
Eurocentric models of education, 158, 159
Europe
European models, 29
China, influences on, 39–40
diverse educational contributions, 3–4
Plato, 31–34
state schooling systems, 29
European Community, 18, 93
European countries, 5, 340, 341
European Union, 337
Evans, Mark, 20, 234–267, 394, 395
experiential learning, 165, 240, 255

F
family resources, support, 49, 134, 191, 195–196
Fanon, Frantz, 310
Farrell, Joseph P., 11, 13, 18, 20, 59–87, 129, 225, 312, 363–398
fathers, 196–197
Federation of Women Teachers' Association of Ontario, 205
feminist approaches, 16
feminist standpoint theory, 187–188
First International Mathematics Study, 369
foreign aid, 317, 322, 380
Foster, Philip, 309
France
centralized educational system, 8
entry examinations to Grandes Écoles, 4
free primary education (FPE), 123, 320, 322, 326
Freire, Paulo, 16, 168, 216, 217, 218, 226, 228, 240, 272, 273, 311
French-Israeli school, 338
Frochel, Hans, 168

Fullan, Michael, 65, 140, 142, 145, 397
functionalist arguments, functionalism 305–306

G

Galtung, Johan, 17,45,269,271
Gandhi, Mahatma, 217,228,311
Gardner, Howard, 79
Gellner, Ernest, 271
Gender and gender equity
  anti-sexist philosophies and initiatives, 206
  Canada, gender inequality in education in, 202–206
  definitions of gender, 183, 184
  educational statistics, 189–193
  disparities at secondary school level, 192
  Eritrea case study. *See* Eritrea
  Gender bias, 204
  gender differences, 355, 367
  gender discrimination, bias, 184, 220t, 222
  gender equity, 184, 189–190, 206, 319
  gender inequality and Aboriginal people, 202–206
  gender parity, 184,190–192
  human reproduction, 184
  liberal equalitarian assumptions about, 206
  out-of-school children, 190
  sex-role stereotyping, 205
  social construction of, 183
  equalitarianism, 186–188
  feminist standpoint theory, 187–188
  postmodernist approach, 188–189
  theoretical approaches, 184–189
Geneva, 7, 177, 215, 339,
Geneva Declaration for the Rights of the Child, 7
Genocide, genocidal violence, 277
Germany, 4–7, 10, 12, 39, 134, 340, 370, 373, 377
Ghana, 131,135,188
Global Campaign for Education (GCE), 213
global citizenship education
  social justice citizenship, 236
  attention to global dimensions in education, 234–235
  UNESCO, 247–253
  In the Arab World, 245–247
  Canadian schools, 242–245
  contrasting perspectives and challenges, 253–257
  core themes, 237t
  current characterizations, evolving understandings, 235–241, 274–280
  educational approaches, 241–257
  teaching and learning goals, 245–250
  implementation, 256–257
  multiple citizenship, 278–279
  teaching practices, 239–240
  worldmindedness, 237t, 238,241
Global Classroom Initiative (CIDA), 283
Global Education Centres, 243
Global Education Digest, 365
Global teachers, 346, 349
globalization
  Africa, crisis of educational development in, 312–316
  challenge to traditional focus, 18
  and comparative education, 17–20
  definitions of, 17
  dialectic between local and global, 19
  and East Asia, 46
  economic globalization, 18, 313

Index

educational reforms, 18, 314–315
  effect of, 10
  fiscal constraint, 18
  skeptic approaches, 317
  international assessments
    and, 373–380
  local communities and, 19
  postcolonial theories
    regarding, 19
  pro-economic approaches,
    317
  transnational advocacy, 321
Greece, 3, 31–32, 281
Gross National Income (GNI), 68,
  68t, 91t, 193, 367
Gu Mingyuan, 13–15, 44
Guatemala, 277
Guinea, 272
Guinea-Bissau, 272

H
Hague Agenda for Peace and Justice for the 21st Century, 273
Halsey, A.H., 309. *See* Britain
Hampton, Eber, 166, 170
Hans, Nicholas, 6
harambee, 320
Hayhoe, Ruth, 1–26, 29–58, 394
Henderson, James (Sákéj)
  Youngblood, 166
Bosnia & Herzegovina, 276
hidden curriculum, 250
history education, 277–276
comparative education, history of,
  2–20
  and gender, 183, 217–218
  and school improvement,
    innovation 119–122
Holland, 4, 5, 6
Holmes, Brian, 13, 29–31, 34
home-schooling, 65, 71
Hong Kong
  See also East Asia

Cantonese dialect, 44
Confucian heritage societies, 30,
  36, 46
decolonization, 36–37
educational investments, 44
imperialism, effects of, 46
Mandarin dialect, 44
development of modern
  educational system, 30, 36,
  43–44
honouring (ceremonies), 167
Horio, Teruhisa, 38
Hudson, Anne Hickling, 19,
human capital (theory), 14–15,
  187,308
  East Asia, educational
    investments in, 44–45
Human Resources and Skills
  Development Canada (HRSDC),
  380–381, 384
human rights education (HRE),
  211–229
human rights and legal education
  [HRLE], 211,212, 225, 226, 227
Human Rights and Legal Services
  (HRLS), 225, 227, 231
Hungary, 133,281
Husen, Torsten, 369,372

I
IB (International Baccalaureate)
  advanced certificate in Leadership
    Research, 355
  IB certificate in Leadership
    Practice,355
ideal types, 13, 29–30, 34–35, 51,66
identity, identities, 277, 281–282
Illich, Ivan, 218, 310
imperialism, 6, 14–17, 30, 36, 44–45,
  52, 254, 306, 310
India
  Bridge International Academies,
    131

citizen-led assessments,379
colonial India, 216–217
Human Rights Education (HRE),
  211, 213, 214–224, 225
low-fee private schools, 135–136
lower castes, violence against, 276
People's Watch, 222, 218–220,
  222, 228, 229
out-of-school children, 190
South Asia, 212–213, 216–217
literacy and gender, 217
Indian state of Kerala, 217
Indian state of Tamil Nadu,220
Indigenous, as term, 156
See also Aboriginal people;
Indigenous group, 156, 161, 221
Indigenous ways of knowing and
  learning, 19, 155
  Indigenous knowledges,
    categories of: traditional,
    empirical, oral, 165–167
  vs. imported, Eurocentric
    educational systems, 157–159,
    167
  Learning and knowledge, 159–164
  purpose of knowledge, 169–170
  representation of, in comparative
    education, 155–156
  The fourth way, 170–172
    Epistemology, 156, 158–160,
    164–168, 174
  human relationship with the
    earth, 163
  implications for teachers, 174–176
  worldviews, 160, 164
  language, 166
  life-wide and lifelong education
    and learning, 164
  educational reform, 174
  medicine wheel, 161, 162f, 164,
    166, 175f, 176
  sense of place, 161–162

spiritual dimension of education,
  160, 166
Indigenous education infusion
  (initiatives), 166, 168, 169, 172,
  173, 175f, 176
indoctrination, 97t, 102, 273
information technology, 369
inner school segmented market,
  348–349
innovation, adoption and
  implementation, 2,17, 94, 113,
  119–122, 129, 143, 144, 246, 314
intercultural (studies), 338
Institute for Human Rights
  Education (IHRE), 220–224
integrated schools, 280
integration, 17, 29, 216, 249, 277,
  306, 340, 342, 344
integrity, 106–108
inter-group, ethnic, identity-based
  conflict, 259, 275
inter-group contact, 278–279, 281,
  285
intergovernmental (organizations),
  8, 18
international aid, 308,322
International assessments
  Adult Literacy and Lifeskills
    Survey, 383t
  large-scale assessment, birth of,
    369–373
  Canada, a guide to, 382t–383t
  criticisms, 385–386
  in developing world, 379–380
  globalization and politics of
    league tables, 373–380
  International Association for the
    Evaluation of Educational
    Achievement (IEA), 11, 369,
    370, 371, 372, 373, 374, 375
  large-scale assessment, 373–380
  regional indicator and
    assessment programs, 379

Index

International Baccalaureate (IB), 335, 336, 337, 338, 339, 340, 342, 343, 344, 345, 348, 355
International Bureau of Education (IBE), 7–8, 271, 365
International Civics and Citizenship Study (ICCS), 381, 382t
international consensus about education, 317, 371, 382t
International education, evolution of, 338–341
International General Certificate of Secondary Education (GCSE), 338
international indicators
 Indicators, definition and description, 364–369
 Canada and, 380–384
 described, 364
 growth in funding, 369
 literacy rates, 367–368
 what teachers need to know, 385
International English-medium schools, 348
International Institute for Comparative Education, 5
International League for New Education, 7
International Monetary Fund (IMF)
 advocacy against, 315, 316–317
 belt tightening and liberalization reforms, 314
 education, renewed attention on, 317
 impact of IMF conditionalities, 315
 pro-economic globalization approaches, 317
International schools
 evolution of, 336–338
 International American schools, 348
Internationalization of schooling, 335–336, 340–341, 355

Globalization and internationalization, 341–342
International Standard Classification of Education (ISCED), 365–366t
Inuit, 156
Iraq, 395
Ireland, 5, 254, 274, 276, 279, 347. *See also* Northern Ireland
Islam(ic), 69, 92, 94, 95, 102, 104, 110, 111
Ismaili Muslim, 90,102
Israel, 274, 276, 278, 279, 280, 338, 341, 370
 French/Franco-Israel(i) schools, 337, 338, 345
Italy, 7,12, 39

J
Jadid, 102
Japan
 See also East Asia
 China, influenced by influences on, 39–41
 Confucian heritage societies, 36, 46, 51, 52
 Dewey's ideas, 34
 Education in, 37–39
 "examination hell," 39
 imperialism, experiences of, 45
 Meiji Enlightenment, 37, 39
 modern educational system, development of, 36–39
 teachers in, 38
 history text, 277
Jefferson, Thomas, 4
Johns Hopkins University, 129
joint venture programs, 340
Jordan, 246, 395
Jullien, Marc Antoine, 4, 5, 6, 15, 45
Justice
 restorative, 283
 retributive, punitive, 324
 transitional, 282

K
Kandel, Isaac, 7–8, 10
Kelly, Gail P., 16
Kenya
   Aga Khan Foundation-sponsored initiatives, 130
   cost-sharing policies, 321
   Education for All (EFA), Tanzania and Kenya, 304, 319–324
   free primary education promises, 322
   harambee, 320
   low-fee private school, 135
   neoliberal economic and educational reforms, 321
   out-of-school children, 190
   quality of learning, 323
   user fees in health and education, 314
   student enrolment, 323
   Tanzania, contrasted with, 319–325
Khusraw, Nasir, 102, 111
King, Edmund, 12
Knowledge
   Confucius, 32
   Dewey, 34, 35
   empirical knowledge, 165
   See also Indigenous knowledge
   Plato, 32–34
   purpose of knowledge, 169
   revealed knowledge, 165
   in Soviet Communism, 35
   traditional knowledge, 164, 171
   Western, Eurocentric evaluation of knowledge, 167
Korea
   See also East Asia
   Confucian heritage societies, 36, 46, 51, 52
   Japan, colonization by, 36, 37, 43, 45
   modern educational system, development of, 36–39
Kosovo, 274, 276
Kyrgyzstan
   See also Central Asia, 90–95
   pedagogies, teaching styles, 95–103

L
language, 86, 136, 145
   Aboriginal, 166
   English-language, 69, 91, 340, 346, 347, 348, 349, 354,
   Local language(s), 95,100t, 103,218, 348
Lao Zi, 31,33
Latin America
   Conscientization see also Freire, 16, 272, 311
   democratic and peacemaking education, 284
   dependency theory, 16–17
   educational improvement, 121–122
   gender disparities, 192
   government transitions, 249
   Indigenous populations, communities, 69
   violence levels, 272, 282
   literacy levels, 368–369
   regional indicator and assessment programs, 379
Latin American Laboratory for Evaluating the Quality of Education, 379
Lê Thàn Khôi, 13–14
League of Nations, 7
league tables, 383–386, 373, 375
Lederach, John Paul, 274, 275
legal aid, 224, 225, 227
legal literacy, 224
Lertzman, David, 164, 166

Index

liberal equalitarian, 206
literacy
   adult literacy rate(s), 91*t*, 192, 367, 368
   China, 40
   gender disparities, 192
   Latin America, 368–369
   lowest rates 192
   mathematical, scientific, and reading literacy, 373, 375, 382*t*
   PISA definition, 374
Little Bear, Leroy, 160,162
low-fee (private) schools, 135, 136, 324, 348, 398

M

Maarifa ni Ufunguo, 321
Macao
   See also East Asia
   comparative reflections, 44–46
   Confucian heritage, 36, 46
   modern educational system, development of, 36–37
   Portuguese colonial legacy, 46
Macedonia, 280
macroeconomic reforms, 315
Madjidi, Katia Sol, 19, 80, 155–182, 310, 395
Mainland China.
   See China
   Education in Mainland China and Taiwan, 39–42
Mak, Grace, 17
Malawi
   free primary education,123
   macroeconomic reforms, 315
Maldives, 212
mandatory standards. *See* standards and accountability
Mann, Horace, 5
Mao Zedong, 41
Maori *Nga hau e wha,* 161

Marginalized groups, communities, 79, 214, 221, 229, 398, 212, 216, 269, 319
market choice, market-driven, 132, 339, 344
Marx, Karl, 14, 31, 34
   Marxist perspective
      feminist critique, 188
      See neo-Marxist perspective
      on spread of schooling in West, 51
   conflict-free view of schooling, 305
masculine norms, masculinity, 89, 172, 204
Masemann, Vandra Lea, 12–13, 17, 19, 158, 170, 183–210, 396
mathematical literacy, 368, 375
matriarchal societies, 202–203
Mazrui, Ali, 17
McCauley, Clark, 273
McGlynn, Claire, 274, 280
McGregor, Deborah, 169
medicine wheel, 161–162*f*, 164, 166, 175, 176,
medieval period, 3–4
Meiji Enlightenment, 37, 39
Mencius, 31, 32
Merelman, Richard, 275
Middle class, 217, 222, 317, 335, 338, 344, 345
Middle Years Programme (MYP), 339
Millennium Development Goals (MDG), 190, 316, 319
Ministry/ministries of Education, 38, 50, 60, 71, 77, 193, 198, 284, 368, 243, 375, 380, 381
mobile teachers, 336, 346, 347, 349–351
   cultural challenges, 351–353
   pedagogical challenges, 353–355
   mobile teacher training, 355–356
   modernization theories, 308

Montessori, Maria, 79, 168, 171
Montessori, alternative schooling, 171
Mother Earth, 161, 166, 168
motivation for learning, 33
Muhammad, 102
multicultural, 10, 20, 235, 236, 281, 341, 353, 354, 393, 396, 397
multiculturalism, 2, 93, 236, 243, 335
Mundy, Karen, 1–26, 59, 79, 123, 159, 213, 303–334, 363–391, 396
Muslim (countries), 352

N
A Nation at Risk, 372, 373
national curriculum, 38, 40, 49, 50, 64*t*, 72, 277, 354
Nekhwevha, Fhulu, 164
neocolonial, 15
neo-colonialism, 310
neo-imperialism, 310
neoliberalism, neoliberal education policies, 236, 343, 344
neo-Marxist, 10, 16, 188, 306, 310
Nepal, 21, 191, 208, 212
nepotism, 107, 313
Netherlands, Dutch 114, 336, 340, 344, 345
New Zealand, 133, 143, 283, 346, 347, 377
Ngugi wa Thiong'o, 310
Nicaragua, 272
Nigeria, 131, 135, 190, 370
Niyozov, Sarfaroz, 13, 20, 88–118, 396
Nkrumah, Kwame, 310
No Child Left Behind, 138, 342
Noah, Harold, 10, 13
Nobel Peace Prize, 213, 230
Noddings, Nel, 79
non-formal education, 80, 219, 224, 230, 249, 255, 276, 322
non-governmental organizations (NGOs), 60, 134, 135, 213, 219, 228, 238, 317

normal school(s), 48, 204
North America. *See* Canada; United States
North Korea, 36*f*, 46
 See also Korea
Northern Ireland, 254, 274, 276, 279
Nyerere, Julius, 310, 311

O
Office of the High Commissioner for Human Rights (OHCHR), 215
Olson, David, 65
online resources and online teaching 176, 260
Ontario, 132, 138, 140, 145, 172, 175, 177, 184, 202, 203, 204, 205, 206, 344, 377, 380, 381, 383, 384, 393, 396, 397
Ontario Public School Teachers Federation, 205
Ontario Secondary School Teachers Federation, 205
Organisation for Economic Co-operation and Development (OECD), 18
 Education at a Glance, 374
 influence of, 18
Osborne, Ken, 243
Other Schools and Ours (King), 1, 12
out-of-school children, 190, 191, 318, 319, 322
Oxfam International, 259, 395

P
Pakistan, 70, 92*f,* 114, 116, 117, 130, 131, 134, 135, 147, 148, 149, 150, 190, 212, 213, 224, 230, 288, 337, 379, 393
Palestine, 246, 276, 289. *See also* Israel
parental support, 195–198
peace
 See also conflict resolution
 culture of peace, 272, 273

Index

peace and conflict education, 20, 272, 275
positive peace, 270, 271, 274
peacebuilding, community based, 266–268
peacekeeping, 271, 272, 274, 282, 284
peacemaking, 270, 271, 274, 281, 283, 284, 285
restorative justice, 173, 283
pedagogies
   See also Central Asia,
   child-centred, learner-centred, 80, 89, 171, 144,
   See also Indigenous ways of knowing and learning
   Pedagogy of the Oppressed (Paulo Freire), 217
   Soviet era pedagogy of cooperation, 101
Peking University, 40
People's Watch (human rights organization), 214, 217, 218, 220, 222, 228, 229
Perestroika, 100t, 102, 109
Peru, 208
Pestalozzi, Johann, 4, 79, 168
phenomenology, 12
Philippines, 6, 36f, 224
philosophy
   Chinese vs. Western educational values, 30–36
   Confucius, 3, 31–32
   Deweyan ideal type, 35
   ideal types, 13, 29, 30, 34, 35, 51, 66
   Marxist ideal type, 35
   Plato, Platonic ideal type, 35
Piaget, Jean, 8
PISA. *See* Programme for International Student Assessment (PISA)
Plato, 3, 31, 32, 33, 34, 35

Pluralism, pluralist, 220t, 243, 281
political development, 15, 308
political socialization (see socialization), 275
Polo, Marco, 3
Popper, Karl, 13
positivistic phase, 9
post-colonial (theories), 10, 19, 189
post-compulsory education, 12
postmodernism, postmodernist, 19, 186, 188
postmodernity, 10,
poverty, 43, 70, 218, 220t, 224, 268, 312
Preschool in Three Cultures: Japan, China and the United States (Tobin), 53
Primary Years Programme (PYP), 339
Programme for International Student Assessment (PISA), 11, 50, 53, 374, 375, 376, 377, 378, 379, 381, 382t, 283, 384, 385
Progress in Reading Literacy Study (PIRLS), 382t, 380, 381
Protestant Reformation, 33
Prussia, 5, 159, 305
lycée, public, 344

Q

qualitative research, (see also anthropological methods, ethnography), 184, 188, 192, 193, 206
Quebec, 66, 132, 243, 281, 381

R

racism, (*See* also anti-racist multicultural, anti-bias ed) 258, 273, 278,
Reardon, Betty, 273
   comparative education societies, 9
regional indicator and assessment programs, 379

regional organizations, 18–19
religious difference, intolerance, 220t
Report Card on child poverty, 369
Republic of Tajikistan. *See* Tajikistan
The Republic (Plato), 3
Restoule, Jean-Paul, 19, 80, 155–182, 310, 397
results-based school improvement plans, 141
revolution, 4, 16, 14, 39, 41, 44, 45, 59, 102, 217, 243
  indigenous rights, 220t
right to education, 2, 19, 213, 228, 230, 303, 304, 319, 324, 369
rites of passage, 164, 169, 178, 179,
role models, 49
Roma, 280
Ross, Marc, 269
Rossello, Pedro, 8
Rotton, Elisabeth, 7
Royal Commission on Learning in Ontario, 205
Royal Commission on the Status of Women in Canada, 205
Rudaki, 102, 111
Russia
  See also Central Asia; Soviet Union
  devaluation, and rewriting of history, 103
  educators' search for educational ideas, 5
  rural post-Soviet realities, 110
Rwanda, 320f, 276

S
sacred (practices), 166–167
The Sacred Tree, 161
Sadler, Michael, 5
safe schools (initiatives), 244
Satyarthi, Kailash, 213
School Act (Canada), 203

Schola Europaea, 337
school-based management (SBM), 170–173, 126–129, 144, 343
school choice, 125, 130, 132–133, 134, 144, 314, 375, 387, 398
school councils, 126, 127
school effectiveness, 122–125, 127, 144, 393
school improvement approaches, 170
  comprehensive school reform (CSR), 128–130
  conventional approach, 161
  corporate Actors, 130–131
  centralization and decentralization, 126–128
  effective schools, 122–125
  future of, 144
  historical perspective, 120–121, 122–125
  Low-Fee Private Schools, 135–136
  Professional learning communities and networks, 141–143
  progressive innovation, 121
school improvement plans, 125, 126, 137, 141
school-based management (SBM), 125, 126–127, 144, 343
standards and accountability-driven improvement, 136–141
school ranking and labelling, 138
school leadership, 135, 144, 393
school ranking, 201–205
schooling
  elite, 203, 304, 340, 345
  formal education, 61–67, 64t, 63t, 76, 77, 80, 212, 216, 242, 246, 247, 268, 275, 277, 282
  functionalist arguments, 305–306
  legitimation role, 306
  Marxist and critical sociological perspectives, 305

national development, 9, 306, 309
  in non-Western world, 306
  popular movements, 46, 306, 306
  refugees and war-affected
    children, 271
  spread of, in the West, 305–306
  world culture, world
    institutionalism (theory), 170,
    214, 306
  right to education, 50
Schultz, Theodore, 187
Schwartz, Benjamin, 31
science literacy, 208
scientific method, 9–14, 165
Scotland, 5
Sears, Alan, 2343
Second Information Technology in
  Education Study (SITES), 383*t*
Sendai, Japan, 48
sex-role stereotyping, 205
  See also gender
Shinto, Shintoism, 37
Sierra Leone, 72, 131, 208
Singapore
  See also East Asia
  Confucian heritage, 36
  modern educational system,
    development of, 36, 43–44
  social development, 34, 42, 48, 308,
    310, 319, 394
social equality, 19, 308, 309, 315
social (in)justice, 111, 213, 221, 236,
  237*t*, 238, 241, 250, 253*t*, 254, 255,
  257, 393, 396
social mobility, 33, 342, 344–345, 394
social movements, 19, 214, 220*t*
social order, 35, 111
social rates of return, 11
social reproduction, 189, 305, 392,
  344, 345
socialization. *See* child socialization
socio-economic status, 309, 367, 376

solidarity, 17, 229, 249, 250, 273, 281
Somalia, 72, 320*f*
South Africa, 133, 240, 258, 346, 347,
  393
South America, Latin America 69, 71,
  121, 192, 217, 249, 258, 347, 352,
  393
  See also Colombia, Mexico,
    various other countries
South Asia, 30, 121, 131, 149, 211,
  212, 213, 214, 216, 217, 218, 219,
  231
South Korea, 30, 44, 46, 357, 376
  See also Korea
  Dewey's ideas, 34
  modern educational system,
    development of, 36, 42–43
Southern and Eastern African
  Consortium for Monitoring
  Educational Quality (SACMEQ),
  379
South Sudan, 190, 224
Soviet Union, 4, 6, 36*f*, 37, 39, 91, 92*f*,
  103, 393
  See also Russia
  China, influences on, 41–42, 45
  collapse, effect of, 10, 103
  educational culture, 102
  moral and ethical aims of
    education,129
  patterns of modern Soviet
    education, 34
  Perestroika, 100*t*, 102, 109, 261
Spain, 337, 377, 386
Sri Lanka, 212, 258, 260, 276, 277,
  296
Stambach, Amy, 19
standardized testing, 133, 137, 140,
  377
standpoint theory, 187–188
The State of the World's Children
  (UNICEF), 192, 366

state-funded schools, 339, 340, 344, 345
(nation-)state schooling systems, 29
Statistical Yearbook, 365
Statistics Canada, 380, 381
Status of Women Canada, 205
Steiner-Khamsi, Gita, 20, 115, 259,
Stevenson, Harold, 48
Stigler, James, 48
Stromquist, Nelly P., 16
Strong-Boag, Veronica, 243
Structural Adjustment Programs, 314
structural theory of imperialism, 17, 45
structural violence, 269, 270, 271, 272
student-centred, learner-centred, 96, 102, 168, 239, 285, 354
Success for All (Johns Hopkins University), 129
Sun Yat Sen, 45
superordinate identities, 281
Sustainable Development Goals, 190, 213, 325, 380
student mobility, 354
student-teacher relationship, 105
Sweden, 12, 133, 134, 340, 370, 372

T
Taipei, Taiwan, 42–45, 48
Taiwan
  See also China; East Asia
  Confucian heritage, 39–42, 47–48
  Dewey's ideas, 34
  educational investments, 39
  Japan, colonization by, 36, 37, 45
  modern educational system, development of, 36, 39–42
  multi-party democracy, 40
Tajikistan
  See also Central Asia

  Teachers' moral commitment, vision and teaching, 106–108
  relevance, and teaching, 108–111
  rural post-Soviet realities, 110
  subject matter, 103–104
  teaching as relationships, 104–106
  teaching styles, pedagogical methods, 95–103
Tanzania
  African socialism, 319, 321
  Aga Khan Foundation-sponsored initiatives, 130
  cost-sharing policies, 321
  crisis of educational development, 321
  educational opportunity and benefits, 316, 320
  free primary education, 320, 322, 324, 326
  Julius Nyerere, 310, 311
  Kenya, contrasted with, 320
  neoliberal economic and educational reforms, 321
  primary school enrolments, 123, 190
  quality of learning, 323
  user fees in health and education, 314–316, 321, 322
Tawil, Sobhi, 271
Thailand, 36f, 316, 337, 340, 370, 379
teachers and teaching
  in alternative models, 63, 63t, 64t, 66
  authoritarian practices, 96
  pedagogical methods in Central Asia, 95–103
  teacher development and learning, in North America, 77–78
  disempowerment, 99
  in East Asia, 43
  gendered histories, 215

Index

in Japan, 38
relevance and context
  dimensions, 101–111
standards and accountability
  approach, 78, 139
teacher-centred and transmissive
  practices, 96, 97*t*,
  images of teachers, 88–90
teacher-centred learning/
  teaching, 54
teaching as relationships, 104–106
transactive teaching practices,
  100*t*
transformational/transformative
  teaching, 99, 100*t*
Western, Eurocentric methods, 165
Teacher job market, 336, 346–349
Teachers' unions, 19, 38, 76, 204, 205
Teasdale, Robert, 91
Tel Aviv, 337, 345, 397
television, 279, 280
terrorist, terrorism, 238, 269
Third World countries, 123
  See developing countries
time to study, 199–201
Tobin, Joseph, 53
*Towards a Science of Comparative
  Education* (Noah and Eckstein), 11
transformative human rights
  education, 214, 216, 218, 219,
  227, 228, 229
transnational advocacy
  (organizations), 321
transnational corporations, 336, 337
Trends in International Math and
  Sciences Study (TIMSS), 371, 373,
  382*t*
  Countries that participate, 373,
    379, 381
  Differences between PISA and
    TIMSS, 375
  TIMSS test, 375

Truth and Reconciliation
  Commission (TRC), 157, 278
Turkey, 91

U
ubuntu, 259
Uganda, 72, 123, 130, 131, 224, 320
UNESCO
  creation of, 304
  cross-national data collection and
    reporting, 365
  *Education for All Global Monitoring
    Report*, 92, 369
  functions, post World War II, 8
  Statistical Yearbook, 365
UNESCO Associated Schools, 337
UNESCO Institute for Statistics (UIS),
  366
UNICEF
  development aid, 58
  education, gradual inclusion of, 9
  gender, and educational data,
    189, 192
  Report Card on child poverty, 369
  The State of the World's Children,
    366
  See also alternative model case
    analysis
Union of Soviet Socialist Republics
  (USSR). *See* Soviet Union
United Indians of All Tribes
  Foundation, 171
United Arab Emirates, 337
United Kingdom. *See* Britain
  Global citizenship education, 247,
    341
United Nations (UN)
  Decade for Human Rights
    Education, 215, 220
  General Assembly, 215
  High Commissioner for Human
    Rights, 186, 215

United Nations Educational, Scientific, and Cultural Organization. *See* UNESCO
United Nations Children's Fund. *See* UNICEF
United Nations Convention of the Rights of the Child, 294, 237t, 238
United Nations Universal Declaration of Human Rights, 185, 213, 215, 304
United States
  alternative school movement, 65
  Chicago school district, 127
  China, influences on, 39–40
  Cold War and education, 308
  community responsibility, 40
  comparative studies, 5–6, 7, 9–10
  comprehensive school reform movement (CSR), 128–129
  decentralized educational administration, 126–127
  Dewey's ideas, 40
  educational reforms, failed attempts at, 62
  effective schools movement, 122
  equal education opportunity policies, 185
  home-schooling, 65, 171
  No Child Left Behind, 138, 342
  organization of schooling, 21
  school choice, voucher programs 134
  history of schooling in, 159
  socio-economic status, 309
  standardized tests and accountability, 139
  teachers in, 45, 250
United States Agency for International Development (USAID), 9, 308, 312
universal access to education 53, 58, 62, 167

United World Colleges (UWC), 337,
Universal Declaration of Human Rights. *See* United Nations Universal Declaration of Human Rights
universal primary education, 123, 307, 316
University of Asmara, 199
University of Montreal, 366
USAID. *See* United States Agency for International Development (USAID)
user fees, 314, 316, 321, 322
Ushinsky, K.D., 5

V
values, value orientations, 29
  in American education, 34
  Chinese vs. Western educational values, 30–36
  core values, 51
  ideal types, 24–25
  in peace and conflict education, 273, 274, 275
Verspoor, Adriaan, 121–122
Vienna Conference Declaration and Program of Action, 215
Vietnam
  See also East Asia
  Confucian heritage, 36
  educational investments, 40–46
  French colonialism, 42
  imperialism, experiences of, 45
  Marx's ideal society, 34
  modern educational system, development of, 42, 43
  socialist market economy, 30
  Vietnam War, 42
violence
  See also conflict
  armed conflict, 269, 271, 274, 277, 285
  bullying, 99, 285

Index

cultural violence, 269, 270, 275
education and violent conflict, 269–270
genocide, genocidal violence, 277
gender-based harassment and violence in schools and safe schools initiatives, 207, 280
legitimate violence, 272
against lower-caste, 276
structural violence, 269, 270, 271, 272
von Fellenberg, Philipp, 4
voucher programs, *See* school choice

W
wage gap, 206
Wales, England, 133, 354
Waldorf approach, schools, 171
War,
  Civil war(s), 40, 109, 269
  Cold War, 30, 41, 42, 45–46, 215, 308, 373
  post war, 10, 38
  World War, first, 7, 40
  World War, second, 2, 8, 9, 30, 38, 42, 44, 70, 212, 243, 303, 365
Weber, Max, 29, 305
welfare state, 306, 308, 313
Welmond, Michel, 19
Western concepts of education
  and Education for All (EFA), 316–319
  epistemology, 156–159
  vs. Indigenous ways of knowing, 78–90, 158–172
  knowledge, evaluation of, 167
  literate mode, 165
  man *[sic]* as dominant, 163
  purpose of knowledge, 169
Western education, 217, 310
Whole School Improvement Program (WSIP), 130

Wide Angle (PBS), 326
women
  See also gender
  and AIDS/HIV epidemic, 254
  and culture of peace, 272–273
  in Eritrea. See Eritrea case study
  mothers and motherhood, 183
Women, Education and Development in Asia: Cross-National Perspectives (Mak), 17
World Bank
  Africa, reform measures in, 314–315
  belt tightening and liberalization reforms, 314
  cost-benefit analysis, 11
  development aid, 312
  education, gradual inclusion of, 9
  Escuela Nueva model, 71, 82
  gender, and educational statistics, 224, 189–193
  Indigenous knowledge, recognition of, 171
  influence of, 18
  international assessments, support for, 377
  and IMF, 314, 317
  loan conditions, 321
  pro-economic globalization approaches, 317
  school improvement, role in, 121,127
  Verspoor study of World Bank funded projects, 121
  World Development Report, 366
world citizenship. *See* global citizenship education
world-class education, 344
World Conference on Education for All, 316
World Council of Comparative Education Societies, 9

world culture theory, 107
  See also world systems theory, 10, 81
World Declaration on Education for All, 379
World Development Report, 366
World of Thought in Ancient China, (Schwartz), 31
World Order Models Project (WOMP), 17
World Programme for Human Rights Education, 215
world system theory, 10, 189
World Trade Organization (WTO), 18
worldmindedness, 237–238, 241, 237*t*
WTO. *See* World Trade Organization (WTO)

X
Xenophon, 3
Xun Zi, 31, 32, 47

Y
Yale University, 129
Yemen, 194*f*
Yousafzai, Malala, 213, 230

Z
Zambia, 320*f*
Zhuang Zexuan, 8
Zimbabwe, 370, 395